Freelance Graphics For Windows® 95 F...

COMPUTER BOOK SERIES FROM IDG

When You Don't Know What to Do Next...

Freelance Graphics has the following helpful tools you can use as you create presentations.

Tool	Location	What It Does
Tour command	On the Help menu	Provides automated demonstrations of the most often-used features
Help Topics command	On the Help menu	Provides a list of topics in the Freelance Graphics Help database, making it easier to find specific information
Guide Me button	Above the current slide	Brings up context-sensitive Help
ToolTip	Appears on a menu	Contains information about each button or tool
Content Advice button	In the Current Page view	Provides a summary of what information the current slide type should contain
Click Here area	On a page	Adds slide elements with a single mouse click

Shift keyboard combinations

(Hold down the Shift key and then press the other key.)

Keystroke	What it does
Shift+F4	When a drawing tool is active, pressing this keyboard combination is the same as choosing View⇨Set View Preferences to toggle between crosshair sizes.
Shift+F6	Same as choosing Edit⇨Points Mode. Allows you to edit Bézier points on an object drawn with a line tool.
Shift+F7	Turns off the Snap to grid option
Shift+F8	Brings a selected object forward one level in a stack of objects
Shift+F9	Returns you to Edit Presentation from Edit Backdrop mode
Shift+Insert	Same as choosing Edit⇨Paste. Pastes a cut or copied object on the Clipboard onto the current page.
Shift+Delete	Same as choosing Edit⇨Cut. Removes a selected object(s) to the Clipboard.
Shift+Tab	In a bulleted list, moves the item one level to the left, demoting the point one level.

Function Keys (keys labelled F1, F2, and so on)

Keystroke	What it does
F1	Opens context-sensitive Help
F2	Displays text cursor in a selected text block so you can edit text
F4	Same as choosing Edit⇨Select All
F7	Same as choosing Create⇨Page. Add new page to layout by opening Page Layout dialog box.
F8	Sends an object back one level in a stack of objects
F9	Same as choosing View⇨Redraw. Refreshes the screen.
F10	Activates the menu bar so that when you hover your mouse cursor over a menu label, you get a description of what the commands on the menus do

Copyright © 1996 IDG Books Worldwide, Inc. All rights reserved.
Cheat Sheet $2.95 value. Item 236-8.
For more information about IDG Books, call 1-800-762-2974.

IDG BOOKS WORLDWIDE

...For Dummies: #1 Computer Book Series for Beginners

Freelance Graphics® 96 For Windows® 95 For Dummies®

Cheat Sheet

Ctrl Keyboard combinations

(Hold down the Ctrl key and press the other key.)

Keystroke	What it does
Ctrl+A	Same as choosing Edit⇨Select All
Ctrl+B	Turns selected text or text you're about to type to bold
Ctrl+C	Same as choosing Edit⇨Copy. Copies selected objects to the keyboard.
Ctrl+E	Centers the paragraph where the text cursor is positioned or a block of selected text
Ctrl+G	Same as choosing Edit⇨Go To. Allows you to choose a page to jump to.
Ctrl+I	Turns selected text or text you are about to type to italic
Ctrl+J	Justifies text left and right in a paragraph or selected text block
Ctrl+L	Left-justifies a paragraph or selected text block
Ctrl+N	Same as selecting Normal when formatting text. Removes formatting from selected text.
Ctrl+O	Same as choosing File⇨Open. Displays the Open dialog box so that you can open a presentation.
Ctrl+P	Same as choosing File⇨Print. Opens the Print dialog box, allowing you to print your presentation, outline, audience handouts, or speaker notes.
Ctrl+R	Right-justifies a paragraph or a selected text block
Ctrl+S	Same as choosing File⇨Save. Saves a presentation or, in an untitled presentation, opens Save As.
Ctrl+U	Underlines text
Ctrl+V	Same as choosing Edit⇨Paste. Pastes a copied or cut object onto the current page from the Clipboard.
Ctrl+W	Same as choosing File⇨Close. Closes the current document.
Ctrl+X	Same as choosing Edit⇨Cut. Removes selected object(s) to the Clipboard.
Ctrl+Z	Same as choosing Edit⇨Undo. Reverses the last action.
Ctrl+F2	Same as choosing Edit⇨Check Spelling. Opens the Spell Check dialog box, allowing you to spell check a presentation.
Ctrl+F3	When an object is selected, pressing this keyboard combination is the same as choosing Edit⇨Replicate.
Ctrl+F6	Brings the next open Freelance Graphics window to the front when you have multiple presentations open

Alt keyboard combinations

(Hold down the Alt key and press the other key.)

Keystroke	What it does
Alt+F1	Allows you to use ANSI codes to enter characters that you cannot enter directly from the keyboard
Alt+F4	Same as choosing File⇨Exit Freelance Graphics. Quits Freelance Graphics.
Alt+F7	Same as choosing Page⇨Duplicate Page. Makes a copy of the current page.
Alt+F9	Toggles between displaying the presentation in color or in black and white, same as color⇨monochrome button at bottom of screen
Alt+F10	Same as choosing Presentation⇨Run Screen Show or clicking the Run Screen Show From Beginning SmartIcon.

...For Dummies: #1 Computer Book Series for Beginners

References for the Rest of Us!®

COMPUTER BOOK SERIES FROM IDG

Are you intimidated and confused by computers? Do you find that traditional manuals are overloaded with technical details you'll never use? Do your friends and family always call you to fix simple problems on their PCs? Then the ...*For Dummies*® computer book series from IDG Books Worldwide is for you.

...*For Dummies* books are written for those frustrated computer users who know they aren't really dumb but find that PC hardware, software, and indeed the unique vocabulary of computing make them feel helpless. ...*For Dummies* books use a lighthearted approach, a down-to-earth style, and even cartoons and humorous icons to diffuse computer novices' fears and build their confidence. Lighthearted but not lightweight, these books are a perfect survival guide for anyone forced to use a computer.

> "I like my copy so much I told friends; now they bought copies."
> — Irene C., Orwell, Ohio

> "Quick, concise, nontechnical, and humorous."
> — Jay A., Elburn, Illinois

> "Thanks, I needed this book. Now I can sleep at night."
> — Robin F., British Columbia, Canada

Already, hundreds of thousands of satisfied readers agree. They have made ...*For Dummies* books the #1 introductory level computer book series and have written asking for more. So, if you're looking for the most fun and easy way to learn about computers, look to ...*For Dummies* books to give you a helping hand.

IDG BOOKS WORLDWIDE™

FREELANCE GRAPHICS® 96 FOR WINDOWS® 95 FOR DUMMIES®

FREELANCE GRAPHICS® 96 FOR WINDOWS® 95 FOR DUMMIES®

by William Harrel and Roger C. Parker

IDG Books Worldwide, Inc.
An International Data Group Company

Foster City, CA ♦ Chicago, IL ♦ Indianapolis, IN ♦ Braintree, MA ♦ Southlake, TX

Freelance Graphics® 96 For Windows® 95 For Dummies®

Published by
IDG Books Worldwide, Inc.
An International Data Group Company
919 E. Hillsdale Blvd.
Suite 400
Foster City, CA 94404

Text and art copyright © 1996 by IDG Books Worldwide, Inc. All rights reserved. No part of this book, including interior design, cover design, and icons, may be reproduced or transmitted in any form, by any means (electronic, photocopying, recording, or otherwise) without the prior written permission of the publisher.

Library of Congress Catalog Card No.: 96-75118

ISBN: 1-56884-236-8

Printed in the United States of America

10 9 8 7 6 5 4 3 2 1

1E/QY/QU/ZW/IN

Distributed in the United States by IDG Books Worldwide, Inc.

Distributed by Macmillan Canada for Canada; by Computer and Technical Books for the Caribbean Basin; by Contemporanea de Ediciones for Venezuela; by Distribuidora Cuspide for Argentina; by CITEC for Brazil; by Ediciones ZETA S.C.R. Ltda. for Peru; by Editorial Limusa SA for Mexico; by Transworld Publishers Limited in the United Kingdom and Europe; by Al-Maiman Publishers & Distributors for Saudi Arabia; by Simron Pty. Ltd. for South Africa; by IDG Communications (HK) Ltd. for Hong Kong; by Toppan Company Ltd. for Japan; by Addison Wesley Publishing Company for Korea; by Longman Singapore Publishers Ltd. for Singapore, Malaysia, Thailand, and Indonesia; by Unalis Corporation for Taiwan; by WS Computer Publishing Company, Inc. for the Philippines; by WoodsLane Pty. Ltd. for Australia; by WoodsLane Enterprises Ltd. for New Zealand.

For general information on IDG Books Worldwide's books in the U.S., please call our Consumer Customer Service department at 800-762-2974. For reseller information, including discounts and premium sales, please call our Reseller Customer Service department at 800-434-3422.

For information on where to purchase IDG Books Worldwide's books outside the U.S., contact IDG Books Worldwide at 415-655-3021 or fax 415-655-3295.

For information on translations, contact Marc Jeffrey Mikulich, Director, Foreign & Subsidiary Rights, at IDG Books Worldwide, 415-655-3018 or fax 415-655-3295.

For sales inquiries and special prices for bulk quantities, write to the address above or call IDG Books Worldwide at 415-655-3200.

For information on using IDG Books Worldwide's books in the classroom, or ordering examination copies, contact the Education Office at 800-434-2086 or fax 817-251-8174.

For authorization to photocopy items for corporate, personal, or educational use, please contact Copyright Clearance Center, 222 Rosewood Drive, Danvers, MA 01923, or fax 508-750-4470.

Limit of Liability/Disclaimer of Warranty: Author and Publisher have used their best efforts in preparing this book. IDG Books Worldwide, Inc., and Author make no representation or warranties with respect to the accuracy or completeness of the contents of this book and specifically disclaim any implied warranties of merchantability or fitness for any particular purpose and shall in no event be liable for any loss of profit or any other commercial damage, including but not limited to special, incidental, consequential, or other damages.

Trademarks: All brand names and product names used in this book are trademarks, registered trademarks, or trade names of their respective holders. IDG Books Worldwide is not associated with any product or vendor mentioned in this book.

is a trademark under exclusive license to IDG Books Worldwide, Inc., from International Data Group, Inc.

About the Authors

William Harrel

William Harrel started designing documents and creating computer graphics back in the days of 8088 XTs with 10MB hard drives and amber monitors. In those days, graphics artists and designers sometimes waited up to 10 minutes or longer for the screen to redraw each time they made a change to a document. Printing graphics often took hours. We've come a long way since then.

Harrel writes for a host of computer magazines, including *PC World, Publish,* and *Home Office Computing,* in which his column "Design Doctor" provides monthly electronic design solutions for readers in the small office-home office (So-Ho) community. Harrel has authored fourteen books on computer graphics and multimedia-related topics. He also owns a successful Southern California desktop publishing firm that specializes in multimedia presentations and World Wide Web site design.

Harrel started using Freelance Graphics long before it was a Windows application — before the Windows 3.*x* revolution. In those days, Freelance Graphics was a companion program to the very popular Lotus 1-2-3 spreadsheet and worked very much like 1-2-3. Looking back on those horse-and-buggy years of computing, Harrel wonders how he and his peers ever got any work done. They spent a lot of time fighting their machines and drooling over the Macintosh graphical environment. Freelance Graphics, Windows, and graphics on a PC have come a long way. Faster computers have opened a whole new world of possibilities for the future. It's an exciting time to be involved with computers.

Harrel lives in Port Hueneme, California, with his new wife Heidi. He still contributes regularly to several international computer magazines. When not working on articles and books, he authors multimedia applications and tries to stay abreast of the ever-expanding Internet — much to the chagrin of his two sometimes-neglected golden retrievers.

Roger C. Parker

More than 750,00 desktop publishers and software users throughout the world own books by Roger C. Parker. In addition to frequently contributing to a variety of publications, including *Graphics Solutions, Publish, Technique,* and *x-height,* Parker has written numerous books on desktop publishing and design.

Roger has conducted presentations throughout the world for organizations such as the Consumer Electronics Show, Apple Computer, Creative Seminars, the State Street Bank, Yamaha Audio, and the University of Illinois. During the past few years, Roger has been the keynote speaker and lead presenter at PageMaker conferences conducted throughout the United States. He is active with the Boston Computer Society.

Roger's recent books for IDG Books Worldwide include *Desktop Publishing & Design For Dummies, Harvard Graphics 2.0 For Windows For Dummies, WordPerfect 6.0 (DOS) Secrets* (with David Holzgang), *WordPerfect 6.0 For Windows Power Techniques,* and *Microsoft Office For Windows 95 For Dummies.*

Acknowledgments

The authors would like to thank Colleen Rainsberger, Barb Terry, William A. Barton, Diana R. Conover, Greg Robertson, Rebecca Whitney, and all the folks at IDG Books Worldwide, Inc., who helped make this book a reality.

(The Publisher would like to give special thanks to Patrick J. McGovern, without whom this book would not have been possible.)

ABOUT IDG BOOKS WORLDWIDE

Welcome to the world of IDG Books Worldwide.

IDG Books Worldwide, Inc., is a subsidiary of International Data Group, the world's largest publisher of computer-related information and the leading global provider of information services on information technology. IDG was founded more than 25 years ago and now employs more than 7,700 people worldwide. IDG publishes more than 250 computer publications in 67 countries (see listing below). More than 70 million people read one or more IDG publications each month.

Launched in 1990, IDG Books Worldwide is today the #1 publisher of best-selling computer books in the United States. We are proud to have received 8 awards from the Computer Press Association in recognition of editorial excellence and three from Computer Currents' First Annual Readers' Choice Awards, and our best-selling ...For Dummies® series has more than 19 million copies in print with translations in 28 languages. IDG Books Worldwide, through a joint venture with IDG's Hi-Tech Beijing, became the first U.S. publisher to publish a computer book in the People's Republic of China. In record time, IDG Books Worldwide has become the first choice for millions of readers around the world who want to learn how to better manage their businesses.

Our mission is simple: Every one of our books is designed to bring extra value and skill-building instructions to the reader. Our books are written by experts who understand and care about our readers. The knowledge base of our editorial staff comes from years of experience in publishing, education, and journalism — experience which we use to produce books for the '90s. In short, we care about books, so we attract the best people. We devote special attention to details such as audience, interior design, use of icons, and illustrations. And because we use an efficient process of authoring, editing, and desktop publishing our books electronically, we can spend more time ensuring superior content and spend less time on the technicalities of making books.

You can count on our commitment to deliver high-quality books at competitive prices on topics you want to read about. At IDG Books Worldwide, we continue in the IDG tradition of delivering quality for more than 25 years. You'll find no better book on a subject than one from IDG Books Worldwide.

John Kilcullen
President and CEO
IDG Books Worldwide, Inc.

VIII WINNER
Eighth Annual
Computer Press
Awards ≥ 1992

IX WINNER
Ninth Annual
Computer Press
Awards ≥ 1993

IDG Books Worldwide, Inc., is a subsidiary of International Data Group, the world's largest publisher of computer-related information and the leading global provider of information services on information technology. International Data Group publishes over 250 computer publications in 67 countries. Seventy million people read one or more International Data Group publications each month. International Data Group's publications include: **ARGENTINA:** Computerworld Argentina, GamePro, Infoworld, PC World Argentina; **AUSTRALIA:** Australian Macworld, Client/Server Journal, Computer Living, Computerworld, Digital News, Network World, PC World, Publishing Essentials, Reseller; **AUSTRIA:** Computerwelt, PC TEST; **BELARUS:** PC World Belarus; **BELGIUM:** Data News; **BRAZIL:** Annuário de Informática, Computerworld Brazil, Connections, Super Game Power, Macworld, PC World Brazil, Publish Brazil, SUPERGAME; **BULGARIA:** Computerworld Bulgaria, Networkworld/Bulgaria, PC & MacWorld Bulgaria; **CANADA:** CIO Canada, ComputerWorld Canada, InfoCanada, Network World Canada, Reseller World; **CHILE:** Computerworld Chile, GamePro, PC World Chile; **COLUMBIA:** Computerworld Colombia, GamePro, PC World Colombia; **COSTA RICA:** PC World Costa Rica/Nicaragua; **THE CZECH AND SLOVAK REPUBLICS:** Computerworld Czechoslovakia, Elektronika Czechoslovakia, PC World Czechoslovakia; **DENMARK:** Communications World, Computerworld Danmark, Macworld Danmark, PC World Danmark, PC World Danmark Supplements, TECH World; **DOMINICAN REPUBLIC:** PC World Republica Dominicana; **ECUADOR:** PC World Ecuador, GamePro; **EGYPT:** Computerworld Middle East, PC World Middle East; **EL SALVADOR:** PC World Centro America; **FINLAND:** MikroPC, Tietoverkko, Tietoviikko; **FRANCE:** Distributique, Golden, Info PC, Le Guide du Monde Informatique, Le Monde Informatique, Reseaux & Telecoms; **GERMANY:** Computer Business, Computerwoche, Computerwoche Extra, Computerwoche Focus, Electronic Entertainment, GamePro, I/M Information Management, Macwelt, PC Welt; **GREECE:** GamePro, Macworld & Publish; **GUATEMALA:** PC World Centro America; **HONDURAS:** PC World Centro America; **HONG KONG:** Computerworld Hong Kong, PCWorld Hong Kong, Publish in Asia; **HUNGARY:** ABCD CD-ROM, Computerworld Szamitastechnika, PC & Mac World Hungary, PC-X Magazine; **INDIA:** Computerworld India, PC World India, Publish in Asia; **INDONESIA:** InfoKomputer PC World, Komputek Computerworld, Publish in Asia; **IRELAND:** ComputerScope, PC Live!; **ISRAEL:** PC World 32 BIT, People & Computers; **ITALY:** Computerworld Italia, Computerworld Italia Special Editions, Lotus Italia, Macworld Italia, Networking Italia, PC Shopping, PC World Italia, PC World/Walt Disney; **JAPAN:** Macworld Japan, Nikkei Personal Computing, SunWorld Japan, Windows World Japan; **KENYA:** East African Computer News; **KOREA:** Hi-Tech Information/Computerworld, Macworld Korea, PC World Korea; **MACEDONIA:** PC World Macedonia; **MALAYSIA:** Computerworld Malaysia, PC World Malaysia, Publish in Asia; **MEXICO:** Computerworld Mexico, GamePro, Macworld, PC World Mexico; **MYANMAR:** PC World Myanmar; **NETHERLANDS:** Computable, Computer! Totaal, LAN Magazine, Macworld, Net Magazine; **NEW ZEALAND:** Computer Buyer, Computerworld New Zealand, MTB, Network World, PC World New Zealand; **NICARAGUA:** PC World Costa Rica/Nicaragua; **NIGERIA:** PC World Africa; **NORWAY:** Computerworld Norge, Computerworld Privat, CW Rapport Klient/Tjener, CW Rapport Nettverk & Telecom, CW Rapport Offentlig Sektor, IDG's KURSGUIDE, Macworld Norge, Multimedia World, PC World Ekspress, PC World Nettverk, PC World Norge, PC World's Produktguide, Windows Spesial; **PAKISTAN:** Computerworld Pakistan, PC World Pakistan; **PANAMA:** GamePro, PC World Panama; **PARAGUAY:** PC World Paraguay; **P. R. OF CHINA:** China Computerworld, China Infoworld, Computer & Communication, Electronic Product World, Electronics Today, Game Camp, PC World China, Popular Computer Week, Software World, Telecom Product World; **PERU:** Computerworld Peru, GamePro, PC World Profesional Peru, PC World Peru; **POLAND:** Computerworld Poland, Computerworld Special Report, Macworld, Networld, PC World Komputer; **PHILIPPINES:** Computerworld Philippines, PC Digest, Publish in Asia; **PORTUGAL:** Cerebro/PC World, Correio Informático/Computerworld, Mac•In/PC•In Portugal; **PUERTO RICO:** PC World Puerto Rico; **ROMANIA:** Computerworld Romania, PC World Romania, Telecom Romania; **RUSSIA:** Computerworld Rossiya, Network World Russia, PC World Russia; **SINGAPORE:** Computerworld Singapore, PC World Singapore, Publish in Asia; **SLOVENIA:** MONITOR; **SOUTH AFRICA:** Computing S.A., Network World S.A., Software World; **SPAIN:** Computerworld España, COMUNICACIONES WORLD, Dealer World, Macworld España, PC World España; **SWEDEN:** CAP&Design, Computer Sweden, Corporate Computing, Mac World, Maxi Data, MikroDatorn, Nätverk & Kommunikation, PC/Aktiv, PC World, Windows World; **SWITZERLAND:** Computerworld Schweiz, Macworld Schweiz, PCtip; **TAIWAN:** Computerworld Taiwan, Macworld Taiwan, PC World Taiwan, Publish Taiwan, Windows World; **THAILAND:** Thai Computerworld, Publish in Asia; **TURKEY:** Computerworld Monitör, MACWORLD Turkiye, PC WORLD Turkiye; **UKRAINE:** Computerworld Kiev, Computers & Software Magazine, PC World Ukraine; **UNITED KINGDOM:** Acorn User, Amiga Action, Amiga Computing, Amiga, Appletalk, CD Powerplay, CD-ROM Now, Computing, Connexion, GamePro, Lotus Magazine, Macaction, Macworld, Open Computing, Parents and Computers, PC Home, PC Works, The WEB; **UNITED STATES:** Cable in the Classroom, CD Review, CIO Magazine, Computerworld, Computerworld Client/Server Journal, Digital Video Magazine, DOS World, Electronic InfoWorld, I-Way, Macworld, Maximize, MULTIMEDIA WORLD, Network World, PC World, PUBLISH, SWATPro Magazine, Video Event, WebMaster; **URUGUAY:** PC World Uruguay; **VENEZUELA:** Computerworld Venezuela, GamePro, PC World Venezuela; and **VIETNAM:** PC World Vietnam   10/17/95a

Credits

Senior Vice President and Publisher
Milissa L. Koloski

Associate Publisher
Diane Graves Steele

Editorial Director
Myra Immell

Brand Manager
Judith A. Taylor

Editorial Managers
Kristin A. Cocks
Mary Corder
Seta K. Frantz

Product Development Manager
Mary Bednarek

Editorial Executive Assistant
Richard Graves

Editorial Assistants
Constance Carlisle
Chris H. Collins
Jerelind Davis
Kevin Spencer

Marketing Assistant
Holly N. Blake

Acquisitions Assistant
Gareth Hancock

Production Director
Beth Jenkins

Production Assistant
Jacalyn L. Pennywell

Supervisor of Project Coordination
Cindy L. Phipps

Supervisor of Page Layout
Kathie S. Schnorr

Supervisor of Graphics and Design
Shelley Lea

Reprint/Blueline Coordination
Tony Augsburger
Patricia R. Reynolds
Todd Klemme
Theresa Sánchez-Baker

Media/Archive Coordination
Leslie Popplewell
Melissa Stauffer
Jason Marcuson

Project Editors
Colleen Rainsberger
Barb Terry

Editors
William A. Barton
Diana R. Conover
Greg Robertson
Rebecca Whitney

Technical Reviewer
Samuel Faulkner

Associate Project Coordinator
Regina Snyder

Graphics Coordination
Gina Scott
Angela F. Hunckler

Production Page Layout
E. Shawn Aylsworth
Linda M. Boyer
Dominique DeFelice
Jane E. Martin
Drew R. Moore
Marti Stegeman
Michael Sullivan

Proofreaders
Sandra Profant
Gwenette Gaddis
Dwight Ramsey
Carl Saff
Robert Springer

Indexer
Sharon Hilgenberg

Cover Design
Kavish + Kavish

Contents at a Glance

Introduction 1

Part I: Gearing Up for Success 5
Chapter 1: Choosing the Right Presentation Format 7
Chapter 2: Familiarizing Yourself with Freelance Graphics 96 19
Chapter 3: Creating Your First Presentation 37
Chapter 4: Working with the Freelance Graphics Outliner 51

Part II: Adding Visuals 61
Chapter 5: Translating Numbers into Visuals: Adding Charts and Graphs 63
Chapter 6: Fine-Tuning Text Charts, Charts, and Graphs 79
Chapter 7: Working with Tables and Organization Charts 103
Chapter 8: Adding Symbols and Manipulating Text Shapes 121
Chapter 9: Working with Freelance Graphics' Drawing Tools 139

Part III: Fine-Tuning Your Presentation 155
Chapter 10: Oops! Reviewing and Reorganizing Your Presentation 157
Chapter 11: Being Your Own Art Director: Modifying Existing SmartMasters
and Creating New SmartMasters 171

Part IV: Printing and Rehearsing Your Presentation 189
Chapter 12: Preparing and Printing 35mm Slides 191
Chapter 13: Working with Overhead Transparencies 201
Chapter 14: Creating and Delivering Electronic Presentations 207
Chapter 15: Preparing Files for Remote Viewing 229
Chapter 16: Preparing and Printing Speaker's Notes 239
Chapter 17: Preparing and Printing Audience Handouts 247

Part V: The Part of Tens 253
Chapter 18: Ten Questions to Help You Define Your Presentation Goals
and Strategies 255
Chapter 19: Ten Tips for Polishing Presentation Content 261
Chapter 20: Ten Things You Need to Know to Use TeamReview Effectively 267
Chapter 21: Ten Ways to Look and Feel More Confident 273
Chapter 22: Ten Things You'll Like about Freelance Graphics 96 281
Chapter 23: The Ten Most Important SmartIcons 285
Chapter 24: Ten Keys to Good-Looking, Easy-to-Read Overheads 289

Index 293

Reader Response Card .... Back of Book

Cartoons at a Glance

By Rich Tennant • Fax: 508-546-7747 • E-mail: the5wave@tiac.net

page 5

page 189

page 61

page 253

page 155

Table of Contents

Introduction *1*

    About This Book 2
    How to Use This Book 2
    How This Book Is Organized 2
        Part I: Gearing Up for Success 3
        Part II: Adding Visuals 3
        Part III: Fine-Tuning Your Presentation 3
        Part IV: Printing and Rehearsing Your Presentation 3
        Part V: The Part of Tens 3
    Icons Used in This Book 4
    Where to Go from Here 4

Part I: Gearing Up for Success *5*

Chapter 1: Choosing the Right Presentation Format 7

    Choosing the Right Presentation Format 7
    Knowing When to Use 35mm Slides 10
    Knowing When to Use Overhead Transparencies 11
    Knowing When to Use Electronic Screen Shows 13
    Recognizing the Importance of Planning Ahead 17

Chapter 2: Familiarizing Yourself with Freelance Graphics 96 19

    The Freelance Graphics Screen 19
    The Freelance Graphics Tools 22
        Using the Pointer (selection) tool 23
        Using the Text tool 25
        Using the drawing tools 26
        Using Text Shapes 27
        Using Connectors 27
    What's on the Freelance Graphics Menus? 28
    Customizing the Freelance Graphics Work Environment 29
        Customizing the SmartIcons bar 29
        Customizing the active SmartIcons set 30
        Using Freelance Preferences to further customize
          your work environment 31
    Getting Around in Freelance Graphics 34
        Getting around in Current Page 34
        Getting around in Page Sorter 35

Chapter 3: Creating Your First Presentation 37
Creating Your First Presentation the Easy Way 37
Saving Your Presentation 43
    More about saving your work 44
    Doing incremental saves 45
Printing Your Presentation 45
    Changing the print options 46
    Previewing and printing selected pages 48
Closing a Presentation 49
Reopening a Presentation 49
Previewing Your Pages 49

Chapter 4: Working with the Freelance Graphics Outliner 51
Deciding to Work in the Outliner 51
Creating a New Presentation in the Outliner 54
Promoting and Demoting Topics in the Outliner 56
Rearranging Slides in the Outliner 57
Changing the Looks of the Outliner 57
    Expanding and collapsing an outline 57
    Changing the way text appears in the Outliner 58
    Adding elements to the Outliner 58
Printing Your Outline 59

Part II: Adding Visuals 61

Chapter 5: Translating Numbers into Visuals: Adding Charts and Graphs 63
Which Chart with What Data? 63
Creating Charts and Graphs 65
Creating Charts from Data in Other Programs 68
Importing a Chart from a Spreadsheet 70
    Using the 1-2-3 Named Chart command 71
    Using Paste to import a 1-2-3 chart 72
    Using Paste to import charts from other spreadsheets 73
Knowing When to Link by Using Paste Special 74
    Creating a link by using Paste Special 74
    Deciding when to use links 76
    Deciding when to use embedded charts 77

Chapter 6: Fine-Tuning Text Charts, Charts, and Graphs 79
Fine-Tuning Text Chart Line and Paragraph Spacing 79
    Increasing or decreasing line spacing 80
    Increasing or decreasing paragraph spacing 81
Adding Borders and Backgrounds to Charts 81
    Adding a border to a chart 82
    Changing a chart's background 83

Changing Chart Fonts, Type Size, Color, and Position 84
Changing Chart Series Borders and Colors 86
   Changing a series fill and color 86
   Changing a series border 87
Adding, Removing, and Modifying X- and Y-Axis, Tick Marks, and Grids 88
   Showing and hiding a chart's axes, tick marks, and grids 90
   Hiding, showing, adding, and removing axis labels 90
   Hiding, showing, adding, and removing axis tick marks 91
   Working with a chart's scale 93
   Hiding, showing, adding, and removing gridlines 94
Making X- and Y-Axis Information Easier to Read 95
   Adjusting X-axis label orientation (angle) 97
   Changing Y-axis title and subtitle position and orientation 97
   Getting rid of Y-axis labels 98
   Changing the number type of Y-axis labels 99
Combining Chart Types 100
   Displaying two charts on the same slide 101
   Creating mixed charts 101

Chapter 7: Working with Tables and Organization Charts 103

Using Tables 103
   Creating a table 104
   Adding, removing, and moving columns and rows 105
   Resizing column widths and row heights in tables 108
   Adding text to tables 108
Changing Table Text, Borders, and Fills 108
   Changing text attributes in tables 109
   Adding and modifying table borders 110
   Changing table-cell backgrounds 111
Using Organization Charts 112
   Creating an organization chart 112
   Modifying organization-chart text, borders, fills,
      and connector lines 116
   Changing the entire chart style 120

Chapter 8: Adding Symbols and Manipulating Text Shapes 121

Working with Text Shapes 121
Adding Text to Text Shapes 123
   Typing into a Text Shape 123
   Resizing Text Shape text 125
   Changing Text Shape fonts 125
   Changing Text Shape font colors 127
   Making really fast font and Text Shape formatting changes
      by using styles 127

Recoloring Text Shape Colors and Line Weights 130
Resizing, Rotating, Layering, Aligning, and Grouping Text Shapes 132
    Resizing Text Shapes 133
    Rotating objects 133
    Layering multiple objects 135
    Aligning objects 136
    Grouping objects 137

Chapter 9: Working with Freelance Graphics' Drawing Tools 139

Creating Drawings in Freelance Graphics 139
Working with the Drawing Tools 140
Creating Attention-Grabbing Text Effects in Freelance Graphics 142
    Using Freelance Graphics' preset curve options 142
    Curving text around your own shapes 143
Using Freelance Graphics' Clip Art 144
    Bringing clip art into your document 144
    Modifying clip art 145
Using Images from Other Programs 147
    Importing images into Freelance Graphics 148
    Modifying bitmaps in Freelance Graphics 149
    Preparing graphics for different media types 151
    Preparing graphics for slide recorders 154
    Printing graphics 154

Part III: Fine-Tuning Your Presentation 155

Chapter 10: Oops! Reviewing and Reorganizing Your Presentation 157

Reviewing Your Presentation 157
    Setting up a self-running screen show 157
    Adding a control panel to your self-running screen show 159
    Running the screen show 159
Identifying Wordy Slides and Weak Points in Your Argument 160
    Watch for wordy, cluttered slides 160
    Maintain a logical data flow 160
    Watch out for weak points in your arguments 161
Revising Your Presentation 162
    Moving slides around in Page Sorter 162
    Rearranging your presentation in Outliner 163
    Moving slides around in Outline view 164
Avoiding Embarrassing Spelling Errors 165
    Watching for misspellings that the spell checker can't catch 166
    Watching for misused words 166

Using the Freelance Graphics Spell Checker 167
    Starting a spell-check session 168
    Managing the Freelance Graphics dictionary 169

Chapter 11: Being Your Own Art Director: Modifying Existing SmartMasters and Creating New SmartMasters 171

How to Modify SmartMasters 172
    Opening a SmartMaster Look file 172
    Saving a SmartMaster Look file 173
How to Modify SmartMaster Background Colors 174
How to Use the Right Fonts 175
    A typeface by any other name 175
    Serif and sans-serif typefaces 175
    How to change SmartMaster fonts 176
How to Change SmartMaster Bullets 177
How to Add a Logo to Each Slide 178
How to Add SmartMaster Elements 178
How to Create a SmartMaster and Save It as a Default Template 179
    Beginning your new SmartMaster 180
    Starting from scratch 180
    Adding a bitmap image to the backdrop 181
    Changing and creating new color palettes 183
    Adding and modifying "Click here" placeholders 184

Part IV: Printing and Rehearsing Your Presentation 189

Chapter 12: Preparing and Printing 35mm Slides 191

Where Slides Come From 191
    A slide recorder by any other name 191
    Off to the service bureau? 193
    Printing your slides in-house 193
How to Prepare a Presentation for Printing at the Service Bureau 195
    What to do if your service bureau has Freelance Graphics 96 195
    What to do if your service bureau doesn't have
        Freelance Graphics 96 196
How to Print Your Slides In-House 198

Chapter 13: Working with Overhead Transparencies 201

Why Overhead Transparencies? 201
Color or Black-and-White Transparencies 203
How to Print Your Transparencies 205

Chapter 14: Creating and Delivering Electronic Presentations 207

Using Builds and Transitions 207
    Using fancy transitions between slides 208
    Creating bullet builds 209

Building slide elements 212
Assigning transitions to charts, tables, and diagrams 213
Launching Other Applications and Using OLE2 214
Launching another application from an electronic screen show 214
Using OLE2 during screen shows 215
Creating a hot link with Paste Special 216
Editing an OLE2 object in Freelance Graphics 218
Adding Sound and Movies 219
Knowing which types of sounds and movies
Freelance Graphics supports 219
Working with sound 220
Working with movies 220
Adding movies to slides 221
Delivering Your Presentation 224
Setting up your screen show 224
Setting up a screen show to be both self-running and self-looping 226
Delivering an electronic screen show 227
Taking Your Presentation on the Road 228

Chapter 15: Preparing Files for Remote Viewing 229

Creating Presentations for Remote Viewing: An Overview 229
Distributing a presentation to a few people you know 230
Distributing presentations when you don't know where
they'll be shown 232
Creating a Run-Time Version of Your Presentation 232
Distributing the Mobile Screen Show Player 234
Finding the Mobile Screen Show Player 234
Using the Mobile Screen Show Player 234
Delivering Presentations Remotely with TeamShow 236
Are you a sender or a receiver? 237
Connecting and sending a file 237
File, file, who's got the file? 237
Creating Self-running Presentations for Kiosks and Trade Shows 238

Chapter 16: Preparing and Printing Speaker's Notes 239

Understanding Why Speaker's Notes Are Important 239
Creating and Formatting Speaker's Notes 240
Knowing What to Include in Your Speaker's Notes 242
Using an outline format 242
Including information that doesn't fit on a slide 244
Printing Speaker's Notes 244

Chapter 17: Preparing and Printing Audience Handouts 247

Understanding Why You Should Use Audience Handouts 247
Formatting and Printing Audience Handouts 248
Adding page numbers, dates, and other information
to handout pages 251
Adding a border to handouts 252

Part V: The Part of Tens 253

Chapter 18: Ten Questions to Help You Define Your Presentation Goals and Strategies 255

Who Is Your Audience? 255
How Much Does Your Audience Know about the Topic
  of Your Presentation? 256
What Action Do You Want Your Audience to Take? 257
What Is Your Audience's Position on This Subject? 257
What Top Three Points Do You Want Your Audience to Remember? 258
What Questions and Objections Are Your Audience Members
  Likely to Have? 258
What Control Do You Have over the Presentation Environment? 259

Chapter 19: Ten Tips for Polishing Presentation Content 261

Avoid Awkward Formatting 261
Avoid Incorrect and Awkward Line Breaks 262
Correct Lines That Stick out Too Far 262
Avoid Breaking Lines between Proper Names and Company Names 262
Avoid Hyphenation 262
Look Professional by Using Special Characters 263
Use Em Dashes 263
Use Typesetter Fractions 263
Use Legal Characters 264
Get Rid of Excess Modifiers 264
Get Rid of Idle, Nonworking Words 264
Get Rid of Flabby, Long Words 264

Chapter 20: Ten Things You Need to Know to Use TeamReview Effectively 267

How You Can Begin a Review Session 267
How You Can Distribute Review Drafts to Coworkers Electronically 268
How You Can Post a Presentation Draft to a Notes Database 268
How You Can Post a Presentation Draft to a Public Network Directory 269
How You Can Preview Reviewers' Comments 269
How You Can Complete the Review Process 270
How You Can Publish Your Presentation on the Internet 270
How You Can Send a Presentation via E-Mail 271
How You Can Start TeamMail or TeamReview to Send a Presentation 271
How You Can Route a TeamMail Presentation 272

Chapter 21: Ten Ways to Look and Feel More Confident 273

Practice Makes Perfect 274
Watch Your Presentation from the Audience's Perspective 275
Anticipating Objections and Preparing Optional Slides 276
Looking Good by Preparing Notes and Handouts 277
Looking Good by Getting a Good Night's Sleep 277

Freelance Graphics 96 For Windows 95 For Dummies

    Looking Good by Introducing Yourself to Audience Members
      Ahead of Time 278
    Looking Good by Focusing Your Eyes on Potential Supporters 278
    Looking Good by Ignoring People Who Leave or Look Bored 278
    Looking Good by Answering Questions Properly 279
    Looking Good by Never Bluffing 280

Chapter 22: Ten Things You'll Like about Freelance Graphics 96 281

    Attractive, All-Purpose SmartMasters 281
    Content SmartMasters 282
    Easy-to-Use "Click Here" Slide Creation 282
    Three Easy-to-Navigate Views 282
    View Presentations in Color or Black and White 283
    Rehearsing Made Easy by Rehearse Mode 283
    Bullet Magic with AutoBuilds and Flying Bullets 283
    Looking Good with Fancy Electronic Transitions 284
    Working with Team Members 284
    Lotus SmartSuite Integration 284

Chapter 23: The Ten Most Important SmartIcons 285

    The New SmartIcon 285
    The Open SmartIcon 286
    The Save SmartIcon 286
    The Print SmartIcon 287
    The Create a Chart SmartIcon 287
    The Check Spelling SmartIcon 287
    The Create a Text Block SmartIcon 288
    The Run Screen Show SmartIcon 288
    The Place Logo on Every Page SmartIcon 288

Chapter 24: Ten Keys to Good-Looking, Easy-to-Read Overheads 289

    Why You Should Use the Right Transparency Film 289
    Why You Should Use Light Backgrounds 290
    Why You Should Use Dark Text 290
    Why You Should Use Sans-Serif Type 291
    Why You Should Use Simple (or No) Borders and Clip Art 291
    Why You Should Avoid Using Portrait Page Orientation 291

Index 293

Reader Response Card .... Back of Book

Introduction

Freelance Graphics and programs like it place you smack dab in the Information Age. These programs provide beginners and professional presenters alike a fast, efficient means for creating and delivering meaningful, colorful, content-rich presentations — a means for looking good, and for looking good quickly and on a budget.

No longer is it necessary to send your ideas out to the art department or print shop and wait two or three weeks to get the materials back. You can do it all — create slides, transparencies, or electronic screen shows resplendent with graphics, charts, even sound and animation — right on your desktop computer or notebook. Freelance Graphics lets you do it all, from simple word slides and transparencies to full-blown multimedia extravaganzas.

The beauty of the desktop-presentation program is that not only do you get the material on *your* time and when you need it, but also your presentations can be dynamic, ever-changing, living entities. As situations and conditions change, you can easily update your presentation to reflect your fast-track environment. Information stays fresh and pertinent. If sales jump by several million units one week, you can incorporate the data into your monthly sales meeting materials in a matter of minutes. If you make presentations to groups that have slightly different interests or agendas, you can easily change your presentation to address their interests.

With Freelance Graphics, *you,* the presenter, are the art director. And there really is no easier way to design a presentation than with Freelance Graphics. Lotus' "click here" approach to creating slides and electronic screen shows is by far the easiest way to go.

Most people don't do presentations regularly enough to remember how the program works from session to session. Lotus knows this and provides a wealth of hand-holding, such as SmartMaster templates that not only help you with the aesthetics of your design but also guide you through creating content. The program comes with several content SmartMasters that walk you through a logical information flow. You don't have to be a writer or professional presenter to create great presentations with easy-to-follow, meaningful content.

For the professional and the adventurous, Freelance Graphics provides a wealth of high-end design options that allow you to create your own look and identity. It also lets you integrate data created in other programs, such as spreadsheet, database, and word processing programs, into your presentations.

As easy as it is, though, Freelance Graphics is still a computer program. And, unfortunately, none of us are born knowing how to use computers and software. That's where this book comes in. Between Freelance Graphics' built-in ease-of-use and this book, you'll be creating beautiful presentations in no time. We promise.

About This Book

If you sit down and read any computer book from cover to cover, let's face it, you need to get a life. Few people (nobody we know) have time for that. Most of us need the information to solve the problem at hand, and then we move on to the next problem. We pick up a book like this one only when the solution is not self-evident.

So, we haven't deluded ourselves that you'll sit up one night enthralled, enthusiastically flipping through these pages as you would your favorite novel. *Freelance Graphics 96 For Windows 95 For Dummies* is not *War and Peace*. We know that you'll pick it up only when you need to work through a problem with the software. We can live with that. And we're glad we can be of assistance.

How to Use This Book

This book is designed as a painless reference. You should use it when you have a problem to solve. Open the book, find the solution, and then get back to work.

We have designed the book by procedures. How to do this. How to do that. Why you should do it our way. And so on. You'll find hundreds of step-by-step procedures, along with design tips and other tidbits to make your life easier.

Use the table of contents to find specific topics and procedures. If you want to narrow down the search, try the index.

You can make finding information easier if you read the next section, "How this book is organized," which provides an overview of how the information in this book flows.

How This Book Is Organized

This book is divided into five parts. Each part is divided into chapters. As much as we could, we tried to make each chapter a stand-alone module. In the few instances where you need information covered in another chapter, we refer you back to the place in the book where the information can be found.

Part I: Gearing Up for Success

This part familiarizes you with Freelance Graphics. Basic concepts, such as presentation media — 35mm slides, transparencies, electronic screen shows — are discussed, as well as when to use each type. You'll also find information on creating your first presentation and using Freelance Graphics' Outliner to control the information flow.

Part II: Adding Visuals

Now we get into the fun stuff, such as using Freelance Graphics' powerful charting feature to create dramatic charts, graphs, organization charts, and diagrams. After creating charts and graphs, you often need to tweak them to get them just right for your audience (or your taste). This part also discusses adding Freelance Graphics' multitude of symbols and flowcharting objects (as well as tables, clip art, and images from other programs) to your slides and using the program's drawing tools.

Part III: Fine-Tuning Your Presentation

After you get the basic framework of your presentation laid out, you need to fine-tune, or "revise," it (as we writers often hear from our editors). This part discusses rearranging, reorganizing, and spell-checking a presentation. This section also looks at modifying Freelance Graphics' SmartMaster templates to meet your own needs or creating your own templates to conform to your organization's established identity.

Part IV: Printing and Rehearsing Your Presentation

Now that you've got the presentation just the way you want it, it's time to print the masterpiece and practice your delivery. This part begins by describing the three basic presentation formats — slides, overheads, and electronic screen shows. It covers printing issues for each medium and reveals how to assure success. Then we discuss preparing self-running screen shows that you distribute to remote viewers, either on disk or online. Using speaker notes during a presentation and preparing audience handouts are also considered.

Part V: The Part of Tens

No ...*For Dummies* book would be complete without a "part of tens." This part is a collection of useful tidbits to make working with Freelance Graphics — and presentations in general — easier. The topics include ten questions to help you define your presentation goals and strategies; ten ways to polish your presentation; ten ways to help combat stage fright, and so forth. You get the idea.

Icons Used in This Book

What would a *...For Dummies* book be without its share of goofy little pictures in the margins? These are, of course, icons. And we've used our share of them. Here's a list of the icons used in this book and the types of information that you find beside them:

All computer books have tips. You know, those bits of information that the writer couldn't logically squeeze into the main text. This book has a bunch of them. Wherever you see a tip, you'll find a little trick or technique designed to make your life easier — such as a simpler way to do something.

Freelance Graphics is a graphics program. We don't assume that you know how to create presentations or that you're a graphics artist. Nope. So, whenever we thought of a nifty way to spruce up your pages (or the presentation as a whole), we passed it on to you.

Here's an easy one to figure out. Basically, this means: Don't try this. We already have, and we can tell you from experience that it can be disastrous (or at least cause problems). When you see a warning, read it. It could save you some anguish.

Most often, a note signifies an exception, or it contains additional information. Sometimes, for example, a procedure may not, depending on various software settings, always work the way we explain in the text. A note might point out the exceptions when a procedure may not work or what to do if it doesn't work for you.

Nerdy stuff appears beside this icon. You can skip it without feeling guilty.

Where to Go from Here

If you're not familiar with Freelance Graphics, go to Chapter 2, "Familiarizing Yourself with Freelance Graphics 96." It'll get you started. Chapter 3, "Creating Your First Presentation," shows you what to do next. After that, it's just a matter of what you want to do with your presentations. Whatever it is, you can find a way in the other chapters in this book.

Have fun!

Part I
Gearing Up for Success

The 5th Wave By Rich Tennant

"SO, HOW DO YOU LIKE THE NEW HIGH PERFORMANCE VIDEO CARD?"

In this part . . .

Most people don't care about the history of a software application, so we won't spend a lot time boring you with the history of Freelance Graphics. It's noteworthy, though, that Freelance Graphics is one of the world's first presentation graphics programs, dating back to the pre-Windows (prehistoric) days.

Since then, the folks at Lotus have premiered many firsts with each update of the program. The first version of Freelance Graphics for Windows, for example, introduced the "click here" approach to entering text, graphics, and other presentation elements onto a slide. You just click on a placeholder and get to typing, defining a chart or graph, or placing a picture or clip art image. It just doesn't get any easier.

This painless way of designing presentations revolutionized the presentation software market — now they all use this method. And, as you'll see throughout Part I, this truly is a not-so-daunting way to design computer programs.

Not only is Freelance Graphics easy, it's powerful. It enables you to create all types of presentations, from simple overhead transparencies to full-blown interactive multimedia extravaganzas, and nearly every other kind of slide show type in between.

This section introduces you to what you can do with Freelance Graphics 96, pointing out along the way how easily the program helps you reach your goals. It introduces the Freelance Graphics interface, which truly is a joy to work in. You use some of the program's templates and automatic features to create your first slide show. You simply won't believe how easy the process is in Freelance Graphics.

Chapter 1
Choosing the Right Presentation Format

In This Chapter
- Choosing the right presentation format
- Knowing when to use 35mm slides: power
- Knowing when to use overhead transparencies: economy and convenience
- Knowing when to use electronic slide shows: razzle-dazzle
- Recognizing the need to plan ahead

The hype on the software packaging box attempts to make you believe that all you need is *this* program and you're up and running — creating slides and electronic screen shows comparable to those produced by a professional presenter. Freelance Graphics provides many tools to make the transition from concept to successful presentation easier, but you still have to know a lot.

This chapter takes a close look at the basic presentation formats — slides, overheads, and electronic screen shows — and the advantages and disadvantages of each one. After looking at which formats are best for you and your prospective audience, the chapter goes over some basic design issues for each format type. Slides and computer screens, for example, are capable of displaying many more colors and special effects than are achievable from laser or inkjet printers. You can save yourself many headaches if you plan ahead, and this chapter helps you do that.

Choosing the Right Presentation Format

A number of factors determine which presentation format you should use. Freelance Graphics supports three different types of output media:

- Slides
- Transparencies
- Computer screens and other types of monitors (LCD panels, TVs, and multimedia presentation systems)

Your presentation has the best chance of success if you use the right format. Although several factors can affect your final output decision, the two most important are where you will be delivering your presentation and the availability of equipment. Often, these two factors are the same. You cannot deliver a full-scale multimedia electronic screen show in a large auditorium, for example, without access to a multimedia presentation system that supports a computer video and audio hookup. Usually, this isn't the kind of equipment you bring with you (not without a good-sized truck and a band of engineers); instead, the equipment must be available at the presentation site. On the same note, you cannot deliver a slide show without a slide projector — and in many cases, you must bring your own.

Think logistics. Sure, you can give your presentation on your notebook computer, but only when the audience consists of a few people. Otherwise, many people in the audience won't be able to see your stupendous work, or they'll

The razzle-dazzle factor

Do you know what the third most important format-determining factor is? The razzle-dazzle effect. When planning your presentation, ask yourself, "How can I best impress my audience?" (Actually, if the first two factors — location and equipment — are easily solved, the third factor becomes the *most* important factor, unless, of course, money is an issue, which it so often is. Don't you just hate it when that happens?)

The medium you use to deliver your presentation can make a significant impression on your audience. Slides, for example, are usually prettier and of higher quality than transparencies (and they're more expensive). And, provided that the equipment and location conditions are right, electronic screen shows with fancy wipes and fades, sights, sounds, and flying bullets speak louder than slides.

All this depends, though, on the quality of the presentation and how well you fit the presentation format to the delivery environment. The best multimedia presentation ever created is a flop if you play it on a 9-inch notebook computer screen through tiny speakers in an overcrowded room.

If you don't think that the presentation medium is important, just ask the Olympic site-selection committee. The city of Atlanta recently razzle-dazzled them with a resplendent multimedia show, complete with animation, video, and sound. Many of the committee members admitted that they were persuaded by the quality of the presentation. So now, Atlanta is gearing up to host the Olympics.

The more engaging the presentation, the more powerful and persuasive your message. We're all looking to host the Olympics, in a manner of speaking.

have to crowd around the computer. When audience members are stepping on each other's toes and are worried about whether they have bad breath, they can't give your masterpiece the attention it deserves.

Just as important as where you deliver your presentation is how you output it or what medium you print it on — another equipment consideration. Slides and overheads must be printed on a slide recorder or desktop printer before you can use them. Electronic presentations are output on computer monitors or some other type of screen. As you can see, it helps to know where you're going and how you can get there before you start creating your presentation.

Table 1-1 shows the different presentation media and the equipment required to create them.

Table 1-1 Output Media and Equipment Needed to Create Them

Output Media	Equipment Needed to Create Them
Slides	35mm slide recorder*
Transparencies	Laser, inkjet, thermal wax, or dye sublimation printer
Electronic Screen Shows	Notebook computer and desktop monitor** or LCD screen and overhead projector*** or television and analog-to-digital converter** or multimedia presentation system

*Slides are usually output at a service bureau or film developing service.
**To play sound clips, you also need sound capabilities and speakers.
***In a large-audience setting, you need a helper to change overheads so that you, the presenter, can remain facing the audience, by the microphone. (Because changing transparencies is time-consuming and distracting, you'll have better luck if you bring a helper, anyway.)

Table 1-2 shows the output media used for different sizes of audiences.

Table 1-2 Output Media and Equipment Needed to Make a Presentation Based on Audience Size

Audience Size	Slides	Transparencies	Electronic Screen Shows
1–5 people	Slide projector*	Overhead projector***	Notebook computer and desktop monitor**
			LCD screen and overhead projector***
			Television and analog-to-digital converter**

(continued)

Table 1-2 *(continued)*

Audience Size	Slides	Transparencies	Electronic Screen Shows
5–20 people	Slide projector*	Overhead Projector***	Desktop monitor of at least 17"**
			LCD screen and overhead projector***
			Television and analog-to-digital converter**
20–50 people	Slide projector*	Overhead projector***	LCD screen and overhead projector***
			Television and analog-to-digital converter**
			Multimedia presentation system
50–500 people	Slide projector*	Overhead projector***	LCD screen and overhead projector***
			Multimedia presentation system

*Slides are usually output at a service bureau or film developing service.
**To play sound clips, you also need sound capabilities and speakers.
***In a large-audience setting, you need a helper to change overheads so that you, the presenter, can remain facing the audience, by the microphone. (Because changing transparencies is time-consuming and distracting, you'll have better luck if you bring a helper, anyway.)

Knowing When to Use 35mm Slides

Several factors affect whether you should use 35mm slides. Provided that you have access to a slide projector, this medium is one of the easiest and most reliable, for the following reasons:

- In most cases, all you need to know about the presentation site is that it has a room big enough to hold your audience. (And electricity, of course, unless you're presenting in the woods, in which case you'll also need a very quiet generator.) You don't have to worry about computer — compatibility issues.

- The slides themselves are small and compact, making them easy to carry and store.

- The projector (and screen, if one is not available at the presentation site) is relatively light and easy to carry.

- When produced correctly, 35mm slides can be beautiful, impressive, and effective.

Chapter 1: Choosing the Right Presentation Format

- Slide projectors are easy to operate during a presentation, allowing you to concentrate on your delivery.

Slides do have their drawbacks, though. Check out the following list of reasons *not* to use them:

- You have limited control over the flow of information. Slide shows provide information in a linear fashion, one slide after another in the order you place them in the slide projector carousel. It's difficult (and distracting for you and the audience) to change the sequence or to search for a slide out of the linear order. You must plan the flow of information and stick to your plan.

- In large presentation settings — say, more than 500 people — slides are difficult to see and ineffective.

- Slides are the most expensive medium to produce. Unless you own a slide recorder (reasonably fast ones cost more than $1,000), you must take the slides to a service bureau for processing, which usually costs about $5 to $10, or more, per slide. This cost quickly adds up.

TIP

Okay. So you did the math from the preceding bullet point. Assume that your slides cost $10 each to process. It wouldn't take but a few 40-slide screen shows to pay for a slide recorder, right? Well, that's only partly right. Even if you *do* have a slide recorder, the slides must be developed and mounted, which accounts for about 25 to 50 percent of the slide-processing cost, depending on where you take them for finishing.

- You should base the resolution of your slides (2K, 4K, 8K, 12K, and so on) upon the size of the audience and the size of the presentation site. The more the projector must magnify the slides, the higher the resolution must be to maintain quality. Often, one set of slides that works well in one setting does not work nearly as well in another. The solution is to print all your slides at high resolution. But this takes more time and costs more — often much more — per slide.

- Slide recorders are not foolproof devices. We've had more than one occasion in which all our slides didn't print the first time through and had to be run again. If you're on a tight schedule, this delay can be a nuisance, even disastrous.

Knowing When to Use Overhead Transparencies

Transparencies are double-edged swords. Sometimes they are easy and inexpensive to generate and print, but they are difficult to display during the presentation. However, under certain circumstances, they are expensive to print (depending on the output device) and difficult to manipulate during presentations, but you can write on them while delivering the presentation, which is a great way to point out important points and clear up difficult concepts. Anyway, here's a list of advantages to using transparencies:

- Transparencies are easy to design, especially if you're printing them on a low-resolution inkjet or laser printer. Because these devices have severe limitations, you can't really get yourself into trouble by creating gawky designs — provided that you understand the limitations, that is. (Check out Chapter 13.)
- The delivery equipment (overhead projector and screen) is inexpensive and reliable. You don't have to worry about breakdowns and incompatibilities at the presentation site.
- When printed on your desktop printer, transparencies are relatively inexpensive. Mistakes aren't so costly, either.
- To illuminate points, you can write on the sheet of glass covering your transparency.
- Because transparencies are placed on the projector by hand, one at a time (unlike slides), controlling the flow of information is easier.

Sound good so far? Check out the following list of disadvantages. (Perhaps you've noticed that at least one of us isn't much impressed with transparencies as a presentation medium — it's Bill. He's into the glitter, flash, and hard work of multimedia presentations.)

- Changing transparencies during a presentation is cumbersome. You must remove and replace each one manually, distracting you and your audience. (You can alleviate this impediment partially by using a helper to change the transparencies. But make sure that you practice your delivery *with the helper* so that he or she knows when to swap the transparencies. Otherwise, you'll be just as distracted by instructing your assistant.)
- Your design choices are severely limited. Because most slides are printed on inkjet or black-and-white laser printers, you can't really incorporate a lot of color, fancy gradients from one color to another, or full-color photographs. (You can improve your design choices by printing the transparencies on a thermal-wax or dye-sublimation printer, which increases quality. If you don't have one of these devices, however, you must take your presentation to a service bureau, which dramatically increases the cost of your transparencies. Thermal-wax runs cost about as much as 35mm slides. Dye-sublimation transparencies can cost as much as $25 to $40 each.)
- Your audience size is limited. No matter what kind of printer you use for your transparencies, you can magnify them only so much without serious degradation of quality. How much you can magnify a transparency largely depends upon what's on it. But if your audience is more than about 500 people, you should consider another medium.

- Except in small, intimate settings, transparencies are an unimpressive, almost goofy, choice of format, especially when you have so many other options. We live in a highly technical age; overheads are low-tech — '60s and '70s technology, appropriate only when that's all you can afford, and are associated with some suspicious, old teacher (in some hot, boring classroom) who covers half the transparency so you can't read ahead.
- Transparencies are not as durable as slides and electronic presentations. They are easily scratched, and their colors fade quickly.

Knowing When to Use Electronic Screen Shows

If Bill had his way, you would use them all the time. Although this presentation medium is the most impressive and versatile, it's also the toughest to design and the most problematic. To work effectively and without embarrassing incidents, all conditions must be checked and rechecked. And, depending on how sophisticated your presentations are, the more you must know to create and deliver them. If you want to include multimedia clips, for example, you've got to understand basic multimedia technology.... You get the picture.

Here's a list of advantages to using electronic screen shows over other formats:

- If you've already got the equipment, electronic presentations are inexpensive to produce. You don't have to print them out on hard copy media, such as slides or transparencies.
- Electronic screen shows are the most impressive medium. The nature of this format makes it the most powerful means for delivering your message for the following reasons:
  - Electronic screen shows provide the most design options. You can include vibrant color blends, gradients, photographs, and multimedia files (provided that you have the right playback equipment).
  - Freelance Graphics contains several built-in options to enhance your electronic screen shows, such as sophisticated transitions between slides, flying bullets (bullets that move onto the slide from various directions), and build slides that display points one at a time, as shown in Figure 1-1.
  - You can launch other applications during your presentation to further explain and clarify points. If, for example, you want to display a 1-2-3 spreadsheet linked to a certain graph on a slide, a click of the mouse brings up the spreadsheet.

- You gain better control over the flow of the information. Rather than being forced to display information linearly, you can easily jump around in presentations or create hot links to other slides containing related data. You can link to other applications, even to another Freelance Graphics presentation. (Figure 1-2 shows the Page Sorter, which is only one of the ways Freelance Graphics makes moving to various slides in your presentation easy.)

✔ You can run electronic presentations on almost any computer, provided it is properly equipped. In other words, you can run the presentation on your notebook computer before a small audience, on a desktop computer before a larger audience, or even for a huge audience in a full-blown multimedia-equipped auditorium. Remember, though, that a number of considerations, including availability of multimedia equipment, exist. Also, presentations resplendent with 24-bit, full-color images don't display well on 256-color notebook computer screens. (Chapter 14 discusses these and other pitfalls.)

✔ Electronic presentations are easy to distribute over a network or on disk.

✔ Electronic presentations are dynamic. Changing information without having to print new slides or overheads is easy.

✔ With the right setup, you can display speaker notes on your computer (notes that the audience cannot see) during the presentation, as shown in Figure 1-3. The notes make delivering the presentation easier. Chapter 14 shows you how to make this happen.

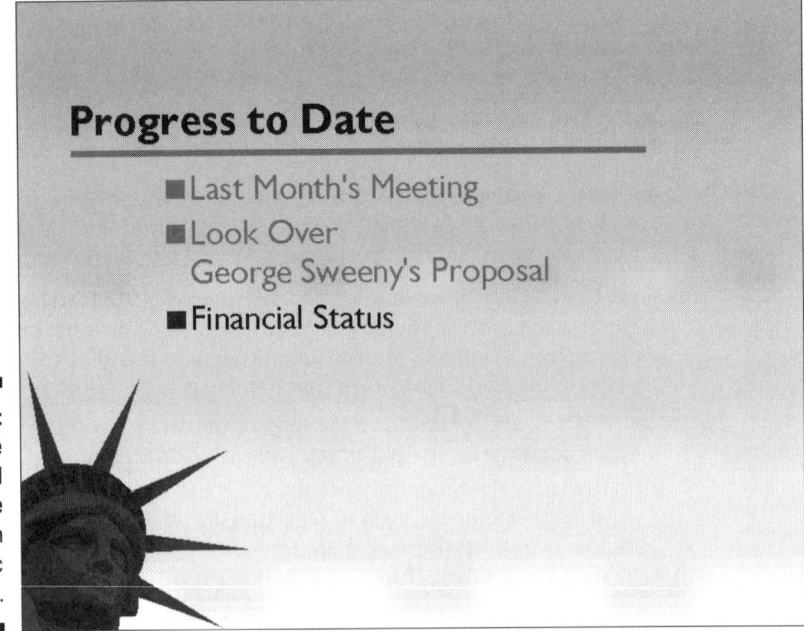

Figure 1-1: An example of a build slide during an electronic presentation.

LCDs — a marriage of old and new technology

A popular device for delivering electronic slide shows to medium-sized audiences is the LCD panel. A flat, partially transparent screen you connect to the video adapter on your notebook or desktop computer, the LCD lies on an overhead projector. Similar to overhead transparencies, the projector magnifies and displays the image on the LCD (the image on your computer) onto a wall or screen.

The LCD provides an easy and relatively inexpensive way to display electronic slide shows.

Plus, you get the benefit of flying bullets, build slides, transitions, even animation and video — options not available with slides and transparencies. A drawback is that the LCD itself does not do sound. You can, however, use your computer's sound capabilities, but that doesn't work well with a large audience unless you plug into some sort of amplified sound system. Also, the quality of your video and animation clips probably won't be as good as you'd like, depending on the level of magnification.

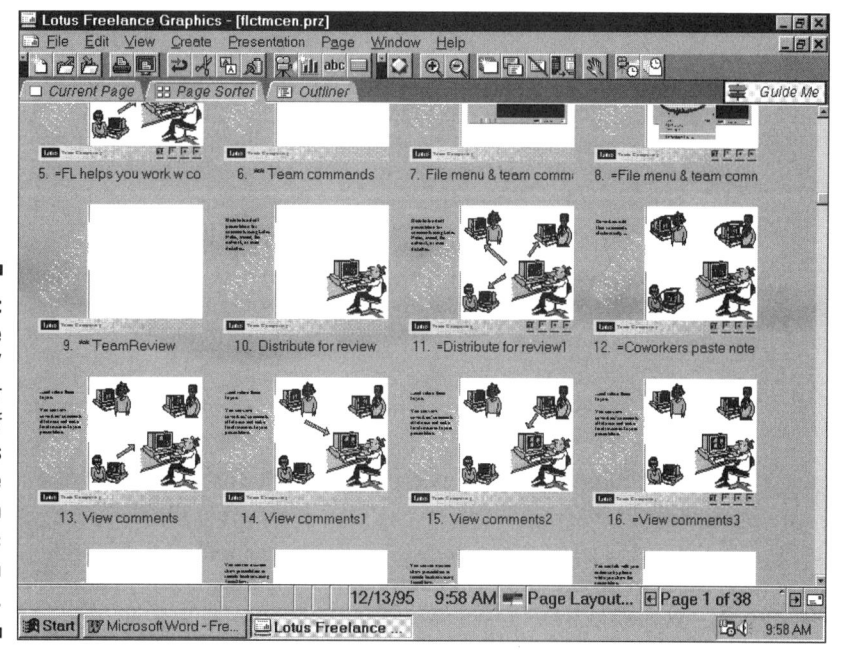

Figure 1-2: Freelance Graphics' Page Sorter is just one of many ways to navigate an electronic screen show.

Figure 1-3: When you make an electronic presentation, Freelance Graphics gives you the option of viewing your speaker notes while delivering the presentation.

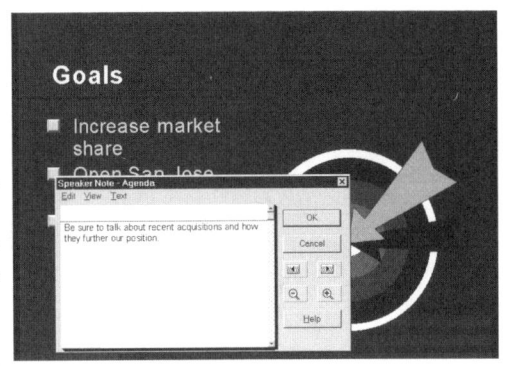

The list of reasons to recommend electronic screen shows seems pretty exhaustive, doesn't it? Here are some reasons not to use them:

- Unless you deliver the presentation on the computer that you created it on, getting it to run properly on another computer can be problematic. For example, if you use fonts that have not been installed on the presenting computer, your text won't display properly.
- Different types of computers display colors and graphics differently. Your slides may look swell on your desktop computer but all wrong on your notebook computer.
- Presentations designed on monitors set at one resolution may not display properly on monitors of different resolutions.
- The equipment to run electronic presentations, especially for large audiences, is expensive.
- Plugging into LCDs, televisions, and multimedia presentation systems brings up a multitude of compatibility issues. You should always do a trial run a day or so before the presentation to ensure that all systems are go and to make sure that you have everything you need.

Recognizing the Importance of Planning Ahead

If you've spent much time with computers, you're a firm believer in Murphy's Law (you know, if something can go wrong, it will). Computers, however, are seldom really at fault. Most mishaps occur because the user doesn't have all the information needed to achieve success. Creating presentations in Freelance Graphics is easy but hardly foolproof. Each type of presentation contains its own pitfalls, all of which you can avoid if you decide on a presentation format *before* you begin working and then make sure that you are aware of potential snafus.

This section provides a list of the most common pitfalls. You should also read the chapters in this book covering each format type for additional information on achieving success with the presentation medium you choose.

- When printing transparencies on a 300-dpi (dots per inch) inkjet or laser printer, you shouldn't use gradients and small-serif fonts. When magnified on a projector, gradients appear grainy and interfere with the other information on the page. Thin type appears broken and jagged. You can get better quality on 600-dpi devices, but you still can't go hog wild. One of the reasons that these printers are inexpensive is that they have limitations.

- Keep your presenting medium in mind when designing visuals, such as charts and graphs. Slides projected onto a screen, for example, can contain more data than screen shows targeted for delivery on a notebook computer, simply because the slide show screen is larger than the computer monitor.

- When creating self-running presentations for distribution on (and display on) other computers, keep the following points in mind:

    - Make sure that you use fonts installed on the presenting computer or include the fonts when you distribute the presentation file.

    - When preparing images (photographs) for presentations targeted for screen shows (or slides), set the resolution at 75 dpi. Computer monitors cannot display higher resolutions, so don't waste your CPU's processing time. (Larger images take forever to print on a slide recorder, with no quality improvement.)

    - Don't use images with a color depth higher than the presenting computer is capable of. If your notebook computer can display only 256 colors (8-bit) or HiColor (16-bit), the only thing a 16.7-million-color image will do is slow down your presentation and take up too much disk space.

- When creating an electronic screen show for distribution on floppy disks, don't include sound and other multimedia clips. They're too large to fit on the disk. (Okay, if your presentation is not too big to fit on a disk, you can get by with a short sound effect or two.)

- When including animation and video files, make sure that the presenting computer contains the appropriate drivers and playback utilities. (Apple QuickTime for Windows drivers for QuickTime movies, for example.)

- When designing presentations for your notebook computer on your desktop computer, set the desktop to the same resolution as your notebook's screen.

✔ When designing slides for output at a service bureau, call the service bureau to get formatting information and the device driver for the intended target device.

✔ Never try to get too much information on one slide. If it looks crowded, it is. Create another slide and move some of the data to the new slide. Or delete some of the data and move it to your speaker notes.

Chapter 2

Familiarizing Yourself with Freelance Graphics 96

In This Chapter

▶ The Freelance Graphics screen
▶ The Freelance Graphics tools
▶ The Freelance Graphics menus
▶ Customizing your work area
▶ Getting around in Freelance Graphics

A major concept behind Windows is that — wherever possible — each application designed for the Windows *graphical user interface* (GUI, pronounced *gooey*) should work and look alike. Freelance Graphics 96 conforms nicely to the Windows 95 environment. And, because Freelance Graphics is also part of the Lotus Office Suite, it has several features in common with other programs in the Suite, such as the SmartIcons that span the top of the Freelance Graphics window. If you also use Lotus WordPro and Lotus 1-2-3, you'll find a similar set of buttons in those programs, as well as many other like features.

However, programs are designed to perform varying and specific tasks; they can't operate completely the same. If they *were* all the same, we wouldn't need so many computer applications. We would have to learn only one program, and life would be wonderful. But our computers wouldn't do nearly as much.

This chapter delves headlong into the Freelance Graphics interface. We open some menus and dialog boxes and take a look around, starting with a description of the Freelance Graphics screen.

The Freelance Graphics Screen

Look at the example of the Freelance Graphics main screen in Figure 2-1. The best way to approach this interface is from a page-layout perspective. Imagine yourself sitting down at a page paste-up easel. Everything you need to lay out

Part I: Gearing Up for Success

your presentation — page by page — is here, including pens, pencils, cutting knives, stencils, rulers, charts and graphs, and clip art images. All you have to do is use them.

Easy so far, right? Well, Freelance Graphics makes it even easier. The program doesn't assume that you are a graphics designer. It provides you with the basic structure for the different types of pages (or slides) in your presentations. Figure 2-1, for example, shows the title slide for your presentation. You don't have to make difficult design decisions, such as where to place elements and what size they should be. First, you fill in the content; in this case, the title of your presentation, the subtitle, and the company logo. Then click on a "Click here" *placeholder,* and the program guides you to the next step in the process.

If you want to, you can actually lay out a simple presentation without delving into Freelance Graphics' powerful menus and dialog boxes. But if you want to customize your presentation — making it unique, your own — Freelance Graphics provides the muscle to get the job done, and then some. Now look again at Figure 2-1.

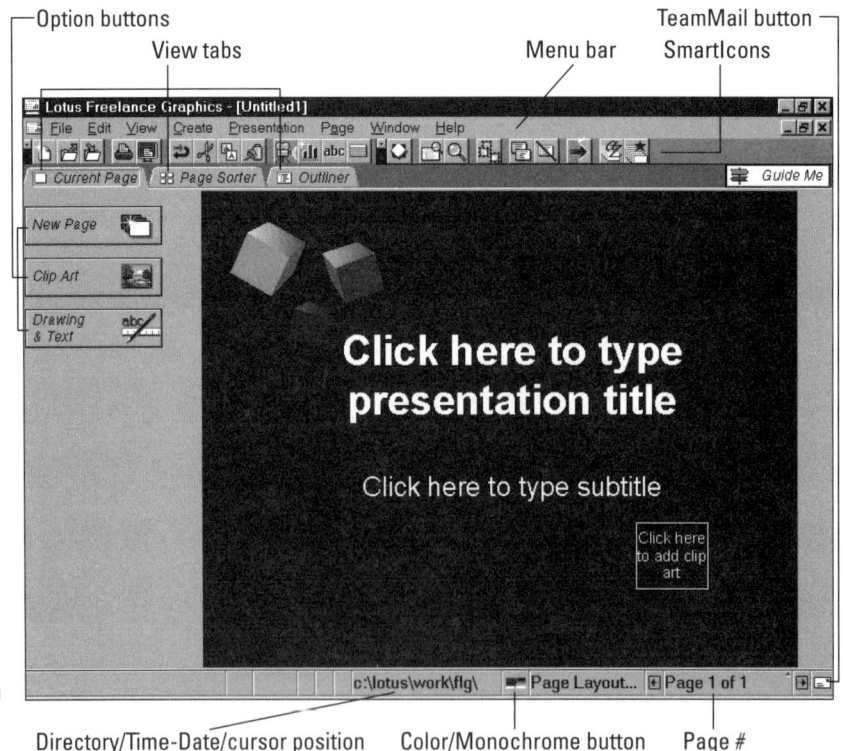

Figure 2-1: The Freelance Graphics Current Page main screen.

Chapter 2: Familiarizing Yourself with Freelance Graphics 96

The following list provides a brief description of the Current Page (main screen) elements:

- **Menu bar:** You probably recognize the menu bar — it's where Freelance Graphics stores all the commands and options. We look closer at the menus in the next section.

- **SmartIcons:** These icons are shortcuts to often-used features, such as printing, copying, cutting, pasting, and many others. You can design your own sets of SmartIcons for specific types of presentations and tasks. Suppose that some of your presentations contain many organizational charts. You can create and save a set of SmartIcons specific to working with organizational charts. The "How to Customize Your Work Area" section of this chapter explains SmartIcon sets.

  What do all those icons mean? Windows 95's Tool Tip feature (stolen from the Macintosh) makes it easier to identify SmartIcon buttons. Simply point to any button on the SmartIcon bar with your mouse. Within a second or two, you get a bubble containing a short description of what the button does. If your Tool Tip isn't working, you can turn it on by choosing User Setup from the File menu, choosing SmartIcon Setup, and then checking the box beside Show Icon Descriptions.

- **View Tabs:** These three tabs below the SmartIcons bar toggle the display between the three main Freelance Graphics views. Current Page, the one in Figure 2-1, is the Slide Design view. Page Sorter displays small "thumbnails" (miniature versions) of all the slides in your presentation. You can use this view to find a specific slide or to rearrange the slides in your presentation. Outliner takes you to the Freelance Graphics Outline view, which enables you to control the flow of information in your presentation. Each view is discussed in more detail in the "Getting Around in Freelance Graphics" section of this chapter and in other chapters throughout this book.

- **Option buttons:** These buttons along the left side of the screen provide instant access to often-used options, such as new slides and drawing and text-formatting tools. This area of the screen is *context-sensitive,* which is another of those $25 computer terms. It means that the program tries to anticipate your needs and provide the appropriate options.

- **Directory/Time-Date/Cursor Position:** This button at the bottom of the Freelance Graphics screen toggles between three options — showing you the directory and filename for the current presentation, the time and date, or the X- and Y-axis of the mouse cursor on the slide — each time you click the button.

  One thing about graphics applications that confuses many users is the X- and Y-axis stuff. It seems like a highly technical mathematical formula. Well, thank goodness it's not nearly *that* complicated. X- and Y-axis refers to page coordinates — a particular position on the page. *X* refers to the horizontal position, and *Y* refers to the vertical position. Where these two points meet, or intersect, is the *X- and Y-coordinate.*

Clear as mud, right? Look at it this way: If you place your cursor 1 inch down and 1 inch over from the upper-left corner of the page, you are at the 1" × 1" X- and Y-axis. Freelance Graphics and most other graphics applications measure X- and Y-axis from the upper-left corner of the page or screen.

- **Color/Monochrome:** Using this button enables you to switch between a monochrome and color view of your slide. You can use it to see how your slides will look in black and white. Also, page elements on some colored slides are difficult to see on some monitors. Switching to black and white makes it easier to edit text and other dark elements.

- **Page Number:** These three buttons enable you to navigate the pages in your presentation. The right- and left-pointing arrows advance and go back one slide. The Page # of # button brings up a pop-up menu that allows you to select from a list of slides in the presentation.

- **TeamMail:** You use this button to send messages, an entire presentation, or specified pages to members of your team. When you click it, the TeamMail for Freelance Graphics dialog box opens, providing you with several options for sending your presentation over the network.

The Freelance Graphics Tools

All graphics applications have toolboxes, and Freelance Graphics has a good one. It contains tools for working with text; tools for drawing lines, boxes, circles, and polygons; tools for creating flowcharts; and shape tools. The only tool that's missing is one for reading your mind. (Lotus says it's working on that one.) This section looks at the various kinds of tools and how to use them.

The majority of Freelance Graphics' tools are in the tool palette, which you get to by clicking the Drawing & Text button (see Figure 2-2). From this palette, you choose the tool you want and then draw or place the desired object on your slide.

Figure 2-2: The Freelance Graphics text, drawing, shape, and connector tools.

Using the Pointer (selection) tool

The Pointer tool is the first tool in the toolbox (Tools). You use it for selecting, moving, and resizing objects on your slides. (You must select an object before you can edit it — whether you want to resize it by using the Pointer tool or one of the menus, buttons, or dialog boxes.) You can tell that you've successfully selected an object when it has eight *handles* around the object (see Figure 2-3). Do they look like handles to you? Not to me either. They look like little square boxes.

Figure 2-3:
You know that you've selected an object when it has eight little boxes around it.

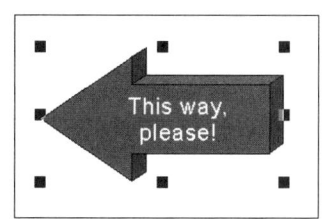

Selecting an object with the Pointer tool

The Pointer tool (arrow) is Freelance Graphics' default tool — the one the program assumes you want to use unless you tell it otherwise. The Pointer tool is active even when the toolbox is not displayed. To select an object with the Pointer tool, click the object. When the eight handles appear, you know it's selected.

To select two or more objects, use one of these methods:

- Click the first object, then hold down the Shift key and click the subsequent objects.
- Hold down the mouse button and drag a box around all the objects you want to select. (This procedure is known as *marquee* selecting. La-de-da.)

The box you draw when you're marquee selecting must encompass all portions of the objects you want to select. Freelance Graphics is very particular; it does not select an object when a portion of it is outside the marquee.

When you select more than one object, each has its own set of handles. To deselect an object when multiple objects are selected, Shift+click the object you want to deselect (that is, hold down the Shift key as you click the object with the mouse). You can move the objects as a group or recolor them, but you cannot resize them using your mouse.

Moving objects with the Pointer tool

Here's an easy one. To move an object, place the Pointer tool anywhere on the object itself (not the handles), press and hold down the mouse button, and pull the pointer to the location you want. In computerese, this procedure is called *dragging*. Clever, no?

To drag multiple selected objects, drag any one of the objects in the group of selected objects.

Resizing objects with the Pointer tool

Those eight handles we've been talking about actually do serve a purpose other than indicating that an object is selected. You use them to resize and reshape objects. To resize an object both horizontally and vertically, drag one of the corner handles. To resize in one direction, drag one of the middle handles. The left and right handles resize horizontally. The top and bottom handles resize vertically.

Be careful, though: dragging the middle handles also distorts the object. Figure 2-4 shows some highly distorted objects.

Figure 2-4: When you use the middle handles to drag an object, you distort it, you pervert you.

You can also use the Reduce, Enlarge, and Equal SmartIcons to resize objects (see Figure 2-5). The Reduce and Enlarge SmartIcons resize proportionally by about 20 percent. The Equal SmartIcon forces multiple selected objects to the same size.

Chapter 2: Familiarizing Yourself with Freelance Graphics 96 25

Figure 2-5:
The Enlarge, Reduce, and Equal SmartIcons for quick resizing.

Using the Text tool

The Text tool is the button in the toolbox next to the Pointer tool — the one, appropriately enough, with the *abc* on it. This tool becomes active when you click a text placeholder on a slide, when you click a Text Shape (discussed next), or when you select the Text tool from the toolbox.

Figure 2-6 shows the Text tool activated after clicking the title placeholder. Now all you do to enter text is begin typing. The bar across the top of the text entry area enables you to adjust the type size in preset increments that are set in the SmartMaster and fully customizable. Notice that the Page menu on the menu bar changed to the Text menu. From the Text menu, you can change type style (bold, italic, and so on), alignment (left, center, right), and many other settings.

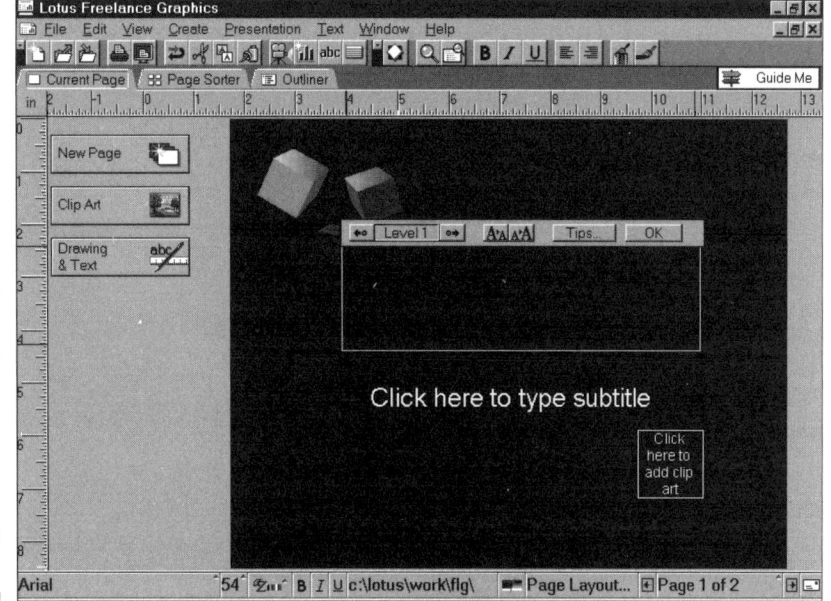

Figure 2-6: The Freelance Graphics screen when you activate the Text tool.

Part I: Gearing Up for Success

> **TIP:** Notice, too, in Figure 2-6, the bunch of new buttons across the bottom of the Freelance Graphics screen. You can use the buttons to change the text point size, style, and color, which is faster than using the Text menu. Chapter 8 takes a look at formatting text.

You can also place text anywhere on a slide by selecting the Text tool, clicking where you want the text, and then typing the words.

Using the drawing tools

Freelance Graphics comes with a slew of drawing tools, which are all the other tools in the same group with the Pointer and Text tools. Using them, you can draw to your heart's content. You can draw circles, boxes, polygons, and even arrows. Let's hope that you're a better artist than whoever drew Figure 2-7. This section is an overview of using these tools. For a more detailed description of how to create all types of fancy artwork with the drawing tools, check out Chapter 9.

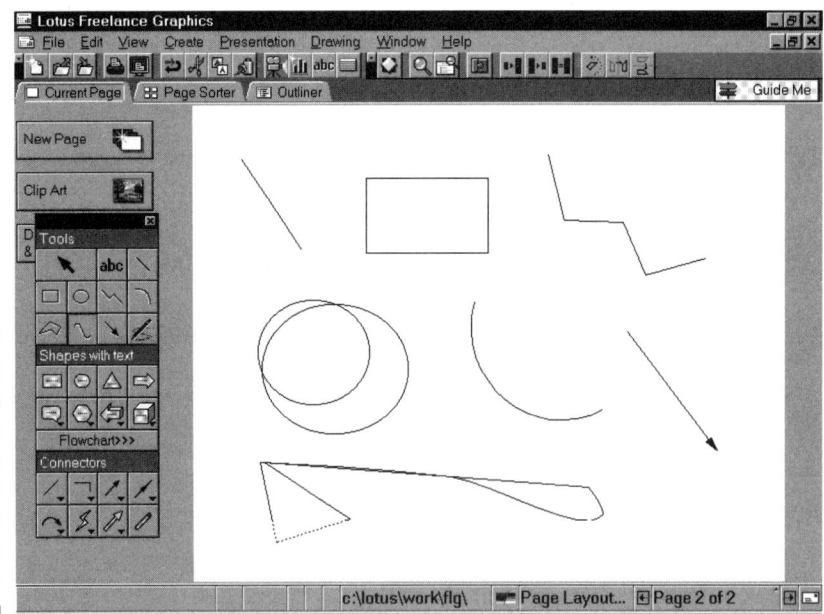

Figure 2-7: Shapes drawn with the Freelance Graphics drawing tools.

To use a drawing tool, select the desired tool and start drawing on the slide. When you draw a shape with the drawing tool, Freelance Graphics automatically selects it, and the Page menu becomes the Drawing menu. From the Drawing menu, you can change a drawing's color, line weight, and many other attributes.

Using Text Shapes

Text Shapes are all those funny-looking arrows and boxes in the second portion of the toolbox. There are actually two sets of Text Shapes. If you click the Flowcharts button, you get a set specifically for working with flowcharts, as shown in Figure 2-8. They're called Text Shapes because you can type text into them and the text remains centered in the shape, no matter how you resize or move the shape around on the screen. Text Shapes make great buttons and callouts.

Figure 2-8: Clicking the Flowcharts button brings up this set of Text Shapes.

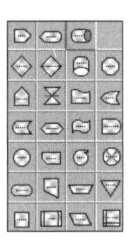

Some of the Text Shape buttons have down arrows on them, indicating that you can find even more shapes on a pop-up subpalette.

To use a Text Shape, click the Drawing & Text option button and then click the shape you want. Click again on your slide. Freelance Graphics assumes that the next thing you want to do is resize the shape. After resizing the shape, click the shape again to type your text into it (see Figure 2-9).

You can change the size and appearance of your text by using options on the Text Shape menu or from the buttons at the bottom of the Freelance Graphics screen. (Chapter 8 contains a detailed description of using Text Shapes.)

Using Connectors

Connectors are the lines and flow arrows used in flowcharts and other diagrams that show the relations between objects, such as the lines that connect the boxes in a top-down organizational chart. To use one of these lines, select the one you want, click the slide where you want it, and then drag the end points to the two objects you want to connect. The connectors then remain connected to the two objects, no matter where you move either one of the objects, kind of like Siamese twins. (Chapter 7 has a discussion of connectors.)

28 Part I: Gearing Up for Success

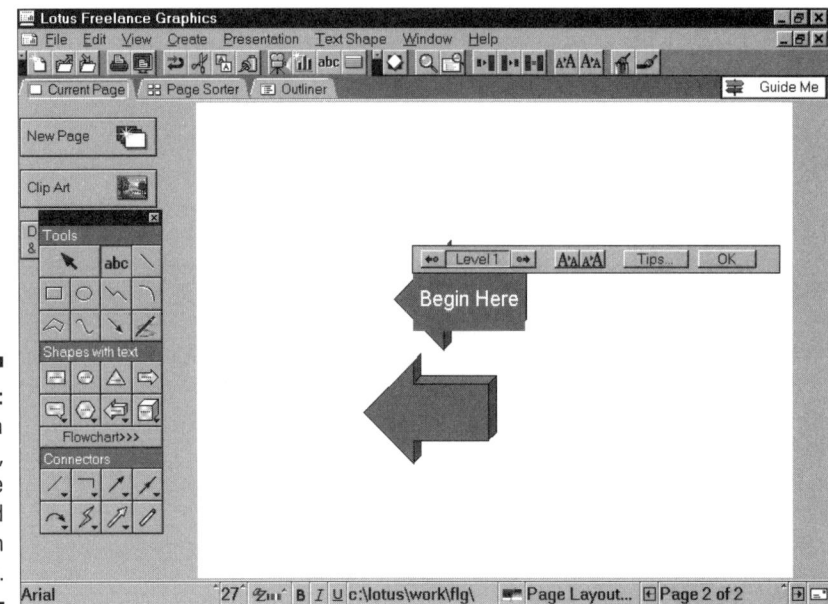

Figure 2-9: To type in a Text Shape, click the shape and then begin typing.

What's on the Freelance Graphics Menus?

Sometimes you can't tell, I know, but software developers really do try to design software that's easy to use and figure out. One way they arrange the software so that it's user-friendly is to make the command structures on the menus logical; the Freelance Graphics developers did a good job. However, the Page menu can be tricky. It is *context-sensitive;* that is, it knows what element you're working with and changes submenus to match that element. If you've selected text, for example, the Page menu becomes a Text menu. Spooky, huh? Table 2-1 lists the submenus that seem to appear from out of nowhere but really are connected to the Page menu.

Table 2-1	Context-Sensitive Page Submenus	
Submenu	*What's Selected*	*Contains Commands for . . .*
Page	Nothing	Changing page properties and layout of the current page
		Creating, deleting, and moving pages in a presentation
		Creating speaker notes, bullets, and slide transition effects
Text	Text	Changing type style, size, color, and other properties

Submenu	What's Selected	Contains Commands for ...
Text Shape	A Text Shape	Changing the appearance of the shape
		Changing the text within a shape
		Applying screen show effects to Text Shapes
Connector	A connector	Changing the properties of connectors
Drawing	A drawing	Changing the properties of a drawing
Group	A group	Grouping objects
Collection	A collection	Making collections of objects
Chart	A chart	Changing the properties of a drawing
Org Chart	An organizational chart	Changing the properties of a drawing
Sound	A Sound icon	Changing the way sound — well, sounds
Movie	A Movie icon	Handling movies such as *Gone with the Wind* — not!

Customizing the Freelance Graphics Work Environment

Freelance Graphics provides several ways you can make your work easier by customizing the program's working environment. You can add SmartIcons to and remove them from the button bar, for example, or you can create entire sets of icons for working on specific tasks, such as one for creating screen shows and another for working with transparencies. You can also tell Freelance Graphics to display certain screen elements, such as rulers, all the time and to save your work automatically every so often.

Customizing the SmartIcons bar

Okay. So SmartIcons are a great help. But half of the stuff you need isn't available as an icon, or the icons currently available are wrong for the way you work. Take heart. You can display almost every Freelance Graphics command and feature on the SmartIcons bar. You can even create sets for certain tasks and tell Freelance Graphics to display them in specific contexts — say, a set of icons for working with text that appears when you're working in Outline view or on a text object, or maybe a set for customizing charts in Chart view. And, if you don't like the icons themselves, you can even modify them using the Edit Icon option. It just doesn't get any more flexible!

You can customize SmartIcons in the SmartIcons Setup dialog box, shown in Figure 2-10. To get to this dialog box, click the File menu, and then choose SmartIcons Setup from the User Setup submenu. In this dialog box, you can customize an existing SmartIcons set or create a new one. The right side of SmartIcons Setup shows available icons. The left side provides options for managing SmartIcon sets.

Figure 2-10: Use SmartIcons Setup to customize Freelance Graphics SmartIcons and to create SmartIcon sets for specific tasks.

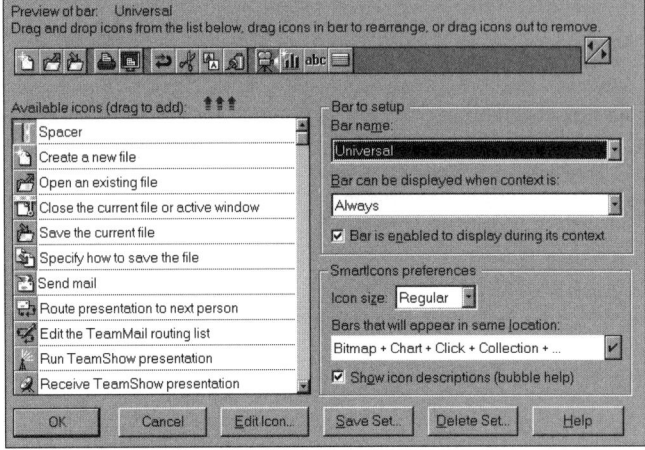

Customizing the active SmartIcons set

The active SmartIcon set is the one displayed when you open SmartIcons Setup. You can change the active set from within the dialog box by clicking the drop-down list under Bar Name in the right side of the dialog box.

Displaying SmartIcons

The number of SmartIcons Freelance Graphics can display depends on the resolution of your display system. Typically, resolutions range from 640 × 480 pixels to 1280 × 1024 pixels, with a couple of settings in between. Most modern computers support 640 × 480, 800 × 600, 1024 × 768, and some support 1280 × 1024.

Depending on the number of SmartIcons your system can display, you may want to remove some icons before placing new ones on the bar. To remove a SmartIcon, drag it off the bar. It disappears. Poof.

Chapter 2: Familiarizing Yourself with Freelance Graphics 96

To add an icon to the active set, scroll through the list of available icons and then drag the one you want to the bar. When you let go of the mouse button, the icon appears as part of the set. Just like that.

Arranging SmartIcons on the icon bar

If you've ever played one of those little slider puzzles, you already know how to arrange the icons on a SmartIcon bar. Drag the icon to the position you want. All the other icons move to make room for it. Polite, aren't they? You can arrange icons in distinctive groups by using the Spacer icon. Drag the Spacer icon from the list and place it between the icons you want to separate.

When you've finished designing your SmartIcon bar, be sure to save it; otherwise, all your hard work will be lost. Freelance Graphics asks whether you want to save the set with a new name or use the existing name. The choice is yours, but if you use the existing name, the original set is overwritten.

Designating when context-sensitive SmartIcon sets appear

To tell Freelance Graphics to display certain icon sets in specific situations, first select the set name in the Bar Name drop-down list. Then select the context where you want the bar to appear in the Bar can be displayed when context is list.

If your screen has room, you can display several sets at once. Keep this in mind when designing your SmartIcon sets. The larger you make them, the fewer that appear at once.

You can also control the appearance of your SmartIcons bars by using the drop-down lists beside each set on the bar. You can hide or display sets assigned to a current context, hide all SmartIcons, or open SmartIcons Setup.

Using Freelance Preferences to further customize your work environment

Preferences, sometimes called *defaults,* control several aspects of how a computer program works or what the program does if you don't tell it to do something else. For example, if you don't tell Freelance Graphics to do automatic backups of your work, it doesn't do them.

Freelance Graphics enables you to change several of its defaults through the Freelance Graphics Preferences dialog box as shown in Figure 2-11. This section looks at several of the customization options in Freelance Graphics Preferences, which you can get to by clicking the File menu and then selecting Freelance Preferences from the User Setup submenu.

Figure 2-11: Use the Freelance Graphics Preferences dialog box to change several of the program's defaults.

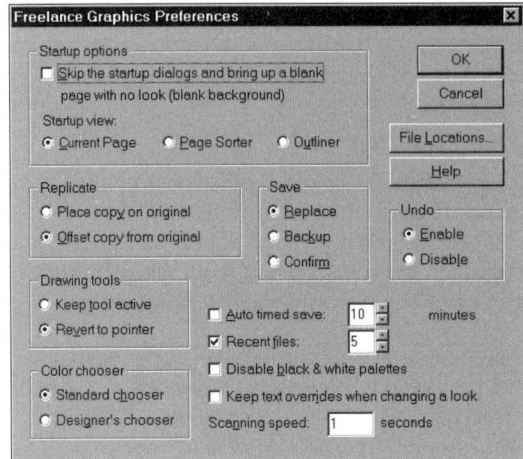

Getting rid of those pesky startup dialog boxes

The startup dialog boxes are those sets of prompts that come up when you first open Freelance Graphics — you know, the ones that allow you to choose whether you want to open an existing presentation or begin a new one, and then choose a look and a context. They are helpful for some people, but those of us who have been using Windows for a while often prefer using the File menu for starting or opening presentations. If you don't like wading through that sequence of dialog boxes before getting to the program's interface, you can turn them off by selecting the first option in Startup Options in the Freelance Graphics Preferences dialog box.

Getting a better view

Not everyone works the same way. Bill, for example, likes starting and managing his presentations from the Outline. Roger prefers working from Current Page. You can control which view Freelance Graphics displays on startup by selecting the desired view under Startup view in Startup options in the Freelance Graphics Preferences dialog box.

Telling Freelance Graphics where to keep your presentation files

It's hard to understand how computers store and manage computer files, which in turn can make it difficult to find the files when you need them. You can tell Freelance Graphics where to keep and look for specific types of files by clicking the File Locations button, which immediately runs away and gets the File Locations dialog box, shown in Figure 2-12. In this dialog box, you can tell Freelance Graphics where to put presentation files, SmartMasters (templates), clip art, and backup files. And, believe you me, Freelance Graphics will obey your instructions to the *T*.

Figure 2-12: The File Locations dialog box.

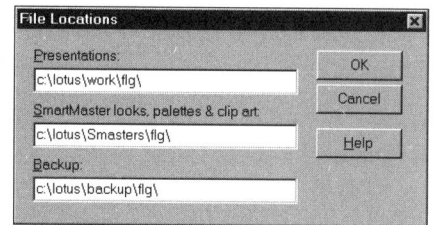

You can either accept the defaults or assign the locations to directories that are easier to remember, such as C:\FREELANCE GRAPHICS PRESENTATIONS. You are using Windows 95, after all, and you may as well take advantage of the capability to use long (up to 255 characters) filenames.

Telling Freelance Graphics to automatically save your work

If you've ever lost two or three hours (or more) worth of work because of a computer crash or power failure, you can appreciate this option. You can tell Freelance Graphics to do incremental backups of your presentations while you work. To do so, check the box beside the Auto timed save option in the Freelance Graphics Preferences dialog box. You can then use the up or down arrows next to the option to set the time between automatic saves.

Use these guidelines when you want Freelance Graphics to automatically save your files:

- If you set too long an interval between saves, you'll lose a lot of work if disaster strikes. Set this option to the amount of work you can comfortably lose without pulling your hair out. For us, it's about 15 minutes.

- If you set too short an interval between saves, you'll wind up doing more waiting for the computer to save your presentations and less time working. This is especially true of presentations containing large, full-color photographs that take a long time to save.

If you noticed that we didn't cover all the options in the Freelance Graphics Preferences dialog box, you're astute. Many of these options are pointed out in tips at various places throughout the book, where they are pertinent to the discussion. In the meantime, if you see something in the dialog box that requires an immediate answer, click the Help button. You'll find your answer.

Getting Around in Freelance Graphics

The Freelance Graphics interface contains several different modules, or views, including: Current Page, Page Sorter, Outliner, SmartMaster (templates), and Chart. The program also provides several ways to move around in a presentation, from Current Page view and from many of the other views. In this section, we look at the Freelance Graphics interface from the following perspectives:

- Navigating the Freelance Graphics interface
- Getting around in your presentations

Although Freelance Graphics has places to go and see, getting to them is not difficult. The interface provides many easy and convenient ways to get around in the program.

Unless you change the startup view in the Freelance Graphics Preferences dialog box, the program starts in Current Page view. You can change to the other various views and modules from here in a number of ways. The easiest way to get back and forth between the three main views — Current Page, Page Sorter, and Outliner — is by clicking the tabs in the upper-left corner of the presentation window, beneath the SmartIcons.

You can also change views by selecting the corresponding command on the View menu.

Getting around in Current Page

Current Page, or the screen where you design your specific slides, is, for the most part, the Freelance Graphics main screen. You use it to navigate from slide to slide and zoom in and out on the page.

Getting from slide to slide

Freelance Graphics provides a number of ways to navigate to and from various slides in your presentations. The easiest way is using the three page buttons in the lower-right corner of the screen. The left and right arrows move backward and forward one page in the presentation. Following are some other ways to get around in Current Page:

Chapter 2: Familiarizing Yourself with Freelance Graphics 96

To Go...	Do This...
To a list of slides in the current presentation, from which you can select a specific slide in the list	Click Page # of # button
To the Go To Page dialog box, from which you can select a specific slide from a list of slide titles	Click the Go To SmartIcon *or* press Ctrl+G *or* choose Edit➪Go To *or* choose Page➪Go To Page
Ahead one slide	Press PageUp *or* choose Page➪Previous Page
Back one slide	Press PageDown *or* choose Page➪Next Page

Zooming in and out on the page

When doing close work on specific areas of slides, such as working on small type or graphics, zooming in on the area enables you to see your work and not strain your eyes. You also need to zoom out to see how an entire slide looks. In Freelance Graphics, you have several options for zooming in and out on slides.

- To zoom in, you can use the Zoom In SmartIcon (large magnifying glass) to increase the zoom level incrementally, which is the same as selecting View➪Zoom In. You can also use Zoom to Actual Size on the View menu, which blows up the page and increases the zoom level.

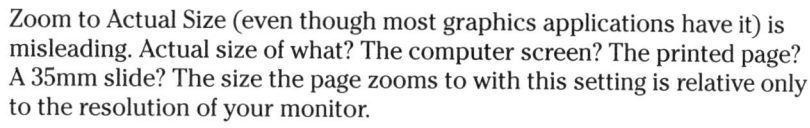

  Zoom to Actual Size (even though most graphics applications have it) is misleading. Actual size of what? The computer screen? The printed page? A 35mm slide? The size the page zooms to with this setting is relative only to the resolution of your monitor.

- To zoom out, you can choose View➪Zoom Out or Zoom to Full Page from the menu or click the Zoom to Full Page SmartIcon (small magnifying glass).

  To return to the last zoom level, choose View➪Last Zoom.

Getting around in Page Sorter

The Page Sorter, shown in Figure 2-13, displays your entire presentation in thumbnail view. You can go to a specific slide or rearrange (or sort) your presentation from this view. Table 2-2 tells you how to perform specific tasks.

Part I: Gearing Up for Success

Table 2-2	Navigating in Page Sorter
To . . .	*Do This . . .*
Go to a specific slide and return to Current Page	Double-click the slide thumbnail.
Move one slide to another location	Drag the slide to the new location. All other slides move and repaginate (renumber) automatically.
Move two or more slides to another location	Click the first slide, Shift+click each subsequent slide, and then drag the group to the new location.

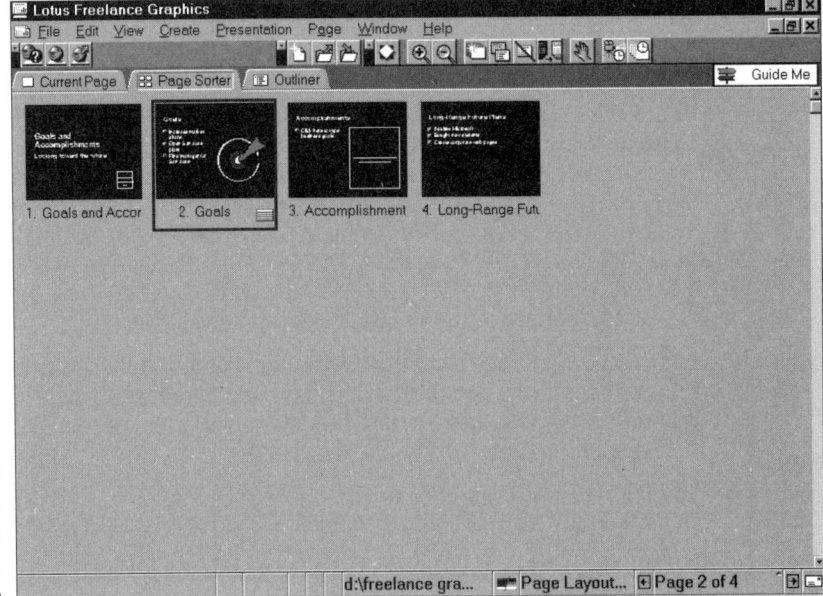

Figure 2-13: The Page Sorter.

In long presentations, you sometimes have to scroll through thumbnails looking for the right slide. You can use the techniques discussed in the preceding section to move around in Page Sorter.

Chapter 3
Creating Your First Presentation

In This Chapter
- Creating a new presentation the easy way, with SmartMasters
- Saving a presentation
- Printing a presentation
- Closing a presentation
- Reopening a presentation
- Previewing your presentation

*F*reelance Graphics provides simplicity for the novice and sophistication for the seasoned professional. This chapter proves the first part of this statement. In these few short pages, you learn how easy creating a presentation can be — you can literally do it in minutes!

If you've ever attended a presentation where the speaker seemed unprepared and disorganized, you've got an idea of how embarrassing it can be for both the presenter and the audience. You can avoid this kind of disaster by following these two simple rules:

- Plan your presentation.
- Become as familiar with the presentation material as possible.

Creating Your First Presentation the Easy Way

Freelance Graphics offers two ways to create presentations: SmartMaster content templates and the Freelance Graphics Outliner. This section presents the one that provides a plan as you create — SmartMaster content templates. Chapter 4 discusses the Freelance Graphics Outliner.

Part I: Gearing Up for Success

To create a presentation using SmartMaster content templates, follow these steps:

1. **Start Freelance Graphics from the Windows 95 Start menu by clicking Start, scrolling up to Programs, scrolling over to Lotus SmartSuite, and then clicking Lotus Freelance Graphics 96.**

2. **In the Welcome to Lotus Freelance Graphics dialog box, click the Create a New Presentation Using a SmartMaster tab.**

   The New Presentation dialog box, as shown in Figure 3-1, appears. The first box lists *SmartMaster contents*, or 30 or so of the most common scenarios on which to base your presentation. To the right of the content list is a description of the currently highlighted content.

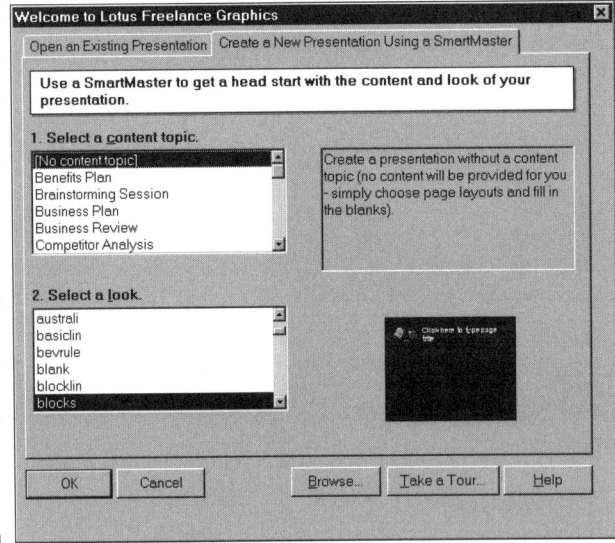

Figure 3-1: In the New Presentations tab you can choose a content and look for your slides.

3. **Using the scroll arrows on the content list, scroll down until you see a SmartMaster content template that appeals to you —** `Meeting - Team`**, for example.**

4. **Click the SmartMaster to select it.**

   Freelance Graphics displays a description of the SmartMaster in the box on the right and suggests a look in the list below.

5. **Scroll through the list of looks.**

   In the box on the right, Freelance Graphics displays a thumbnail view of the look.

6. **Find the look that you want (**`pencil2`**, for example) and select it.**

When you chose a Smart Master content, Freelance Graphics automatically suggested a look. However, you don't have to use its suggestion. Keep the target output device foremost in your mind. For example, SmartMasters containing a lot of color often don't print well on 300-dpi inkjet printers or black-and-white laser printers. Also, SmartMasters with a great deal of white — which is actually clear on most media — are designed for transparencies. 35mm slides and electronic screen shows with white backgrounds are not very attractive and are often too bright to view comfortably.

> Oh, yeah. Another consideration is that you simply may not like the look that Freelance Graphics suggests. Feel free to change it. Be careful, though. Don't choose inappropriate backgrounds for serious subjects. Using the Festive SmartMaster to announce that your company is on the verge of going belly-up seems a little strange, for example.

7. **Click OK.**

   Freelance Graphics displays the New Page dialog box, as shown in Figure 3-2. From here, you choose the first page of your presentation. Notice that Freelance Graphics has given you several choices, or topics, based on the content of the SmartMaster.

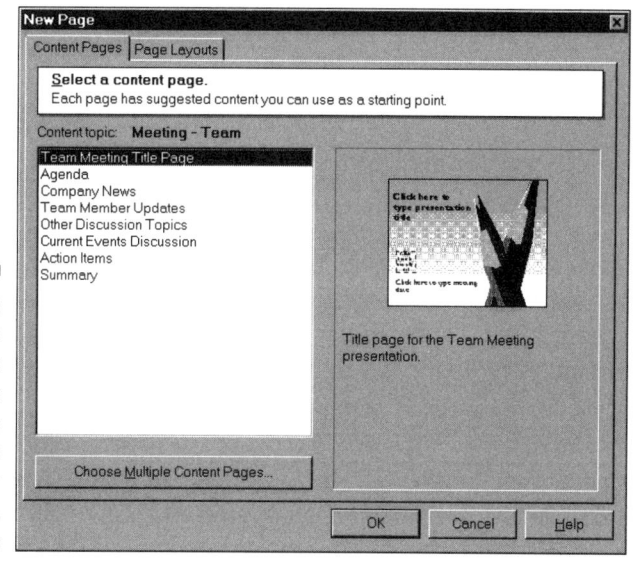

Figure 3-2: Use the New Page dialog box to select the first page of your presentation.

8. **Select the first content page that the SmartMaster lists (Team Meeting Title Page, for example), and click OK.**

   The first page in your presentation is now ready to receive your information, as shown in Figure 3-3.

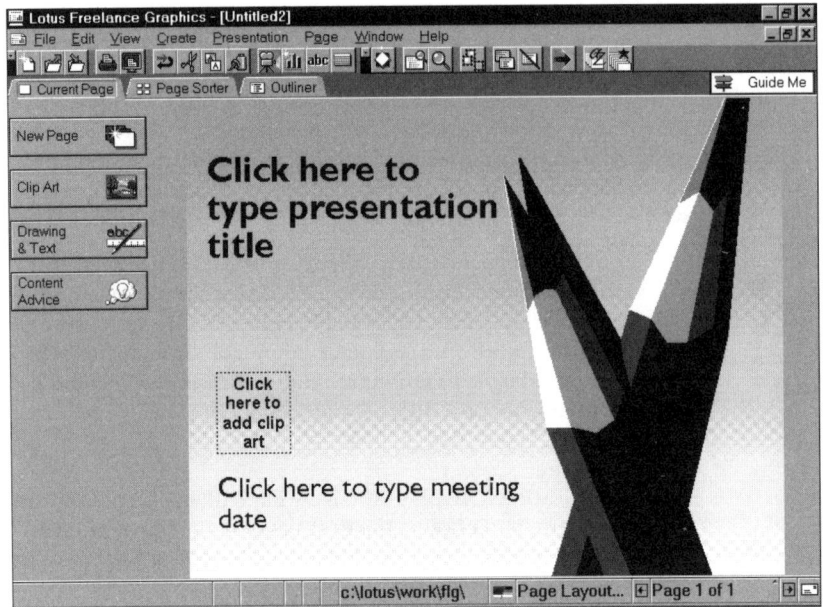

Figure 3-3:
The first slide in a presentation.

9. **To add text to your page, click the placeholders and type the information you want to appear on the page.**

    When you click a text placeholder, such as the title text, Freelance Graphics goes into a text-editing mode that enables to you type and format text. Chapter 8 discusses formatting text.

    Each SmartMaster, be it Corporate Strategy, Business Plan, or whatever, requires a slightly different information flow, and Freelance Graphics provides content advice for each. To get more information about the SmartMaster you're working on, click the Content Advice button on the left side of the screen.

10. **Click a blank place on the slide to clear the white text box.**

11. **To add clip art to the page, click the** click here to add clip art **placeholder.**

    The Add Clip Art or Diagram to the Page dialog box opens. In it, you can select from a catalog of symbols and diagrams that come with Freelance Graphics.

    The Scan button between the arrows scrolls through the catalog automatically, displaying one page of images after another.

    Granted, the Freelance Graphics clip art catalog is extensive, but it often won't have the images you need. (We're not all that impressed with the quality of some of the Lotus clip art, anyway.) Chapter 8 explains how to create and add your own symbols and diagrams to the clip art catalog.

12. **Scroll through the drop-down list to find the category you want (`commobjt`, for example) and then select it.**

    You now have a page displaying clip art. The notation at the top of the page (beneath the spiral binding) shows the number of images in this category. `commobjt` has 34, for example. As you select each image, the notation changes, telling you the name of the selected image and its position in the list. The Burn Candle at Both Ends image, for example, is 1 of 34.

13. **Select the image you want (the pot of gold and rainbow, for example, is 7 of 34).**

14. **Click OK.**

    The clip art is now placed on the slide. It's not really big enough to see well, however, so you need to resize it.

15. **Drag the upper-right object handle (one of the eight boxes surrounding the image) until the clip art image is a little larger (see Figure 3-4).**

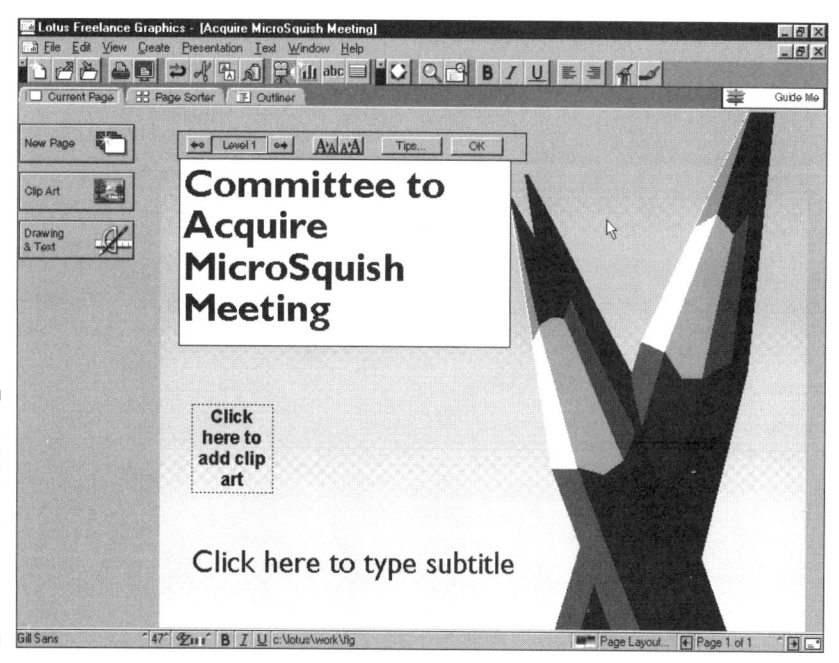

Figure 3-4: Clip art is now positioned and sized onto your slide.

16. **Finish the first page that the SmartMaster suggests by filling in any placeholders you want to use with text or graphics.**

17. **Click the New Page option button on the left side of the screen.**

    You've seen this dialog box before. The SmartMaster suggests the next page based on your choice of contents.

18. **Click OK to accept the SmartMaster suggestion.**
19. **Finish the page by typing your agenda one bullet point after another, pressing Enter each time you complete a point.**

    Each time you press Enter, Freelance Graphics starts a new bullet point.

The procedure for adding new slides based on the content built into the SmartMaster is the same from slide to slide. Simply click the New Page button and accept the default slide.

We hear what you're thinking: *This content progression is great, but what if I want to add charts and other visuals?* You are quite astute. Few presentations consist of text slides, one right after another. How boring. You can sneak out of the SmartMaster dance at any time by selecting the Page Layouts tab in the New Page dialog box and selecting the type of slide you want from the list, such as 1 Chart or Diagram (see Figure 3-5). When you finish that slide and click the New Page option button again, Freelance Graphics returns to the original SmartMaster flow without skipping a beat, keeping your presentation nice and orderly.

Also, you can create several pages at once by clicking the Choose Multiple Content Pages option button in the New Page dialog box.

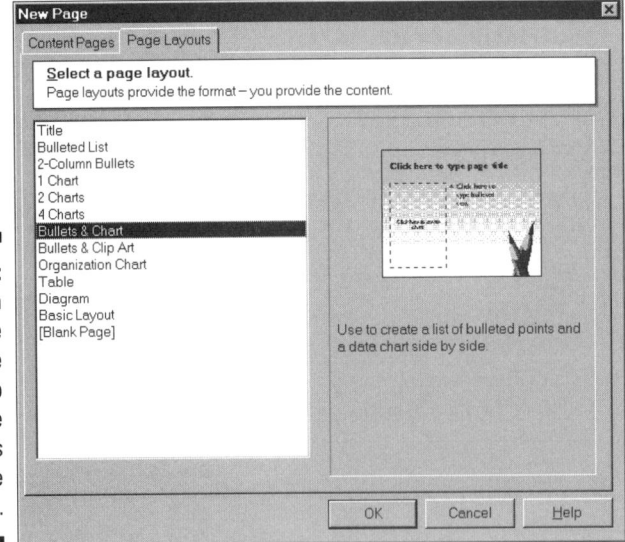

Figure 3-5: You can click the Page Layouts tab to choose from various page templates.

Saving Your Presentation

To save your presentation, follow these steps:

1. **Press Ctrl+S or choose File⇨Save from the menu bar.**

    If this is the first time you have saved the presentation, the Save As dialog box shown in Figure 3-6 appears, asking you to name the file.

    Figure 3-6: Use the Save As dialog box to name and save your presentation files.

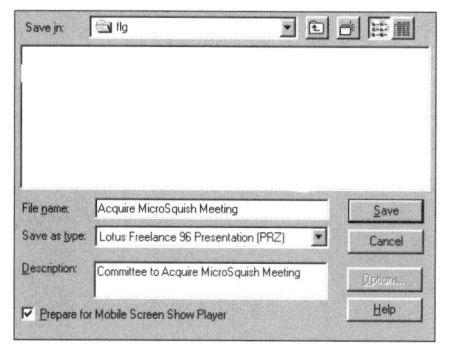

2. **To save to the default directory, type a name in the File name field.**

    In Windows 95, you can type filenames up to 255 characters long. So go ahead and type a description that means something to you. Also, you do not need to give the file the Freelance Graphics 96 .PRZ extension. The program does that automatically.

    If you want to save to another directory on your system, type the path (the drive letter, a colon, a backslash, and the directory name) before you type the name you're giving the file.

3. **If you are the forgetful type, you may want to add a description of the file in the Description field.**

    As you create numerous presentations and save them on your hard disk, you might forget what each one is about. You can create notes to yourself (and others on your team) in the Description field at the bottom of the Save As dialog box. By default, the Description field contains the title from the title slide. You can change the text in the Description field or add more information simply by clicking in the field and typing.

4. **Make sure that Prepare for Mobile Screen Show Player is not checked (see Figure 3-7).**

5. **Click Save.**

    Freelance Graphics saves your work and returns you to the presentation screen. Notice that the name of your presentation now appears in the title bar at the top of the Freelance Graphics window.

Part I: Gearing Up for Success

More about saving your work

Usually, the process just described is how you would save all your presentations. Occasionally, however, you may need to make other settings in the Save As dialog box. You may need to save the presentation in a different Freelance Graphics version. Suppose that you have created a presentation in Freelance Graphics 96, for example, and you have an associate who uses an earlier version of Freelance Graphics. For the associate to review the file on his or her computer, you must save the file in the version of the earlier format.

The Save as type drop-down list in the Save As dialog box, as shown in Figure 3-7, gives you several export options. You can also save a presentation as a SmartMaster Look or SmartMaster Content template, and Freelance Graphics enables you to save specific pages of your presentations in various graphics formats. (Chapter 11 covers saving SmartMasters.)

Figure 3-7: You can save your presentation in several file formats simply by selecting the format from this list and saving the file normally.

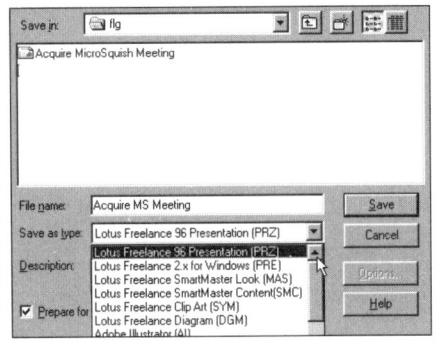

Earlier versions of Freelance Graphics do not support Windows 95's long filenames. When you open a file with a long filename in earlier versions of the program (Versions 1.x and 2.x), the name is *truncated* (shortened) to the old DOS convention of eight characters with a three-character extension (*xxxxxxxx.xxx*). The earlier versions of Freelance Graphics are unable to resave the file with a long filename.

Doing incremental saves

After you save a file the first time, you can save it as you work without having to use the Save As dialog box. Just press Ctrl+S every so often, and Freelance Graphics saves the file without disrupting your work while you wait for a pesky dialog box to open. The only time Save (Ctrl+S) opens the Save As dialog box is when you use it on an untitled, unsaved presentation.

> Although it's good practice to get into the habit of pressing Ctrl+S every ten minutes or so while you work, even the best of us forget now and then. Freelance Graphics' automatic backup feature, discussed in Chapter 2 in the "Using Freelance Preferences to further customize your work environment" section, enables you to tell Freelance Graphics to save your work automatically. You don't have to remember to save it. After all, you have enough to think about already.

Printing Your Presentation

To print a presentation, follow these steps:

1. **Select File⇨Print from the menu bar.**

    The Print dialog box opens (see Figure 3-8).

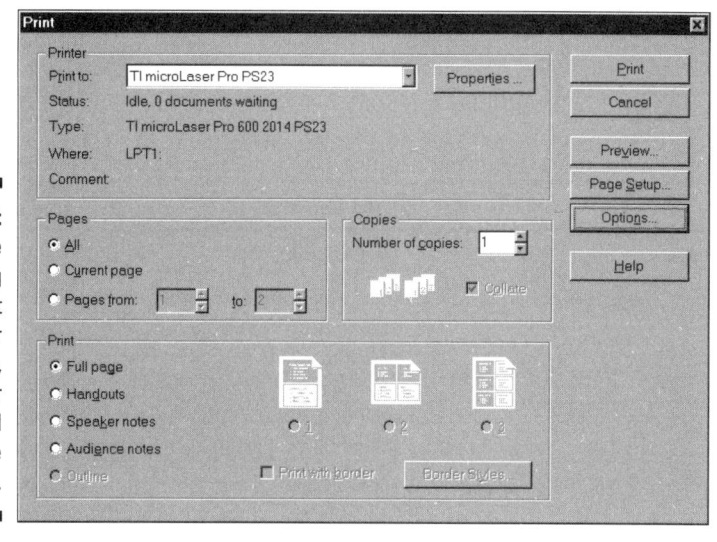

Figure 3-8: Use the Print dialog box to print your presentations, speaker notes, and audience handouts.

2. **Make sure that the correct printer is selected in the Print to drop-down list.**

      If the wrong printer is selected, click the down arrow beside the list, find the correct one, and select it.

   3. **In the Pages portion, tell Freelance Graphics which pages to print.**

      All prints the entire presentation.

      Current page prints the page displayed when you chose File⇨Print.

      Pages from prints the page range you specify in the two fields.

   4. **Specify the Number of copies you want to print.**

   5. **For now, select Full page in the Print portion at the bottom of the dialog box.**

      This portion of the dialog box looks more complicated than it really is. Use it when printing handouts, speaker notes, audience notes, or an outline. The chapter presenting each type of presentation also explains how to print it.

   6. **Click Print.**

      Your presentation prints. It's that easy!

Changing the print options

Sometimes the limitations of printers can affect the appearance of your slides. Freelance Graphics offers three print options for controlling whether certain design elements print, described in Table 3-1 and shown in Figure 3-9, thus working around your printer's limitations. To change the print options, choose Print⇨Options.

Table 3-1	Print Options
Option	*Description*
Adjust output library for printing	Uses an alternate color library to make the printed color match the displayed color, compensating for differences in color definitions of printers and monitors. The default setting is on. Turn the option off when you're using devices that have built-in color libraries, such as slide recorders.
Print graduated fills as solid	Makes colors solid rather than gradually changing from one color to another. Turn this option on when you can't read the text and graphics objects because of the changing color around them.

Option	Description
Print with blank background (no look)	Turns off the SmartMaster backgrounds, printing just the presentation elements. Turn this option on to convert a colorful presentation to a black-and-white format.

Figure 3-9: These options enable you to control whether Freelance Graphics prints certain design elements on printers that cannot reproduce them well.

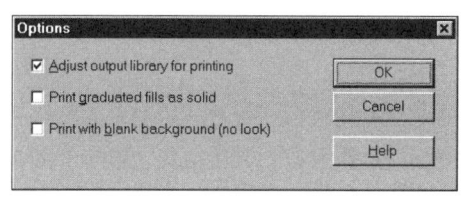

Freelance Graphics contains alternate color libraries for the following printers:

- Canon BubbleJet BJC-800
- Hewlett-Packard (HP) Color LaserJet
- HP DeskJet 500C
- HP DeskJet 550C
- HP DeskJet 560C
- HP DeskJet 1200C
- HP PaintJet XL
- HP PaintJet XL300
- IBM Color Jetprinter PS 4079
- Kodak Colorese PS Printer
- NEC Super-VGA Screen
- QMS ColorScript 100 Model 10
- QMS ColorScript 100 Model 30
- QMS ColorScript 230
- Seiko ColorPoint PS
- Tektronix Phaser II SDX
- Tektronix Phaser II 200i
- Xerox 5775 Digital Color Copier

Freelance Graphics automatically uses a default library for printers not on this list.

Part I: Gearing Up for Success

> **NOTE:** The default setting for this option is on. You turn it off when you're using devices with printer drivers that have their own color libraries built in, such as most slide recorders.

Previewing and printing selected pages

Previewing your presentation before you print it is always a good idea and sometimes you may want to print only a page here or there. You can use the Preview option in the Print dialog box to do both.

To preview or print specific pages, follow these steps:

1. **Choose File⇨Print from the menu bar.**
2. **Click Preview.**

   The Print Preview dialog box appears.

3. **Choose First Page to preview the presentation from the beginning, or choose Current Page to preview the page that was displayed when you opened the Print dialog box.**
4. **Click OK.**

   The full-screen preview appears, shown in Figure 3-10.

5. **Click Previous to move back, Next to move ahead, or Print to print the slide.**
6. **Click Quit to end the preview.**

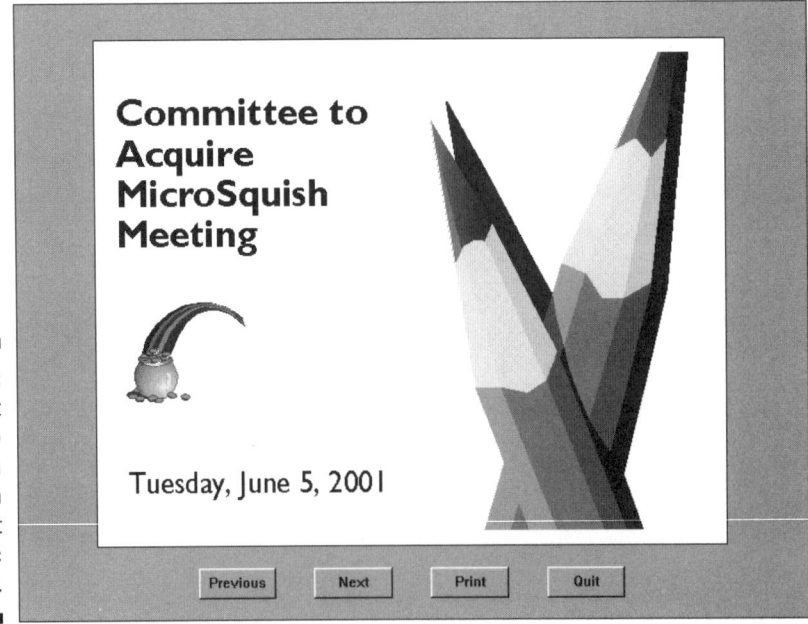

Figure 3-10: Use Print Preview to navigate a presentation and to print specific slides.

Closing a Presentation

There's more to your life than creating presentations in Freelance Graphics. Maybe you have other work to do. Wouldn't it be nice to see a movie? When you finish a presentation or want to work on something else, you should close your presentation (if for no other reason than to get it out of the way). Freelance Graphics offers several ways to close a presentation, but you want to know only the easiest and safest way, right? Follow these steps:

1. **Double-click the Control menu icon beside the File menu.**
2. **If Freelance Graphics prompts you to save the presentation, click Yes.**

   Freelance Graphics saves the presentation and closes.

Reopening a Presentation

Okay. So, you've got some time to work on your presentation. How do you find it and get it open in Freelance Graphics again? Freelance Graphics offers many ways to open a file in Windows 95, but the easiest is to follow these steps:

1. **Open Freelance Graphics from the Start menu by clicking Start, clicking Lotus SmartSuite, and then clicking Lotus Freelance Graphics 96.**
2. **In the Welcome to Lotus Freelance Graphics dialog box, find your presentation in the list and double-click it (see Figure 3-11).**

   If you have several presentations in the list, you can get a thumbnail preview of the first page of any of them by highlighting the filename in the list.

Figure 3-11: A Freelance Graphics presentation file icon.

Previewing Your Pages

If you're like us, it's often difficult to tell how a slide looks when it's surrounded by all the components of the Freelance Graphics screen, such as the menus and option buttons. Sometimes you just need to get rid of all the clutter so that you can focus on the slide. To see your presentation full-screen, follow these steps:

> ### What's the shortest distance between you and your presentation?
>
> When working on a presentation that you will be opening and closing often, you can create a Windows 95 shortcut and place it on your desktop. Then you can open the presentation at any time simply by double-clicking the shortcut. To create a shortcut, use My Computer or Windows' Explorer to go to the directory containing the presentation file. Click the right mouse button on the presentation file icon, and then select Create Shortcut. Windows 95 copies the icon and places it in the current directory.
>
> You can tell a shortcut in two ways: First, shortcuts contain a small arrow in the lower-left portion of the icon. Second, Windows 95 names shortcuts with the word *shortcut* at the end. For example, your Acquire MicroSquish Meeting icon shortcut would be named *Acquire MicroSquish Meeting shortcut*.
>
> To move the shortcut to your desktop, highlight the shortcut, click the right mouse button, and then choose Cut from the menu. Go to your desktop, place the cursor where you want the shortcut to appear, click the right mouse button, and then choose Paste.
>
> Another quick way to open a presentation you've worked on recently is to use the Documents option on the Windows 95 Start menu. Simply select Start/Documents and then select the presentation.

1. **Click the Run Screen Show SmartIcon.**

   After a moment, Freelance Graphics displays a full-screen view of the page. You can navigate from slide to slide by using PageUp and PageDown or by clicking the mouse buttons. Press the left button to move ahead one slide, and press the right mouse button to move back one slide.

2. **Press Esc to return to Freelance Graphics.**

   The Screen Show Pages dialog box appears. From here, you can quit the screen show, return to the current page, or go to a specific page by double-clicking the slide you want to go to.

3. **Click Quit Screen Show.**

Chapter 4
Working with the Freelance Graphics Outliner

In This Chapter
▶ Deciding to work in the Outliner
▶ Creating a new presentation in the Outliner
▶ Promoting and demoting topics in the Outliner
▶ Rearranging slides in the Outliner
▶ Changing the looks of the Outliner
▶ Printing your outline

*P*lanning is an important part of creating an orderly, effective presentation. Freelance Graphics provides several ways to help you plan presentations. One important planning tool is the SmartMaster content template, presented in Chapter 3. This chapter looks at another of Freelance Graphics' planning tools, the Outliner, or Outline view. In addition to helping you plan your presentation, Outliner also provides powerful controls for arranging and managing your masterpieces.

Deciding to Work in the Outliner

Ask any creative professional, from writer to presenter to film director, and they'll probably tell you that they create from some kind of outline during the planning stage of their work. All the magazine articles and books that we write originate from an outline, as do Bill's multimedia titles and presentations. So should yours. Why? Because outlines help you organize the information you want to present.

52 Part I: Gearing Up for Success

In many ways, a presentation is nothing more than an outline that you, the presenter, follow to deliver your message to your audience. Many of the slides in your presentation come directly from an outline.

Check out the outline on back pain in Figure 4-1. Notice that the topics are arranged in titles, major points, and minor points.

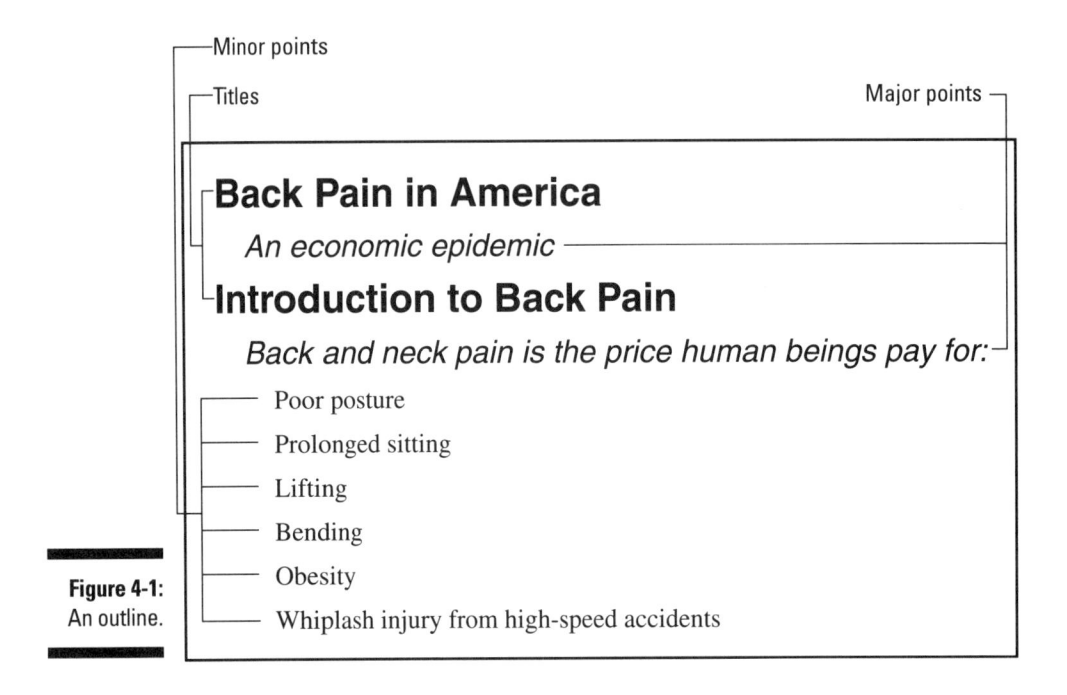

```
                  ┌─ Minor points
                  │ ┌─ Titles                              Major points ─┐
                  │ │
                  │ │  Back Pain in America
                  │ │    An economic epidemic ─────────────────────
                  │ └─ Introduction to Back Pain
                  │      Back and neck pain is the price human beings pay for: ─┘
                  │         ─── Poor posture
                  │         ─── Prolonged sitting
                  │         ─── Lifting
                  │         ─── Bending
                  └         ─── Obesity
                            ─── Whiplash injury from high-speed accidents
```

Figure 4-1: An outline.

Now look at the same outline in Freelance Graphics' Outliner in Figure 4-2. Each topic head is now a slide title. Each major point in the outline is a major topic on the slide, and each minor topic is a bullet point. Notice how the structure of the outline is nearly identical to the structure of the presentation. The information flow is the same. Figure 4-3 shows one of the slides, complete with the title, major topic, and bullet points.

Chapter 4: Working with the Freelance Graphics Outliner   **53**

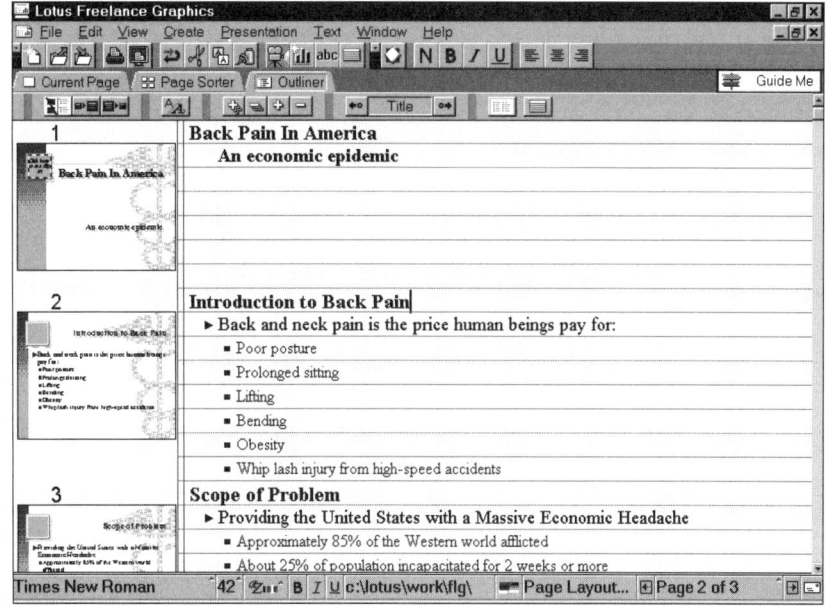

Figure 4-2: An outline in the Freelance Graphics Outliner.

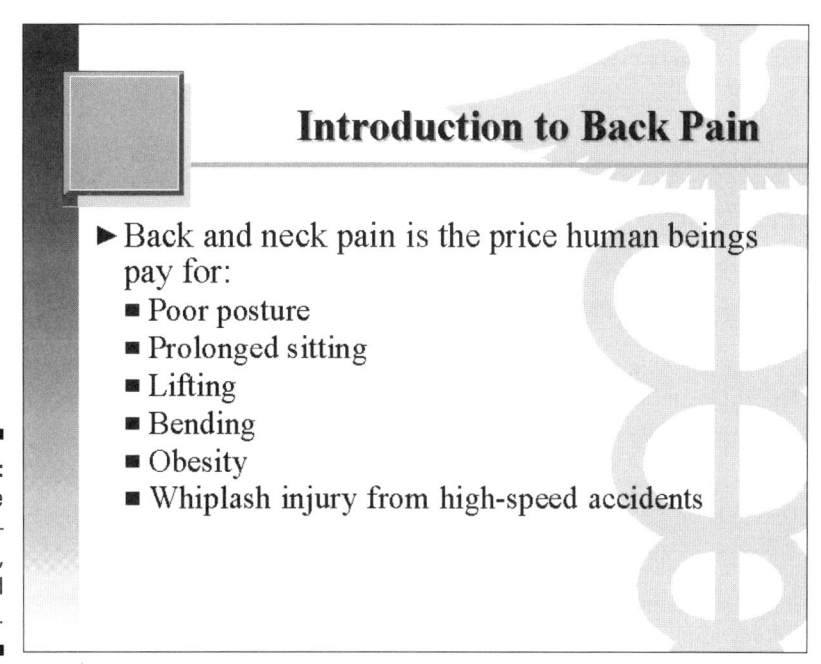

Figure 4-3: From outline to slide — a smooth, logical transition.

Creating a New Presentation in the Outliner

Beginning and planning a presentation in Freelance Graphics' Outliner is easy and fast. Follow these steps:

1. **Open Freelance Graphics by clicking Start, and then clicking Programs, Lotus SmartSuite, and Lotus Freelance Graphics 96.**

2. **In the Welcome to Lotus Freelance Graphics dialog box, click the Create a New Presentation Using a SmartMaster tab to begin a new presentation.**

3. **In the Select a Content Topic list, select No Content Topic.**

   Because you're going to design your presentation from scratch in Outliner, you create your own information flow rather than depend on built-in content. (For information on creating a slide from a SmartMaster content template, see Chapter 3.)

4. **In the Select a Look list, scroll down and select a look — currency, for example.**

5. **Click OK.**

6. **In the New Page dialog box, make sure that Title is selected and then click OK.**

   You now have a blank presentation from which to begin designing your information flow.

Moving text from WordPro to Freelance Graphics' Outliner

If you've outlined a report or presentation in WordPro, Lotus SmartSuite's word processing program, you can copy and paste an outline into Freelance Graphics' Outliner for an instant presentation. Just open WordPro and Freelance Graphics at the same time, select the outlined text in WordPro and then select the Copy SmartIcon (or press Ctrl+C). Switch to Outliner in Freelance Graphics, place the text cursor on the line where you want the outline pasted, and click the Paste SmartIcon (or press Ctrl+V).

Each topic head becomes a slide title, with the subsequent levels becoming major points and bullet points, up to five levels deep. Note that you can also paste text from other word processing programs or import ASCII text. Freelance Graphics recognizes tabs at the beginning of lines and formats accordingly. Text with no tab is a title, text with one tab is Level 1, and so on.

Chapter 4: Working with the Freelance Graphics Outliner

7. Click the Outliner tab.

The screen shown in Figure 4-4 appears. The thumbnails, little pictures on the left side of the screen, show each individual slide. The lined tablet on the right arranges the text on the slides in an outline format.

8. If you see icons on the left and not thumbnails, click the first button below the Current Page tab to turn them on.

Your screen should look like the one in Figure 4-4.

You can change the size of the thumbnails by clicking on one of the three thumbnail icons shown in Figure 4-4. Use the large size to get a better idea of what your slides look like; use the smaller size or no thumbnails if you want to focus on the outline rather than the slides.

9. Type the title for your first slide — We're in the Money Now, for example.

Notice that the text appears on the thumbnail as a title.

10. Press Enter to move to the next line.

Because you were on the Title level, Freelance Graphics assumes that you want to type the subtitle, or Level 1, next. Slide titles are always Title level whether you are working on title slides or bullet slides. Level 1 is a subtitle on title slides and a major topic on bullet slides.

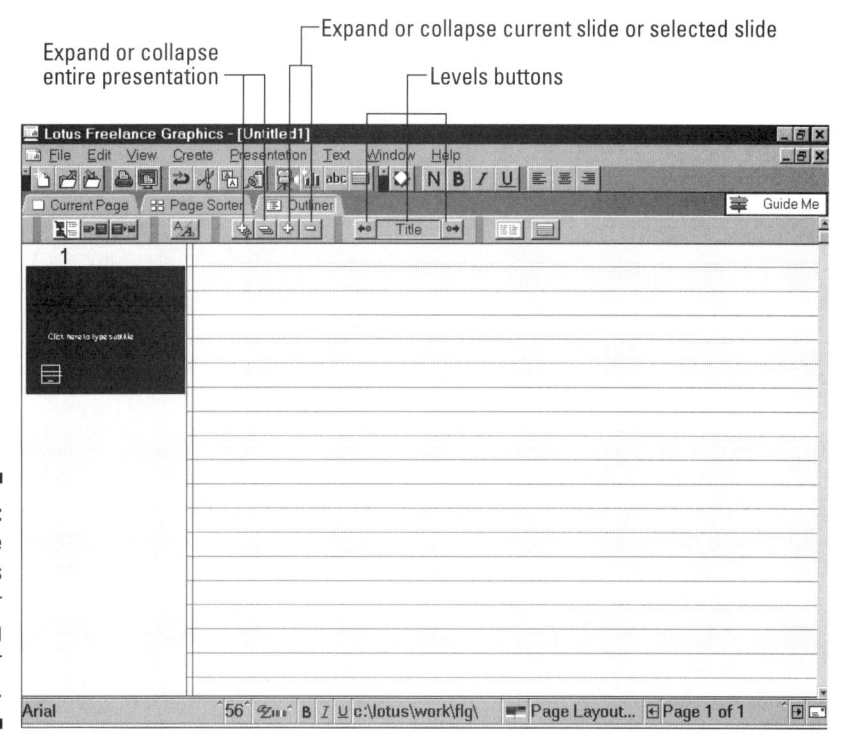

Figure 4-4: The Outliner's screen for designing your presentation.

Part I: Gearing Up for Success

> **TIP**
>
> 11. **Type the subtitle** — From rags to riches in 30 days, for example.
> 12. **Choose Create⇨Page from the menu bar or press F7.**
>
>   Freelance Graphics adds a new slide. By default, the new page is titled Bulleted List.

> **TIP**
>
> You can change to any of the slide layouts by clicking the Page Layout button at the bottom of the screen, selecting the layout you want, and clicking OK in the Switch Page Layout dialog box.

13. **Type the points that you want on your slide, pressing Enter after each one.**
14. **When you have created all the slides you want, save the presentation.**

Promoting and Demoting Topics in the Outliner

In an outline, topics are organized in levels. The Title level, is the title of the slide, with supporting levels expanding on the topic. Freelance Graphics supports up to six topic levels — the Title level plus five sublevels.

Table 4-1 lists the ways you can change levels of text using the Levels buttons shown in Figure 4-4 or the keyboard. Promoting a line of text to Title creates a new slide.

Table 4-1	Changing the Level of Text
To Do This:	*Do This:*
Move text up one level	Click the left arrow or press Shift+Tab
Move text down one level	Click the right arrow or press Tab
Move several lines to the same level at one time	Select them all with the I-beam and click the Levels button or press Tab or Shift+Tab

> **DESIGN**
>
> Hey, all this topic and subtopic stuff is great, right? You can list virtually every point you want to cover right on the slides! Wrong. You rarely should go more than three levels deep when listing bullet points. The slide becomes too cluttered and too difficult for your audience to follow. If you need reminders of all the salient points, list them in a separate outline that your audience doesn't see or in your speaker notes, discussed in Chapter 16.

Rearranging Slides in the Outliner

Freelance Graphics has a convenient feature. If you don't like where you placed a slide in your presentation, you can pick it up and move it to another location. Just follow these steps:

1. **Click the thumbnail of the slide you want to move.**
2. **Drag the thumbnail up or down until the grabbing hand cursor is where you want to position the slide.**

   You can tell where the slide is to be inserted by the colored bar that appears between slides.
3. **Release the mouse button.**

   The slide you wanted to move is now in the new position.

You can also move several adjoining slides at once by clicking the first one to select it, Shift+clicking the subsequent slides to select them, and dragging the slides to their new positions.

Changing the Looks of the Outliner

Freelance Graphics enables you to change its Outliner so that it meets your needs. You can change the number of levels displayed in the Outliner, you can alter the way the text looks, and you can add elements to the Outliner.

Expanding and collapsing an outline

As you fill your presentation with bullet points, you may not be able to see the overall picture from a slide-by-slide perspective. Also, moving slides around is easier when the pages aren't separated by so many bullet points. In these cases, it's often easier to work from a collapsed view of an outline. A *collapsed view* shows only the slide titles. Freelance Graphics lets you collapse a single slide or an entire presentation.

You expand and collapse presentations by clicking the + (plus) and – (minus) buttons below the Outliner tab, as shown in Figure 4-4. The two buttons on the right (the ones without the drop shadows) collapse the current slide or selected slides. (You can select more than one slide by Shift+clicking each one.) The two buttons on the left collapse the entire outline.

Table 4-2   Changing Your View of an Outline

To do this:	Do This:
Collapse the entire outline	Click the – (minus) button on the left
Expand the entire outline	Click the + (plus) button on the left
Collapse the current slide	Click the – (minus) button on the right
Expand the current slide	Click the + (plus) button on the right
Remove the outline completely	Click the No Thumbnails icon under the Current Page tab

When only the titles are displayed, the slide numbers in the thumbnail section of the screen that have plus symbols beside them contain subtopics.

Changing the way text appears in the Outliner

Text attributes are type style, point size, boldface, italics, and so on. You can change text attributes in Outliner the same way you change text on slides. Follow these steps:

1. **If you're in collapsed view of an outline, click the plus sign with the drop shadow to expand the entire outline.**
2. **Select the text to be changed.**
3. **Click the appropriate formatting icon (*I*), for example, at the bottom of the Freelance Graphics screen.**

    The text is now formatted the way you chose.

TIP

To see how the text looks on the slide, turn on the thumbnails or double-click the Current Page tab.

Adding elements to the Outliner

You can add speaker notes and other elements in the Outliner. To add speaker notes, for example, place the text cursor in the slide where you want to create a note, click the Speaker Notes icon (the SmartIcon that looks like an index card), and start typing. (Chapter 16 is full of information about speaker notes.)

Chapter 4: Working with the Freelance Graphics Outliner

Printing Your Outline

You may want to have a printed version of your outline with you as you make a presentation. Having the outline in front of you can increase your confidence and keep you on track — you'll always know what slide is coming up next, and you won't have to look away from the audience to see the screen.

To print your outline, follow these steps:

1. **From any view, choose File⇨Print from the menu bar.**

   The Print dialog box, shown in Figure 4-5, appears.

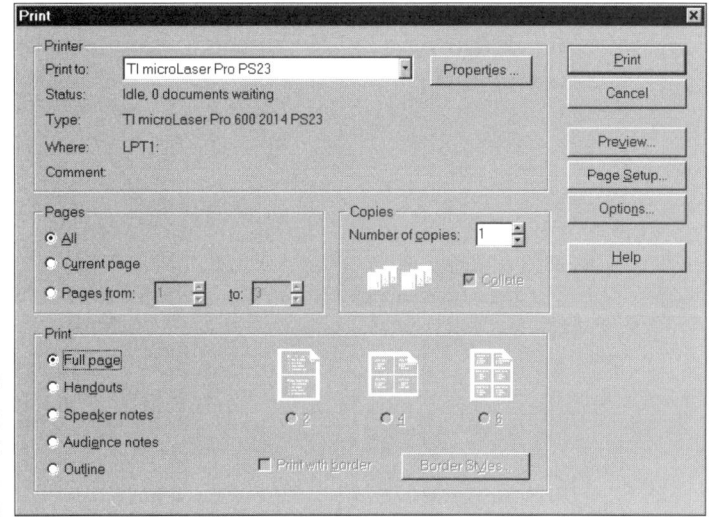

Figure 4-5: The Print dialog box.

2. **In the Print section at the bottom of the Print dialog box, select Outline.**
3. **Click Print.**

   The outline prints.

Part II
Adding Visuals

The 5th Wave   By Rich Tennant

"Of course graphics are important to your project, Eddy, but I think it would've been better to scan a _picture_ of your worm collection."

In this part . . .

Now this part has the real meat of Freelance Graphics —creating charts and graphs, working with text, adding symbols, and even drawing. We won't promise that you'll walk away with a Master of Fine Arts just by reading this part, but you will be a lot closer!

Chapter 5

Translating Numbers into Visuals: Adding Charts and Graphs

In This Chapter
- Choosing the right chart or graph
- Translating numbers into charts and graphs
- Creating charts from data in your spreadsheets
- Importing charts and graphs created in a spreadsheet program
- Knowing when to use Copy and Paste and linking with Paste Special

Presentations, especially business presentations, work best if they are rich in visuals. Numbers and statistical data are much easier to digest when viewed in chart form rather than as text. For example, compare the following text example to the visual interpretation shown in Figure 5-1:

> "Last year the Northern Division sold 15,560 units, or 24.9 percent of the entire company volume. Southern Division sold 14,460 units, or 23.1 percent. Eastern Division sold 20,008 units, or 32 percent. And Western Division sold 12,566 units, or 20 percent."

Any question about which format is easier to understand? In this chapter, you find out how to turn numbers into meaningful visuals. We also spend some time with design issues, such as when to use what kind of chart and how to use colors and fills.

Which Chart with What Data?

Freelance Graphics provides many types of chart and graph variations, more than you may ever use or care to use — unless you're a statistician or an alien. You can, for example, create stacked horizontal or vertical bar charts, multiple-pie charts, or combination line and area charts. The list goes on and on. But you really have only a few basic ways to organize and display information in a chart or graph, as presented in Table 5-1. Everything else is fluff.

Part II: Adding Visuals

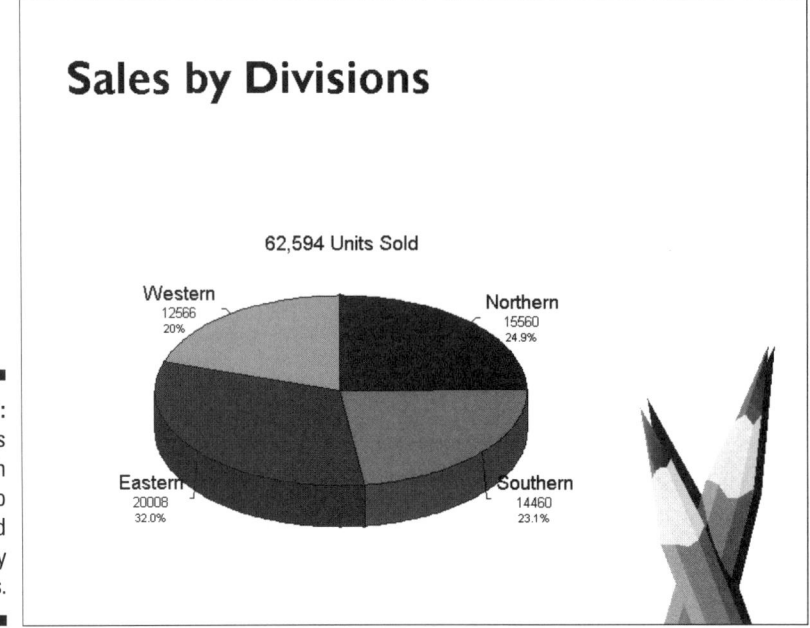

Sales by Divisions

62,594 Units Sold

- Western: 12566, 20%
- Northern: 15560, 24.9%
- Eastern: 20008, 32.0%
- Southern: 14460, 23.1%

Figure 5-1: Charts are much easier to understand than wordy explanations.

TECHNICAL STUFF

Before going any farther, we need to dispense with what by now must be a nagging question: What's a chart, and what's a graph? Technically, a *chart* displays data in tabular form, or columns, and a *graph* shows data in linear form, comparing variables and their relationships.

Table 5-1		Which Chart Does What?
Type	*Description*	*Use It When You Want to*
Table	Displays information in columns and rows	Show data in organized groups rather than in paragraphs of text
Bullet	Displays topics and subtopics sequentially	Present a message topic by topic
Build Bullet	Has topics appear on a slide one at a time	Discuss each point before you present the next one
Organization chart	Displays hierarchical relationships in an organization	Demonstrate who has what responsibilities or who answers to whom

Chapter 5: Translating Numbers into Visuals: Adding Charts and Graphs

Type	Description	Use It When You Want to
Bar chart	Displays data in horizontal or vertical bars	Show trends, compare sales numbers, and so on
Pie chart	Displays data in a segmented circle	Show percentages or parts of a whole
Line graph	Displays data in points connected by lines	Show trends
Area chart	Displays data in blocks of color	Show trends

TIP

The Create Chart dialog box gives you a preview of the charts that Freelance Graphics offers.

Creating Charts and Graphs

To create a chart by using the Create a Chart SmartMaster, follow these steps:

1. **Click the New Page button.**

    The Content Pages section of the New Page dialog box appears (see Figure 5-2). Rather than a content page, though, you want a chart layout page.

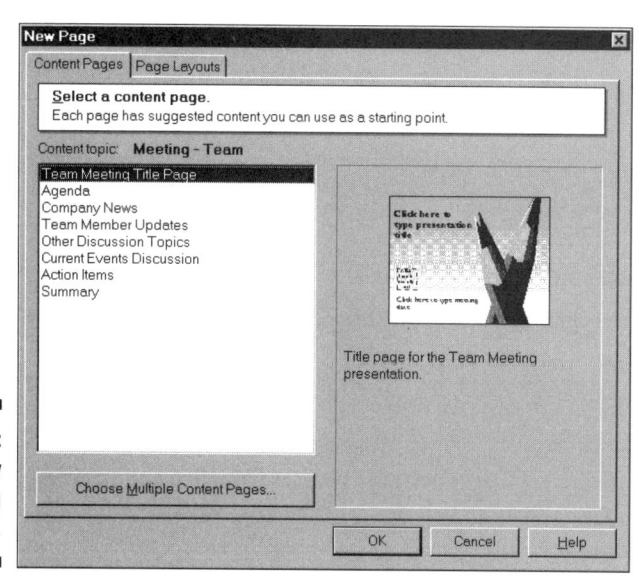

Figure 5-2: The New Page dialog box.

Part II: Adding Visuals

2. **Click the Page Layouts tab and select the desired page layout.**

   For a chart or graph, choose 1 Chart. For a bullet chart, choose Bulleted List. For a table or organizational chart, choose the appropriate layout. If you want to put more than one chart on the slide, choose 2 Charts or 4 Charts. Remember that the only reason you would really want to use more than one chart on a slide is to compare groups of data.

3. **Click OK.**

   Freelance Graphics displays a new slide with a chart placeholder. If you chose 2 Charts or 4 Charts, you have more than one placeholder.

   TIP: Some of the layouts in SmartMasters have SmartCharts associated with them. SmartCharts are an easy way to create charts. All you do is double-click the chart and then replace the existing data with your own numbers.

4. **Click the** `Click Here to Create Chart` **placeholder.**

   The Create Chart dialog box appears, as shown in Figure 5-3. The Select a chart type list contains the ten chart types that Freelance Graphics supports. The buttons to the right of the list enable you to toggle between variations of the chart type. You can, for example, change a bar chart from vertical to horizontal, add 3-D effects, and so on.

Figure 5-3: Use the Create Chart dialog box to select the chart type and effect.

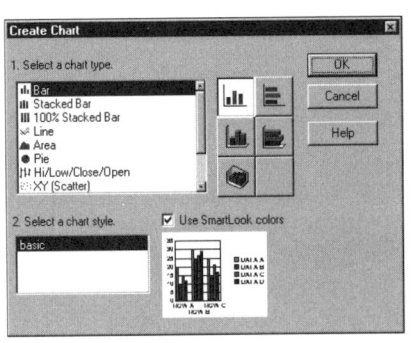

As you click the chart types and buttons, the preview window at the bottom of the dialog box displays how the finished chart appears.

5. **Select the chart type from the list.**
6. **Select the desired chart effect by clicking the appropriate button.**
7. **Click OK.**

   The Edit Data dialog box appears into which you enter legends, labels, and data in a spreadsheet-like form (see Figure 5-4).

8. **To create titles (or legends) for your chart, click the cell labeled Legend A, and type a title.**

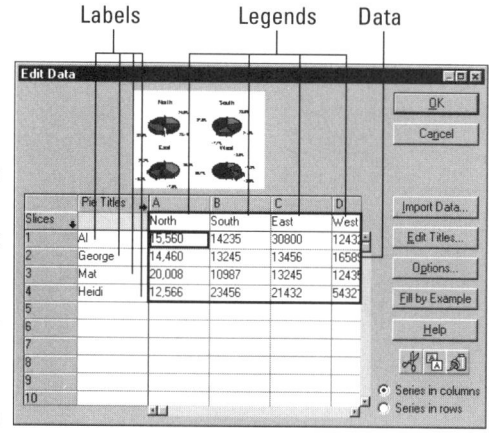

Chapter 5: Translating Numbers into Visuals: Adding Charts and Graphs 67

Figure 5-4: Use the Edit Data dialog box to create your charts and graphs.

Figure 5-4 shows the legends North, South, East, and West, which serve as titles for the data.

 9. **Press Tab to move to the next cell and type a title, continuing until the dialog box has all the legends for your chart.**

   Notice that each time you press Tab, the preview changes, showing how the entry affects your chart. You can watch the progress of your chart in this window.

10. **Click the cell labeled Labels 1 and type the label you want to use for the first set of data.**

    The labels in Figure 5-4 are Al, George, Mat, and Heidi.

11. **Press the down-arrow key to move down to the next label and type it until the dialog box has all the labels for your chart.**

    You can switch where labels and legends appear in the Edit Data dialog box by clicking the Series in columns and Series in rows buttons in the lower-right portion of the dialog box.

12. **In the remaining cells, type the data for your chart.**

    Freelance Graphics uses the data entered in these cells to create your chart. When Series in columns is active, each column represents one group of data. For a pie chart, each column is one pie. In a bar chart, each column represents a group of bars. In a line chart, each column represents one line, and so on. If you switch to Series in rows, each row takes on these characteristics.

13. **Click the Edit Titles button.**

    The Edit Titles dialog box appears (see Figure 5-5).

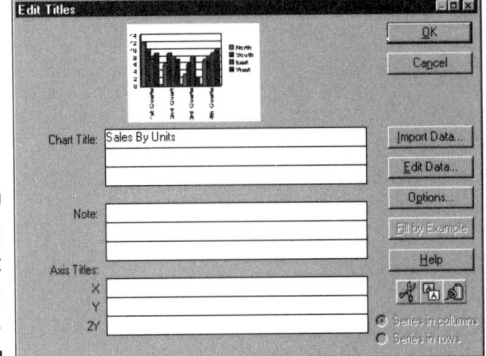

Figure 5-5:
The Edit Titles dialog box.

14. In the first line of the Chart Title cell, type the title of your chart.
15. In the Note cell, you can type any information that you want to add to the chart.
16. In the X-axis title cell, type a description of the labels, such as Salesperson.
17. In the Y-axis title cell, type a description of data represented by the legends, such as Sales Units By the Thousands.
18. Click OK to return to the slide and see your chart.

Creating Charts from Data in Other Programs

Freelance Graphics comes to the rescue of those of us who hate repetition! By using Freelance Graphics, you can create charts from data in spreadsheets, databases, and word processing programs. To use data from other programs, follow these steps:

1. **Click Import Data in the Edit Data dialog box.**

   Freelance Graphics displays an Open dialog box, in which you can search for the name of the file you want to use.

2. **Double-click the filename to open it.**

   The Edit Links dialog box (as shown in Figure 5-6) appears, displaying the spreadsheet and, depending on how the spreadsheet is set up, enabling you to define how Freelance Graphics uses the data to create the chart. Notice that the spreadsheet is very similar to the form in the Edit Data dialog box for setting up charts.

Chapter 5: Translating Numbers into Visuals: Adding Charts and Graphs   69

Linking is a way to connect two applications so that data originally stored in a file in the first application (the *server*) is displayed in a file in the second application (the *client*). As you change the data in one application, the change is reflected in the other application.

Figure 5-6: Use the Edit Links dialog box to define how Freelance Graphics uses the spreadsheet data to create a chart.

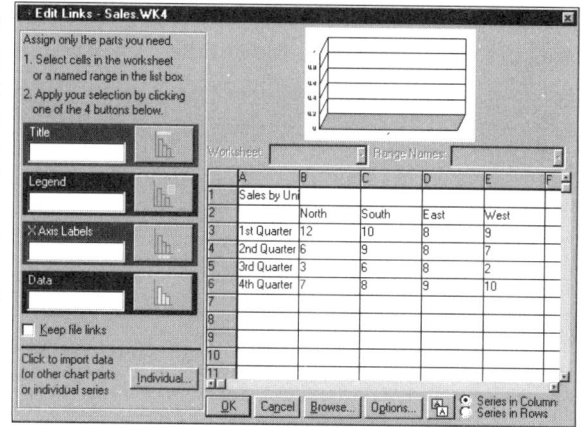

   3. To use your spreadsheet title as the title of your Freelance Graphics file, select the cells containing the title and then click the Title button.

   The field on the title button shows you which cells you selected, and the preview displays the title, as shown in Figure 5-7.

Figure 5-7: To define a title, select the cells containing the title text and then click the Title button.

   4. To define the Freelance Graphics legends, select the row of cells containing the legends in the open file and then click the Legend button.

   The range of cells appears in the field on the Legend button, and the legends are shown in the preview.

Part II: Adding Visuals

5. **To define the Freelance Graphics X-axis labels, select the row of cells containing the labels in the open file and then click the X-Axis Labels button.**

   The range of cells appears in the field on the X-Axis Labels button, and the label appears in the preview.

6. **To define the data for the Freelance Graphics chart, select the row of cells containing the data in the open file and then click the Data button.**

   The range of cells appears in the field on the Data button, and the bars, lines, or pies show up in the preview, as shown in Figure 5-8.

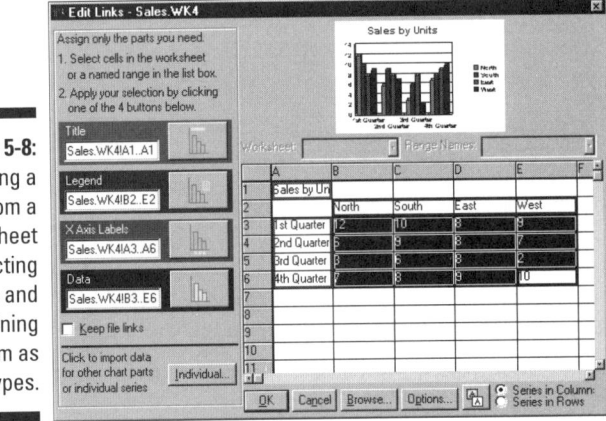

Figure 5-8: Creating a chart from a spreadsheet by selecting cells and defining them as chart types.

TIP

Sometimes your charts may come from spreadsheets that contain data that changes periodically. If you check the Keep file links option, Freelance Graphics maintains a link to the spreadsheet file. Then when you click Import Data again, Freelance Graphics automatically opens the spreadsheet from which your chart was created.

7. **After you finish defining your data, click OK to return to the Edit Data dialog box.**

8. **Click OK again.**

There you have it: You created a chart from a spreadsheet. Easy, wasn't it?

Importing a Chart from a Spreadsheet

Sometime you may want to use a chart from your spreadsheet in a Freelance Graphics presentation. The easiest way to place the chart into Freelance Graphics is to copy the chart in your spreadsheet and paste it into your presentation.

If you use Lotus 1-2-3, you find a tighter integration between Freelance Graphics and your spreadsheet than between Freelance Graphics and other programs, such as Microsoft Excel. If you copy a 1-2-3 chart into a Freelance Graphics presentation, for example, the chart automatically assumes the color and formatting used in the Freelance Graphics SmartMaster, saving you from making time-consuming changes to the graphic. The chart also becomes a Freelance Graphics chart, enabling you to edit it in your presentation without going back to 1-2-3.

This easy match between 1-2-3 and Freelance Graphics does not mean, however, that you cannot use charts from other spreadsheets, such as Excel. But you may find that using the Import Data feature, discussed in the preceding section, is a bit more efficient. When pasting a chart from another spreadsheet application, Freelance Graphics cannot convert the chart colors. The only way to do so is by ungrouping the chart and then recoloring each part of the chart separately. Using this method, however, breaks the Windows OLE link to the chart so that you cannot update it from Excel. (A brief discussion of OLE follows, but OLE is covered more thoroughly in the following section.)

As you paste a graphic from another application into Freelance Graphics, the program establishes a link between the graphic and your Freelance Graphics presentation. This link, established through Windows' Object Linking and Embedding 2 (OLE2), enables you to launch the application where the graphic originated. You can then use the OLE2 link to edit the graphic inside Freelance Graphics. This way, you don't ever need to go back and reimport the graphic.

As you discover in Chapter 14, OLE2 has broad applications if you are working with electronic presentations. In creating other types of presentations, however, using OLE2 is mostly a matter of convenience. As you can see later in this chapter, you can use Paste Special to create a link that automatically updates your charts as they change in the host application, such as 1-2-3.

Using the 1-2-3 Named Chart command

The Create⇨1-2-3 Named Chart command is handy for taking one chart out of a 1-2-3 file that contains many charts. If you use this method, the chart becomes a Freelance Graphics chart that you can then edit and modify however you like. To insert a 1-2-3 chart using this command, follow these steps:

1. **Make certain that the slide where you want the chart is the active slide and then choose Create⇨1-2-3 Named Chart from the menu bar.**

   The Create a 1-2-3 Named Chart dialog box shown in Figure 5-9 appears. Select the spreadsheet file from which you want to extract a file.

Figure 5-9: Use the Create a 1-2-3 Named Chart dialog box to select a 1-2-3 chart to use in your Freelance Graphics presentation.

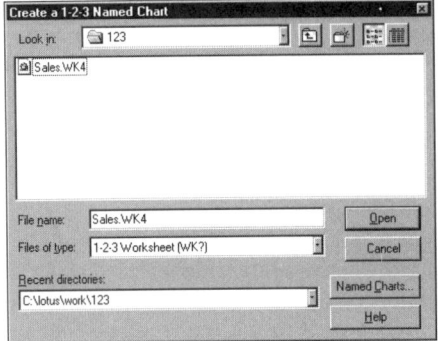

   2. **Click the Named Charts button to view a list of charts contained in the 1-2-3 file.**

   3. **Select the chart name from the list and click OK.**

      If you did not give the charts specific names in 1-2-3, they are named Chart 1, Chart 2, and so on. Of course, you must know in advance which chart you want.

   4. **Click Open.**

      Freelance Graphics imports the chart, changes the chart to conform with the current SmartMaster formatting, and then places the chart. You may need to move the chart a little to position it exactly where you want it, though. Rough, huh?

Using Paste to import a 1-2-3 chart

Use the Paste command to place a chart in your presentation if you are working in both 1-2-3 and Freelance Graphics simultaneously. To paste a 1-2-3 chart into Freelance Graphics, follow these steps:

   1. **Open Freelance Graphics and then open Lotus 1-2-3 and select the chart you want to copy.**

   2. **Choose Edit➪Copy from the 1-2-3 menu bar.**

   3. **Return to Freelance Graphics, make sure that you are on the correct page, and choose Edit➪Paste from the Freelance Graphics menu bar.**

The process is that easy. Freelance Graphics imports the graphic and converts it to Freelance Graphics format so that you can edit the data and modify the colors and formatting as you would any other Freelance Graphics chart.

Chapter 5: Translating Numbers into Visuals: Adding Charts and Graphs 73

Using Paste to import charts from other spreadsheets

Although the procedure for pasting charts created in Excel or other spreadsheets is similar to that of using the Paste command with 1-2-3, the results are somewhat different. If you paste an Excel chart into a Freelance Graphics presentation, the chart is not converted to Freelance Graphics format. Instead, the chart maintains the color, font, and other formatting assigned to it in Excel.

Pasting Excel charts from the Windows Clipboard into Freelance Graphics creates a link between Excel and the chart. You can edit the chart, but you must do so in Excel rather than in Freelance Graphics. To edit the chart, follow these steps:

1. **Double-click the chart.**

   The Freelance Graphics menus and SmartIcon bars change to Excel menus and button bars, as shown in Figure 5-10. The chart itself, however, is still in context on the Freelance Graphics presentation page.

   While in this state, Freelance Graphics acts like the spreadsheet application, right down to the actions performed by keyboard shortcuts and right-mouse-button actions.

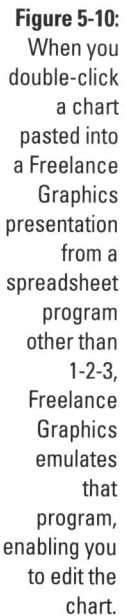

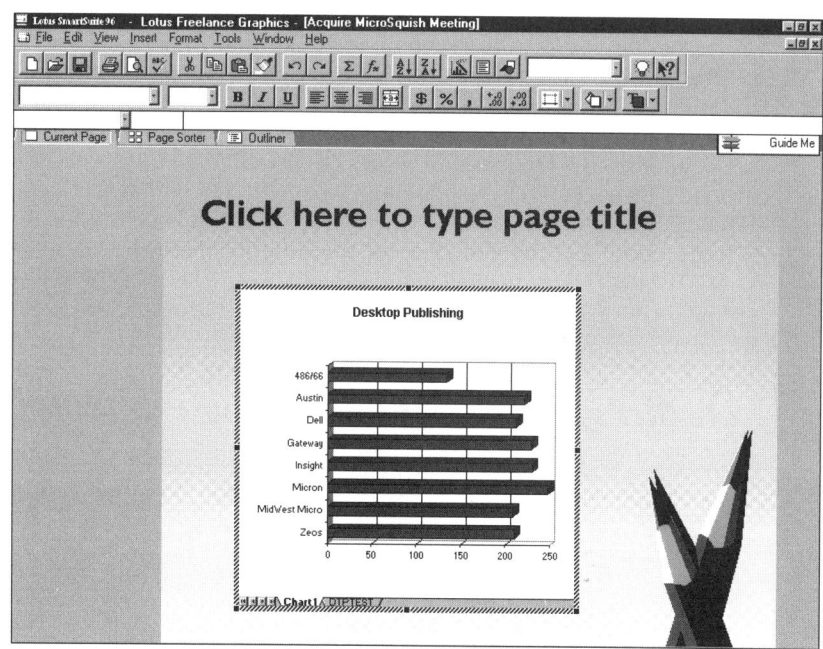

Figure 5-10: When you double-click a chart pasted into a Freelance Graphics presentation from a spreadsheet program other than 1-2-3, Freelance Graphics emulates that program, enabling you to edit the chart.

2. **Make your changes to the chart.**
3. **Click a blank area of the presentation page.**

   Excel closes, and you return to Freelance Graphics.

Technical Stuff: This last bit seems like something out of *Star Wars,* huh? Linking to other applications so that Freelance Graphics assumes the menus and buttons of those applications is a Windows Object Linking and Embedding (OLE) feature. For this feature to work, the spreadsheet must be an OLE2 application, common with today's software. The following section discusses OLE2 further.

Knowing When to Link by Using Paste Special

Often the 1-2-3 and Excel charts that you use in your presentations are linked to data that changes periodically, based on the variables that the numbers represent. In a manufacturing environment, for example, the number of units completed probably changes from week to week. This, in turn, means that somebody, perhaps one of your team members, periodically changes the spreadsheet to reflect the new numbers.

If the graph in your presentation is based on these ever-changing numbers, your graph can become obsolete each time the spreadsheet changes. These changes can be difficult to keep up with, especially if you are working in a group and somebody else is making the changes to the spreadsheet data.

The ideal situation, therefore, is to have a link to the spreadsheet that automatically updates the Freelance Graphics chart each time the spreadsheet changes. Sound like magic? Well, no; it's simply a function of Windows' OLE2. If you use Paste Special, rather than Paste, to import your 1-2-3 and other spreadsheet charts, each time that you open the presentation, Freelance Graphics checks to see if the chart has changed in the spreadsheet. When it detects a change, the program automatically updates the chart in your presentation.

Creating a link by using Paste Special

To create a link to a spreadsheet chart, text, or drawings, you use the Paste Special command rather than the Paste, 1-2-3 Named Chart, or Object command. However, you need to meet these conditions:

Chapter 5: Translating Numbers into Visuals: Adding Charts and Graphs

> **TECHNICAL STUFF**

Object linking and embedding — OLE

Windows has always enabled you to move graphics from one Windows application to another on the Clipboard by using Cut and Paste. OLE (and OLE2), however, takes this concept several steps farther. Not only can you copy and paste graphics, text, and other objects between applications, but you can also create *hot links* between the originating application, or OLE *server*, and the receiving application, or OLE *client*.

The advantage of *object linking* is that you update objects — such as a 1-2-3 chart — automatically, no matter how many applications or documents they are linked to. If you link an Excel chart to a Freelance Graphics presentation, the linked chart in the Freelance Graphics presentation is updated automatically each time you change it in Excel — without having to import the object again.

Unlike linking, *object embedding* enables you to temporarily launch a second application from within a Windows program and use it to create a new object. Typically, you do this by using the client application's Object menu command. (In Freelance Graphics, the Object command is on the Create menu.) After you finish creating the object, it is pasted into the original, or client, application — in this case, Freelance Graphics. You can then edit the object anytime simply by double-clicking it in Freelance Graphics. The server application — in this case, a spreadsheet — opens to enable you to edit the embedded object. (Notice that you embed the object as either a document or an icon that opens the server application.)

After you close the server application, the object is updated. In order for linking and embedding to work, both applications must be OLE-aware. Nowadays, most Windows applications support OLE2. Freelance Graphics does, as do Lotus 1-2-3 and Excel.

- Both programs, Freelance Graphics (the client) and the source (or server application), must support OLE.
- The file containing the chart must have been saved (that is, the file cannot be an "untitled" file).
- The source, or server application, must be kept open.

To use the Paste Special command to create a link, follow these steps:

1. **Start the source application and open the file that contains the chart you want.**

2. **Choose Edit⇨Copy from the menu bar to copy the chart to which you want to link.**

3. **Open the Freelance Graphics presentation in Current Page view on the page in which you want the chart to appear.**

4. **Choose Edit⇨Paste Special from the menu bar.**

Part II: Adding Visuals

This command opens the Paste Special dialog box, as shown in Figure 5-11.

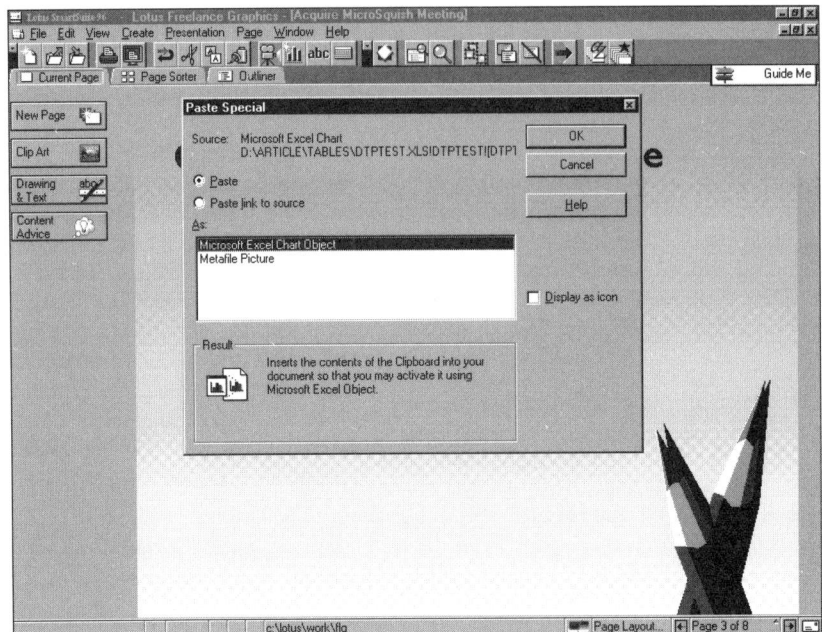

Figure 5-11: Use Paste Special to import a chart into a presentation.

   5. **Select the Paste link to source radio button.**
   6. **In the As list, select how you want to import the data.**

      In almost all cases, you choose to import the object as is or in its original format. In Figure 5-11, for example, you import the chart as a Microsoft Excel Chart Object rather than as a metafile. (A *metafile* is simply an image file that you really couldn't edit from inside Freelance Graphics with OLE except to change colors.)

   7. **Click OK.**

Deciding when to use links

You should use links in the following situations:

   ✔ When you need to share data between Windows applications
   ✔ When you expect the chart data to change
   ✔ When you need to update the chart after the original data changes

Chapter 5: Translating Numbers into Visuals: Adding Charts and Graphs

Suppose that you use a chart from a 1-2-3 file in a Freelance Graphics presentation, and the chart changes weekly. You can create OLE links in the Freelance Graphics presentation to the chart in the 1-2-3 file. Then whenever you open the Freelance Graphics presentation, it automatically displays the latest 1-2-3 chart.

You should not use links in the following situations:

- When you use the chart only in Freelance Graphics
- When you do not expect the chart to change
- When you do not need (or want) to update the chart when the original changes

Deciding when to use embedded charts

An *embedded chart* is created in a spreadsheet application but stored in a file (sometimes called the *container file*) created by using Freelance Graphics. The embedded object can be either a document or an icon that opens the server application.

Use embedded objects in the following situations:

- When you use the chart in only one application
- When you expect to edit or update the data

If you create a Freelance Graphics presentation containing a chart from an Excel document, for example, you can embed the Excel chart into the presentation. If you distribute the chart for review online and your reviewers want information from the Excel document, they can simply double-click the Excel icon to open Excel and the file.

Chapter 6
Fine-Tuning Text Charts, Charts, and Graphs

In This Chapter
- How to fine-tune text chart line and paragraph spacing
- How to manipulate charts and graphs by adding borders and backgrounds
- How to modify chart fonts, type size, text color, and position
- How to change chart series borders, fills, and colors
- How (and why) to add and remove X- and Y-axis, tick marks, and grids
- How to make X- and Y-axis information easier to read
- How to combine charts

Freelance Graphics' default chart settings are fine for many applications. But if you're like us, you want to personalize the way your presentations look by manipulating the charts and chart text. If so, this chapter is for you.

Maybe you just need to tweak a chart to get it to look more like the other documents your company publishes. In any case, Freelance Graphics provides hundreds of ways to manipulate your charts' fonts, colors, backgrounds, as well as their overall appearance.

Fine-Tuning Text Chart Line and Paragraph Spacing

The preceding chapter tells you that bullet slides are technically bullet *charts*. Although Freelance Graphics' default method of laying out a bullet slide is adequate and, in some cases, aesthetic, it's not always appropriate to your taste or design needs.

In these cases, you want to edit the line and paragraph spacing for your bulleted lists. For example, in Figure 6-1, the bullet points are so close together that it's difficult to tell where one begins and the other ends. The lines are so close together that the text is difficult to read. Furthermore, that short list sitting next to the long chart looks out of balance. This chart would be much easier to read and would look better if you add just a little more space between each item on the list.

Increasing or decreasing line spacing

To increase the spacing between lines of text (sometimes called *leading* — pronounced "ledding") in the same paragraph, you use the Text Properties dialog box. You can get to Text Properties by selecting the bulleted list and then choosing Text➪Text Properties from the menu bar. You can also right-click and then choose Text Properties. (If you're working on a bulleted list that is part of the presentation's level scheme, you can also use Text➪Text Properties by Level on the menu bar. Remember that Freelance Graphics automatically creates levels if you use a Bulleted List SmartMaster page layout.)

The Text Properties dialog box is separated into several different sections. To change line spacing, click the Alignment tab, which is the one with several horizontal lines centered between two vertical lines, as shown in Figure 6-2.

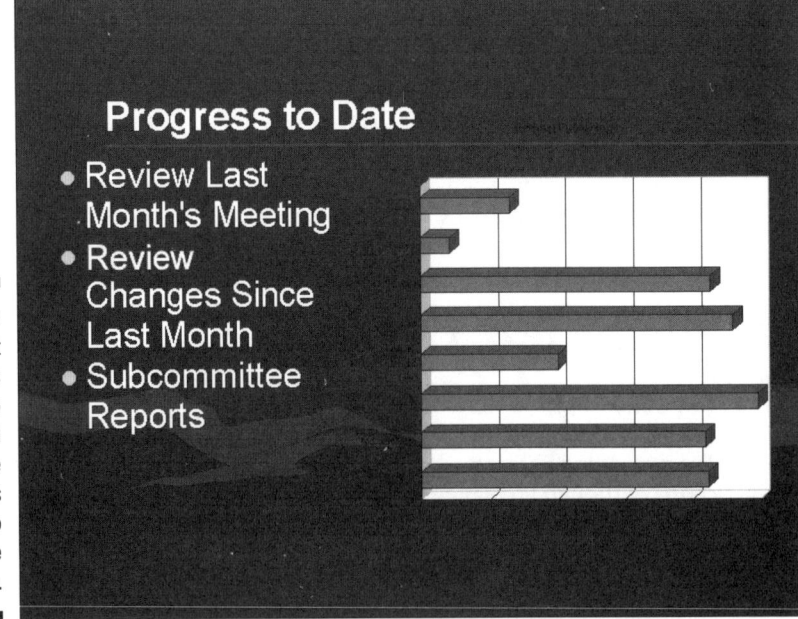

Figure 6-1: This bullet chart is difficult to read because the bullet points are too close together.

To change the line spacing for the selected text block, you can either click the Lines drop-down list and choose one of the preset options or select the text in the field and type in a value.

Figure 6-2: Use the Alignment tab of the Text Properties dialog box to change line spacing.

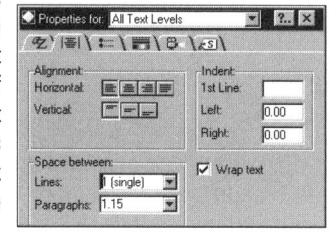

Line spacing is measured in line-widths, or the width of the line of text, similarly to a typewriter. For example, 1.5 equals a line and a half of space. If you choose, say, 1.15, the lines of text will separate by 1 and 15/100s of a line.

Increasing or decreasing paragraph spacing

Like line spacing, you adjust paragraph spacing in the Text Properties dialog box. The only variation from the preceding procedure is that, instead of changing the Lines option, you change the value in Paragraphs.

Adding Borders and Backgrounds to Charts

Another way to tweak your charts and graphs is by adding borders and backgrounds. Basically, you have two reasons for adding borders and backgrounds to charts: to make them easier to read or for aesthetics. Sometimes the background on a slide is too busy to place a chart over it. The background interferes with parts of the chart. In these cases, you would use a chart background to blot out the page background, leaving the chart to sit in a calm, blank area. At other times, you just may like the way a border and background make the chart look.

Part II: Adding Visuals

If you're using a SmartMaster look for your presentation, Freelance Graphics automatically adds backgrounds to some page layouts designed for charts. You can edit the background by changing the fill and color, as you see in the following section. If you use the Chart command or the Create a Chart SmartIcon command to place charts on slides that don't have chart placeholders, they do not automatically have backgrounds, but you can add backgrounds easily enough.

Adding a border to a chart

You add borders to charts in the Chart Properties dialog box, which you access by choosing Chart➪Chart Properties on the menu bar. (Remember that the Page or Text menu changes to the Chart menu after you select a chart.) You can also access Chart Properties with the right mouse button, but you must be careful not to click a chart element. If you do, instead of the Chart Properties dialog box, you get a Properties dialog box for the element you click, such as X-Axis Properties or Series Properties. To get a Chart Properties dialog box from the right-mouse-button menu, click inside the chart's bounding box (inside the eight handles), but away from chart elements.

After you're inside the Chart Properties dialog box, click the Line & Fill Color tab, the third tab from the left, as shown in Figure 6-3. To add a border, follow these steps:

   1. **First choose one of five border styles from the Style drop-down list.**
   2. **Choose the line width from the Width list.**
   3. **Choose a color from the Color list.**

Figure 6-3: The Line & Fill Color tab of the Chart Properties dialog box.

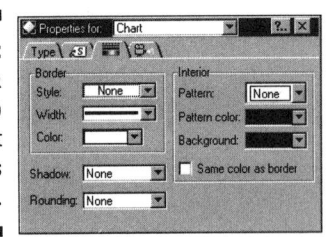

As you work in Chart Properties, Freelance Graphics makes the changes to your chart, enabling you to see your changes as you go. This features enables you to try various combinations on the fly.

Chapter 6: Fine-Tuning Text Charts, Charts, and Graphs 83

> **TIP:** You can round the corners of your chart borders by using the Rounding option at the bottom of the Chart Properties dialog box. Freelance Graphics provides three rounded-corner options: High, Medium, and Low. Rounding corners is a great special effect.

Changing a chart's background

As for a chart's outline, you change backgrounds from the Borders and Backgrounds section of Chart Properties. The procedure is to first define a fill and then to define a pattern and background color for the fill. Using this method, you can add solid backgrounds, tints, cross-hatching and other patterns, or gradients. (Remember that a *gradient* is one color graduating into another.)

By default (even when the chart is given a background by a SmartMaster layout), a chart has no fill. To add a background to chart, follow these steps:

1. **Define a fill from the Fill drop-down list, as shown in Figure 6-4.**

   The first two rows of the drop-down list consist of a solid fill and several screens, or tints. The next three rows are pattern fills, and the last four are gradients. When you define a pattern, the foreground color is the dark elements, and the background colors are the light areas of the fills.

Figure 6-4: Use this drop-down list to define a fill for your background.

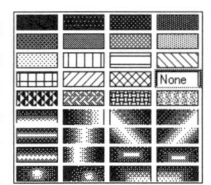

2. **Choose a pattern color from the Pattern color drop-down list.**
3. **Choose a background color from the Background drop-down list.**

> **TIP:** You can also add a drop shadow to the chart background, giving it a 3-D effect. To add a drop shadow, simply choose one of the four options under Shadow. The location of the shadow simulates a light source. When the shadow is bottom-right, for example, the simulated light source is upper-left.

As you work in Chart Properties, Freelance Graphics displays the effects on your chart, enabling you to experiment with colors and patterns. When you get the right look, simply close Chart Properties. Figure 6-5 shows a chart with a new rounded border, a gradient background, and a drop shadow.

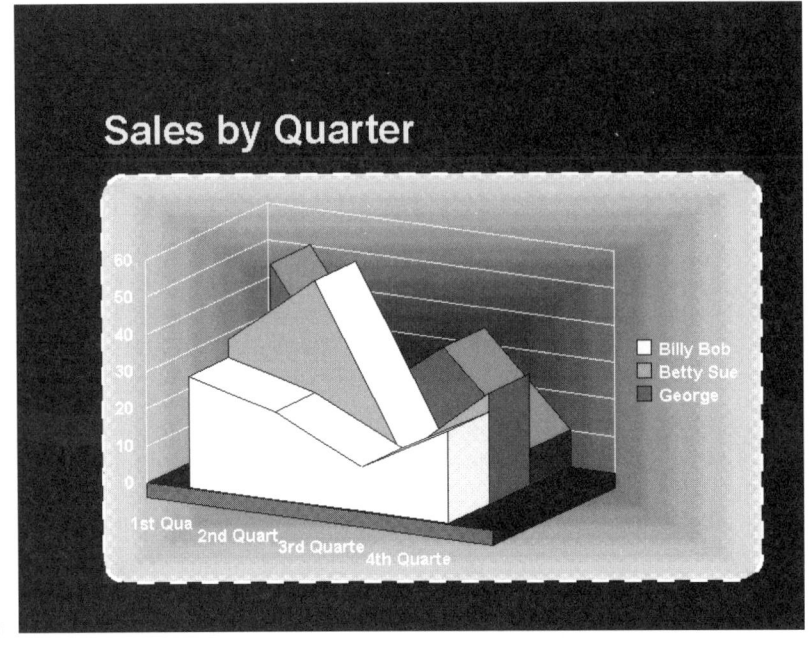

Figure 6-5:
A chart with a new gradient background, a rounded border, and a drop shadow.

By now you see that Freelance Graphics provides a wealth of options for creating dynamic design effects for your charts. Our advice, though, is that you use these options sparingly. If you put the wrong fill patterns or colors behind a chart, the chart becomes difficult to read, even garish. Keep in mind that sometimes less is good.

Changing Chart Fonts, Type Size, Color, and Position

You may want to change the text associated with your chart for a number of reasons. You may, for example, want some elements to stand out more than others. Or maybe you just want your presentation to be different from that of the next guy using Freelance Graphics.

Changing font properties is easy. All you do is click the element you want to change and then select the appropriate Properties command. For example, after you click the chart legend, Freelance Graphics' Chart menu displays Legend Properties. After you select X-axis labels, the Chart menu displays an X-axis

Chapter 6: Fine-Tuning Text Charts, Charts, and Graphs

Properties command, and so on. You can also open the appropriate Properties command by clicking the right mouse button on the element you want to edit. Or you can choose the desired element, such as Legend, Axis, and so on, from the commands on the Chart menu.

You edit text attributes from the Font and Color section of the Properties dialog box, as shown in Figure 6-6. To change the font, simply choose a new font under Font Name. To change the type size, choose a new size under Size or type in a new value. To change the color, choose a new color from the Color drop-down list. You get the idea, right?

Figure 6-6: Use this dialog box to change font attributes in charts.

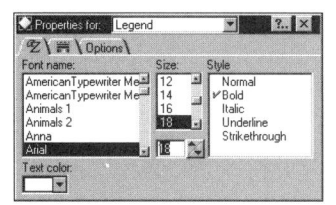

Here are a couple of things about Chart Properties you should know that make your life easier. You can easily change to all the various Chart Properties contexts from the Properties For drop-down list in the menu bar, as shown in Figure 6-7. Also, some contexts contain Option sections. Legend, for example has an Option section that enables you to change the position of the legend block.

Figure 6-7: You can use this drop-down list to change the aspect of the chart you are working on.

Changing Chart Series Borders and Colors

As you can modify chart borders, backgrounds, and fonts, you can also edit other aspects of your chart, such as series (bars, pie sections, and so on) colors.

Series are the actual bars, pie sections, lines, and so on that depict your data. You can change the series lines, colors, and fills similarly to changing background lines, colors, and fills — by selecting the series you want to change and then choosing Chart➪Series from the menu bar. You can also click the object you want to change with the right mouse button and then choose Series Properties.

This action opens the Properties dialog box. By default, the Properties dialog box opens at the Options section. To modify lines, colors, and fills, click the Line & Fill Color tab, which opens the dialog box shown in Figure 6-8. Use the Interior section of this dialog box to define fills and change colors. Use the Border section to change borders.

Figure 6-8:
Use this dialog box to change series borders, fills, and colors.

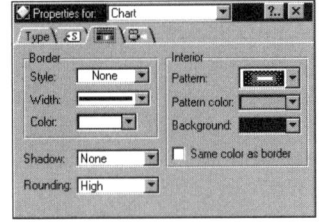

Changing a series fill and color

Usually, the default fill for a series of objects is solid. To change a series fill and color, follow these steps:

1. **Define a new fill from the Pattern drop-down list.**

    The first three rows of the drop-down list consist of no fill (*T* for *transparent*), a solid fill, several screens (or tints), and patterns. The last row is gradients. In the patterns, the foreground colors are the dark elements of the pattern, and the background colors are the light areas of the fills. In gradients, the pattern color graduates into the background color.

2. **Choose a pattern color from the Pattern color drop-down list.**
3. **Choose a background color from the Background drop-down list.**

Changing a series border

You also change borders from the Line & Fill Border section of Properties. To change a series border, follow these steps:

1. **Choose one of five border styles from the Style drop-down list.**
2. **Choose the line width from the Width list.**
3. **Choose a color from the Color list.**

As you work in Chart Properties, Freelance Graphics displays the changes to your chart, enabling you to see your new design as you go. This capability enables you to experiment with various combinations.

TIP

After you finish working on a series, you can change to another from the Option tab of Properties, as shown in Figure 6-9, or by clicking the new series in the chart. This enables you to make numerous changes to your chart without having to close the Properties dialog box.

You can also hide and show a selected series, which is a good way to point out specific data. Say, for example, you want to display data for one or two employees. You can turn off the others by selecting the Show Series check box.

You can modify your chart further, making it even more dynamic and meaningful, by displaying some aspects of the chart in different types of series, such as combination area and bar chart, for example, as shown in Figure 6-10. Notice how the combination bar and gradient fill causes data for Billy Bob to stand out compared to the others.

Figure 6-9: Use this drop-down list to change between series.

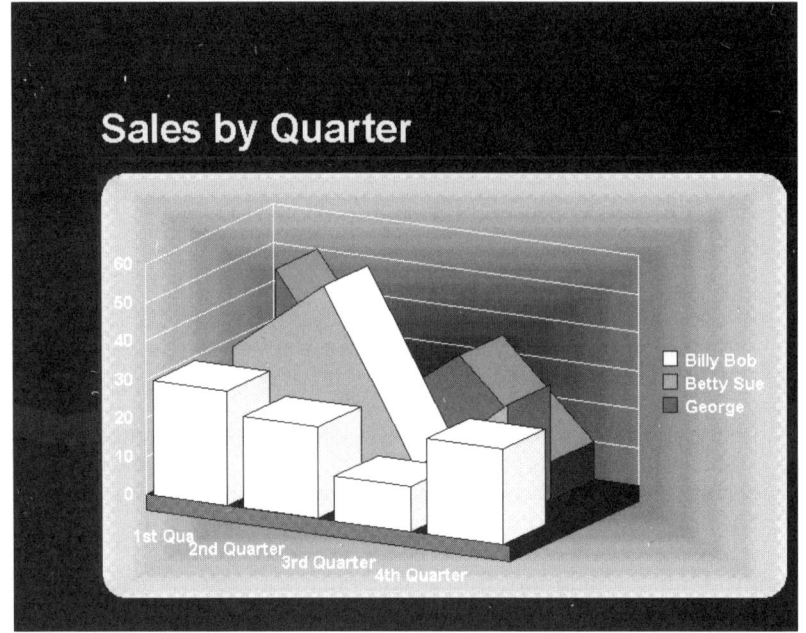

Figure 6-10: Changing a series type and fill makes it stand out.

Adding, Removing, and Modifying X- and Y-Axis, Tick Marks, and Grids

Sometimes you may want to increase or reduce the chart axes and gridlines for clarity or aesthetics. Other times you may want to remove them altogether. For example, it's not always necessary for you to display the Y-axis. Suppose that you included data labels at the top of each bar, as shown in Figure 6-11. Hiding tick marks and grids can be either a design enhancement, to make the chart less cluttered, for example, or to make data easier to understand.

Tick marks, of course, are the lines on the charts that mark off the data. In a bar chart, for example, tick marks are the marks that measure the data the bars depict. Grids are the lines that connect the tick marks from one side of the chart to the other.

Is this confusing? Well, then, look at Figure 6-12. Tick marks show where the numbers fall on the Y-axis. The grid is the series of white lines that run from the Y-axis to the right side of the chart.

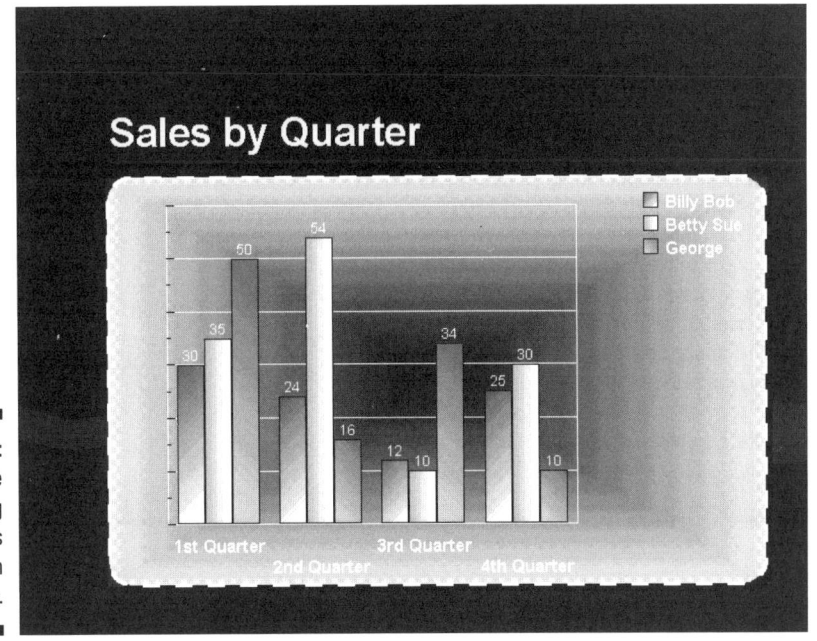

Figure 6-11: An example of using series labels rather than axis labels.

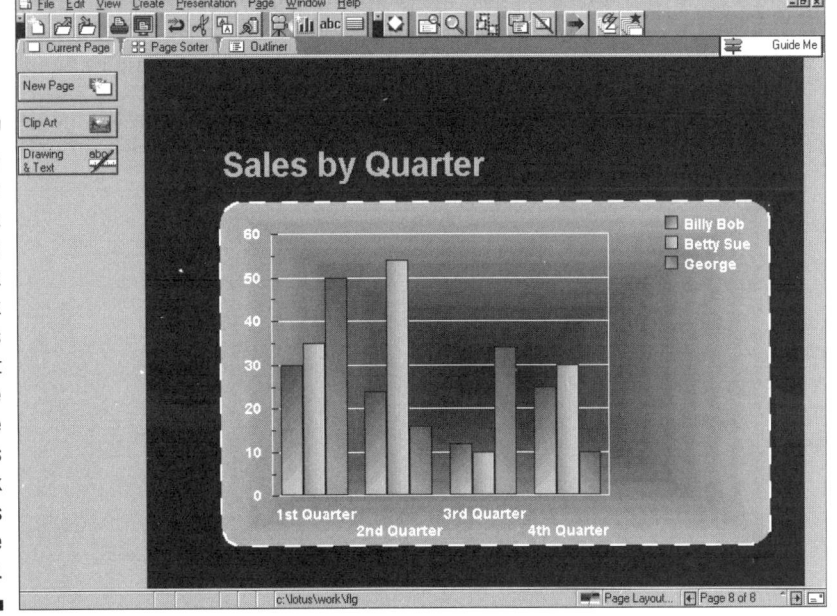

Figure 6-12: An example of tick marks and a grid. Tick marks mark the numbers that measure the bars; the grid marks the tick marks across the chart.

Axes mark the spots

Bar charts, line graphs, and area charts are structured around a framework of two axes — one vertical, the other horizontal. A scale for measuring the quantities is plotted along the vertical, or *Y-axis*. Usually, the Y-axis displays how much money, the number of pieces or units, and so on. Typically, the scale starts at zero and is subdivided evenly into units that are appropriate for the data you're plotting, such as tens, hundreds, or thousands. Freelance Graphics enables you to modify the scale along the Y-axis to suit your needs.

The horizontal axis, or *X-axis*, plots the scale for time or another category that serves as a basis for comparison, such as corporate divisions or regions.

Freelance Graphics charts are usually built on evenly divided units spaced at regular intervals along the axes. These units are called the *scales*.

Showing and hiding a chart's axes, tick marks, and grids

You show and hide these objects from the Properties dialog box for axes, which you can access by choosing Chart⇨Axes and Grids from the menu bar or by clicking the right mouse button on the axis labels you want to modify and then choosing Y-axis (or X-axis) Properties. This Properties dialog box is shown in Figure 6-13. Depending on the aspect of the axis you want to change, you use different tabs within this dialog box. You change axis labels by choosing Chart Properties⇨X-axis and making your changes.

Figure 6-13: Use this dialog box to hide and show axis elements.

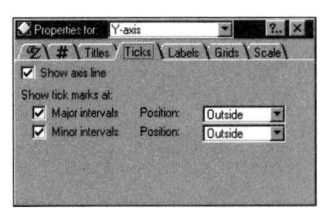

Hiding, showing, adding, and removing axis labels

To hide axis labels, follow this procedure:

1. Make sure that the Properties dialog box is open to the Labels tab.
2. Click the Show scale labels every _ ticks option to turn it off (uncheck it).

To turn the labels on again, simply click the Show scale labels every _ ticks option to check the box again.

You can add axis labels in even increments by clicking the increase and decrease arrows next to the Show scale labels every _ ticks field. If your chart already displays labels at every tick, however, this method does not work. In these instances, you need to add them manually, as discussed in the following section.

To add axis labels, click the increase (up) arrow next to Show scale labels every _ ticks field until you have the desired number of labels per tick mark, or select the text in the field and type in a new value. The chart displays the effects.

To remove axis labels, click the decrease (down) arrow next to Show scale labels every _ ticks field until you have the desired number of labels per tick mark, or select the text in the field and type in a new value. The chart displays the effects.

When working with the X-axis, you can change the labels from the bottom of the chart to the top from the Scales portion of Properties, which is yet another way to change the look of your chart.

Hiding, showing, adding, and removing axis tick marks

Tick marks measure data along the Y-axis. Just imagine setting a ruler beside your chart, and you should get the idea behind tick marks. To modify tick marks, you use the Ticks tab of Properties, as shown in Figure 6-14. From here, you can turn on major and minor tick marks and determine where they appear in relation to the Y-axis line. You can place tick marks inside the axis line, outside it, or across it.

Adjusting where the tick marks sit on the axis line is primarily a design decision affecting aesthetics. Deciding whether to show minor or major points can be an aesthetics issue, too. But you can also use this option to make charts easier to understand. Depending on the nature of the data, too many ticks can be difficult to read. By the same token, so can too few. Remember that good design is a tradeoff between aesthetics and clarity.

To hide and show tick marks, simply check or uncheck the corresponding check box. Click Minor Intervals to turn off minor ticks, and click Major Intervals to turn off major ticks.

Part II: Adding Visuals

Figure 6-14:
Use this section of the Properties dialog box to hide and show tick marks.

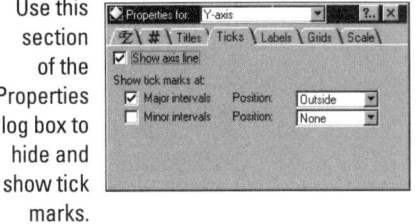

Figure 6-15 shows the result of decreasing tick marks. Use this option primarily as a design procedure to make your chart less cluttered. Notice from the figure that this also decreases the number of gridlines.

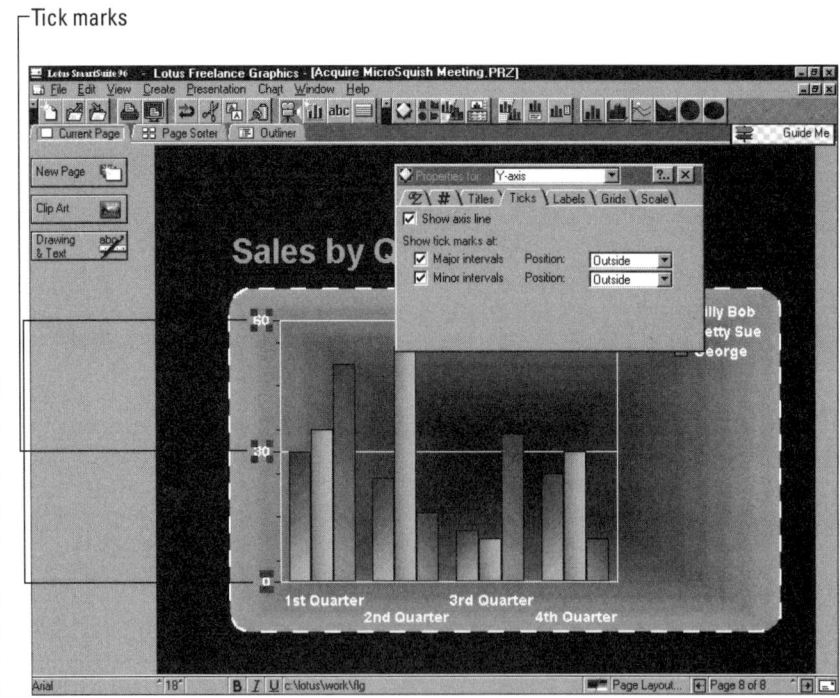

Figure 6-15:
Decrease the number of tick marks to make your chart appear less cluttered.

Working with a chart's scale

By default, Freelance Graphics makes some good design decisions when creating your charts. Usually, the scale on which your Y-axis is based is right on target. Sometimes, however, it isn't. For example, there may be times when you want your data to be measured from a base (minimum) number other than zero. Or maybe you want to change where major and minor tick marks fall on the chart.

You control the chart scale from the Scale tab of the Properties dialog box, as shown in Figure 6-16. The following is a description of the options on the Scale tab and how to use them:

- Under **Scale Manually,** you control on what number the axis begins and ends. To use numbers other than the defaults — which Freelance Graphics determines from the data you use to create the chart — simply change the Minimum and Maximum fields. To adjust where tick marks appear, change the Major Ticks and Minor Ticks settings. A common use for changing the Maximum scale is to display a goal and then to use your bars or lines to show how close the actual performance is to the goal, as shown in Figure 6-17.

- The **Direction** drop-down list enables you to display data from the top down. This actually turns your chart scale upside down.

- The **Position** drop-down list enables you to change the position of your labels and tick marks. Your choices are Left, Right, and Both. Sometimes moving the tick marks or displaying them on both sides can make charts easier to read.

- The **Type** drop-down list enables you to change the chart type between Linear, Log, and 100%.

- The **Units** drop-down list enables you to choose a unit of measurement ranging between thousands and trillions.

Figure 6-16:
Use the Scale tab to change how Freelance Graphics sets up the measurement system and axis options for your charts.

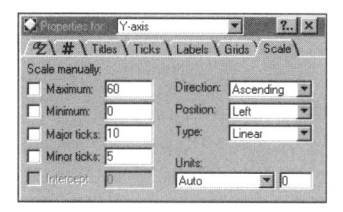

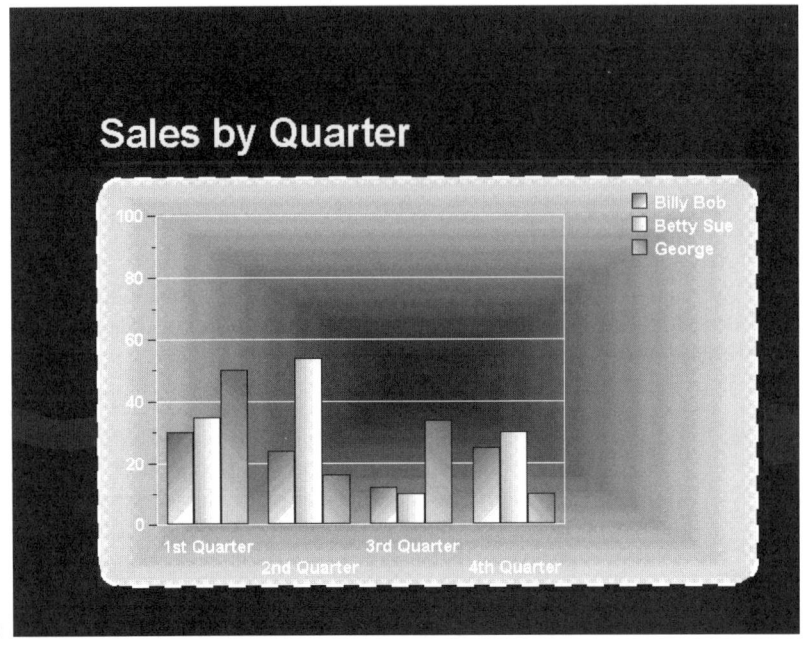

Figure 6-17:
You can change the Maximum axis for your chart to show a goal. Then you use bars or lines to depict performance in relation to the goal.

Hiding, showing, adding, and removing gridlines

Gridlines are extensions of the tick marks that span the chart to make the data easier to read. You control gridlines from the Grids section of the Properties dialog box for Y-axis, which you access by clicking the Grids tab. You can also get there by clicking the chart grid with the right mouse button and then selecting Y-axis Properties. The Grids tab of the Properties dialog box is shown in Figure 6-18.

Figure 6-18:
Use the Grids tab of Properties for Y-axis to hide, show, add, and remove gridlines.

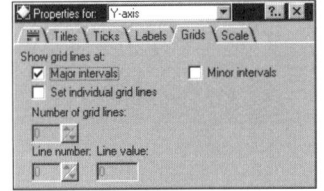

To hide and show minor and major gridlines, simply click the corresponding Major intervals and Minor intervals check boxes. You can also add gridlines individually by selecting Set individual grid lines and then adjusting the values in Number of grid lines, Line number, and Line value. These three options have the following effects on your grid:

- **Number of grid lines** tells Freelance Graphics how many lines to add to the grid. If, for example, you type **1** in this box and then change the Line value to 15, you get one new gridline at tick mark 15. This is a great way to highlight important value positions on your chart.

- **Line number** designates which line in the grid you are setting a value for. Lines are numbered from the bottom up.

- **Line value** tells Freelance Graphics where to place the gridline for the current line designated in Line number. If you change a value from 5 (5,000) to 10 (10,000), Freelance Graphics moves the line up the scale and gives it a new value.

Making X- and Y-Axis Information Easier to Read

As your charts increase in sophistication, some elements, such as Y-axis titles and subtitles and X-axis labels, can be difficult to read. Take, for example, the chart shown in Figure 6-19. You almost have to turn your head sideways to read the Y-axis title "In Units of Tens." And the series labels at the bottom of the chart are a bit awkward as well. As you can see in Figure 6-20, a few minor adjustments make the chart much easier to figure out.

As described earlier in this chapter, one way to make chart text easier to read is by making fonts bigger and changing text color. Another way is to adjust the position and orientation of labels, as demonstrated in Figure 6-20.

Part II: Adding Visuals

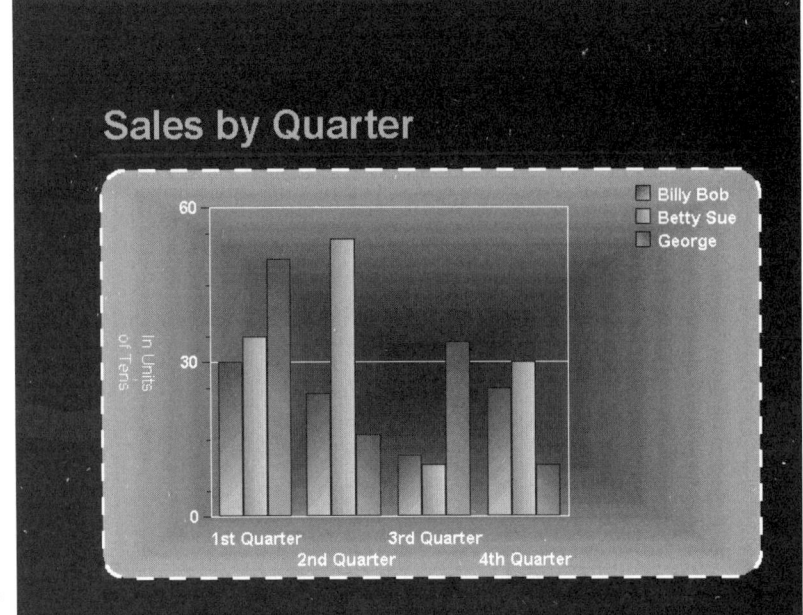

Figure 6-19: The labels in this chart could certainly be easier to read than they are now.

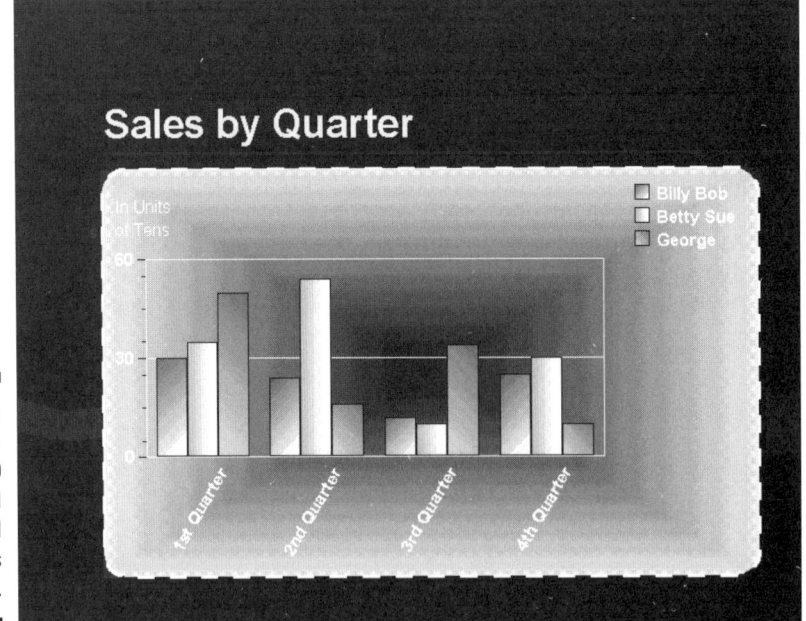

Figure 6-20: The chart in Figure 6-19 with revised X- and Y-axis labels and titles.

Adjusting X-axis label orientation (angle)

Freelance Graphics enables you to set your X-axis labels at five angles: horizontal, staggered, slanted, vertical, and down. The program also enables you to define a number-of-characters limit per label. This restricts, or truncates, the number of characters each label can contain, cutting down some of the confusion if labels are too long to display comfortably.

These controls reside in the Properties for X-axis dialog box, as shown in Figure 6-21. You can get here by choosing Chart⇨Axes and Grids from the menu bar or by clicking the right mouse button on the X-axis labels. If you are already in the Properties dialog box, select X-axis from the Properties for drop-down list.

Figure 6-21: Use this version of the Properties dialog box to adjust X-axis orientation.

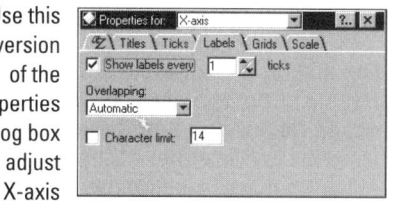

When the Overlapping option is set to Automatic, Freelance Graphics tries to calculate the best fit for the labels. However, the program is not always right. To change the angle, simply change the setting in the Overlapping drop-down list. When you make a new selection, the chart labels change, enabling you to see the effect of your choice.

Changing Y-axis title and subtitle position and orientation

When you created your chart, you may have defined a title and subtitle for the Y-axis. Typically, the title and subtitle explain what the numbers mean. For example, your title could say "In Units" and your subtitle may say "of Tens." (Depending on how you print the slides, you may or may not want to keep the subtitle.) Sometimes Freelance Graphics doesn't automatically place the title and subtitle at the optimal position and angle. You can change where and how they appear on the Titles tab of Properties for Y-axis, as shown in Figure 6-22.

Figure 6-22: Use this tab of Properties for Y-axis to adjust the position and orientation of titles and subtitles.

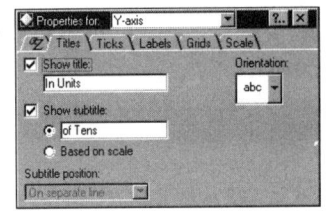

If you didn't add a title and subtitle, you can do so at any time from the Properties for Y-axis dialog box. Simply click Show title and then type a title in the field provided. To create a subtitle, click Show subtitle and type in a subtitle.

Much of the control here results from the Orientation drop-down list. The horizontal option turns the text upright and positions it at the top of the chart. The other two options place the text in a landscape (sideways) orientation and place the text at the side of the chart. When you choose either of the landscape options, Freelance Graphics also gives you the choice of placing the subtitle on the same line as the title or on the next line. Control this option by using the Subtitle position drop-down list. Based on scale makes the adjustment automatically.

Getting rid of Y-axis labels

Another way to make your Y-axis labels easier to read is by scrapping them altogether and using series labels, as shown in Figure 6-23. This cleans up the chart some, giving it more area to stretch out in. This is a particularly slick trick when working with small charts that don't contain a lot of data.

You create series labels by selecting the chart and then choosing Chart⇨Series Labels from the menu bar. This action displays the Properties for Series labels dialog box, as shown in Figure 6-24. From here, you can add labels for each series by selecting Show value labels, and you can change the position and orientation of the labels by using the Position and Orientation drop-down lists. You can also select Show percent labels to display the labels as percentages rather than as values.

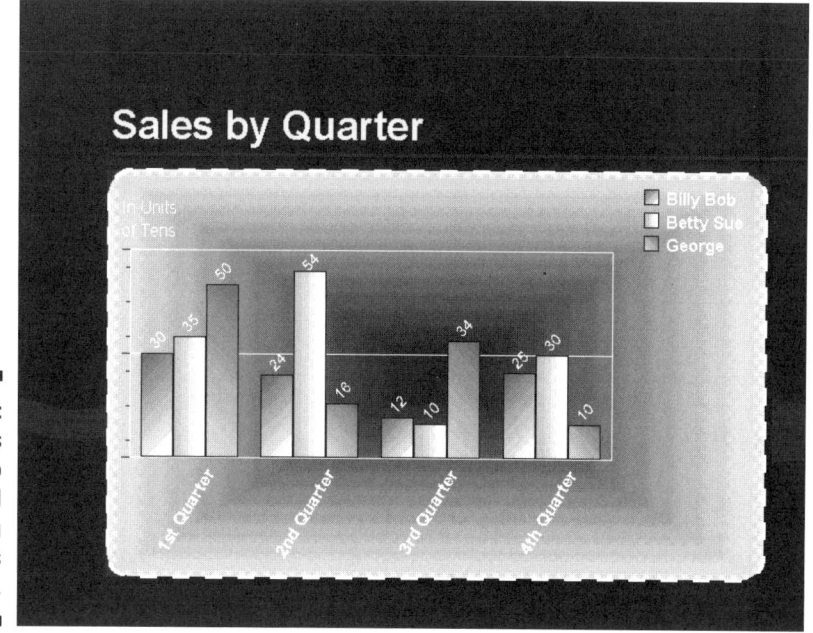

Figure 6-23: Make charts easier to understand by using series labels.

Figure 6-24: Use this section of the Properties dialog box to add and manipulate series labels.

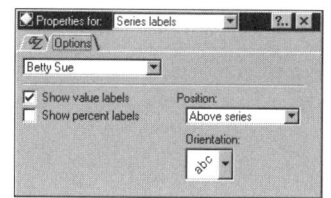

Changing the number type of Y-axis labels

Freelance Graphics enables you to display numbers in many ways, such as percentages, currency, scientific formulas, date, time, and a few others. To change the data type, simply use the Number portion of the Properties for Y-axis dialog box, as shown in Figure 6-25. Use the Format type list on the left to choose the type of numbering system. Then use the Current format list to choose a variation of the format type. For the Currency format type, for example, you can choose among several different currencies, by country. You can also place parentheses around numbers to show negative values, and you can change the decimal point position by using the Decimal places option.

Figure 6-25: Use this tab of the Properties dialog box to change the numbering format.

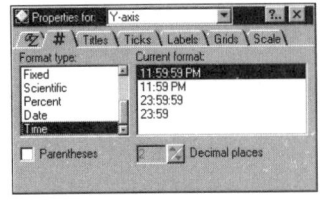

Combining Chart Types

Sometimes data is easier to understand if you display it more than one way. For example, sales data is more meaningful if you show how much each person sold *and* what percentage of the total sales the same person is responsible for, as shown in Figure 6-26. In this example, the sales numbers for all three salespeople are displayed in the first chart, and the second chart shows the numbers for a specific salesperson.

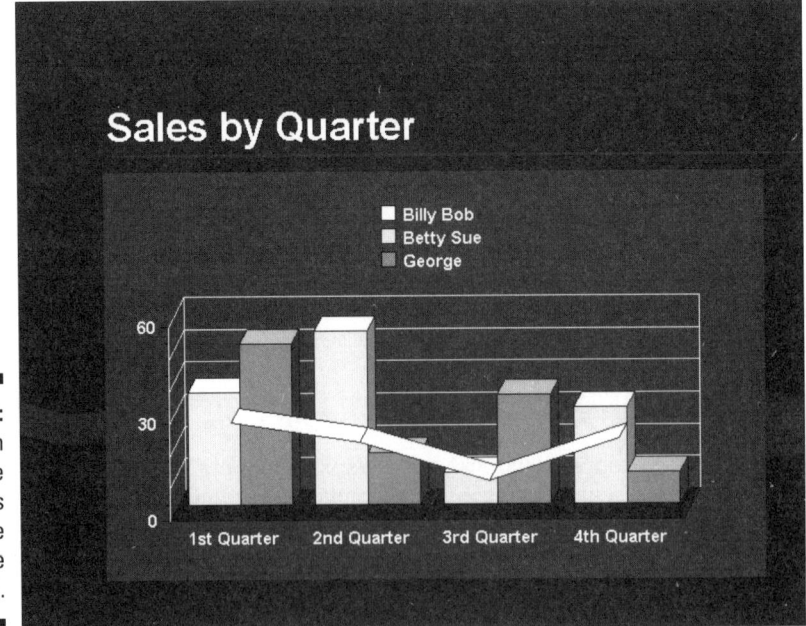

Figure 6-26: You can combine two charts to make data more meaningful.

Displaying two charts on the same slide

There are two ways to do this. You can use a page layout designed for two charts, or you can place two charts on any page layout by using either the Create⇨Chart command from the menu bar or the Create a Chart SmartIcon.

To use the page layout for two charts method, follow these steps:

1. **Add a new page.**
2. **Use the Page Layouts section of the New Page dialog box to choose the 2 Chart template.**
3. **Click the first chart placeholder, and design the first chart.**
4. **Copy the data from the first chart to the Clipboard.**
5. **Click the second chart placeholder.**
6. **Paste the data from the Clipboard into Edit Data form presented in Chapter 5.**
7. **Change to the desired chart type.**

You can also apply a 2 Chart layout to an existing page by using the Page⇨ Switch Page Layout command on the menu bar or by clicking the Page Layout button at the bottom of the screen.

Creating mixed charts

Another way to display data effectively is by mixing the way series are displayed within the same chart, as shown in Figure 6-27. Effectively, this chart shows the sales performance for two of the salespeople on a quarterly basis and highlights the performance of Billy Bob by showing not only a quarterly performance, but also by graphing his performance over the entire year.

The easiest way to create a mixed chart is to right-click the series you want to change and then choose Series Properties. Then, in the Mixed Type drop-down list of the dialog box that appears, choose the type you want the selected series to become: Area, Line, or Bar.

It would be irresponsible for us to leave this chapter without mentioning Freelance Graphics' chart style feature. After you've gone to all the work of designing a chart you like, wouldn't it be nice if you could define all your charts the same way with a simple mouse click or two? Well, you can. Simply save the chart settings as a *style*.

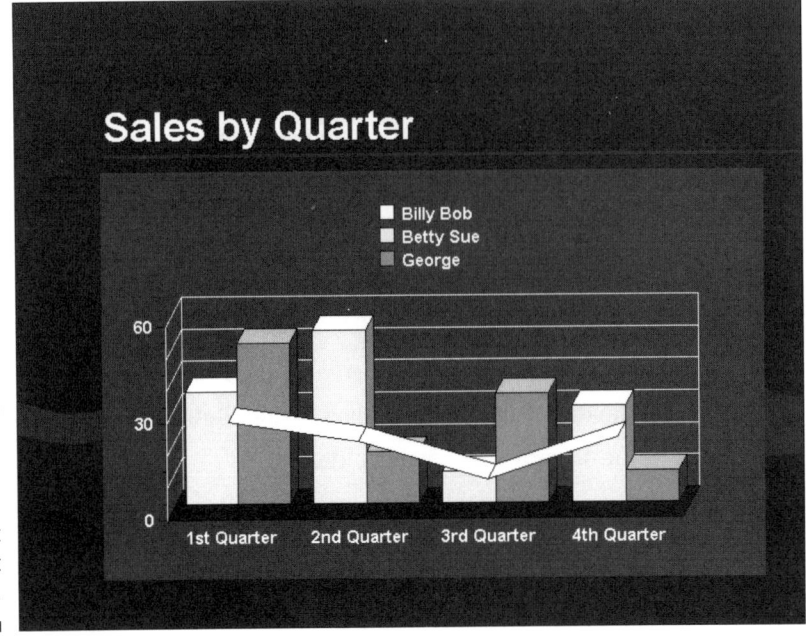

Figure 6-27: Use mixed charts to highlight important data.

You create chart styles in the Properties for Chart dialog box — in the Styles section, which is the second tab (the one with the little tag on it). To define a chart based on the current chart settings, click Create Style. A Create Chart Style dialog box opens, asking whether you want to save the current settings as a style. (The Make This Your Default Chart check box also enables you to create all new charts with the current settings.)

Click OK. Then, in the Save As dialog box, name the style and click Save. The new style is added to the Style list. You can now apply it to any chart simply by selecting the chart and then selecting the style.

Chapter 7
Working with Tables and Organization Charts

In This Chapter
- How to create tables
- How to modify table text, borders, and fills
- How to create organization charts
- How to modify organization-chart text, borders, fills, and connector lines

*P*receding chapters describe how charts and graphs make numbers easier to grasp. Graphical presentations are more interesting and easier to understand than word-heavy slides and overheads, which are boring and difficult to follow. You should use every tool at your disposal to display information graphically.

This chapter discusses how to display information in tables and organization charts. Tables are similar to spreadsheets in that you arrange data in rows and columns. *Organization charts,* or *top-down charts,* are used to show structure or process. Most often, corporations use these charts to display the company's hierarchical structure — who is whose boss, and so on.

Using Tables

Tables are a powerful medium for showing time periods, figures, currency, and concepts. You can use tables to show data organized in groups rather than display the data in text blocks. You also can use tables to present schedules, timetables, and price lists.

Tables enable you to present complicated information organized in row-and-column format so that the information is easier for the audience to find and associate with other data. Using tables is preferable to trying to explain relationships in long, wordy text blocks, especially in presentations.

Part II: Adding Visuals

In a typical table, a matrix of words and/or numbers replaces the bars and lines that would be used in a chart (see Figure 7-1). Like charts, tables work in two directions, showing the points at which two variables meet. Although tables usually are text-oriented, they are structured like charts. Picture a chart window with labels down the left side and across the top — that's the table format.

Sales by Quarter

	Things	Widgets	Stuff
1st Quarter	30	35	50
2nd Quarter	24	54	16
3rd Quarter	12	10	34
4th Quarter	25	30	10

Figure 7-1: A typical table works like a chart, but a table displays data in text format rather than graphically.

Creating a table

You can create a table in Freelance Graphics in two ways: Use the Table SmartMaster page layout, or choose Create⇨Table. Both methods display the Table Gallery dialog box, as shown in Figure 7-2. This dialog box enables you to select a table style and to define the number of rows and columns for your table.

Figure 7-2: Use this dialog box to create your table.

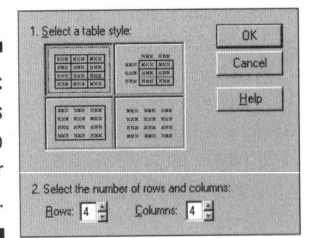

Chapter 7: Working with Tables and Organization Charts

The four options in the Select a Table Style section of the Table Gallery dialog box are as follows (from left to right):

- Borders around every cell
- Borders around data with no borders around labels
- Border around table with no borders around individual cells
- No borders

Creating a table is easy. Simply click the table style that you want to use; then click the up- and down-arrow buttons to define the number of rows and columns. If you need more rows or columns later, you can add them easily, as described in the following section.

Adding, removing, and moving columns and rows

When you select a Freelance Graphics table, the SmartIcon bar changes to enable you to work with tables. The easiest way to add, remove, or move tables is to click a SmartIcon button; you also can use the Insert, Delete, and Move Column/Row commands in the Table menu. (Remember that the Table menu is available only if you have selected a table.)

Adding table columns and rows

To add a row to your table, click the Insert a Row or Insert a Table SmartIcon. (If you don't know which SmartIcon is which, place the mouse pointer on one of the icons without clicking; the ToolTips tells you what each icon does.)

TIP If you want more control over insertions, place the text cursor in one of the cells in the row or column before where you want to insert the new row or column. In Figure 7-3, for example, you want to insert a new row between the second and third rows. Place the cursor in one of the cells in the second row; then click the Insert a Row SmartIcon. Freelance Graphics inserts a row after the second row.

Removing columns and rows

To delete a single column or row, place the text cursor in any of the cells in the column or row that you want to delete; then click the Delete Rows or Columns icon. The Delete Column/Row dialog box appears, as shown in Figure 7-4. This simple dialog box enables you to specify whether you want to delete a column or a row. Choose Column or Row, and then click OK.

To delete multiple columns or rows, first highlight them with the mouse; then click Delete Rows or Columns.

Part II: Adding Visuals

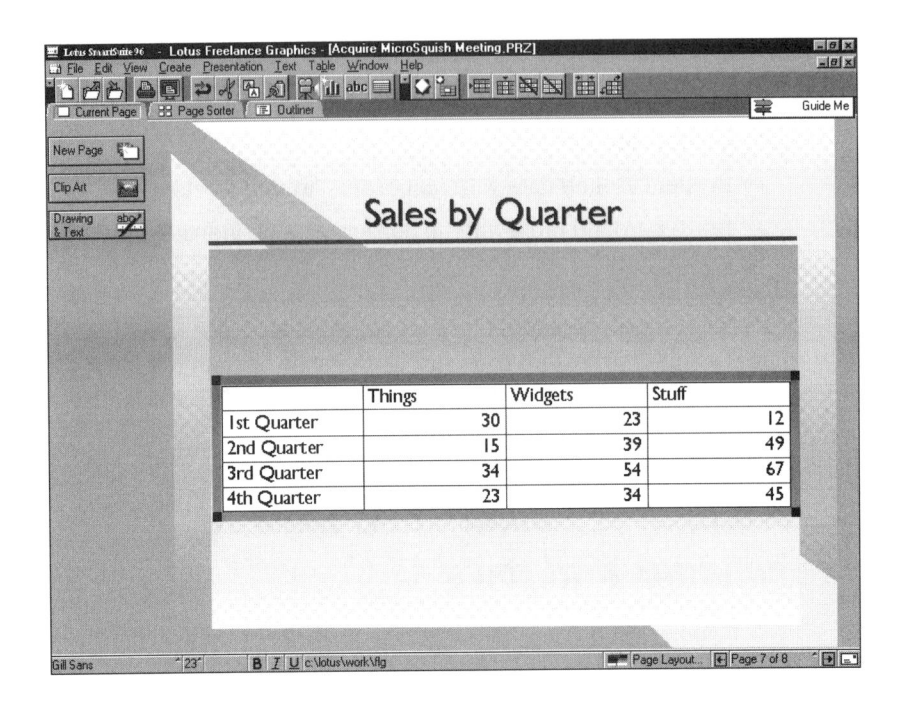

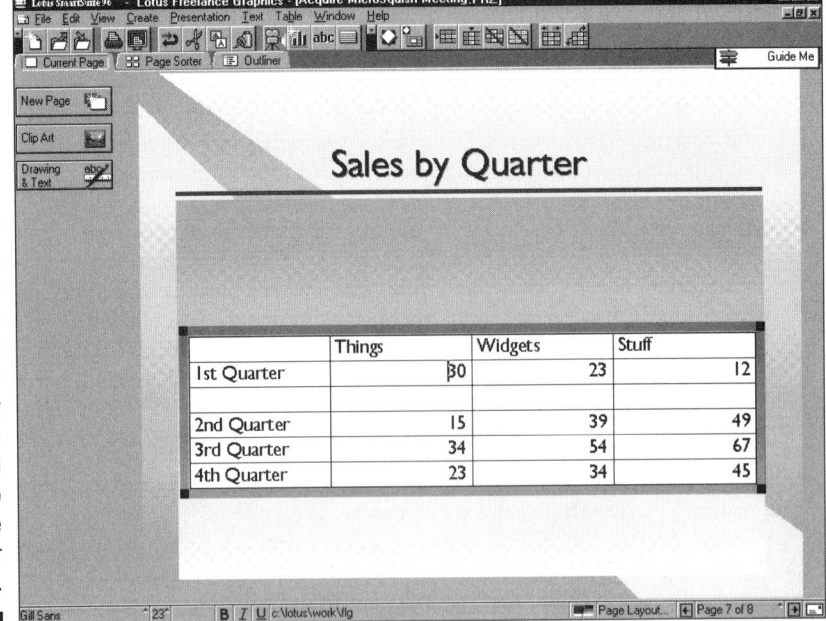

Figure 7-3:
Place the cursor in the row or column directly before where you want to insert the new row or column.

Figure 7-4:
Use this dialog box to tell Freelance Graphics whether to delete a column or row.

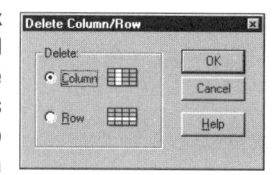

Moving columns and rows

You can use three methods to move the columns and rows in your tables: cutting and pasting, choosing Table⇨Move Column/Row, or clicking the Move Column or Row SmartIcon. If you are moving multiple columns and rows, you should cut and paste. To move one column or row, use either the menu command or the SmartIcon, both of which display the Move Column/Row dialog box (see Figure 7-5). This dialog box enables you to specify where the selected column or row should be placed.

Figure 7-5:
Use this dialog box to tell Freelance Graphics where to move the column or row.

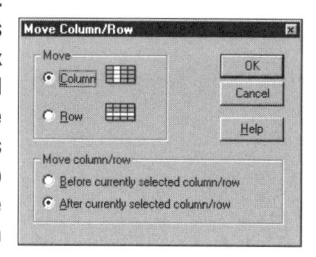

To move multiple rows or columns, highlight them and then choose Edit⇨Cut to remove them from the table. Place your cursor in the cell of the first column of the row to which you want to move the selection; then choose Edit⇨Paste.

> **NOTE** When you cut and paste to move multiple rows or columns, you need to place the cursor *in the cell where you want the new data to begin.* Otherwise, you may not get the desired result. Also, if you select several cells before pasting, Freelance Graphics replaces the data in the selected cells with the pasted data instead of inserting the data by moving rows and columns to make room for the new data.

Resizing column widths and row heights in tables

You can change the column width and row heights in your table by choosing certain options in the Column & Row tab of the Table Properties dialog box. To access the Column & Row tab, select the row(s) or column(s) that you want to resize; then choose Table➪Size Column/Row. Alternatively, right-click the table, choose Table Properties, and then click the Column & Row tab (the fifth from the left) in the Properties dialog box. To make changes for the entire table, select Table from the Properties For drop-down list in the Properties dialog box's title bar.

The Column & Row tab has the following four options:

- **Use Row Height:** Enables you to manually set the row to the desired height.
- **Check Automatic Row Height:** Tells Freelance Graphics to resize the row to match the text size automatically.
- **Column Width:** Enables you to type a new column-width value.
- **Cell Margin:** Enables you to change the cell margin (the distance from the cell border to text) by typing a new value.

Adding text to tables

To add text to a table, simply click a cell and start typing. You press Tab to move from cell to cell, or you can navigate the table in all four directions by pressing the arrow keys.

Changing Table Text, Borders, and Fills

Previous chapters of this book describe how to change the text, borders, and fills for your tables. After you select a Freelance Graphics object, the Page menu changes to accommodate the selected object. If you select text, for example, the Page menu changes to the Text menu. In the case of tables, however, Freelance Graphics changes the Page menu to Text and adds a Table menu because the table itself *and* the text inside it are the two properties that you want to edit.

As you do for most other objects on a Freelance Graphics page, you change the formatting of a table by using the Properties dialog box. To display this dialog box, choose Text➪Text Properties, Table➪Cell Properties, or Table➪Table Properties. Depending on which method you use, the Properties dialog box displays the options that you use to work with a specific aspect of the table.

Chapter 7: Working with Tables and Organization Charts *109*

You can change the context of the Properties dialog box by selecting a new option from the Properties For drop-down list, as shown in Figure 7-6. Selecting Selected Cell(s) affects only the text that is highlighted in the table; selecting Table affects the entire table; selecting Text affects the next text that you type.

Figure 7-6: Use this drop-down list to specify which aspect of table formatting you want to change.

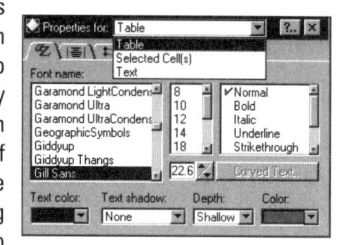

Changing text attributes in tables

You can change either selected text or the text in the entire table. In Figure 7-7, for example, the headings in the first row need to be centered and boldface.

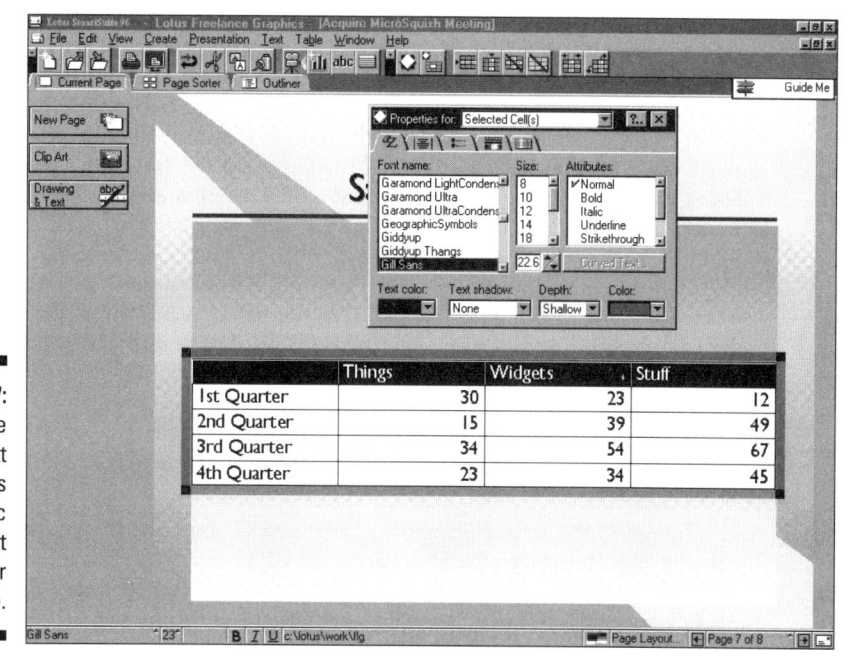

Figure 7-7: To change the text attributes for specific text, select it with your mouse.

Rather than change the headings one at a time, you can select the entire row by highlighting it. If the Properties dialog box is already open, as in Figure 7-7, it changes to work with selected text. If the dialog box isn't open, simply right-click the table and select Cell Properties from the pop-up menu, which opens the Properties dialog box for Selected Cells.

Properties for Selected Cells enables you to make several changes in selected text and cells, including borders and background fills. (See the section "Adding and modifying table borders," later in this chapter.) To change text attributes, you use the tabs in the Properties dialog box: Font & Color, Alignment, and Bullets.

Selecting several cells before opening the Properties dialog box affects only the selected cells. If you want to change all the text in the table, select Table from the Properties For drop-down list.

Changing fonts

Text attributes — typeface, size, and style (normal, bold, and italic, for example) — are controlled from the Font & Color tab of the Properties dialog box. Use the following procedures to change font attributes:

- To change the typeface, select the new font from the Font Name list.
- To change the type size, select a new size from the Size list or click the up- and down-arrow buttons below the Size list. You also can type a new value in the Size box.
- To change the type style, select a new style from the Attributes list. All text but Normal text (text without attributes) can have more than one attribute.

Changing the color of table text

You also can change text color in the Font & Color tab of the Properties dialog box. To change the color of text in selected cells, simply use the palette in the Color drop-down list. Remember that the colors at the top of the palette are the color scheme for the SmartMaster colors; they are designed to work well with the other colors in the presentation.

You can add shadows to the text in your tables from this section of Properties. Use the Text Shadow drop-down list to select where you want to place the shadow in relation to the text. Use the Depth drop-down list to control the size of the shadow and the Color drop-down list to change the color of the shadow.

Adding and modifying table borders

You can modify the line style, width, and color of borders for selected cells or for the entire table. (Use the Properties For drop-down list in the title bar of the Properties dialog box to toggle between Table and Selected Cells.) Control your tables' borders from the Line & Fill Color tab of the Properties dialog box.

Chapter 7: Working with Tables and Organization Charts

To add or modify a table border, follow these steps:

1. **Select one of the five border styles from the Style drop-down list.**
2. **Select the line width from the Width list.**
3. **Select a line color from the Color list.**

Changing table-cell backgrounds

As you do for a table's borders, you change backgrounds from the Line & Fill Color tab of the Properties dialog box. First, define a fill; then define a pattern and background color for the fill. Using this method, you can add solid backgrounds, tints, cross-hatching and other patterns, or gradients. Remember that a gradient is one color gradually changing into another.

By default (even if the table is given a background by a SmartMaster layout), a table has no defined background fill. To add a background to a table, follow these steps:

1. **Select a fill from the Pattern drop-down palette, as shown in Figure 7-8.**

Figure 7-8: Use this drop-down palette to define your table-cell fill pattern.

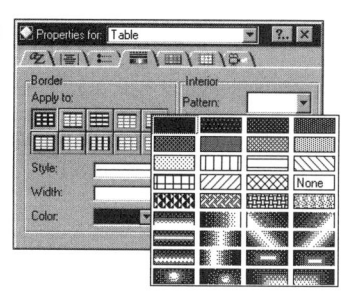

The first two rows of the drop-down palette consist of a solid fill and several screens, or tints. The next three rows are pattern fills; the last four are gradients. When you define a pattern, the foreground color is the dark elements, and the background colors are the light areas of the fills.

2. **Select a pattern color from the Pattern Color drop-down list.**
3. **Select a background color from the Background drop-down list.**

TIP

You can add a drop shadow to the entire table to give it a 3-D effect. To add a drop shadow, select one of the four Shadow options. The location of the shadow simulates a light source. If the shadow is at the bottom right of the table, for example, the simulated light source is from the upper left.

As you work in the Properties dialog box, Freelance Graphics displays the effects you choose on your table, enabling you to experiment with colors and patterns. After you get the right look, simply close the Properties dialog box. Figure 7-9 shows a chart with new text formatting, modified borders, a gradient background in the label cells, and a drop shadow.

Using Organization Charts

Organization charts (sometimes called *top-down charts* or *org charts*) usually display hierarchical relationships among people in a large organization. These charts can also display processes. Big companies like to use organization charts to demonstrate who has what responsibilities and who answers to whom.

Creating an organization chart

You can create an organization chart in Freelance Graphics in two ways: Use the Organization Chart SmartMaster page layout, or choose Create⇨Organization Chart. Both methods display the Organization Chart Gallery dialog box, as shown in Figure 7-10. This dialog box enables you to select a chart style and define how the lowest level of the chart is displayed.

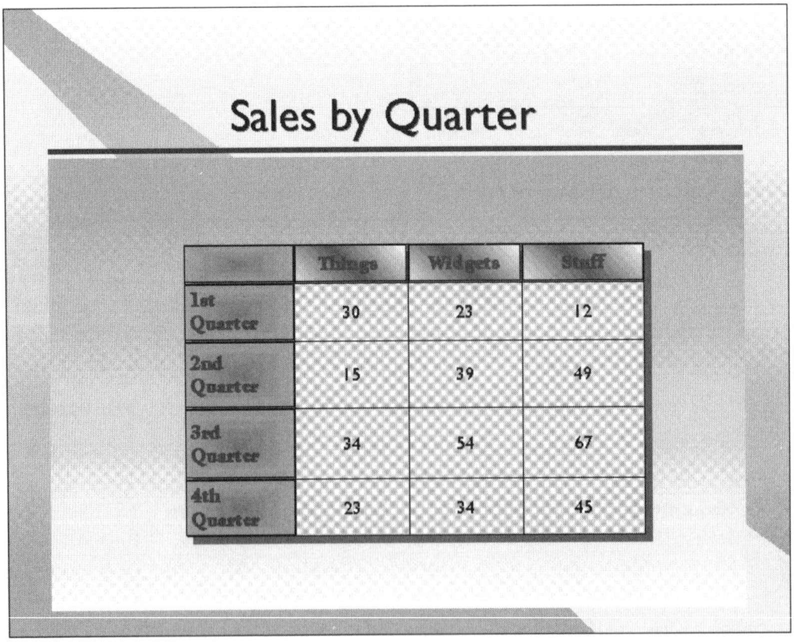

Figure 7-9: Freelance Graphics enables you to create dynamic-looking tables.

	Things	Widgets	Stuff
1st Quarter	30	23	12
2nd Quarter	15	39	49
3rd Quarter	34	54	67
4th Quarter	23	34	45

Sales by Quarter

Figure 7-10: Use this dialog box to define your organization-chart style. The icons show how your chart will look.

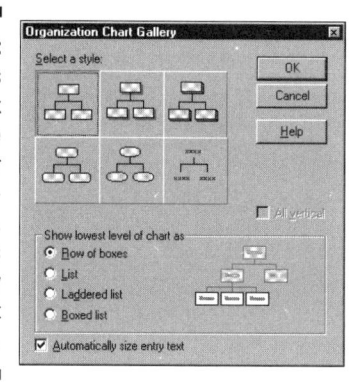

The four options in the Show Lowest Level of Chart As section of the Organization Chart Gallery dialog box enable you to save space in large, complicated charts. To see how each option affects your chart, simply turn it on; Freelance Graphics shows you a preview of how the option works. You should leave the Automatically Size Entry Text check box selected to make sure that the text fits into your organization chart's boxes.

To create an organization chart from the Organization Chart Gallery dialog box, follow these steps:

1. **Select the chart style from the Select a Style section.**
2. **Select an option button from the Show Lowest Level of Chart As section.**
3. **Click OK.**

Adding superiors and subordinates

After you follow the steps in the preceding section, Freelance Graphics displays the Organization Chart Entry List dialog box, which enables you to type labels for each entry in the chart. You can add three types of entries per position: Name, Title, and Comment. You also define the structure of the chart from this dialog box. To define subordinates, press Tab. To create superiors, press Shift+Tab. (Superiors are higher levels; subordinates are lower levels or lower than superiors.) You can define several layers of superiors and subordinates, but remember that you have only so much space and that you must keep the chart simple and easy to understand.

To add entries to your organization chart, follow these steps:

1. **Type your entries in the Organization Chart Entry List dialog box.**

    To add an entry at the same level, press Enter. To create a subordinate entry, press Tab to indent the name (creating a hanging indent with the first line sticking out farther to the left than the other lines). To create a superior entry, press Shift+Tab to outdent the name. To force line breaks in the text, place the insertion point between words and press Ctrl+Enter.

Part II: Adding Visuals

Figure 7-11 shows a completed list and the ensuing organization chart. Notice that superiors are outdented in relationship to the indented subordinates.

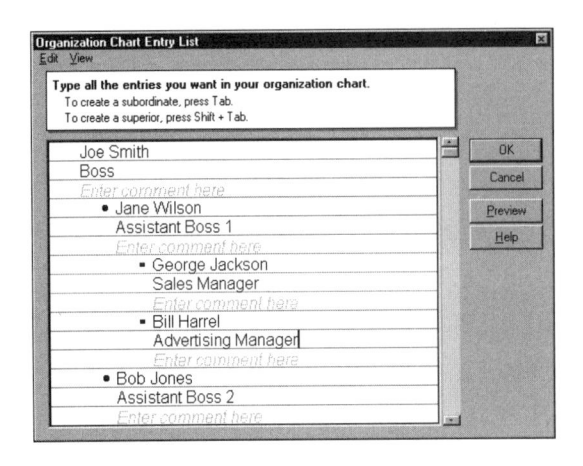

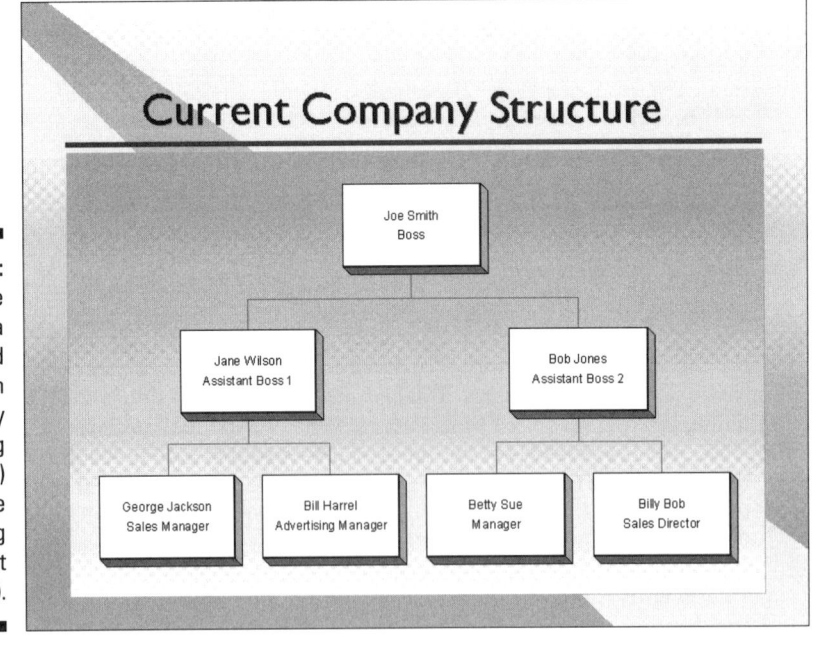

Figure 7-11: An example of a completed Organization Chart Entry List dialog box (top) and the corresponding chart (bottom).

Chapter 7: Working with Tables and Organization Charts 115

> **TIP**
>
> You can preview your work at any time from the Organization Chart Entry List dialog box by clicking the Preview button. To accept the chart and insert it into the slide, click OK. To return to the Organization Chart Entry List dialog box after previewing the chart, click Change.

 2. **After you finish making your entries, click OK.**

   Freelance Graphics creates your organization chart. Now you can format the text boxes to your liking.

Adding a staff member

Freelance Graphics enables you to add one support-staff member per organization chart. The staff member is inserted directly below the uppermost level in the chart, as shown in Figure 7-12. This position reports to the top entry.

To add a staff position (such as an administrative assistant) to an organization chart, follow these steps:

 1. **Choose Edit⇨Staff from the Organization Chart Entry List dialog box's menus.**

   The Organization Chart Staff dialog box appears (see Figure 7-13).

 2. **Fill in the text boxes in the dialog box with the appropriate information.**

 3. **Click OK.**

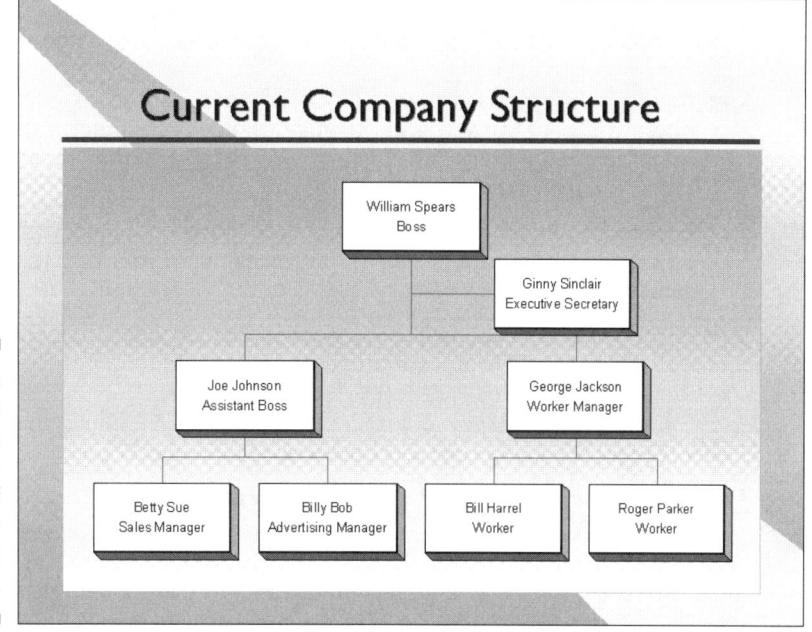

Figure 7-12: An example of a supporting-staff member added to a chart.

Current Company Structure

William Spears — Boss
Ginny Sinclair — Executive Secretary
Joe Johnson — Assistant Boss
George Jackson — Worker Manager
Betty Sue — Sales Manager
Billy Bob — Advertising Manager
Bill Harrel — Worker
Roger Parker — Worker

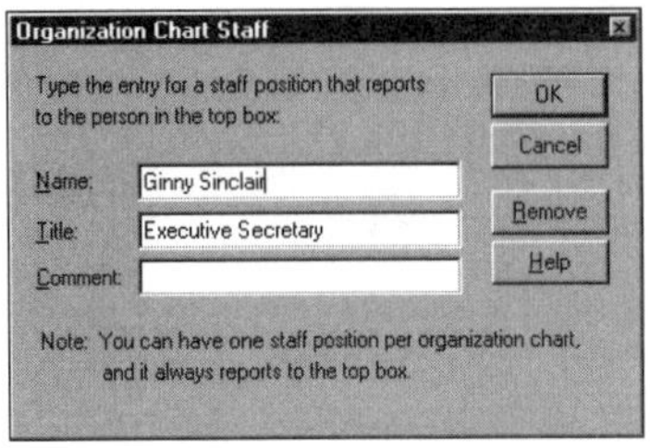

Figure 7-13: Use this dialog box to add a supporting staff member to a chart.

Adding, removing, and editing organization-chart entries

Most companies change personnel from time to time. Sometimes, positions are eliminated; sometimes, new positions are added. When your company or group changes, you need to update your organization chart.

You make additions and deletions to the data in your organization chart in the Organization Chart Entry List dialog box, where you created the chart initially. You can edit the text in the chart by clicking it and retyping the text in the chart itself.

You can reopen the Organization Chart Entry List dialog box by right-clicking the organization chart and then choosing Edit Data or by selecting the chart and then choosing Org Chart⇨Edit Data (see the following section for information on the Org Chart menu).

To add, remove, or edit an organization-chart entry, follow one of these procedures:

- To add an organization-chart entry, place the cursor in the entry behind where you want the new entry to appear; then press Enter. If the new entry is a subordinate, press Tab. If the new entry is a superior, press Shift+Tab. Then type the new entry.
- To delete an organization-chart entry, select the entire entry and then press Delete. Make any necessary adjustments to your data to accommodate the deletion.
- To edit an organization-chart entry, click the entry and then add and delete text as you would in any other text block.

Modifying organization-chart text, borders, fills, and connector lines

You have almost unlimited control of your organization charts. You can change the text to any typeface, size, or style that you like; you can edit the borders and fills of your organization-chart boxes. You can even change the chart style itself. You make these changes in the Properties dialog box.

Chapter 7: Working with Tables and Organization Charts

After you select a chart, the Page menu changes to the Org Chart menu, which provides options for working with organization charts. You can access the Properties dialog box by choosing from the Org Chart menu the command that corresponds with the chart element that you want to edit (Frame, Connecting Lines, and so on) or by right-clicking the chart element itself.

After the Properties dialog box appears, you can switch among chart elements by making selections from the Properties For drop-down list in the dialog box's title bar.

Formatting organization-chart text

You reformat your organization-chart text in the Font & Color tab of the Properties dialog box, as shown in Figure 7-14. You access the tab by clicking the first tab in the Properties dialog box (the one with the letters on it).

Figure 7-14: Use this tab to reformat organization-chart text.

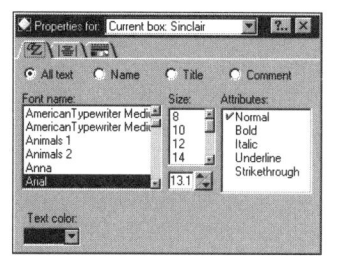

Freelance Graphics provides several options for the text in your chart. You can change only the text in the selected box of the chart, the text in the selected box and its subordinates, or the text in the selected box and its peers. To determine which boxes to change, select Current Box, Current Box Subordinates, or Current Box Peers from the Properties For drop-down list. To change the text for the entire chart, select Organization Chart from the Properties For drop-down list.

You also can choose which parts of the box entries to edit by clicking one of the four radio buttons at the top of the dialog box. Those buttons are as follows:

- ✓ **All Text:** Changes all three entries, or lines of text, in the boxes — Name, Title, and Comment.
- ✓ **Name:** Changes the Name entries, or the first lines of text in the boxes.
- ✓ **Title:** Changes the Title entries, or the second lines of text in the boxes.
- ✓ **Comments:** Changes the Comment entries, or the third lines of text in the boxes.

After you select which text the changes affect, you can use one or all of the following methods to format the text:

- ✔ To change the typeface, select a name from the Font Name list.
- ✔ To change the type size, select a new size from the Size list or change the number in the Size field.
- ✔ To change the type style (Bold, Normal, Italic, and so on), select one or more of the options in the Attributes list. (Notice that you cannot select more than one attribute if you select Normal.)
- ✔ To change the text color, select a new color from the Text Color drop-down palette. Remember that the colors in the top section of the palette are SmartMaster colors, which are designed to work within the current color scheme.

As you make changes, Freelance Graphics automatically applies them to the chart, enabling you to see the effects of your work. Feel free to try different combinations.

> When you create an organization chart, by default, Freelance Graphics fits the text to the boxes and the boxes to the available space. Changing typefaces and text size can affect how text fits in the boxes, giving you an undesired effect, such as uncentered text or even text that flows out of the boxes.

Changing organization-chart borders and fills

When you change borders, you can specify whether to modify the selected box, the selected box's peers, or the selected box's subordinates. You make these specifications by making selections from the Properties For drop-down list. To modify the entire chart, select Organization Chart from the Properties For drop-down list.

Modifying organization-chart borders

Changing borders for organization charts is similar to changing borders for tables and charts. Control your organization-chart borders from the Line & Fill Color tab of the Properties dialog box (the third tab from the left).

To add or modify an organization-chart border, follow these steps:

1. **Select one of the five border styles from the Style drop-down list.**
2. **Select a line width from the Width list.**
3. **Select a color from the Color list.**

Changing organization-chart box fills

As with the organization chart's borders, you change backgrounds from the Line & Fill Color tab of the Properties dialog box. First, you define a fill; then you define a pattern and background color for the fill. Using this method, you can add solid backgrounds, tints, cross-hatching and other patterns, or gradients.

Chapter 7: Working with Tables and Organization Charts   119

By default (even if the chart is given a background by a SmartMaster layout), a chart contains no fill. To add a background to the chart, follow these steps:

1. Select a fill from the Pattern drop-down palette, as shown in Figure 7-15.

Figure 7-15: Use this drop-down palette to define your organization chart's fill pattern.

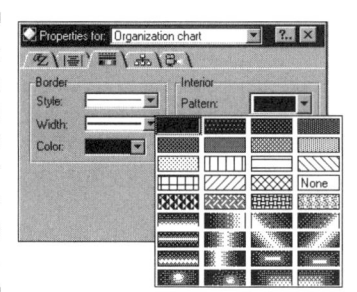

The first two rows of the drop-down palette consist of a solid fill and several screens, or tints. The next three rows are pattern fills; the last four are gradients. When you define a pattern, the foreground color is the dark elements, and the background colors are the light areas of the fills. In gradients, the foreground color graduates into the background color.

2. Select a pattern color from the Pattern Color drop-down palette.

3. Select a background color from the Background drop-down palette.

Modifying organization-chart connecting lines

You can modify the lines that connect the elements of your organization charts. Perhaps you want to make the lines stand out or you just want a different look. You can recolor the lines, make them thicker, and assign one of Freelance Graphics' five line styles to them.

To modify the connecting lines, select the organization chart and then choose Org Chart⇨Connecting Lines or select Connecting Line from the Properties For drop-down list in the Properties dialog box. The Properties dialog box for Connecting Lines has only one section: Line & Fill Color. To modify your connecting lines, follow the procedures in the section "Modifying organization-chart borders," earlier in this chapter.

As you work in the Properties dialog box, Freelance Graphics displays the effects on your chart, enabling you to experiment with colors and patterns. When you get the right look, simply close the dialog box.

Figure 7-16 shows an organization chart with new text formatting, modified borders, a gradient background in the boxes, modified connector lines, and a drop shadow.

Part II: Adding Visuals

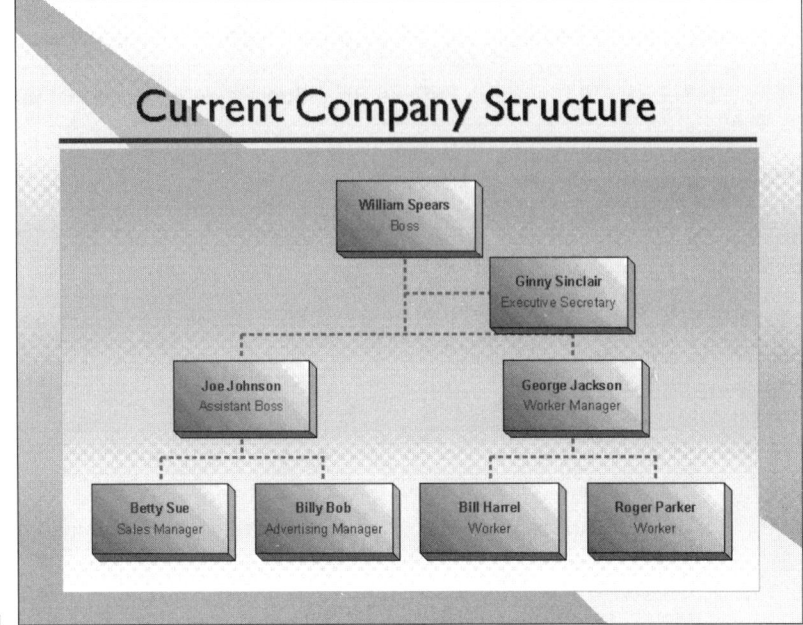

Figure 7-16: A customized Freelance Graphics organization chart.

Changing the entire chart style

When you created your chart, you defined a chart style that included a box shape, a drop-shadow style, and so on. If your page appears to be too full or if you just want a different look, you can change these settings in the Properties dialog box.

In the Properties dialog box, select Organization Chart from the Properties For drop-down list; then click the Layout tab (fourth from the left, with the organization chart on it). The dialog box shown in Figure 7-17 appears. You can select a new chart style from the Layout drop-down list, or you can choose options in the Lowest Level section to change how the lowest levels appear.

Figure 7-17: Use this tab to change the chart style.

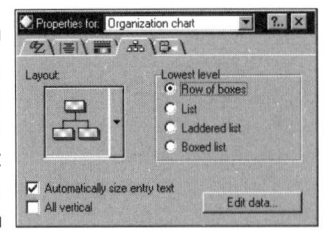

Chapter 8
Adding Symbols and Manipulating Text Shapes

In This Chapter
- Working with Text Shapes and clip art
- Adding text to a symbol
- Recoloring Text Shapes
- Resizing, layering, aligning, and grouping Text Shapes and artwork

Previous chapters of this book describe how to make great-looking text and chart slides. This chapter describes how to make your slides more interesting and attractive by adding symbols, or what Freelance Graphics calls *Text Shapes*. Text Shapes consists of the symbols that appear after you click the Drawing & Text button on the left side of the Freelance Graphics screen.

In this chapter, you discover how to use Text Shapes. You can use Text Shapes "as is," or you can modify them to fit your individual needs. Freelance Graphics provides hundreds of ways to resize, recolor, and otherwise manipulate graphics.

What do you say we stop jawing about it and get down to business?

Working with Text Shapes

Freelance Graphics has a number of ways to get symbols and images into your presentations. The easiest route by far, however, is using the program's built-in Text Shapes.

Another way to spruce up your presentations is with clip art. Clip art, of course, consists of predrawn images — pictures of everything from pandas to howitzers — that you can place on your slides. Freelance Graphics ships with several hundred clip art images that you can access by choosing Create⇨Add Clip Art on the menu bar. As an alternative, you can import other images from clip art collections, such as 3G Graphics' Images with Impact or TMaker's ClickArt. Freelance Graphics also supports drawings and images from various draw and paint programs, such as CorelDRAW, Adobe Illustrator, and Adobe Photoshop. The next chapter discusses using clip art in your presentations.

To get to the Text Shape palette, you click the Drawing & Text button on the left side of the screen. Text Shapes are all those funny-looking arrows and boxes in the second portion of the toolbox that appears. There are actually two sets of Text Shapes. If you click the Flowchart button, you get a set specifically for working with flowcharts, as shown in Figure 8-1. They're called Text Shapes because you can type text into them and the text remains centered in the shape, no matter how you resize or move the shape around on the screen. Text Shapes make great buttons and callouts.

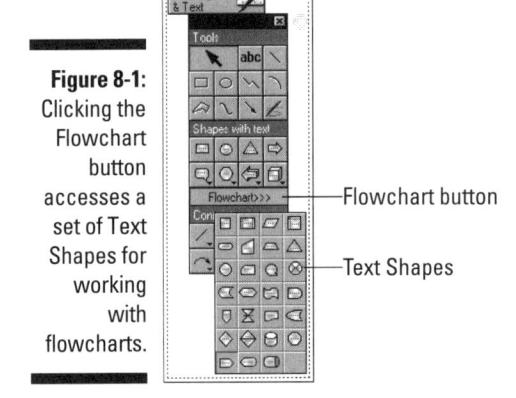

Figure 8-1: Clicking the Flowchart button accesses a set of Text Shapes for working with flowcharts.

Notice also that some of the Text Shape buttons have down arrows on them. This arrow means that there are even more shapes on a pop-up subpalette. So, as you can see, Freelance Graphics provides plenty of shapes.

To use a Text Shape, simply click the Drawing & Text button and then click the shape you want from the palette. Click again on your slide where you want to place the shape. Freelance Graphics assumes that the next thing you want to do is resize the shape. You can resize the shape by dragging one of the eight handles surrounding it. After resizing the shape, click it again to type your text into it, as shown in Figure 8-2.

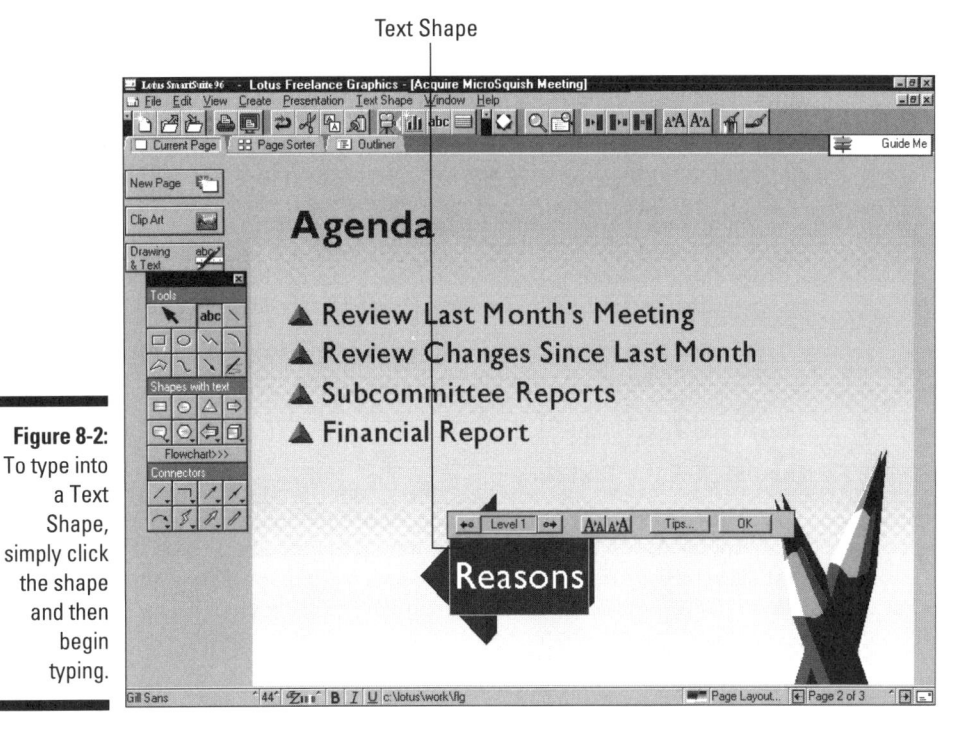

Chapter 8: Adding Symbols and Manipulating Text Shapes *123*

Figure 8-2: To type into a Text Shape, simply click the shape and then begin typing.

You can change the size and appearance of your text by using options on the Text Shape menu or from the buttons at the bottom of the Freelance Graphics screen.

Adding Text to Text Shapes

If everything in life were as easy as adding text to Freelance Graphics' Text Shapes, nobody would ever struggle. (Which, depending on your perspective, can be either good or bad.) To type in a Text Shape, all you do is click it with the Text tool and begin typing. The text automatically stays centered in the shape. You can easily change the font, size, and color of the text. (Be careful, though; too many fancy effects can render the text unreadable.)

Typing into a Text Shape

Before typing into a Text Shape, you must place the shape on the page and resize it. To do so, follow these steps:

Part II: Adding Visuals

1. **In Current Page view, click the Drawing & Text button.**
2. **In the Tools palette, in the Shapes with Text section, select the desired shape and then click the place on the slide where you want the shape.**

   You can make your shape exactly the size you need by clicking and dragging out a rectangular area. You can control both the width and height of the shape by dragging the box to the size and shape you want.

   Oh, yeah. If you don't see the shape you need, try clicking one of the down arrows at the bottom of the buttons in the second row of shapes under Shapes with Text. Voilà! You've got a bunch more shapes.

   To add text to the shape, simply select the Text tool (labeled *abc*) and then click the shape, or double-click the shape.

3. **Resize the Text Shape as desired.**
4. **Double-click the Text Shape.**

   The shape goes into Text mode, just as when you add text to a Click Here placeholder (see Figure 8-3). A text bar spans the shape. Use it to assign a text style or to resize the text. (Text styles are discussed in the section "Making really fast font and Text Shape formatting changes by using styles," later in this chapter.)

5. **Type the text into the shape.**

Figure 8-3: The Text Shape is in Text mode. You enter text here as you do in a placeholder.

Resizing Text Shape text

More often than not, the text in the Text Shape isn't the size you want. You can resize it in three ways: using the reduce and enlarge buttons on the text mode bar spanning the shape, choosing Text Shape⇨Text Shape Properties on the menu bar, or clicking the size button at the bottom of the screen. Only the buttons on the Text mode bar, however, resize the text without your first selecting it. The other two options require you to select the text with your mouse or keyboard before you can resize it.

After you've sized the text inside the Text Shape, you can resize the shape, and the text resizes with it. You cannot resize both the text and shape with the mouse, however, as you can in a draw program. Instead, you should use the commands on the Object Size submenu of the Text Shape menu, as shown in Figure 8-4. You can also change the shape to any other Freelance Graphics Text Shape by using the Text Shape⇨Switch Text Shape Type command on the menu bar, as shown in Figure 8-5.

Figure 8-4: Use these commands to resize the text and the shape at the same time.

Changing Text Shape fonts

Often, the text in your shapes is not in a typestyle you like or that looks good inside the shape. You can change the Text Shape font in three ways: from the Font button at the bottom of the screen, as shown in Figure 8-6; from Create⇨Text Shape Properties; or from Create⇨Fonts & Colors.

To change the font, first select the text with the mouse or keyboard and then click the Font button at the bottom of the screen. If you want to change several attributes at once, use the Properties for Text Shape dialog box, as shown in Figure 8-7. You can get to this dialog box by choosing Text Shape⇨Text Shape Properties or Font & Color from the menu bar.

Part II: Adding Visuals

> **TIP**
>
> You can change font, size, and color before you type text. Then, when you start typing, the text assumes the attributes you set. This approach saves you from having to go back and select the text to change it.

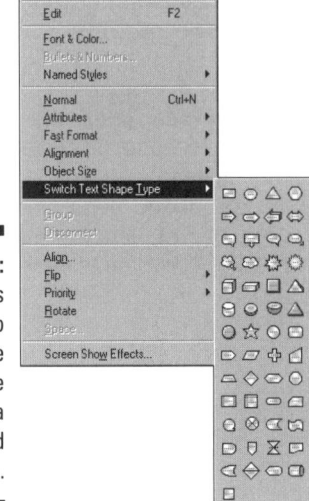

Figure 8-5: Use this submenu to change the shape type of a selected shape.

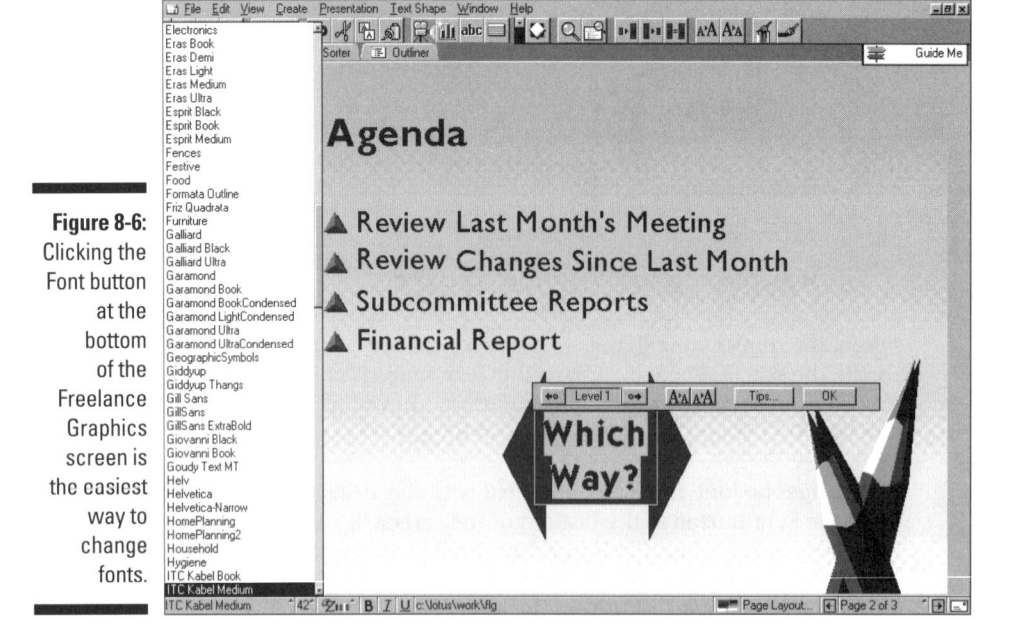

Figure 8-6: Clicking the Font button at the bottom of the Freelance Graphics screen is the easiest way to change fonts.

Figure 8-7:
Use this dialog box to make several text attribute changes at once.

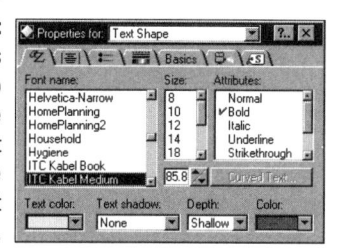

Changing Text Shape font colors

Often, Freelance Graphics' default text colors may not be to your liking. You can easily change the text color with the Color button at the bottom of the screen or from the Properties for Text Shape dialog box. Be careful, though. Make sure that you don't create gaudy color combinations or text colors that are difficult to see from far away.

To change text color, first select the text with the Text tool and then click the Color button at the bottom of the screen (the one with letters and rainbow colors on it), which opens the Freelance Graphics color palette, as shown in Figure 8-8. (This button is available only when an object that can be colored is selected.) The colors across the top of the color palette are the currently active color scheme and are designed to work well together. These are your safest choices. You can also use any of the other colors on the palette. Simply click the swatch for the color you want.

NOTE: You can create your own color schemes, modify existing schemes, or use one of the Freelance Graphics schemes. See Chapter 11 for more information. You should note, however, that the Freelance Graphics schemes are professionally designed to include complementary colors to keep you from using weird, eye-offending combinations.

If you want to change several attributes at once, try using the Text shape⇨Text Shape Properties or Font & Color commands on the menu.

Making really fast font and Text Shape formatting changes by using styles

If your presentation has several symbols containing text, wouldn't it be a drag to go through and format each one manually? You can save loads of time and maintain consistency by using Freelance Graphics' styles. Styles contain sets of text and background formatting information that you can apply to an object with a couple of mouse clicks.

Part II: Adding Visuals

Figure 8-8: Use the Color Palette to change selected text color.

For example, if you frequently use Text Shapes with white, Helvetica 24-point bold text in a purple background, you can save all this information in a style. Freelance Graphics then remembers the style, and you can use it over and over.

Freelance Graphics has two ways to create a style. You can first create the text and background and then choose Text Shape⇨Named Styles from the menu bar. Then click Create on the submenu. This opens the Create Text Style dialog box, as shown in Figure 8-9. In this dialog box, you name the style and click OK. Freelance Graphics then adds the new style name to the style list.

Figure 8-9: Select the object for which you want to create a style, type the name in this dialog box, and click OK to save the new style.

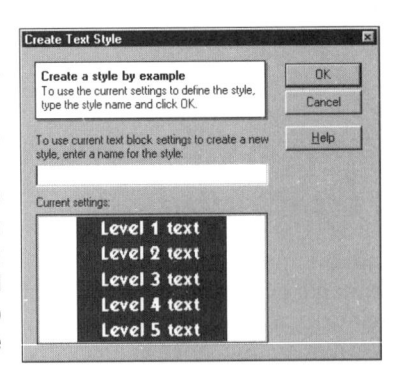

Chapter 8: Adding Symbols and Manipulating Text Shapes

Now you can apply the style to any text object, including Text Shapes. To do so, simply select the object you want to format and then choose Apply from the Named Styles submenu. This opens the Properties for Text Shape dialog box with the Styles section displayed, as shown in Figure 8-10. If the text already has a style assigned to it, that style is highlighted. If not, `None` is highlighted. You can either select one of the styles from the list or use one of the buttons to perform one of the following actions:

- Use the **Create Style** button to create a new style from the selected object.
- Use **Redefine Style** to reconfigure the current style to the settings of the currently selected object.
- Use **Manage Style** to delete styles.
- Use **Reset to Style** to return the currently selected object to the style assigned to it. Use this option when you have made character-level changes to the text (changes where you have selected text and changed attributes). When you click Reset to Style, the Reset to Style dialog box appears, enabling you to determine which text the reset affects. You can choose to reset all text in the presentation back to the formatting contained in its respective styles, or you can reset only the currently selected text. You can also choose which types of overrides to remove (*overrides* are changes you make to text after assigning a style). You can remove only character overrides or remove changes you've made to text formatted as level text. (Remember that *level text* is the text used to format titles and bullet slides.)

Freelance Graphics ships with several predefined styles, such as Numbered List, Presentation Title, and others. You can also modify these styles to suit your needs, such as changing fonts to match your corporate identity.

Figure 8-10: The Properties dialog box for applying styles to Text Shapes.

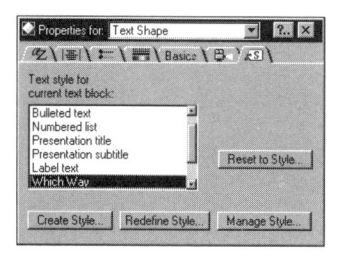

Recoloring Text Shape Colors and Line Weights

Sometimes Freelance Graphics' default colors for Text Shapes don't suit your fancy. It's easy to change a Text Shape's color, fill, and line color. (*Fill* refers to the pattern inside the shape, and *line* refers to the outline.) You can also change the line weight and style of the shape. Line weight is the width of the outline around the shape. Line weights are measured in points. There are 72 points per inch.

You control Text Shape colors and line weights from the Properties for Text Shape dialog box, which you can reach by using the Pointer tool to select the Text Shape and then choosing Text Shape⇨Text Shape Properties from the menu bar. You then click the Line and Fill tab (fourth from right) to work with the shape's color and line attributes. This displays the dialog box shown in Figure 8-11. The left side of the box enables you to work with borders (or outlines), and the right side enables you to change the interior of the shape (or fill style).

Figure 8-11: Use this dialog box to change line styles, widths, and fill colors for Text Shapes.

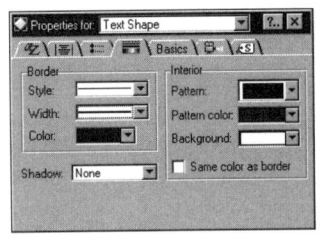

The following is a list of procedures for working with this dialog box:

- ✔ To change an outline's style, click the Style drop-down list and then choose from one of the five line styles.

- ✔ To change a line weight, click the Width drop-down list and select the desired weight. You should be careful not to choose too thick of a line, though, because most objects look funny with big ol' outlines.

Chapter 8: Adding Symbols and Manipulating Text Shapes

- ✓ To change the outline color, click the Color drop-down list and choose the desired color.

- ✓ To add a drop shadow to the shape, click the Shadow drop-down list and choose the desired position for the shadow. (Drop shadows provide a dynamic, 3-D effect and can make objects stand out more, as shown in Figure 8-12.)

- ✓ To add a gradient (one color graduating into another), cross-hatch, or another type of Freelance Graphics fill, click the Pattern drop-down list and then choose the desired fill.

- ✓ To change the pattern, or foreground, color of a Text Shape, click the Pattern Color drop-down list and then choose the desired color. The foreground color is the hue Freelance Graphics uses for the dark parts in a pattern. The background color is the color to which the gradient graduates.

- ✓ To change the background color for the pattern fill, click the Background drop-down list and choose the desired background.

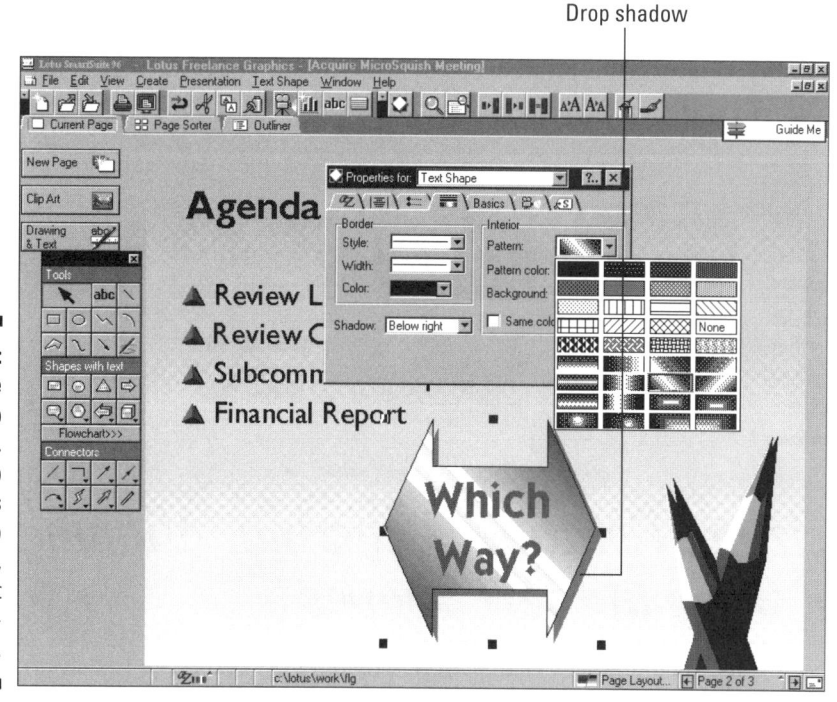

Figure 8-12: An example of a drop shadow. Drop shadows add depth to an object, making it seem three-dimensional.

Part II: Adding Visuals

> **DESIGN**
>
> Freelance Graphics enables you to get pretty creative with your Text Shape fills. You should be careful when designing Text Shapes to make sure that the foreground and background colors do not clash. One way to do so is to use the combinations of the 16 colors at the top of the various color palettes. These colors are designed to go together. Also important is that you not design fills that are so busy your audience can't read the text in the shape. Look at the several examples in Figure 8-13 to see what we mean. In the top row, you can hardly read the text for the background. The boxes in the bottom row are much better.

✔ To automatically make the fill the same color as the border, select the Same Color As Border check box. This choice tells Freelance Graphics to make the pattern, or foreground color, the same color as the outline.

> **TIP**
>
> Yet another way to make quick formatting changes to Text Shapes is by using Text Shape➪Fast Format on the menu bar. This command remembers attributes, such as color, size, line weights, and so on, and applies them to other objects. To use this feature, use the Pointer tool to select the object you want to copy attributes from and then choose Text Shape➪Fast Format/Pickup Attributes from the menu bar. Next select the Text Shapes to which you want to apply the attributes and then choose Text Shape➪Fast Format/Apply Attributes from the menu bar. The shapes assume the attributes of the object from which you picked up attributes. (You should note that this feature also works with objects you draw by using Freelance Graphics' drawing tools.)

Figure 8-13: Use fills that emphasize your text.

Resizing, Rotating, Layering, Aligning, and Grouping Text Shapes

Freelance Graphics enables you to manipulate Text Shapes and the objects you draw with the drawing tools in a number of ways. You can resize them with your mouse, stack (layer) them, automatically align them in relation to one another, group them so that they maintain juxtaposition — you name it. In this section, you see how to use these powerful features to create complex objects from multiple objects.

NOTE

The following discussion of Freelance Graphics' Text Shapes and their relationships to one another also pertains to most other Freelance Graphics objects, such as shapes drawn with the drawing tools, text, and clip art. Because we are talking about Text Shapes in this chapter, the commands referenced here are located on the Text Shape menu. Remember, though, that this menu is context-sensitive, meaning that it changes depending on which object is selected. If you select an object drawn with the Freelance Graphics drawing tools, the Text Shape menu becomes the Drawing menu. If you select a chart, it becomes the Chart menu, and so on. In many contexts, the commands discussed here on the Text Shape menu are also available on other menus.

Resizing Text Shapes

All the graphics objects in a Freelance Graphics presentation are resized in the same way, by dragging one of the eight control points, or handles, that surround the object after you select it with the Pointer tool. You use these control points to resize and reshape objects. To resize an object both horizontally and vertically, drag one of the corner handles. To resize in one direction, drag one of the middle handles. The left and right handles resize horizontally. The top and bottom handles resize vertically.

TIP

You can also use the Reduce, Enlarge, and Equal SmartIcons to resize objects. Reduce and Enlarge resize proportionally by about 20 percent. The Equal SmartIcon forces multiple selected objects to the same size. Similar commands are on the Object Size submenu of the Text Shape or Drawing menu (depending on which object is selected). The benefit of using these commands, rather than your mouse, is that text inside a Text Shape resizes proportionally.

Rotating objects

You can create a number of dynamic effects by rotating Text Shapes and other objects. The most useful application for this feature is to rotate arrows and other callouts to position them precisely or to increase the effect. Figure 8-14 shows an example of an arrow Text Shape rotated to call out a bar on a bar chart. You can also use Freelance Graphics' Rotate option to rotate text, graphics drawn with the drawing tools, and clip art.

You rotate objects by choosing Text Shape⇨Rotate. To rotate an object, first select the object using the Pointer tool and then choose Text Shape⇨Rotate. The cursor changes to a rotation arrow. You then can drag anywhere on the object to rotate it. A dotted bounding box shows you how much the object rotates from the original position. After you release the mouse button, the object rotates to the position at which you let go.

> **TIP**
> Wherever you click the object initially becomes the center of rotation, or the point around which the object rotates. So, if you want to rotate an object from a right or left side, begin your rotation from that point. To rotate an object from its center, click in the center of the object to begin and then drag in the direction you want to rotate.

You can constrain the rotation action to 30-degree increments by holding down the Shift key as you rotate the object. If you press Shift, Freelance Graphics does not let you rotate beyond 30-degree movements.

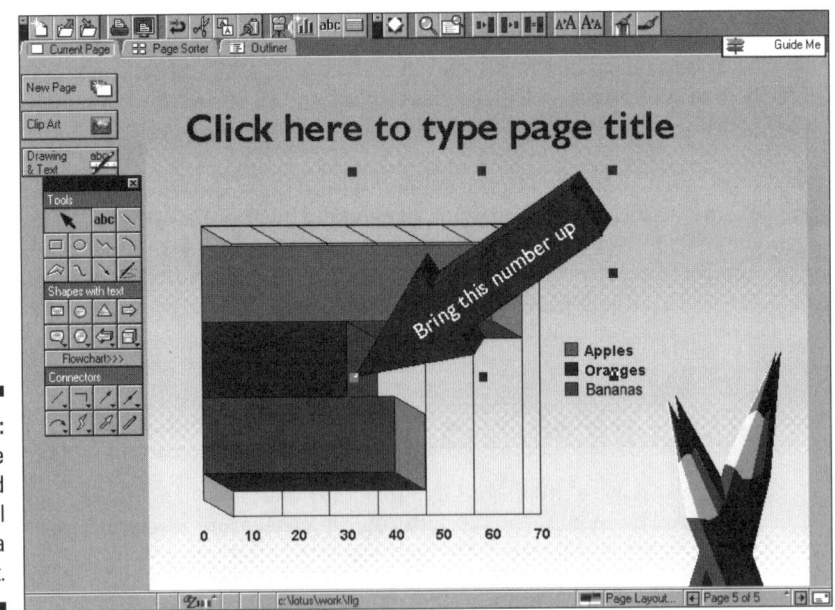

Figure 8-14: An example of a rotated arrow to call out an area on a chart.

Layering multiple objects

Layering refers to the order in which objects are placed on top of one another, or their priority. Each time you place a new object on the page, Freelance Graphics positions that object over existing objects, as shown in Figure 8-15. (Another term for layering is *stacking order*.) Often, you will want to manipulate the stacking order so that objects change positions, placing one or more behind or on top of others. An example may be placing a graphic behind text for a silhouette or watermark effect.

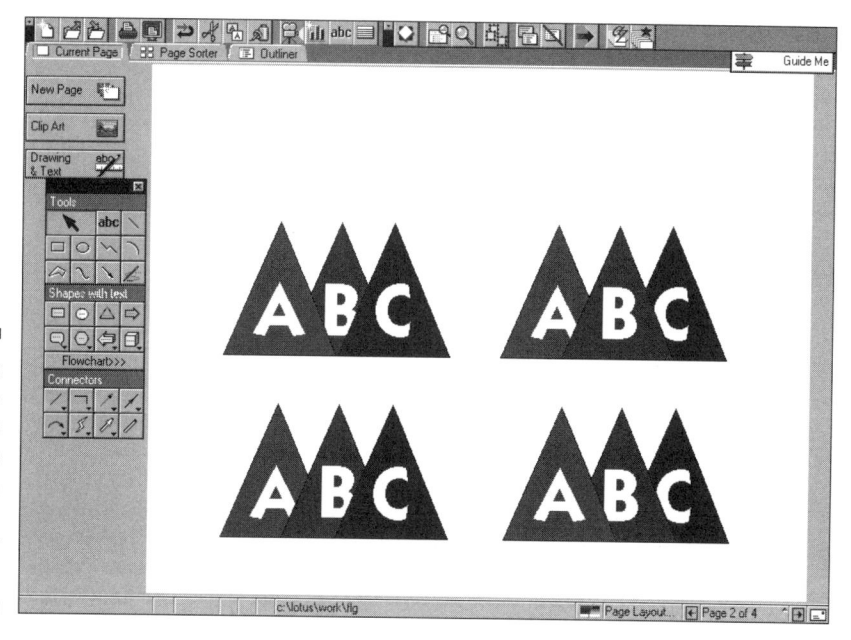

Figure 8-15: Freelance Graphics objects are arranged in a stacking order, or priority.

To change the stacking order, you use Text Shape⇨Priority, as shown in Figure 8-16. Four priority commands perform the following actions:

- **Bring to Front** brings the selected object or objects to the top of a stack of objects.

- **Send to Back** places the selected object or objects on the bottom of a stack of objects.

- **Bring Forward One** brings the selected object or objects one level closer to the top of a stack of objects. In other words, an object three levels deep in a stack of four objects becomes second in the stack, and the second object becomes third.

✔ **Send Back One** places the selected object or objects one level closer to the bottom of a stack of objects. In other words, an object three levels deep in a stack of four objects becomes fourth in the stack, and the fourth object becomes third.

Figure 8-16:
Use these commands to change an object's (or objects') position in the stacking order.

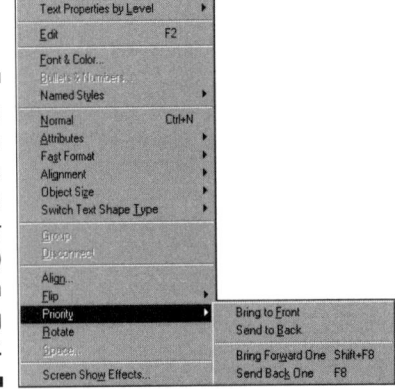

Aligning objects

It can be both frustrating and time-consuming to try to eyeball objects into alignment with one another. Any graphics application worth its salt provides a way to align objects automatically. Freelance Graphics' Align command takes the guesswork out of precisely arranging objects along their bottoms, tops, and sides, and it can center stacked objects in a column, a row, or on top of each other. By using this command in conjunction with Collection➪Space, which evenly spaces objects horizontally and vertically, you can easily create symmetrically precise drawings.

To precisely align objects, you select the objects you want to align and then choose Text Shape➪Align from the menu bar. This choice opens the Align dialog box, as shown in Figure 8-17. The following is a description of how the options in the Align dialog box affect the arrangement of selected objects:

✔ **Align Left Sides** aligns the selected objects along a straight edge on the left side of the objects.

✔ **Align Right Sides** aligns the selected objects along a straight edge on the right side of the objects.

✔ **Align Tops** aligns the selected objects along a straight edge at the top of the objects.

✔ **Align Bottoms** aligns the selected objects along a straight edge at the bottom of the objects.

Chapter 8: Adding Symbols and Manipulating Text Shapes

- ✓ **Center in a Column** aligns the selected objects vertically.
- ✓ **Center in a Row** aligns the selected objects horizontally.
- ✓ **Center on a Point** stacks the selected objects and aligns them from the center of each object.
- ✓ **Center on Page** works in conjunction with the other three options on the right side of the dialog box. If you choose this option, Freelance Graphics aligns the objects vertically and horizontally on the page, in addition to the other option you choose. In other words, if you choose Center in a Column and Center on Page, your objects align in the center of the page vertically.

Figure 8-17: Use the Align dialog box to align objects precisely in relation to one another.

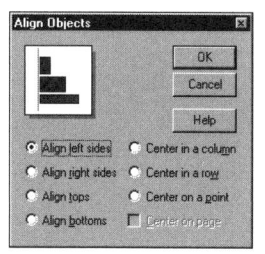

The preview window in the upper-left corner of the dialog box shows you how your selection arranges the objects. After you align your objects, you can use the Space command to place an even amount of space between objects. The Space command, of course, does not work with the Center on a point option.

Grouping objects

Finally, you've got your objects meticulously placed and arranged on the page. Then, all of a sudden, you accidentally select one of them and move it out place! Don't you hate it when that happens? Well, you can maintain several objects' juxtaposition by using the Group command. Group combines all selected objects into one bounding box, or set of control handles, as shown in Figure 8-18. Not only does this help you maintain positional relationships, but you can also move and resize the objects as one. And you can change attributes, such as color, fills, and line weights, all at the same time.

To group objects, select them and then choose Text Shape⇨Group from the menu bar. To ungroup them, choose Text Shape⇨Ungroup from the menu bar. Ungrouping returns each separate object's autonomy. Any changes you made to the group, however, remain with all the ungrouped objects.

Figure 8-18: An example of three grouped objects. The objects are treated as one until you ungroup them.

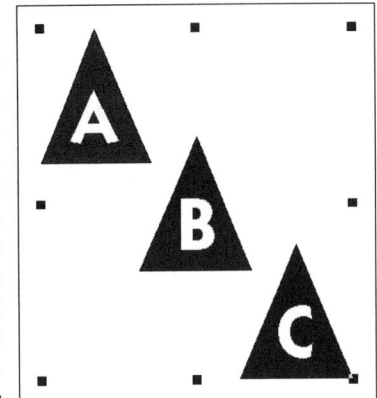

Chapter 9
Working with Freelance Graphics' Drawing Tools

In This Chapter
- Creating drawings in Freelance Graphics
- Creating attention-grabbing text effects
- Using Freelance Graphics' clip art
- Using graphics created in other programs

*I*f you do presentations in an environment where several other people use Freelance Graphics, you may want to avoid having your presentations look like everyone else's. This is also true if you present in an environment where some or all of your audience members see many presentations. After a while — no matter what program you use — presentations created with presentation programs start to take on a canned, out-of-the-box look.

There are many ways to avoid the canned look. We look at several of them, such as editing and creating your SmartMasters, in the next part of this book, which covers fine-tuning presentations. Another way to avoid the canned look is by using Freelance Graphics' drawing tools and clip art to create your own graphic or by importing graphics from other programs, such as CorelDRAW!.

That's the focus of this chapter: personalizing your presentations with some of the many graphics options supported by Freelance Graphics. This is a big topic, so we should get started.

Creating Drawings in Freelance Graphics

Several chapters throughout this book describe how to use the drawing tools. For example, you can find information in Chapter 2 about drawing lines and shapes, using fills, and changing line widths. Many of these procedures are covered in the preceding chapter about working with Freelance Graphics' text

Part II: Adding Visuals

shapes and symbols. Much of that information is pertinent to working with Freelance Graphics' drawing tools. You change line widths and fills for the objects drawn with the drawing tools the same way that you do for shapes and symbols.

So, rather than covering that ground here, this chapter looks at each tool and what it does.

Working with the Drawing Tools

You access the drawing tools by clicking the Drawing & Text option button on the left side of the screen. This opens the palette shown in Figure 9-1. The top group of tools includes the drawing tools. As you can see, several types of tools are available.

Figure 9-1: The first group of 11 tools contains Freelance Graphics' drawing tools.

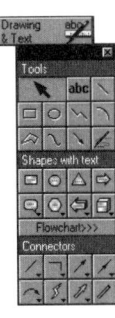

The first two tools, as you probably already know, are the Selection and Text tools. The other nine are drawing tools. The following is a description of each tool, from left to right and top to bottom, and how to use it:

- Use the **Line** tool to draw straight lines. The procedure is to simply start where you want the line to begin and then drag to where you want the line to end. You don't need to worry about being precise; you can adjust either end of the line. You can also constrain the tool by holding down the Shift key as you draw the line. This forces the tool to draw at stringent 45-degree angles. This is a great way to maintain precision.

- The **Rectangle** tool draws squares and rectangles. To constrain the tool to drawing perfect squares, hold down Shift while dragging the tool.

- The **Ellipses** tool draws ellipses and circles. To force the tool to draw perfect circles, hold down Shift while dragging the tool.

- Use the **Polyline** tool to draw multiple-segment lines. The procedure is to click where you want the first segment to begin and then click where you want it to end. Now repeat the process for each segment. Figure 9-2 shows an example of a multiple-segment line.

Chapter 9: Working with Freelance Graphics' Drawing Tools *141*

> **TIP**
>
> You can also use the Polyline tool to create multiple-segment arrows. In the Line & Fill Colors section of the Properties dialog box (choose Drawing⇨Line/Curve Properties from the menu bar after the line is selected), use the Arrowhead section to define the arrow.

- Use the **Arc** tool to draw arcs. The procedure for drawing arcs is to click where you want the arc to begin and then click where you want it to end. You can constrain the arc to 45 degrees by using the Shift key.

- Use the **Polygon** tool to draw multi-sided shapes. This tool works similarly to the Polyline tool, except that you can close the shape by clicking the final end point on the first beginning point. After the object is closed (known in computerese as a *closed path*), you can fill it as you do a circle, rectangle, or symbol. Figure 9-3 shows a polygon drawn with the Polygon tool.

- Use the **Curve** tool to draw curves. The procedure is to click where you want a curve to begin and then click where you want the first segment to end. You can then draw additional curves by dragging the mouse button. The curve will follow the course you draw. You can constrain the Curve tool by holding Shift as you draw.

- Use the **Arrow** tool to draw arrows. The procedure is to click where you want the arrow to begin and then click where you want the arrow to end. The end point is where the arrowhead appears. You change the properties of an arrow, such as give it arrowheads on each end, from the Properties dialog box (choose Drawing⇨Line/Curve Properties from the menu bar, with the arrow you drew selected).

- Use the **Freehand** tool to draw as you do with a pen or pencil.

Figure 9-2: An example of a multiple-segment line drawn with the Polyline tool.

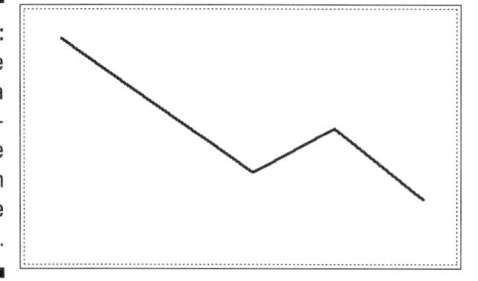

Figure 9-3: An example of a polygon. The final segment closes the shape.

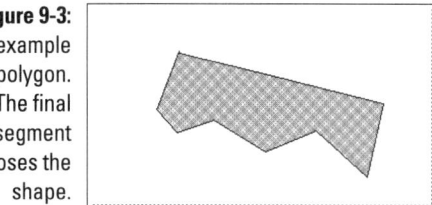

Creating Attention-Grabbing Text Effects in Freelance Graphics

In addition to providing extensive drawing tools, Freelance Graphics enables you to achieve some interesting text effects. The Curved Text option enables you to sculpt text to a path, as shown in Figure 9-4. You can choose from several preset shapes or wrap text to your own shapes.

Using Freelance Graphics' preset curve options

Chances are, Freelance Graphics provides all the curve text shapes you need. If, after reading this section, you don't find the one you need, the following section tells you how to wrap text around your own shapes. Either method is a great way to create your own logos and other fancy drawings.

To use the preset curved text shapes, follow these steps:

1. **Type the text you want to curve (or select any text object, including page titles).**

Figure 9-4: Use Freelance Graphics' Curved Text option to create these and several other text effects.

2. **Choose the text in object mode (with control handles) rather than edit text mode.**
3. **Choose Text➪Text Properties from the menu bar.**
4. **Click the Text Format (first) tab.**
5. **Click the Curved Text button.**

    This action opens the Curved Text dialog box, as shown in Figure 9-5. From here, you select the shape you want and then click OK to apply the effect. You can also use this dialog box to see a preview of the effect with your text or to remove an effect.

6. **Select the effect you want.**
7. **Click OK.**

Freelance Graphics automatically sizes the shape to fit your text. If you want to get more control over how your text wraps, such as setting where it begins and ends on the shape, you should create your own shape and then curve the text to it, as discussed in the following section.

Figure 9-5: Use this dialog box to curve text along one of Freelance Graphics' preset shapes.

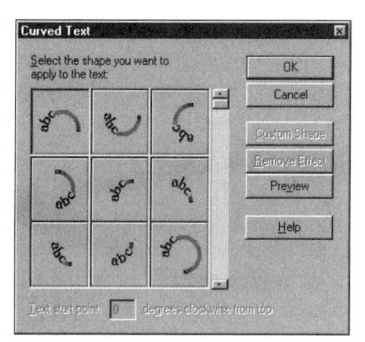

Curving text around your own shapes

You can also use Curved Text to wrap around your own shapes. This is a great way to create dynamic effects, such as wrapping text around chart objects, such as pies. (You cannot actually curve around the pie itself, but you can draw a circle, curve the text, and then delete the circle.)

To curve text around your own object, follow these steps:

1. **Draw the shape that you want to curve text around.**

    You can use any of the drawing tools, including the Rectangle and Ellipses tools. If you use either of these shapes, however, you must convert them to either polylines or lines by using one of the options on the on the Drawing➪Convert submenu.

2. **Select both the text you want to curve and the shape (remembering to use Shift as you click the second object to select it).**
3. **Choose Collection➪Text Properties from the menu bar.**
4. **Click the Curved Text button.**
5. **In the Curved Text dialog box, click the Custom Shape button.**

   The text conforms to the curve, beginning where you started drawing the shape and ending where you finished.

   TIP

   You may be wondering how you edit text after you've contorted it into one of these weird shapes. Well, have no fear. All you do is click the text as you do to edit any other text block. The text straightens out into text-editing mode while you make your changes. After you deselect it, it returns to the curved shape.

Using Freelance Graphics' Clip Art

You can use either Freelance Graphics clip art or import your own to spruce up your documents. This section covers using Freelance Graphics clip art (the art that comes with the program). Importing graphics from other programs is discussed in the section "Using Images from Other Programs," later in this chapter.

Bringing clip art into your document

To bring an image into your document, you can use either a Click here placeholder, or you can start from scratch by using the Create➪Add Clip Art command on the menu bar or the Clip Art button on the left side of the screen. Either option opens the Add Clip Art or Diagram to the Page dialog box, as shown in Figure 9-6. From here, you can choose one of Freelance Graphics' several clip art images or diagrams or you can find a specific file by using the Browse button.

Figure 9-6: Use this dialog box to add Freelance Graphics' clip art to your presentation.

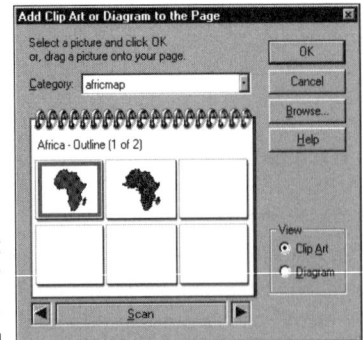

You can select clip art categories in the Add Clip Art or Diagram to the Page dialog box by typing the first letter of the name of a category, or you can skim through clip art sets automatically (in alphabetical order) by clicking the Scan button. Simply click the Stop Scan button to halt the display.

> **TIP:** If the scan option is too fast or too slow, you can change the speed. To change the scanning speed, choose File⇔User Setup⇔Freelance Preferences and then type the number of seconds you want each set of images to be displayed in the Scanning Speed box. You can type values between 0.1 and 100.

You can bring the image onto the page by double-clicking it and then clicking OK or by dragging and dropping from the Add Clip Art or Diagram to the Page dialog box.

> **TIP:** You can create or import a graphic and then add it to the clip art library for later use. Here's how. Draw or import the objects that you want to save as clip art. Select all the objects. If you select more than one object, choose Drawing⇔Group to group them (or Collection⇔Group). Now choose Create⇔Add to Library⇔Clipart Library. Add the clip art to the category of your choice or use CUSTOM.SYM, which is an empty library designed for this purpose. Click Open, and then save the file. Note that if you do not group the objects, they are added to the clip art library as separate objects. See the preceding chapter for a discussion of grouping objects.

Modifying clip art

In addition to modifying clip art as you do other objects — moving and resizing them by using the Selection tool — you can modify clip art in various other ways, such as recoloring and using parts of images.

Say, for example, you want to use only one of the people shown in Figure 9-7.

To use just one of the people, here's what you do:

1. **Bring the image onto the page from the Add Clip Art or Diagram to the Page dialog box.**
2. **Making sure that the object is selected, choose Group⇔Ungroup from the menu bar.**

   > **NOTE:** Group and Ungroup are very handy features for working with clip art and other Freelance Graphics objects. Group enables you to combine several objects into one, which Freelance Graphics then treats as one object. You can move, resize, and perform other modifications to the group all at once. All of Freelance Graphics' clip art consists of multiple grouped objects. For an explanation of Group and how to use it, see Chapter 8. (You also find useful information about aligning and layering objects, which is also pertinent to working with Freelance Graphics' drawing tools and clip art.)

Part II: Adding Visuals

Figure 9-7:
You can use part of this image by ungrouping it.

Typically, Freelance Graphics' clip art consists of groups of groups. In the case of our two people in Figure 9-7, when we ungroup it, we get two groups of objects, one for each person. The Group menu now reads Collection because more than one object is selected.

Often, getting at the objects you want isn't quite this easy. Some clip art images are quite complex. What you should do in these cases is ungroup, click away to deselect the collection, click again the object that you're trying to isolate, and repeat this process until you get the object you want. You know when you have the object itself when the Group menu says Drawing rather than Collection — unless, of course, the object you want is a group. Suppose that you're trying to lift a baseball from a sports scene. The ball could consist of the round shape itself, the threads, and the shadow effect that makes it appear 3-D.

 3. **Click in a blank spot on the page to deselect the collection.**

 4. **Click the object you're trying to isolate.**

 5. **If the object (and only the object you want) is selected, move it away from the rest of the image, if not, ungroup the object again.**

 6. **Repeat this process until you isolate the object or group of objects you want.**

After you finish, you can move the object away from the others, as shown in Figure 9-8. You can then select the other objects and delete them.

Chapter 9: Working with Freelance Graphics' Drawing Tools *147*

NOTE

You can also use this method to recolor objects within a clip art image. Say that you want to recolor a state on the U.S. map. You use the preceding method to isolate the state and then recolor it as you do any other Freelance Graphics object, from the Drawing Properties dialog box. You can then select all the objects and regroup them.

TIP

Need to rotate an object or group of objects? Try using the Rotate command on the Drawing, Collection, or Group menu. Simply select the objects you want to rotate, and then choose Rotate from the menu. Now use the mouse to rotate the objects as desired. Holding down the Shift key constrains the rotation to 45-degree increments.

Figure 9-8: An example of isolating clip art elements.

Using Images from Other Programs

Freelance Graphics supports several of the more popular image file formats, including PCX, TIFF, BMP, and EPS. Using images from these outside sources and clip art and stock photography collections is a sure way to ensure the originality of your presentations, especially if you use a scanner to bring your own photographs and other artwork into Freelance Graphics.

Importing images into Freelance Graphics

You can use the following two methods to import images into Freelance Graphics:

- The Clipboard, by using Paste or Paste Special. (See Chapter 5 for a discussion of the two methods and the advantages of each.)

> **NOTE:** This is the method used for bringing EPS images into Freelance Graphics. Depending on how the image was created, it behaves differently in Freelance Graphics. For a detailed description of using EPS files, search for EPS in Freelance Graphics' Help Topics.

What you should know about computer graphics

Basically, computer graphics come in two different types: vector and bitmapped. The differences between the two are tremendous. Freelance Graphics supports both types in several different formats.

Vector graphics are created in draw programs, such as CorelDRAW!, Adobe Illustrator, and Micrografx Designer. Vector graphics are drawn mathematically, using lines and curves rather than the multiple fixed dots used in bitmaps. The immediate advantage of this format is that files are generally much smaller than bitmaps and usually don't take as long to print.

More important than file size and print times, however, is that vector graphics are scalable and support several artistic effects better than bitmaps. (If an image is scalable, you can resize it without degrading quality.) Vector graphics are much more adept at handling drawings consisting of fine lines and arcs.

Vector graphics also provide more control over the final output resolution, which is important if you are printing on high-resolution film or viewgraphs. Because vector images are *device independent,* they do not have a fixed resolution. In other words, you can print them at any resolution you want and they assume that resolution. Bitmap images, on the other hand, retain the resolution at which they were created, making them *device dependent.* The most widely used vector format is Encapsulated PostScript (EPS).

Bitmapped graphics are created in bitmap editors, or paint programs, such as Corel Photo-Paint or Adobe Photoshop. Nowadays, though, most paint programs are referred to as image-editing or digital darkroom software.

Bitmapped graphics consist of a series of dots in fixed patterns and print in blobs, much like a rubber stamp. Each dot is programmed into a computer file. If the graphic contains a lot of color information and high resolution, the file can be gigantic — 10, 20, 30 megabytes and beyond. And they maintain their resolution, no matter what the capabilities of the device they are printed on. Basically, what this means to you is that they can be difficult to work with because of their size and that they are not easily resized because of their fixed-dot patterns. If you enlarge a bitmap much at all, quality begins to degrade.

This is not to say that bitmaps are not useful. The same characteristics that make them so unruly make them ideal for grayscale and color photographs. They are the format of choice for desktop scanners.

✔ The Create➪Add Bitmap command on the menu bar. Bitmaps (files that have a BMP, TIF, GIF, TGA, or PCX extension) that are imported into Freelance Graphics maintain their original size. If a bitmap is too large to fit on the page, Freelance Graphics repeatedly scales the bitmap by 50 percent, until it fits on the page.

After the image is on the page, you can resize it and move it as you can any other Freelance Graphics object. However, your modifying options are otherwise limited. You really can't do much to bitmap files. Freelance Graphics does provide some control over bitmaps — though you cannot ungroup them. And you should be careful when resizing them because you may distort the image.

Modifying bitmaps in Freelance Graphics

Depending on the type of image (color, monotone, grayscale) and file format, Freelance Graphics provides some control over the bitmaps that you import into your presentations. This section describes those controls and how to use them.

Controlling contrast, sharpness, and brightness

You control contrast, sharpness, and brightness from the Bitmap Properties dialog box, which you can access by selecting the bitmap and then choosing Bitmap➪Bitmap Properties from the menu bar, or by using the right mouse button. This opens the Bitmap Properties dialog box, as shown in Figure 9-9. *Contrast* is the ratio of black to white, similar to the controls on your monitor or TV. *Sharpness* is the degree of line and border definition. *Brightness* is the luminance, or light intensity. The controls range from -5 to 5. Zero is the mid-range.

Figure 9-9: Use this dialog box to control the contrast, sharpness, and brightness of an image.

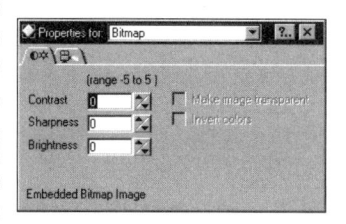

You can change the contrast and brightness for both color and grayscale images. You can change the sharpness only for grayscale images. Contrast, sharpness, and brightness are not relevant to monochrome or black-and-white images.

Making a bitmap transparent

Selecting Make Image Transparent from inside the Properties dialog box turns all pixels except the black ones transparent so that objects or colors that are behind the bitmap show through. This is particularly useful for line art or monotone images because the border of the bitmap image is white. You should use this option to blend bitmaps into your slides. Note that this option doesn't work for all bitmap formats, such as TIFF. If it's not available, the option is dimmed. If you really need this option, take the image into a paint program, such as Windows Paint, and resave it as a BMP file.

Inverting colors

Selecting Invert Colors from inside the Properties dialog box reverses the black-and-white areas of a selected monochrome image, making it a negative image. That is, black areas become white and white areas become black. This works only with monochrome images and does not affect color or grayscale images. You can create some great special effects with this option.

You can also assign transition effects and multimedia events to bitmaps, the same as you do any other object. If you don't know how to assign transition and multimedia events, refer to Chapter 4.

Cropping bitmaps

Cropping means cutting away the outer portions of an image. This is a great way to get rid of unwanted portions of the picture. In a portrait, for example, you may want to cut away the torso and background to bring out the face.

To crop a bitmap, select it and then choose Bitmap➪Crop Bitmap from the menu bar. This opens the Crop Bitmap dialog box, as shown in Figure 9-10. Simply drag inward on the handles in the preview to cut away the unwanted portion of the image. After you click OK, Freelance Graphics crops the image on the page.

Figure 9-10: Use this dialog box to crop bitmaps. Simply drag inward on the handles.

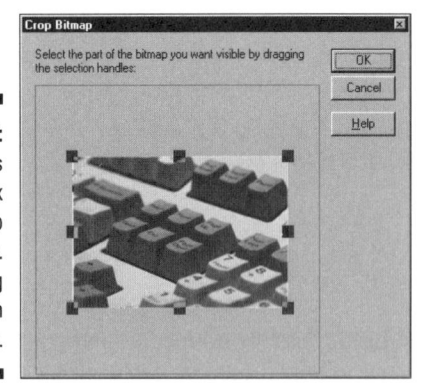

Preparing graphics for different media types

Whether you are printing to slides, transparencies, or your monitor, you should pay special attention to the images you import into your presentations. For example, high-resolution image files can clog a slide recorder and take forever to display on your monitor. This section is packed full of technical stuff about computer graphics that you should consider while creating images for your presentations.

Graphics and your monitor and other display systems

The devices covered here are computer screens, television monitors (including videotape), overhead LCD projectors, and anything else that connects to your computer's display adapter. Because preparing graphics for each device is identical, the word *monitor* used throughout this discussion covers them all.

To display information, be it text or graphics, all computers require two components: a display adapter and, of course, a monitor. Display systems run in various "modes."

Pick a card

Often called a graphics card, the display adapter is usually an incredibly boring-looking circuit board that slips into a bus slot on the motherboard of your computer (some computers have display adapters built onto the motherboard). The display adapter processes information from the computer and sends it to the monitor.

Resolution

On display systems, as opposed to hard copy output, resolution refers to the number of dots, or pixels, on the monitor. The higher the resolution, the more information you can fit on-screen and the better is the image. In Windows, that means that you can view more open windows at the same time, or, in a graphics program such as Freelance Graphics, you get a better what-you-see-is-what-you-get (WYSIWYG) representation of how the page will print. In on-screen presentations, you just plain get better-looking graphics.

Standard VGA has a resolution of 640 pixels across and 480 pixels down (640 × 480). Super VGA mode is 800 × 600. VGA and Super VGA are the most common resolutions, but 1024 × 768 and even 1280 × 1024 (sometimes called Ultra or Extended VGA) are becoming increasingly popular. Some cards support resolutions up to 1600 × 1200. Remember, though, that your monitor must support the resolution of the card to benefit from the additional dots. If you cram too many pixels onto a 14-inch monitor, text becomes too small to read easily. A good rule of thumb is to use a system that approximates the size of the final printed text. Table 9-1 should help you match resolution and monitor sizes.

Table 9-1 **Matching Resolution to Monitor Size**

Resolution	Monitor Size
VGA (640 × 480)	14"
Super VGA (800 × 600)	15" or 16"
Extended VGA (1024 × 768)	17" or higher
1280 × 1024	19" to 21"

Keep in mind that these resolution recommendations are helpful for viewing text. However, no matter what size your monitor, graphics applications benefit greatly from high resolutions. If you edit graphics in CorelDRAW!, Adobe Photoshop, or some other application (and use a small monitor), you can switch resolutions in the Windows Display control panel so that you don't strain your eyes when editing text. Presentations and multimedia applications also benefit from high resolutions. Frankly, graphics just plain look better on a fine display than they do on a coarse one.

Millions of colors

Perhaps even more confusing than resolution is display color. Graphics cards are rated by the number of distinct colors they can display on a screen at one time. The range is from 16 to 16.7 million colors, with 256 being the most common. The number of colors a card is capable of depends on its bits-per-pixel rate. Four bits per pixel, for example, provides 16 colors; 24 bits per pixel provides 16.7 million colors. The 16-color model is the easiest one to use to demonstrate this concept. Because there are four bits per pixel, you have 4 × 4 (16) possible red, green, and blue (RGB) combinations. As the number of bits per pixels increases, the possible combinations also increase substantially.

Today's graphics cards come in four color standards, as depicted in Table 9-2.

Table 9-2 **Color Depth Ratings for Graphics Cards**

Bits Per Pixel	Color Mode Name	Number of Colors
4	Minimum Color	16
8	Pseudo Color	256
16	Hi-Color	32,768 or 65,536
24	True-Color	16.7 million

For most applications, including many presentations and multimedia applications, 256 colors are fine. Most graphics look better at Hi-Color, however, though many multimedia applications and titles don't support more that 256 colors. Most people, except for users of high-end photograph-editing software, such as Photoshop or PhotoStyler, don't really need 24-bit color. Freelance Graphics presentations look fine on Hi-Color displays.

For the most part, graphics cards are comparable when it comes to resolutions and colors supported, with only slight variations. Most, for example support 256 colors at 1280×1024, and most support Hi-Color at 1024×786 and lower.

Refresh rate

If you spend a lot of time at your computer, be on the lookout for a card with a high refresh rate. Your eyes will be forever grateful. The *refresh rate* is the speed at which the screen is repainted. If the refresh rate is too low, your monitor flickers, which is annoying and hard on the eyes. It can cause headaches and long-term visual problems.

Refresh rates are measured in hertz (Hz). A refresh rate of 72 Hz means the screen is refreshed 72 times per second. Anything less than 72 Hz can cause a noticeable flicker. Just because a card claims "up to 72 Hz" doesn't mean it supports that rate in all modes. Match the refresh rate to the number of colors and resolution at which you plan to use the card.

Creating graphics for a monitor

The two drawbacks to creating graphics incorrectly for monitors are slow screen redraws and bad coloring. The first problems can slow down your presentation, making you and your audience wait too long for transitions between slides. The pace and timing of a presentation are very important. The second problem — bad coloring — ruins the quality of your electronic presentations.

Of all the different output devices, preparing graphics for your monitor is easiest. There is no extra processing between what you see on-screen and what comes out of a printer or the slide recorder.

As described in the sidebar "What you should know about computer graphics" earlier in this chapter, there are two basic graphics types: vector and bitmap. Device-independent vector graphics display independently, meaning that they print or display at the resolution of the output device. Bitmaps are device dependent. They print or display at their own resolution, regardless of the output device.

The average monitor displays at 75 dots per inch (dpi). The average bitmap image is 300 dpi. So, you ask, how can you display a 300-dpi image on a 75-dpi monitor? There's the rub. You can't. The image appears at 75 dpi. The problem is that your computer's CPU must process the image at 300 dpi, which requires several times the data processing — for absolutely no gain. You should use your paint software to reduce the resolution.

This is also true of color depth. If your display system can display only 265 colors, there's no need to create your images at thousands or millions of colors. In fact, the way Windows compensates for these color differences can give you some downright ugly pictures. You should use your paint software to reduce the color depth to the bits-per-pixel setting of the device you are presenting on.

Preparing graphics for slide recorders

Believe it or not, preparing graphics for slides is easier than preparing them for monitors. You don't, for example, need to worry about color depth. Slide recorders print all colors.

When using vector graphics, don't worry about resolution. The image prints at the highest possible setting. The only type of image you should treat differently is the bitmapped type. The image you see on your monitor is shrunk several times to fit on a slide.

When scanning or creating images for slides, be it a black-and-white line image or 24-bit photograph, set the resolution to 75 dpi. Higher settings accomplish nothing, except slowing down the slide recorder. This could cost you more money and cause the slide recorder to choke on the images.

Printing graphics

Perhaps the trickiest printing is to your desktop inkjet or desktop printer. The rule of thumb here is to scan or save monotone bitmaps at the resolution of the output device. A 600-dpi laser, for example, prints 600-dpi black-and-white images optimally. Grayscale and color images should be printed at about 150 dpi, no matter what the resolution of the printer. More than that gives you little or no quality improvement, but your files are large and printing is slow.

Part III
Fine-Tuning Your Presentation

The 5th Wave   By Rich Tennant

"I'VE GOT SOME IMAGE EDITING SOFTWARE, SO I TOOK THE LIBERTY OF ERASING SOME OF THE SMUDGES THAT KEPT SHOWING UP AROUND THE CLOUDS. NO NEED TO THANK ME."

In this part . . .

Drats! Don't you just hate it when you're standing in front of the company president, all the other vice presidents . . . practically the whole world . . . and you see a typo on the screen? Or you realize that you have the information in the wrong order? Well, this part can spare you those embarrassing moments. It reveals Freelance Graphics' capabilities for helping you uncover errors before you're put on the spot!

Chapter 10
Oops! Reviewing and Reorganizing Your Presentation

In This Chapter
- Reviewing your presentation
- Identifying text-heavy slides and weak points in your presentation
- Using Page Sorter and Outline views to reorganize your presentation
- Avoiding embarrassing spelling errors

Creating a presentation is a lot like writing a short story or magazine article. First you put the presentation together; then you go back and clean it up. And that's the thrust of this chapter — getting the flow of information and supporting arguments just right.

Reviewing Your Presentation

After you have your presentation laid out, you should go back through it several times to make sure that it delivers the message correctly and that the information flow makes sense and is easy to understand.

The easiest way to review your presentation is with a self-running screen show that allows you to kick back and watch the presentation from your audience's point of view. This section shows you how to set up and run the screen show itself; the next section tells you what to look for.

Setting up a self-running screen show

You use the Set Up Screen Show command in the Presentation menu to create a self-running screen show. Whether you plan to print your presentation on slides or overheads or to show it as an electronic screen show, you can use the Set Up Screen Show command to review your work. Follow these steps:

1. **With your presentation open and in Current Page view, choose Presentation➪Set Up Screen Show from the menu bar.**

   The Set Up Screen Show dialog box appears (see Figure 10-1). From this dialog box, you set the options for a self-running screen show. The dialog box enables you to set up a screen show for an entire presentation or for all new slides. In this example, you want to set up the entire presentation. You also can set a transition effect and use a control panel to help navigate the show, as you can see in a moment.

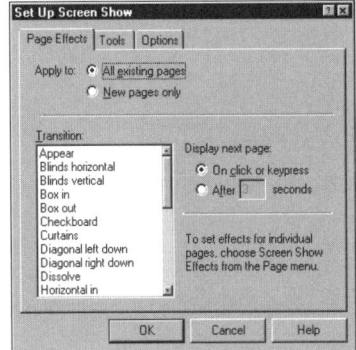

   Figure 10-1: The Set Up Screen Show dialog box.

2. **In the Page Effects section of the dialog box, make sure that Apply to All existing pages is selected.**

   Because all that you're doing is reviewing the presentation, you really don't need to make any fancy transitions from slide to slide. Besides, from this dialog box, all you can do is assign the same transition effect to all slides.

   TIP: If this presentation is targeted to be an electronic screen show, you can set transition effects for individual slides with the Screen Show Effects command (on the Page menu), which is discussed in Chapter 14. You also can set screen-show transitions for individual slide elements, such as a chart or text, also discussed in Chapter 14.

3. **In the Transition list, select Appear.**

4. **In the Display next page section, select After __ seconds and type a number in the text box.**

   This option tells Freelance Graphics to change from slide to slide automatically. The number that you type in the box determines how many seconds lapse between slides. Use a number that gives you enough time to review each slide.

   TIP: You probably need about 30 seconds for each text slide and (depending on your graphics) more for each chart and graph. If your charts and graphs take more than a minute of study to decipher, however, you should

Chapter 10: Oops! Reviewing and Reorganizing Your Presentation

consider revising them. In the context of the actual presentation, when you're speaking to audience members and they're trying to read slides and listen to you at the same time, even a minute could be too long.

5. **Click OK.**

Adding a control panel to your self-running screen show

While you are reviewing a presentation via the self-running screen show, you may need to stop, go backward, or jump forward to go over specific points. Freelance Graphics' Control Panel option enables you to include a set of controls in your self-running presentation.

To include a control panel in your self-running screen show, follow these steps:

1. **From inside the Set Up Screen Show dialog box, click the Tools tab.**
2. **Under Control Panel, check Display Control Panel.**
3. **For Position, select where on the screen you want the control panel to be displayed.**
4. **Click OK to return to Current Page view.**

TIP: Most likely, reviewing the screen show just one time won't be sufficient. You can tell Freelance Graphics to run the show continuously by clicking the Options tab in the Set Up Screen Show dialog box and then making the Run Screen Show in Continuous Loop option (Run Options) active. The screen show runs as many times as you like (forever or until you press the Esc key).

Running the screen show

Running the screen show is even easier than setting it up. Simply choose Run Screen Show from the Presentation menu; then, from the submenu, choose From Beginning. The screen show starts running, displaying slides every few seconds, according to the time that you set in the Set Up Screen Show dialog box.

You can override the timing settings with your mouse. To advance a slide, left-click; to go back a slide, right-click. To leave the slide show, press Esc. Using the mouse to override the timer affects only the current slide. If you don't click the mouse again, the timer resumes control of the presentation.

If you added a control panel to your screen show, you can override the timer by clicking the buttons in the following manner:

- The left- and right-arrow buttons advance and reverse the screen show one slide.
- The button that has several pages on it (the one between the arrows) displays the Screen Show Pages dialog box. From this dialog box, you can go to any slide in the presentation or quit the screen show altogether.
- The last button stops the screen show and returns you to Current Slide view.

Identifying Wordy Slides and Weak Points in Your Argument

The first time or two that you review your presentation, you should be on the lookout for two things: slides that contain too much information and flaws in the information flow. Often, you can correct both of these problems at the same time.

Watch for wordy, cluttered slides

Frankly, if a slide contains more than 30 words or more than 6 bullet points, it's overworked. Each bullet point should not contain more than five or six words, whenever possible. Your audience can't decipher much more material on a slide, and you shouldn't leave people staring at the same slide long enough to cover that much material. Remember that you want the audience to listen to you.

The most common ways to correct cluttered slides are to add more slides, delete material, or move material to your speaker's notes. As you review your presentation, make note of slides that contain too much data. Later in this chapter, you learn how to use Outline view to manipulate the data flow.

Maintain a logical data flow

Though it's not always readily apparent, most presentations have a logical data flow. First, decide what you want to tell your audience (decide whether you want to inform or persuade the audience, or both); then decide how you can do it.

When you design your presentation, use this basic format:

- Tell the members of the audience what you're going to tell them.
- Tell them.
- Then tell them that you told them.

The basic presentation structure is as follows:

- A title slide, stating the title of the presentation. The title should indicate the content and theme of the presentation.
- A few slides that provide the general theme of the presentation or the thesis statement.
- The body of the presentation, which is the information that supports your thesis statement: the charts, bullet slides, and graphics.
- The conclusion, which reiterates crucial points.

The typical approach to delivering this type of presentation is to introduce topics in the form of a crescendo, with one point building on another until the presentation's thesis statement is fully supported.

As you review your presentation, you should make sure that the information comes forth in a logical, sensible manner. Introduce subthemes and subtopics methodically. Make a statement; then use information to support the statement, one topic after another.

If your presentation follows the theme of one of Freelance Graphics' many content SmartMasters, Lotus has provided several very good structures for creating logical presentations. If you apply a content SmartMaster to your work before you begin designing and you follow that structure, you wind up with a pretty logical presentation.

The body of your presentation supports, or proves, your thesis statement. Bring in information only as it supports your thesis. Peripheral data, jokes, and anecdotes that do not pertain to the topic only distract your audience, as do other tangents.

Determining how many slides you need in a presentation is difficult. A good way to estimate is to allow about 30 seconds for each bullet point and 60 seconds for each chart or graph. Detailed graphics, of course, require more time.

Watch out for weak points in your arguments

Never, *never* brush off weak or unsupported parts of your argument with the thought, "Oh, they won't notice." If you ever have that thought, the next logical question should be, "What if they do?" The answer is: your credibility comes into question.

The success of your presentation depends on your credibility. So here are some do's and don'ts that you should keep in mind when you review your presentation:

- ✓ Close up loopholes; don't leave questions in the audience's mind.
- ✓ Support all general statements (or don't generalize).
- ✓ Don't tell half-truths or exaggerate.
- ✓ Be straightforward and genuine.
- ✓ Reveal the pitfalls and risks before somebody else points them out.
- ✓ Use realistic projections and goals.
- ✓ Don't inflate statistics and numbers.

Revising Your Presentation

After reviewing your presentation a few times and jotting down information-flow problems, you're ready to revise your presentation. Freelance Graphics provides two powerful tools that help you revise your work: Page Sorter and Outliner.

You learned about both of these resources in earlier chapters; Chapter 4, for example, concentrated on the Outliner. But those chapters were about creating a presentation. This section explains how to revise your presentation with the Page Sorter and the Outliner.

Moving slides around in Page Sorter

In Page Sorter, you can get an overview of your entire presentation (see Figure 10-2). Each page in the presentation is displayed as a thumbnail. You can select one slide or a group of slides and then move the slides about with your mouse, dropping them into a new pagination sequence.

Use the following procedures to rearrange your presentation in Page Sorter:

- ✓ To move one slide, click the slide and drag it to its new position. As you move the slide over the other slides in the presentation, a dotted box shows you where the slide is at all times, and a black bar shows where the slide is to be inserted after you release the mouse button.

- ✓ To move two or more slides, select the first slide and then Shift+click the others to select them. Next, drag one of the selected slides to the new position; the others will follow. As you move the slides over the other slides in the presentation, a group of dotted boxes shows you where the slides are at all times, and a black bar shows where the slides are to be inserted after you release the mouse button.

You also can drag the Pointer tool around several slides to select them. This procedure is known as *marquee* selecting. All the slides within the ensuing dotted marquee line become selected.

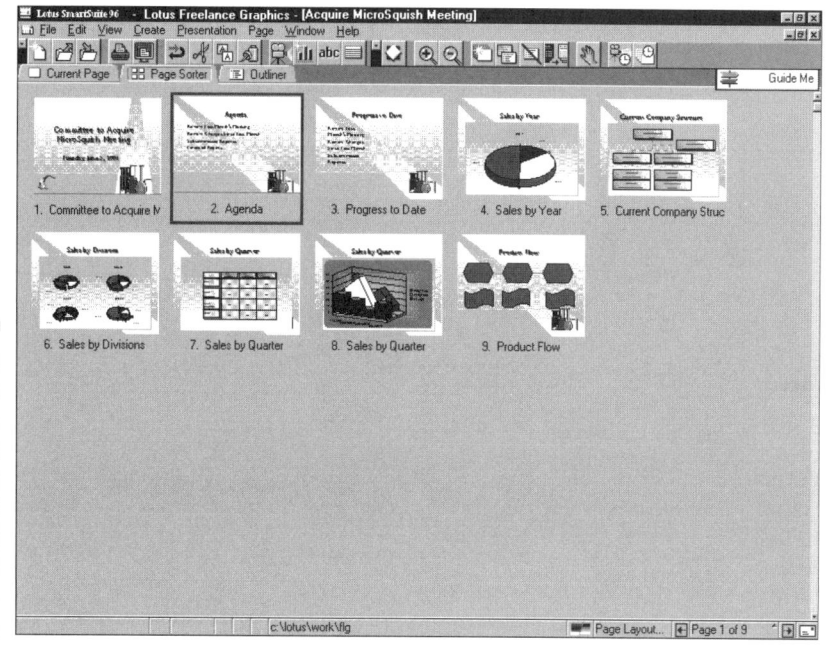

Figure 10-2: Use Page Sorter to move one slide (or a group of slides) around in a presentation.

> ✔ To delete a slide, select it; then press the Delete key or choose Edit⇨Clear from the menu bar. To delete multiple slides, click the first slide, Shift+click the others to select them, and then press Delete. You also can marquee-select multiple slides.
>
> ✔ To add a new slide, first select the slide directly before the location where you want to insert the new slide; then choose Create⇨Page from the menu bar. After the New Page dialog box appears, choose the content master or page layout that you want to use and click OK. Freelance Graphics inserts the page behind the currently selected page.

Rearranging your presentation in Outliner

Unlike Page Sorter, which forces you to treat each page as an independent unit, the Outliner enables you to manipulate the text on slides (see Figure 10-3). You can, for example, promote bullet points to new slides and vice versa. You can edit text or move it around with drag and drop or Copy and Paste, and you can move entire slides around.

Chapter 4 provides an in-depth description of using the Outliner to create presentations. So, to avoid redundancy, this chapter discusses this tool only as it pertains to revising presentations.

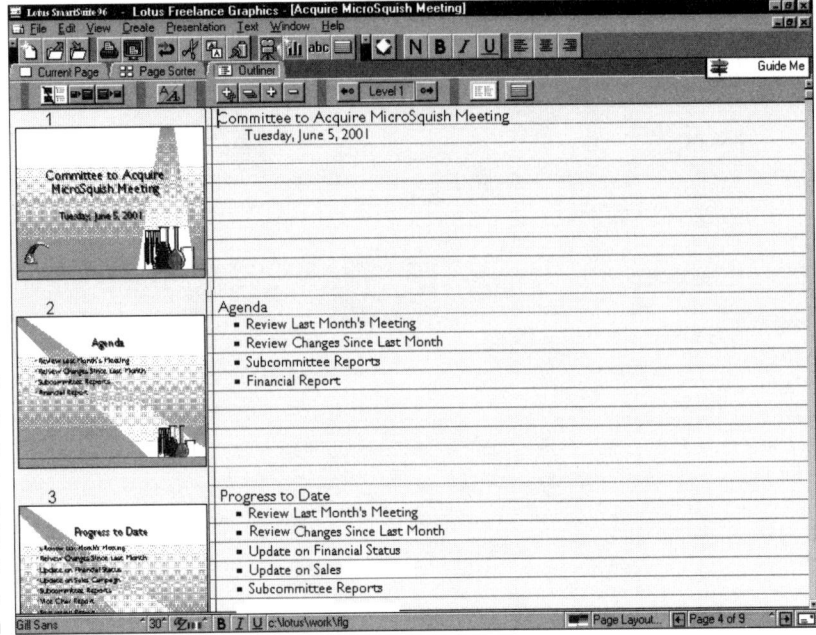

Figure 10-3: Use the Outliner for more detailed presentation revisions.

Some of the most useful revision techniques in the Outliner enable you to demote and promote bullet points and to create new slides.

To break a slide into two slides, follow these steps:

1. **Place the cursor where you want to make the break and press Enter to create a blank line.**
2. **Click the blank line.**
3. **Click the left arrow in the Level indicator so that it reads** `Title` **(it currently reads** `Level 1`**) to create a new slide.**
4. **Type the name of the new slide.**

Another easy method is to select text and drag it to another slide, or you can collapse the outline and move entire slides (or groups of slides) around.

Moving slides around in Outline view

Moving slides in the Outliner is somewhat similar to moving them in Page Sorter. You select the slide icon and move it to its new position, as shown in Figure 10-4. You also can Shift+click multiple slides to move more than one slide at a time. The problem with this method in Outliner is that you cannot see as many slides as you can in the Page Sorter.

Chapter 10: Oops! Reviewing and Reorganizing Your Presentation *165*

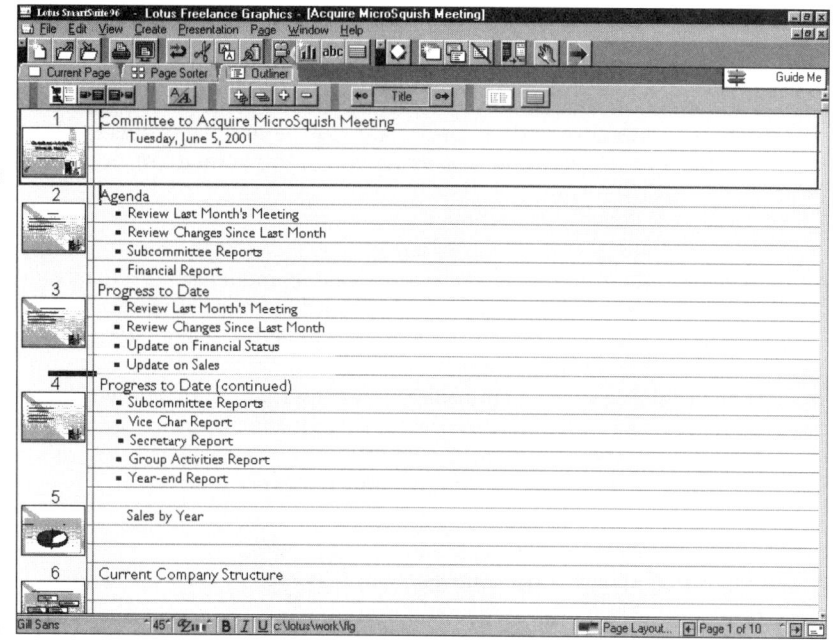

Figure 10-4: To move slides in Outliner, drag the slide thumbnail to its new location, as indicated by the dark bar between slides three and four.

Outliner has a few tricks up its sleeve, however. First, you can switch from large thumbnails to small thumbnails to view more slides at the same time. And if that's not enough, you can turn the thumbnails off altogether. (These controls are the first three icons directly below the Current Page tab. The first one turns off the page thumbnails, replacing them with tiny icons. The second one turns on large thumbnails. The third icon turns on small thumbnails.)

Still not satisfied? You can see even more of your presentation by collapsing the outline. To do so, click the button with several minus signs (–) on it, located directly below the Outliner tab. This button collapses the outline so that only slide titles are shown. You can expand the outline again by clicking the button with multiple plus signs (+). To expand or collapse only one slide (or a group of selected slides), select the slide(s) and then click the button that bears either the single plus or single minus sign.

Again, Chapter 4 has a full description of the Outliner.

Avoiding Embarrassing Spelling Errors

After all your reviewing and revising, imagine yourself standing in front of an audience of 200. Your first slide appears on-screen. You turn and gasp — the second word on the title slide is misspelled.

Well, a definite nick has appeared in your confidence, credibility, and self-esteem.

What's the remedy? Freelance Graphics' spell checker? Well, yes and no. Since the advent of word processors with spell checkers, many people have come to rely on computers to do their thinking for them. A spell checker helps, but it's not the ultimate solution, absolving you of the ultimate responsibility for knowing how to spell.

Look at the way spell checkers work. Freelance Graphics really doesn't know how to spell; instead, it checks each word in a document against a database of correctly spelled words. If the program finds a word in your presentation that's not in the database, it flags the word as being misspelled — even if it's spelled correctly.

The problem with this approach is the fact that important words, such as company names and terms, are not included in Freelance Graphics' spelling list. The good news is that you can add these words easily enough, as you see in the following section about using the spell checker.

Watching for misspellings that the spell checker can't catch

What Freelance Graphics can't do is help you avoid using the wrong word or misusing homonyms. (*Homonyms* are words that sound alike but have different meanings — such as *since* and *sense*, *principal* and *principle*, and *forth* and *fourth*.) A whole slew of homonyms exists, and you probably are aware of most of them. But being aware doesn't always mean that you always use the right word when the time comes. In addition to running the spell checker, make sure that you correctly use words that have homonyms.

Watching for misused words

Spell checkers cannot catch misused words either. If a word is spelled correctly but is the wrong word in context, Freelance Graphics passes right over it. Even well-educated people misuse certain words, including *really* (for *very*) and *specially* (for *especially*).

Providing spelling and diction instruction is beyond the scope of this book. We just want you to be aware that Freelance Graphics' spell checker can't help you with these kinds of problems. Neither can the spell checker catch grammar and punctuation errors; you have to catch them yourself.

Catching many of your own spelling and grammar errors is difficult, especially if you've spent long hours with the document and have become familiar with it. In such a case, catching all the mistakes that may be glaring to somebody who is approaching the piece for the first time is next to impossible. Magazines and book publishers have many editors, so that everything is checked and rechecked. We suggest that you turn your presentation over to somebody else — a friend or coworker, for example — for proofing and comments, because everybody needs an editor. In fact, that topic is covered in Chapter 20.

Using the Freelance Graphics Spell Checker

You can run Freelance Graphics' spell checker from all three views: Current Page, Page Sorter, and Outline. Freelance Graphics enables you to check the spelling in a selected block of text, the current page, or the entire presentation. You also can elect to check only text slides, only data charts, only organization charts, only speaker notes, all these elements, or a combination of elements.

You conduct a spell-checking session from the Spell Check dialog box, as shown in Figure 10-5. To access this dialog box, choose Edit⇨Check Spelling from the menu bar or press Ctrl+F2.

Figure 10-5: Use this dialog box to check the spelling in your presentations.

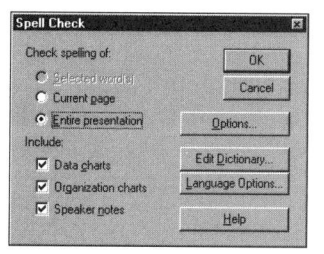

The following list describes the options available in the Spell Check dialog box:

- **Check spelling of.** Use this area to tell Freelance Graphics what to spell-check. The options are Selected Word(s), Current Page, and Entire Presentation. For Selected Word(s) to become active, you first must select some text by using the Text tool. Using this option is a great way to check one word or just a few words.

- **Include.** Use this section to tell Freelance Graphics which parts of the presentation to check. The program automatically checks text slides, titles, and any other text that you type directly onto the page. You also can set Freelance Graphics to check Data Charts, Organization Charts, Speaker Notes, or a combination of these elements.

- **Options button.** This button displays the Spell Check Options dialog box, as shown in Figure 10-6. Use the dialog box to tell Freelance Graphics to check for repeated words, words that contain numbers, and words that start with capital letters. If you turn the last option off, Freelance Graphics skips all words in the presentation that begin with capitals.

Part III: Fine-Tuning Your Presentation

- **Edit Dictionary button.** This button enables you to add words to the Freelance Graphics dictionary by typing them in a dialog box; you find out about this procedure later in this section.

- **Language Options button.** This button enables you to choose a different language dictionary. Freelance Graphics ships with eight dictionaries.

Figure 10-6: Use this dialog box to set up spell-check options.

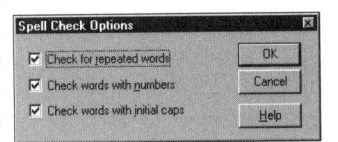

Starting a spell-check session

After you use the Spell Check dialog box to define the parameters for your spell-check session — what to check, options, and so on — click OK to begin checking the document. If Freelance Graphics comes to a suspect word, it stops and displays the word in the dialog box shown in Figure 10-7. From that dialog box, you can replace the word with an alternative from the Alternatives list, skip the word and move on, or add the word to the Freelance Graphics dictionary.

Figure 10-7: Use this dialog box to correct spelling errors.

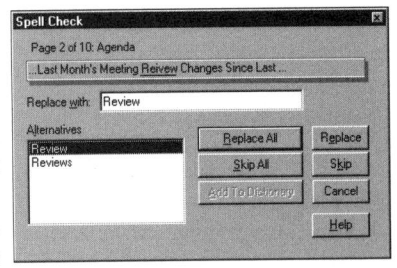

The following list describes the options in this Spell Check dialog box:

- **Replace and Replace All.** Use these buttons to replace the misspelled word with one from the Alternatives list. Click the word you want to use and then click Replace. Clicking Replace All replaces all occurrences of the misspelled word with the one that you select in the Alternatives list.

- **Skip and Skip All.** Use these buttons to move to the next misspelled word without replacing the current one. Skip skips the current occurrence; Skip All passes over all occurrences, without stopping on the word again.

✔ **Add to Dictionary.** This button adds the current word to the Freelance Graphics dictionary. Thereafter, the spell checker does not stop on the word again in any of your presentations.

✔ **Cancel.** This button stops the current spell-check session and returns you to the presentation.

Continue replacing, skipping, and adding words until Freelance Graphics displays the Spell Check Complete dialog box.

Managing the Freelance Graphics dictionary

In addition to adding words to the Freelance Graphics dictionary while conducting a spell check, you can add words directly to the dictionary in a batch by using the Edit Dictionary option in the Spell Check dialog box. This method is a great way to add several words at the same time or to manage a Freelance Graphics dictionary on a network. You also can use this option to remove words from the dictionary.

Use the Edit Dictionary option to add personal names, company names, company terms, and terms that are related to your specific field. To add words to the dictionary, follow these steps:

1. **Choose Edit➪Check Spelling from the menu bar.**

    The Spell Check dialog box appears.

2. **Click Edit Dictionary.**

    The Spell Check User's Dictionary dialog box appears (see Figure 10-8). To add a word, type it in the New word box and then click Add. To remove a word, highlight it in the Current words list and then click Delete.

Figure 10-8: Use this dialog box to enter words in the spelling dictionary.

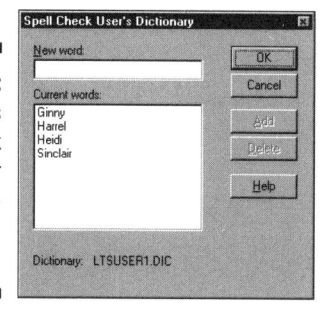

3. Type a word in the New Word box.
4. Click Add.
5. Repeat steps 3 and 4 to add as many words as you want.
6. Click OK to return to the Spell Check dialog box.
7. Click OK in the Spell Check dialog box to return to your presentation.

Chapter 11

Being Your Own Art Director: Modifying Existing SmartMasters and Creating New SmartMasters

In This Chapter

▶ Editing SmartMasters (an overview)

▶ Modifying SmartMaster background colors and patterns

▶ Making intelligent typeface and type-size choices

▶ Changing bullet type, color, size, and spacing

▶ Adding a logo to each slide

▶ Rearranging, adding, and deleting SmartMaster elements

▶ Creating a new SmartMaster and saving it as a default template

A problem with using any program's templates is that you could wind up creating presentations that look a great deal like somebody else's. This situation is especially true in a corporate setting in which everybody uses the same presentation program. To avoid that out-of-the-box look, you can modify Freelance Graphics' SmartMasters to personalize your presentations and give them a distinctive appearance.

Another reason for modifying SmartMasters is to tailor presentations to specific clients. If you are a salesperson, for example, you may want to put the logo, company name, or company colors of a prospective client on each slide. The easiest and quickest way to make these global changes in the entire presentation is to edit SmartMasters. Another way to make these changes is to create new SmartMasters and save them as default templates.

And that's the subject of this chapter: creating your own look and feel either by editing Freelance Graphics' SmartMaster templates or by creating new SmartMasters and saving them as default templates.

How to Modify SmartMasters

Freelance Graphics has two kinds of SmartMasters: SmartMaster Look and SmartMaster Content. You can edit each type. You modify the SmartMaster Look files to make style and appearance changes: colors, backgrounds, fonts, and so on. Editing the SmartMaster Content files alters the flow of information built into the content prompts. This section describes how to modify SmartMaster Look files; modifying Content files is very similar.

SmartMaster Look template files are kept in the LOTUS/SMASTER/FLG subdirectory and contain a MAS file extension. Unless you change the default SmartMaster directory with User Setup, Freelance Graphics always looks for SmartMaster Look files in the same directory when you start a new presentation. The program also expects SmartMaster Look files to have the MAS extension; it does not recognize any other files as SmartMaster Look files.

Opening a SmartMaster Look file

When you use the New Presentation dialog box to start a new document, Freelance Graphics uses the SmartMaster Look file to create a new, untitled presentation. You can make your changes in the untitled presentation and save it as a SmartMaster Look template, or you can open a SmartMaster Look file and edit it directly. No matter which method you use, the process of editing SmartMaster colors, fonts, and so on is the same. The only real variation is in the way in which you save the file, as discussed in the following section. To open a SmartMaster Look file directly, follow these steps:

1. **In the Freelance Graphics window, choose File⇨Open or press Ctrl+O.**

   The Open dialog box appears. This dialog box enables you to open presentations and SmartMasters.

2. **From the Files of Type drop-down list, select Lotus Freelance SmartMaster Look (MAS); then change to the directory in which your Freelance Graphics SmartMasters are stored and select the SmartMaster that you want to modify.**

   As you select a filename, a thumbnail of the SmartMaster appears in the bottom-left portion of the dialog box, as shown in Figure 11-1.

3. **Click Open or double-click the filename in the list of files.**

From this point, you edit the SmartMaster. After you finish editing the SmartMaster, save it as a SmartMaster Look (MAS) file, as discussed in the following section.

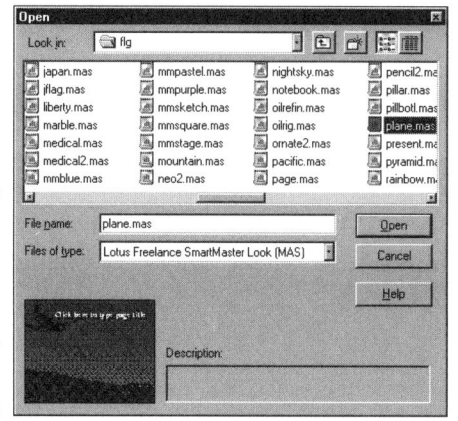

Figure 11-1: Use this dialog box to open the SmartMaster Look file.

Saving a SmartMaster Look file

You can save a presentation or an edited SmartMaster Look file as a SmartMaster Look template. Thereafter, Freelance Graphics recognizes the SmartMaster template and provides it as one of the options in the New Presentation dialog box. To save a SmartMaster Look file, follow these steps:

1. **Choose File➪Save As.**

    The Save As dialog box appears. This dialog box enables you to rename and save the file. You can also add a description to the file that will display in the New Presentation dialog box.

    TIP

    If you are editing an existing SmartMaster file, consider renaming the edited version. If you save the file with the default name, you copy over the existing Freelance Graphics SmartMaster. The only way to get the original SmartMaster back after that is to run the installation program again.

2. **Type a filename in the File name box.**

    You don't need to type the MAS extension; Freelance Graphics adds that automatically.

3. **If Lotus Freelance SmartMaster Look (MAS) is not already displayed in the Save As Type drop-down list, select it from the drop-down list.**

4. **(Optional) Type a description of the new SmartMaster in the Description text box.**

5. **Click Save and choose File➪Close to close the SmartMaster file.**

The next time you use the New Presentation dialog box, your new SmartMaster is one of the template choices.

How to Modify SmartMaster Background Colors

One way to avoid that out-of-the-box look is to change the background colors and patterns of a SmartMaster, giving it your personal touch. This method ensures that your presentations won't look like everybody else's.

Like charts, SmartShapes, and other Freelance Graphics elements, slide backgrounds consist of a background color, a foreground (pattern) color, and a foreground pattern. Follow these steps to change a SmartMaster's background color and pattern:

1. **Open the SmartMaster for which you want to change the background colors and choose Presentation➪Edit Page Layouts to select the Presentation Backdrop layout.**

   If you want the changes to apply to all SmartMaster layouts, you must edit the Presentation Backdrop layout, which will apply to all layouts except Title. You must change Title separately. If you are working on a SmartMaster file directly, as opposed to a standard presentation file, Freelance Graphics displays all the layouts in Layout Sorter view immediately after opening the MAS file. Choose Presentation➪Edit Backdrop to edit all layouts except the Title layout (or double-click the Title layout to edit it).

2. **Choose Page➪Page Properties.**

   The Properties dialog box appears.

   You can change the backdrop fill pattern and colors by making choices in the Line & Color Fill tab of the dialog box. First, define a pattern (if you want to change it); then define a pattern color (foreground) and a background color for the fill. Using this method, you can add solid backgrounds, tints, crosshatching and other patterns, or gradients (colors that graduate into others). You also can add a bitmap graphic, such as a silhouetted company logo, to the background.

3. **Click the Line & Color Pattern tab and select a pattern from the Pattern drop-down list.**

   The first two rows of the drop-down list consist of a solid fill and several screens or tints. The next three rows are pattern fills, and the last four rows are gradients. When you define a pattern, the foreground color is used for the dark elements, and the background color is used for the light areas of the fills.

4. **Select a pattern color from the Pattern Color drop-down list, select a background color from the Background drop-down list, and click the Done button at the left side of the screen; after you make all the changes that you want, save the SmartMaster Look file.**

Changing backgrounds is great, but be careful not to use colors that are too dark or patterns that are too busy to display your presentation elements. You don't want to strain audience members' eyes.

If you want to make the SmartMaster unique, you can add your own graphics to the background.

How to Use the Right Fonts

A common mistake that new presenters and designers make is using all the design elements in their program's arsenal — especially *fonts* — in the same presentation. You really shouldn't use more than four fonts in the same slide — or even in the same presentation, for that matter. This section discusses font technology, tells you when to use what fonts, and tells you how to change the fonts used in your SmartMasters.

A typeface by any other name . . .

Before we start talking about changing typefaces, we need to make sure that you're speaking the same language that we are. A *typeface* is a style of type, such as Arial or Times New Roman. Most typefaces have four attributes (sometimes called *styles*): normal (often called book or roman, depending on the typeface), **bold,** *italic,* and ***bold italic.*** Some typefaces have only one or two styles; others, such as Futura, have as many as eight or more.

The term *font* breaks the typeface distinction down even further. A font actually is a typeface that has a specific set of attributes (for example, Arial Italic). Another term that you need to be familiar with is *point size*. Type height is measured in units called *points*. You have approximately 72 points per inch.

Serif and sans-serif typefaces

Most typefaces are either serif or sans-serif. *Serif* characters have little foundations, or "feet," at the ends of letter strokes. Typically, serif typefaces are used in body copy because they are easy on the eyes. *Sans-serif* means "without serifs." Traditionally, sans-serif fonts are used for headlines, subheads, and titles as well as for presentations' body copy and bullet points because they are easy to make out from far away and print better at low resolutions than do serif fonts. Another typeface distinction is *decorative* (sometimes called *display*), such as Gothic. On the whole, these typefaces are hard to read; they work only for short headlines and titles. Use these typefaces sparingly.

How to change SmartMaster fonts

Another way to change the out-of-box appearance of presentations created with SmartMasters is to change the typefaces. To change SmartMaster typefaces and point sizes, follow these steps:

1. **Open the SmartMaster that you want to change, choose Presentation➪Edit Page Layout, and select Title or another layout.**

   If you are working on a SmartMaster file directly, as opposed to a standard presentation file, Freelance Graphics displays all the layouts in Layout Sorter view immediately after opening the MAS file. Double-click the Title layout.

2. **Select the Click Here to Type a Presentation Title placeholder.**

   At this point, the Page menu changes to the Click Here menu, which is similar to the Text menu. This menu enables you to make many changes in the selected placeholder text — typeface, color, style, size, and so on. Notice that any changes you make in the title affects all other text levels.

3. **Choose Click Here➪Font & Color.**

   The Properties dialog box appears. This version of the dialog box enables you to change the typeface, type style, font size, and text color; set a drop shadow; and make all kinds of other changes in the selected placeholder text, including adding transition effects.

4. **Scroll through the Font Name list until you find the font that you want to use and select it.**

   The Change Named Style dialog box appears. This dialog box gives you two options: rename the existing text style or create a new style. (A *style* is a set of instructions for formatting a block of text quickly. Check out Chapter 6 for more information on styles.) The dialog box also informs you that this change affects all levels of text.

5. **Click OK to redefine the existing style, make your changes (size, attributes, and so on), click the Done button on the left side of the screen, and save the SmartMaster file.**

The next time that you use this SmartMaster, Freelance Graphics substitutes the new typefaces for the old ones.

A faster way to make the same change while you are in Edit Backdrop mode is to choose Presentation➪Change Typefaces Globally. This command enables you to change not only titles and the other five text levels, but also charts and tables. This command also works while you are working on a presentation file, not just on a SmartMaster.

If you want to change typefaces on all but the title slide, edit any of the other page layouts in the manner described in the preceding steps.

How to Change SmartMaster Bullets

You can further personalize your SmartMasters by changing the bullet type, color, size, and spacing. In addition to using bullets from a font set, you can use Freelance Graphics clip art as bullets.

To change SmartMaster bullets, follow these steps:

1. **Open the SmartMaster for which you want to change the bullets, choose Presentation⇨Edit Page Layouts, and choose the Bulleted List layout.**

   You also can click another layout that contains bullets. Changing any bullet-slide bullet affects all bullets.

   If you are working on a SmartMaster file directly, as opposed to a standard presentation file, Freelance Graphics displays all the layouts in Layout Sorter view immediately after opening the MAS file. Double-click Bulleted List.

2. **Select the Click Here to Type Bulleted List placeholder and choose Click Here⇨Click Here Properties.**

   The Properties dialog box appears.

3. **Click the Bullet tab (the third one).**

   The Properties dialog box appears. This dialog box enables you to select a bullet, change its color, add a drop shadow, and add space between the bullet and the text.

   You can use Freelance Graphics clip art as bullets, too. But if you want to use your images as bullets, you need to convert them to Freelance Graphics clip art, as discussed in Chapter 9.

4. **Select a new bullet from the Style drop-down palette.**

   The Change Named Style dialog box appears, enabling you to rename the existing text style or create a new style. The dialog box also informs you that this change affects all levels of text.

5. **Click OK to redefine the existing style.**

   The Properties dialog box reappears.

6. **Make your changes (size, color, and so on) by changing the values in the appropriate drop-down list boxes, click the Done button on the left side of the screen, and save the SmartMaster file.**

The next time that you use this SmartMaster, Freelance Graphics substitutes the new bullets for the old ones.

How to Add a Logo to Each Slide

Follow these steps to place a running logo on the pages of your favorite SmartMasters:

1. **Open the SmartMaster that you want to change, choose Presentation⇨Edit Page Layouts, and select the Presentation Backdrop layout.**

   If you want the changes to apply to all SmartMaster layouts, you must edit the Presentation Backdrop layout, which applies to all layouts except Title. You must change Title separately.

   If you are working on a SmartMaster file directly, as opposed to a standard presentation file, Freelance Graphics displays all the layouts in Layout Sorter view immediately after opening the MAS file. Choose Presentation⇨Edit Backdrop to edit all layouts except the Title layout, or double-click the Title layout to edit it.

   Step 2 puts Freelance Graphics into Edit Backdrop mode. On the left side of the screen, below the Drawing & Text option button, is a step-by-step description of what you should do to complete the process of adding a logo to your SmartMaster pages. You use Freelance Graphics' drawing and text tools to create a logo, import a graphic file, or copy and paste the logo from another application. Chapter 9 presents all these procedures.

2. **Create a logo or import a graphics file by choosing one of the Add commands (or Object) from the Create menu and click Done (the button located below the Drawing & Text button on the left side of the screen).**

   If you scroll through your list of template pages (click Page Layout), you see that the logo is on each page.

3. **If this change is the only change that you want to make, save the SmartMaster.**

A quick way to do this in multiple layouts is to cut and paste. Place a logo on the SmartMaster Presentation Backdrop layout and then put it on the Title layout. After you place the graphic in Edit Backdrop mode in one layout, copy the logo, exit Edit Backdrop mode (by clicking the Done button), go to another layout, and paste the logo into that layout.

How to Add SmartMaster Elements

Yet another way to personalize SmartMasters is to add text and graphics to the layouts. Freelance Graphics enables you to move, add, and delete layout elements at will. To do so, follow these steps:

1. **Open the SmartMaster that you want to change, choose Presentation⇨Edit Page Layouts, and select the layout that you want to modify.**

   Each layout has a different layout scheme, so you should edit each one separately. If you are working on a SmartMaster file directly, rather than a standard presentation file, Freelance Graphics displays all the layouts in Layout Sorter view immediately after opening the MAS file. Double-click the desired layout.

2. **If you want the change to appear on all layouts, edit the Presentation Backdrop layout and then edit the Title layout or vice versa.**

   This step puts Freelance Graphics into Edit Backdrop mode. In this mode, you make changes in SmartMaster layouts as you would in any other slide in a regular presentation. If you change font properties for placeholders, however, those changes apply to all layouts. Placeholders are added in a dissimilar manner, as discussed later in this chapter. The rest of this procedure assumes that you know how to add text and other elements to pages.

3. **Add, delete, and move text and graphics to the layout page, placing and formatting these elements as you normally do.**

   If you are working on the Presentation Backdrop layout, you should not place the new element inside the dotted line that encompasses most of the page; this area is where Freelance Graphics places "Click here" elements. If you need to place the new element in the area occupied by the box, resize the box with the Pointer tool so that "Click here" elements don't overlap the new element.

4. **After you finish, click the Done button on the left side of the screen, repeat these steps to edit the other layouts in the SmartMaster Look file, and save the SmartMaster.**

   A dramatic way to modify SmartMasters is to add, resize, and rearrange "Click here" placeholders. This also is a major part of creating your own SmartMasters and is discussed later in this chapter.

How to Create a SmartMaster and Save It as a Default Template

Sometimes, Freelance Graphics' SmartMasters just won't do. Freelance Graphics provides you nearly unlimited freedom to create your own custom templates and save them as SmartMasters. This section discusses how to incorporate the components — typefaces, colors, and tone — of your company's other advertising media into your own SmartMasters, which you can use over and over to create presentations that are consistent with your organization's identity.

To create a SmartMaster, you can start with an existing presentation or edit an existing SmartMaster. In either case, how you save the file determines whether Freelance Graphics recognizes it as a SmartMaster. This section shows you how to start from scratch, beginning with a blank presentation and modifying it to your taste. You can save a great deal of time, however, by finding a SmartMaster that is close to the design that you want and modifying it to fit your needs.

NOTE: Creating a new SmartMaster is much like creating a presentation; you use many of the same tools and commands, with a few exceptions. So rather than go into many of the details that are already scattered around in this book, this section assumes that you have some working knowledge of Freelance Graphics. Wherever pertinent, though, we refer you to sections of this book where you can find details on procedures discussed in previous chapters.

Beginning your new SmartMaster

You can begin with a standard presentation or with a SmartMaster Look .MAS file. We recommend the latter method because Freelance Graphics provides a few more tools for creating templates when a SmartMaster Look file is open. If you already have a presentation that you want to convert to a SmartMaster template, however, feel free to do so.

To begin your SmartMaster template, choose File➪Open (to open the BLANK.MAS SmartMaster Look file) and choose Presentation➪Edit Backdrop.

NOTE: As you learned earlier, changes that you make in Edit Backdrop affect all layouts except the Title layout. If you want to make the same changes to the Title layout backdrop, you must repeat the procedure for that layout. To do so, choose Presentation➪Edit Page Layouts and then open the Title slide layout.

Starting from scratch

From this point, you can create a set of new layouts or modify existing layouts. You can save a great deal of time if, whenever possible, you edit the existing layouts. The procedures discussed in this section for editing the existing layouts also are pertinent to creating new layouts.

When you need to create a new layout, the procedure changes in the following ways:

- In the Edit Page Layouts dialog box, choose Create rather than Edit; in the Create New Page Layout dialog box, name the new page, and check or uncheck the Use Backdrop option to determine whether this layout should use the existing presentation backdrop.

- You define the number of "Click here" blocks that you want on the page with the Number of Click Here Blocks.
- After clicking OK, you get a blank screen with none of the "Click here" blocks defined. You must define each block, as described in the section "Adding and modifying 'Click here' placeholders," later in this chapter.

We usually use the BLANK.MAS SmartMaster Look template, but you can use any template that you want. In some cases, however — as in the next procedure, in which you add a bitmapped image to the backdrop — you may not get the desired results.

After you finish defining the new layout, Freelance Graphics adds it to the SmartMaster Look library. The layout then appears in the New Presentation dialog box each time you begin a new presentation with the current SmartMaster.

Adding a bitmap image to the backdrop

You add a bitmap to a backdrop much as you add or change a color or pattern: from the Edit Backdrop screen with the Properties dialog box. When you add a bitmap to a backdrop, the graphic becomes the backdrop, and you no longer can edit the pattern or color of the background.

Freelance Graphics supports several bitmap formats, including TIF, BMP, TGA, PCX, and GIF. Before you add a backdrop, you should first do any desired editing and recoloring in a paint program, such as CorelPhoto-Paint or Adobe Photoshop. If you import a colored graphic on a white background, that's what you'll get in Freelance Graphics: a colored graphic on a white background. If you use an image for a backdrop, it should be colored exactly as you want the backdrop to appear in Freelance Graphics.

If you are importing a backdrop based on company colors, be sure to see the section "Changing and creating new color palettes" later in this chapter. The information in that section about defining colors based on color models also is pertinent to image-editing (paint) software.

To add a bitmap image to a backdrop, follow these steps:

1. **From the Edit Backdrop screen, choose Page⇨Page Properties.**

   The Properties dialog box appears.

2. **Select Bitmap from the Pattern drop-down palette.**

   The Use Bitmap for Page Background dialog box appears, as shown in Figure 11-2. This dialog box enables you to place the bitmap image and tell Freelance Graphics how to use it. You can have the image resized to fit the page, or you can tile it.

Figure 11-2: Use this dialog box to define and place the bitmap background.

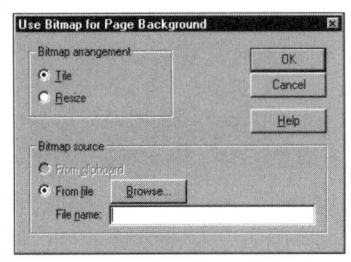

TIP

When you place a bitmap, you have to experiment with the image size in your paint program to get the image to fit properly in Freelance Graphics. We suggest that, as you resize the image in your paint software, you save multiple versions of your changes, so that you can pick the one that fits best. The trouble with being an art designer is that you have to experiment. (That's why we make the big bucks.)

3. In the Bitmap Arrangement area of the dialog box, choose whether to Tile or Resize the image.

TIP

You have the best luck with the Resize option if you create the image the same size as your presentation page; otherwise, the image could get distorted during resizing. Tiled images are kept at their original size, in pixels.

NOTE

In most cases, you gain nothing by importing high-resolution images into your slide and screen-show presentations. Computer monitors display at only about 75 dots per inch (dpi). If your presentation is destined to be a screen show, resample images to 75 dpi in your image-editing software. Likewise, 35mm slides are so small that images larger than about 100 dpi do little but slow the slide recorder and the speed at which your computer screen redraws. About the only time you can benefit from 150- to 300-dpi graphics is when you print on paper or transparencies.

4. Click Browse.

The Browse dialog box appears.

5. In the Files of Type list, select the image type, find the image file, and specify whether to store the image in the presentation file or whether to link to the file under Store in Presentation.

The first option imports a copy of the graphic into the Freelance Graphics presentation file, making the file bigger, which could cause slower navigation and screen redraws. The second option makes the file smaller, but you need to remember to bring the image file if you transport the presentation for printing.

6. Click Open; then click OK.

Freelance Graphics replaces the current background with the bitmap. Now you can use this bitmap as the backdrop for your presentation.

Another way to personalize a backdrop is to change colors and patterns, as discussed previously. Remember, though, that you cannot recolor backdrops that consist of bitmap images.

Yet another way to achieve a similar effect is to import a bitmap image into the backdrop, as you would import any other image in a standard presentation. You then can move the image around and resize it. You also can use this method to recolor and add patterns to the backdrop.

Changing and creating new color palettes

You can change one of Freelance Graphics' existing color palettes or create your own. To create a new palette, you start by editing an existing palette. Follow these steps to change the color scheme for a SmartMaster by editing a color palette:

1. **Open the SmartMaster for which you want to change the colors, choose Presentation⇨Edit Backdrop, and choose Presentation⇨Edit Palette.**

    The Edit Palette dialog box appears. This dialog box enables you to change the colors for various slide elements, including all chart and graph text, grids, bars, lines, pie slices, bullets, and text. As you click a color in the palette, a message at the bottom of the dialog box tells you what object(s) the color is assigned to. To change the basic design colors, you edit cells A1 through A11. These colors are assigned to primary foreground and background objects, such as the slide background itself and drop shadows. The other cells in B – C are specific elements — text, chart and graph elements, and so on.

    If the color scheme for a specific SmartMaster is miles away from the colors that you need, try choosing Presentation⇨Switch Palette. That command displays the Switch Palette dialog box, which enables you to switch among the various palettes designed for that SmartMaster. One of the other palettes may be closer to what you need, so you won't have to make so many changes in the Edit Palette dialog box. In the Switch Palettes dialog box, you can choose a color set and then click Preview to see how the scheme changes the SmartMaster.

2. **To begin making changes in the palette, click a color swatch in a specific cell, read the message that describes the element to which that color is assigned, and then click the Change Color drop-down list.**

    After you click Change Color, the Color Library drop-down list appears.

3. **Select a color from the Color Library drop-down list.**

   The color that you select from the Color Library list replaces the color that you selected in the palette.

4. **Repeat steps 2 and 3 until all the colors that you want to change are replaced by the new colors; then click OK to close the Edit Palette dialog box and save the SmartMaster file.**

> **TIP:** You also can save the modified palette as a new palette by clicking Save. This button opens a dialog box that enables you to name and save the palette. You then can use the color scheme with any of Freelance Graphics' SmartMasters (or with any presentation, for that matter). The advantage of this method is that it preserves the program's original color schemes. To use the new palette, choose Presentation⇨Switch Palettes while you are in Edit Backdrop mode.

> **TIP:** Wouldn't changing all those colors in the Edit Palette dialog box, only to find out that they look terrible together, be a waste of time? You can check your progress as you swap colors in the palette by clicking and holding the Preview button. Freelance Graphics shows you how the changes affect the SmartMaster by applying them to the current slide. When you release Preview, the program returns you to the Edit Palette dialog box and restores the preceding color scheme. The changes that you make in the Edit Palette dialog box are not permanent until you click OK or Save. A disadvantage of using this option to edit a SmartMaster is the fact that the templates usually don't contain many elements, so you don't get to see many of the color changes — usually, only the title text, drop shadow, and background. You get a better preview by using Preview with a presentation that already contains text and chart elements.

Adding and modifying "Click here" placeholders

Earlier in this chapter, you learned how to change typefaces, text color, shadows, and so on in SmartMasters. The procedure is pretty much the same as changing the typefaces in a standard presentation file, except you work in Edit Backdrop. This section explains how to add, delete, rearrange, and modify the "Click here" placeholders — or *blocks,* as Freelance Graphics calls them — themselves.

Freelance Graphics gives you complete control of these template elements, right down to changing what the placeholder text says to prompt the user. You can, for example, change *Click Here to Add Clip Art* to *Click Here to Add Company Logo.*

Adding a new "Click here" block

When you are creating or laying out a new SmartMaster page or creating a new one especially for transparencies or paper output, you can have a better idea about where you are placing objects if you use Freelance Graphics' rulers. To turn on the rulers, choose View➪Show Rulers. You can choose Presentation➪Units & Grids to change the type of measurement system (points, inches, and so on) used in the rulers. To add a new "Click here" placeholder, follow these steps:

1. **Use Edit Page Layouts to choose a layout that you want to modify, or click the Create button to start a new layout.**

   You cannot edit the page title placeholder from here. If you want to create a layout with a new page title placeholder position, you should create a new layout and, in the Create New Page Layout dialog box, deselect the Use Backdrop option. If you use this method, you also have to recreate the backdrop colors and other design elements for the new layout.

   Also, to add a "Click here" block to all layouts, you choose Presentation➪Edit Backdrop. This command enables you to place an element in all layouts except the Title layout. Remember that you must modify the Title layout separately.

   When you are adding elements to a backdrop, you should not place new elements in the dotted box ("Click here" guide). Existing Freelance Graphics layouts use this area to place charts and text blocks. If you need to place elements in this area, you should use the Pointer tool to resize the box.

2. **Choose Create➪"Click here" Block and click the layout in which you want to place the placeholder.**

   By default, this procedure provides a text "Click here" block. You can move, resize, and shape this placeholder as you would any other Freelance Graphics object. You also can replace the current text with other text or change the text attributes.

Modifying the basic properties of "Click here" blocks

You can edit the basic properties of existing "Click here" blocks (or of new ones that you create) by using the procedure described in the preceding section. You can, for example, change a page title to a data chart or to any other type of Freelance Graphics page-layout element. To modify the properties of a "Click here" block, follow these steps:

1. **Begin on the layout that contains the placeholder you want to modify in Edit Backdrop mode, select the "Click here" block that you want to change, and choose "Click here" Properties from the "Click here" menu.**

   The Properties dialog box, which you've seen many times throughout this book, appears. "Click here" properties are changed from the Basics section of Properties, as shown in Figure 11-3. This dialog box enables you to change the type and some other aspects of the placeholder.

Part III: Fine-Tuning Your Presentation

Figure 11-3: Use this dialog box to change the "Click here" properties of a selected placeholder.

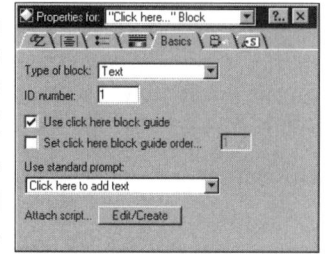

2. **From the Type of block drop-down list, select the kind of "Click here" block to which you want to change.**

   The box properties change, as does the text inside the box. If, for example, you change to a diagram, the text inside the placeholder changes to Click Here to Create a Diagram.

   TIP: If, during your work, the Properties dialog box gets in your way, you don't have to close it to see more of your page; double-click the title bar, and the dialog box collapses. Double-click the title bar again to expand the dialog box.

3. **From the Use standard prompt drop-down list, select the type of prompt that you want the text to have.**

   Again, the box properties change, as does the text inside the box. If, for example, you change to Click Here to Type a Page Title, the text inside the placeholder changes to Click Here to Change a Page Title. Also, the text assumes the formatting that is associated with that text style.

   TIP: Remember that most of the text in a Freelance Graphics presentation is formatted with a style, especially text created from "Click here" blocks. You can change the default formatting for each block of text by modifying the style. To do so, click the Style (S) tab in the Properties dialog box. To modify an existing style, click Redefine Style. To create a new style, click Create Style. You then modify the style in the Properties dialog box as you would any other text.

4. **If you want the block to conform to SmartMaster conventions, choose the Use click here block guide option, move and resize the placeholder as desired, and save the SmartMaster.**

   Remember that you are modifying an existing SmartMaster, giving it a new name so as to avoid copying over the original.

   TIP: Now that you have created a new template, you may want to make it your default SmartMaster — the one that Freelance Graphics always displays when you start a new presentation. Following are three ways to accomplish that task:

Chapter 11: Being Your Own Art Director: Modifying Existing SmartMasters... 187

- Give the new SmartMaster a name that starts with *A* so that it is listed first in the SmartMaster list.
- Delete all SmartMasters except the one that you created.
- Change the directory in which Freelance Graphics looks for SmartMaster files (File/User Setup/Freelance Preferences/File Locations) and save the new SmartMaster to that directory.

About Freelance Graphics' automatic "Click here" block placement

Inherent in each Freelance Graphics SmartMaster is a "Click here" placement scheme. In other words, each SmartMaster has built-in instructions about where each type of placeholder should be placed on the page. When you switch SmartMaster Look files or layouts while you create a presentation, Freelance Graphics automatically repositions the "Click here" elements according to the scheme for the new SmartMaster Look or layout.

A "Click here" block on the Bullets & Chart page layout with an ID of 3, for example, is placed in the position of the "Click here" block with an ID of 3 in the new look's Bullets & Chart page. This is designed, of course, to make sure that elements do not conflict with backdrops and other design elements of each SmartMaster.

Freelance Graphics automatically gives each "Click here" block an ID number when it is created, using the next available ID in the 1–100 sequence. If you create a new look and find that "Click here" blocks do not map properly with existing SmartMaster looks (that is, their positions move when you switch to a new look), you may have to change the ID numbers if you foresee using existing looks with the new one.

If you create new page layouts with "Click here" blocks, keep these things in mind:

- "Click here" text blocks get ID numbers 1–100. The title block should have an ID of 1; the first text block should have an ID of 2; and so on.
- "Click here" graphic blocks get ID numbers 101–999.

When you switch looks and a "Click here" block does not have a matching ID number in the new look, the block remains in its original position on the page.

Part IV
Printing and Rehearsing Your Presentation

The 5th Wave

By Rich Tennant

"WOW! I DIDN'T EVEN THINK THEY MADE A 2000 DOT PER INCH FONT!"

In this part . . .

One of the fun things about the emerging computer technology is that it gives us all a bunch of options for distributing information. No longer do you have to rely on just a typewritten, photocopied handout; you can use slides, transparencies, electronic presentations . . . and who knows what's next. This part gives you the inside scoop on handling the different options available when you use Freelance Graphics 96.

Chapter 12
Preparing and Printing 35mm Slides

In This Chapter
- Where slides come from
- How to prepare a presentation for printing at a service bureau
- How to prepare a presentation for printing in-house

*H*ave you ever wondered how images get from a computer screen to those little pieces of plastic-mounted film that we call 35mm slides? This chapter tells you how and focuses on turning your computer-based presentation into a set of slides that are ready for the slide projector.

Where Slides Come From

You probably already know that slides are printed on devices called slide recorders. But did you know that slide recorders come in several varieties and print at various resolutions? Did you know that you can buy your own slide recorder for less than $1,000? Do you know where to take your slides if you don't have or don't plan to purchase a slide recorder?

Stick around; this section covers those issues, beginning with slide-recorder technology.

A slide recorder by any other name

When it comes to making slides, slide recorders take the place of 35mm cameras nowadays. Basically, you print from a computer to these recorders in much the same way that you print to any other desktop printer.

Slide recorders come in all shapes and sizes, but two basic types exist:

- ✔ Machines that use Adobe's PostScript printer language. These machines typically are more versatile than the second type and are better suited to high-volume settings, in which presentations come in from several sources and different presentation programs. Some small, personal PostScript slide recorders are available, however.
- ✔ Machines that use their own proprietary language. These machines typically are small, low-resolution personal machines that work relatively well for low volume in-house settings.

When you rate slide recorders, the two most significant specifications to consider are *speed* and *resolution*.

No slide recorder is fast enough to break the sound barrier; among personal devices, the best that you can hope for is about one slide per minute. But if you don't create many presentations, printing speed isn't an issue anyway.

More important to presentations is slide resolution. As is true of any output device, resolution greatly affects quality. This concept works a bit differently with slides, however. Slides are rated by the amount of data that they contain: 2K, 4K, and so on, up to 10K and beyond. Another difference is that, unlike other desktop printers, a 2K slide can look just as good as a 12K slide to the naked eye. The size at which the slides are projected determines the quality of the image.

If you project a 2K slide on a large screen in an auditorium that's filled with 1,000 or more people, the image degrades, making your slide look jagged and fuzzy. In such a case, you're better off using an 8K or 10K slide. The 2K slide looks good only if projected from about four or five feet away.

The higher the resolution, the longer the slide takes to print — and, if you're getting the job printed at a service bureau, the more it costs. Personal slide recorders usually have a fixed resolution of 4K, which often is adequate for all but very large audiences.

Of course, the size of the audience does not determine the quality of the images; the size to which the projector increases the images determines the quality. And the size of the images is determined by the slide projector and screen in the presentation setting. Before you get your slides printed, you should find out the size at which the images are to be projected; then ask the service-bureau operator to suggest a resolution for your slides.

If you're printing on a 4K personal recorder, resolution is not, of course, an issue. Your recorder prints at only one resolution. In all but the largest settings, 4K slides are adequate.

Off to the service bureau?

Service bureaus — sometimes called *desktop publishing service bureaus* — are businesses that output computer files on media that customers don't have in-house, such as high-resolution film, color prints, CD-ROMs, and slides. These companies essentially print your files for you.

If you live in a large metropolitan area, you probably have at least one service bureau nearby. If not, several service bureaus around the country accept computer files electronically and ship the slides back to you the next day, if necessary. You can find these businesses listed in the back of many computer magazines, including *MacWorld, Publish, MacUser,* and *PC World.* You also can find several service bureaus on the World Wide Web by searching for the keyword *slides.*

Using a service bureau for slides has several advantages and disadvantages. The primary advantage is the fact that you don't need to mess with cutting the film and mounting the slides after printing. The primary disadvantage is the fact that service bureaus can be expensive, charging $5 to $12 per slide, depending on quantity, resolution, and the service bureau itself. Excluding the cost of the slide recorder, in-house printing and film can cost as little as 50 cents per slide.

Some other disadvantages of using a service bureau are as follows:

- Many service bureaus do not support Freelance Graphics. In such a case, you must create a print file, as discussed in the section "What to do if your service bureau doesn't have Freelance Graphics 96," later in this chapter. This process can be time-consuming.

- Modem transmissions are not always foolproof. You may need to send the file more than one time. If you use an online service (such as CompuServe or America Online) to transmit the slide files, transmitting them could cost some extra online time.

- Depending on how many bitmap graphics and how many slides they contain, presentation files can be extremely large — and, therefore, costly and time-consuming to transmit. (We've created presentations as long as 18MB.) You may need to invest in removable media, discussed in the sidebar "Removable media for transporting large files."

Printing your slides in-house

Printing your slides in-house is not quite as convenient as printing to a desktop printer. The procedure is not simply a matter of walking over to the printer and picking up your slides. After going through the slide recorder, the film must be cut and mounted, which can be somewhat tedious. So the only real benefit of printing your slides in-house may be savings, which are something to think about.

But then again, the savings don't really add up until you print enough slides to pay for the slide recorder. Expect to save about $4.50 to $11.50 per slide by printing in-house. Also, most personal slide recorders support only one resolution, which may be an issue if you show presentations to large audiences.

Removable media for transporting large files

Most presentation and graphics designers who transport computer files to service bureaus use some form of removable medium. *Removable media* are storage devices that have disks or cartridges that you can put in and take out, as you do floppy disks. The difference is that these disks or cartridges are capable of holding many megabytes of data, from about 40MB to more than 1GB.

Following is a list of removable-media devices that many service bureaus support, listed in the order of their prevalence:

- *Syquest.* Perhaps the oldest and most popular form of removable medium is the Syquest drive. Syquest devices use 5-inch disks that can (depending on the drive) hold anywhere from 44MB to more than 200MB worth of data. You probably won't find a service bureau that does not support this type of removable medium. Many vendors make Syquest drives; you can find these drives in many computer outlets. Drive: $200 to $400, disks: $29 to $90.

- *Iomega Bernoulli.* The Bernoulli drive also uses 5-inch disks and is widely supported by service bureaus, although not as widely as the Syquest. These drives can hold about 50MB to more than 200MB worth of data. Only Iomega makes Bernoulli drives. You can get a list of distributors from the company's WWW site at http://www.iomega.com. Drive: $400, disks: $29 to $100.

- *Iomega Zip.* A relatively new drive, the Zip drive uses small, inexpensive, 3-inch, 25MB and 100MB disks and is very fast — about the same speed as the average hard disk. These disks are not in wide use yet, but they are catching on. Only Iomega makes these drives. Drive: $200, disks: $14 and $19.

- *Syquest EZ135.* A relatively new drive, the EZ drive uses small, inexpensive, 3-inch, 135MB disks and is very fast — about the same speed as the average hard disk. These disks are not in wide use yet, but they are catching on. Only Syquest makes these drives. You can get vendor information from the Syquest WWW page at http://www.syquest.com. Drive: $300, disks: $35.

- *Iomega Jaz* and *Syquest SyJet.* These drives are new. Both drives hold 1GB or more worth of data per disk. This new technology is likely to catch on fast. Drive: $500, disks: less than $100.

Another benefit of using a removable medium is the fact that you can use it to back up and archive data. If you choose a removable medium, first decide what service bureau you want to see; then call and ask what devices the service bureau uses.

Keep in mind that Syquest and Bernoulli drives are only backward-compatible. In other words, a 150MB drive can read and write disks that have lower capacities but not disks that have higher capacities. When you ask your service bureau about drives, also ask about the size of the drives. Otherwise, you could find yourself buying special disks just to work with the service bureau.

How to Prepare a Presentation for Printing at the Service Bureau

If you prepare a file to transport or transmit electronically to a service bureau, the way in which you prepare the file depends on a few variables. Keep these issues in mind when you decide how to prepare your file:

- Find out whether your service bureau supports Freelance Graphics 96. If not, you may want to consider using another service bureau or printing to a print file, as discussed in the section "What to do if your service bureau doesn't have Freelance Graphics 96," later in this chapter.

- Determine whether you will be transporting the file physically or sending it electronically.

- Decide on resolution and delivery options. The lower the resolution and slower the turnaround time, the cheaper is the print job.

What to do if your service bureau has Freelance Graphics 96

If your service bureau supports Freelance Graphics 96 and if the presentation is small enough to fit on a 1.44MB floppy disk, all you need to do is take or send the presentation file to the service bureau. If the file does not fit on a floppy disk and you don't have a removable storage medium (or plan to transmit the file electronically), you should consider compressing the file.

TIP

File compression on a PC (as opposed to a Macintosh) typically is handled by a shareware utility called PKZIP. You can download PKZIP from CompuServe, America Online, or the Internet. Simply use the keyword *PKZIP;* several sources come up on each service. PKZIP is a DOS utility, so you also may want to consider downloading WinZIP, a Windows utility that works in conjunction with PKZIP to compress and decompress files. Figure 12-1 shows a file compressed to 64 percent of its original size. Any service bureau that supports Windows machines will have PKZIP.

Sometimes — especially when your presentations contain many bitmap graphics — your files may be too large even when you use PKZIP. In such cases, if you have a fast modem (14.4 or 28.8 Kbps), you can transmit the files. Any files that are larger than about 2MB, however, can take an hour or more to transmit. Some service bureaus do not want you to tie up their phone lines that long, and you may not either, especially if the call is long-distance.

Figure 12-1: Use WinZIP to compress files too large to transmit comfortably or to fit on a floppy disk.

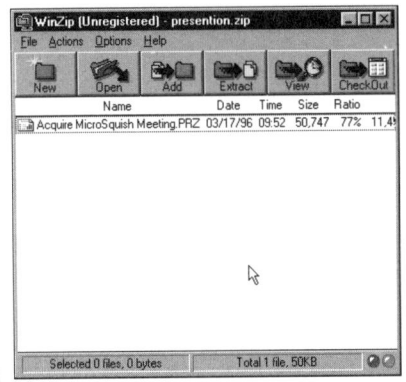

Unless you break down and buy a removable drive, your only alternative is to break the presentation into pieces small enough to fit on floppy disks and then either ship or hand-deliver the disks to the service bureau. To break the presentation into small chunks of slides, choose Edit⇨Cut or Edit⇨Clear to delete a slide from the file and then save the slide under a new name.

Most people don't use many bitmaps in their presentations, and you may not either. Presentation files that do not contain bitmaps usually can contain many slides — 100 or more — and still fit on a floppy disk. If you compress the presentation file, you can get a very large presentation on one disk.

What to do if your service bureau doesn't have Freelance Graphics 96

If your service bureau does not have Freelance Graphics 96, it can still output your slides if you supply a print file. A *print file* is a computer file that contains all the data required to print your slides. The service bureau simply copies the file to its slide recorder.

Follow this procedure to print to a file:

1. **Call the service bureau and ask which slide recorder it uses.**
2. **Use the Windows 95 printer-installation wizard to install the driver for the service bureau's slide recorder.**

Not all slide-recorder drivers ship with Windows 95. If you don't have the appropriate driver, the service bureau can provide it or tell you which alternative to install from the Windows installation disks. Most service bureaus have electronic bulletin boards from which you can download drivers, compression utilities, and other supporting files. Work closely with your service bureau to set up a print-to-file printer.

Chapter 12: Preparing and Printing 35mm Slides

Installing a printer driver in Windows 95 is easy. To do so, choose Start➪Settings➪Printers and then double-click the Add New Printer icon. The Add Printer Wizard window appears, as shown in Figure 12-2. From this point, just follow the prompts. (If you are installing the driver from a third-party source instead of from the Windows installation disks, you should click Have Disk rather than look for the printer in the Add New Printer dialog-box lists.)

Figure 12-2: Use the Windows 95 Add New Printer wizard to add the service bureau's slide recorder to your list of installed printers.

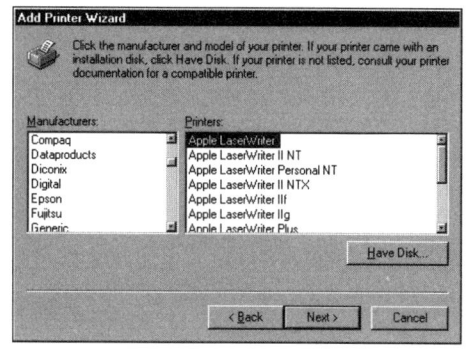

3. **After the printer driver is installed, click Start➪Settings➪Control Panels➪Printers to display the Printers control panel and click the slide-recorder icon to select it.**

4. **Choose File➪Properties➪Details.**

   The Properties dialog box shown in Figure 12-3 appears.

5. **In the Print to the Following Port section, select FILE: (Creates a File on Disk).**

6. **Click OK.**

7. **In Freelance Graphics, choose File➪Print.**

   The Print dialog box appears.

8. **In the Where section, make sure that FILE: is the specified port for your printer.**

9. **Click Print.**

   The Print to File dialog box appears.

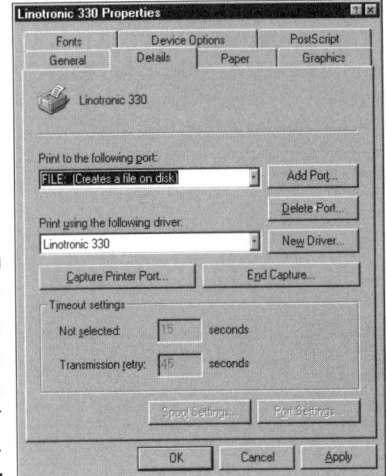

Figure 12-3: Use this dialog box to configure a new printer port.

10. In the File Name box, type the name of the file.
11. In the Save File As Type drop-down list, select the file type that you want to use (Printer files).
12. To specify the path, select the directory in which you want to save the file.
13. Click OK to print to the file and return to Freelance Graphics.

> Print files almost always are large, so you should count on compressing them with PKZIP. Also, if your presentation contains several slides, you should consider printing it in increments of five to ten slides. That way, you wind up with several small files that you can compress in the same archive for transmission or for copying to separate disks. If you print to one large file and the file doesn't print correctly at the service bureau, none of your slides may print, so you must print the file again.

How to Print Your Slides In-House

Providing that the slide recorder is hooked up and installed properly, you don't really have to do much to print in-house. Simply follow these steps:

1. Choose File➪Print.

    The Print dialog box appears, as shown in Figure 12-4. This dialog box enables you to specify what to print, the range of pages to print, and so on.

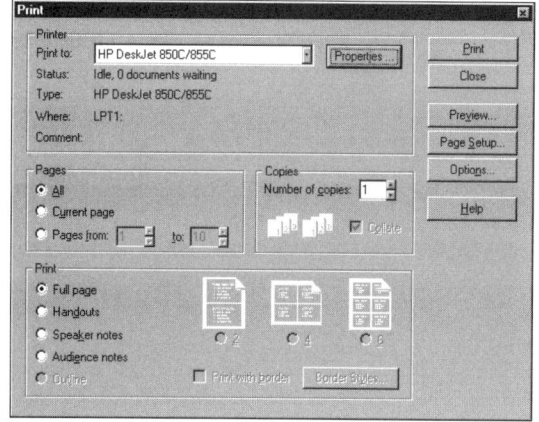

Figure 12-4: Use this dialog box to print your slides.

2. Select the slide recorder in the P<u>r</u>int To drop-down list.
3. In the Print section, make sure that Full page is selected.
4. Select the page range: <u>A</u>ll, C<u>u</u>rrent Page, or Pages <u>f</u>rom.
5. If your slide recorder supports multiple resolutions, click Propert<u>i</u>es and select the desired resolution; then click OK to return to the Print dialog box.
6. Click <u>P</u>rint.

TIP

You can get a preview of the slide in your presentation by clicking the Preview button in the Print dialog box.

Chapter 13
Working with Overhead Transparencies

In This Chapter
- Why overhead transparencies?
- Color or black-and-white transparencies
- How to print transparencies

*T*he old standbys, overhead transparencies, are the fastest and least expensive output option (next to screen shows, of course). You can zip off transparencies on the office laser or inkjet printer in a few minutes and be on your way.

This chapter discusses the advantages of using overhead transparencies and explains how and where to print them for the best results.

Why Overhead Transparencies?

With all the high-tech slides, electronic screen shows, and multimedia extravaganzas out there today, you may think that low-tech overhead transparencies are mediocre and undesirable. Why, then, do so many people use them?

Here are some reasons why:

- Transparencies are inexpensive to produce on a desktop laser printer or inkjet printer.
- The equipment used to display them — an overhead projector and screen — is inexpensive. In addition, most organizations already possess a projector and screen.
- Printing them is fast and easy; you don't need to wait for a service bureau to print and deliver them. (An exception, of course, is having high-resolution viewgraphs printed at a service bureau.)

- Making changes and updating individual pages or entire sections are fast and easy. You don't need to send the changes out for printing.
- You can draw on your graphics during a presentation to illuminate certain points.
- Transparencies are easy to transport.

Some disadvantages of overheads are as follows:

- Changing transparencies during a presentation is cumbersome. You must remove and replace each transparency manually, which distracts both you and your audience.

  You can alleviate this impediment partially by using a helper to change the transparencies. Make sure, however, that you practice your delivery with the helper, so that he or she knows when to swap the transparencies; otherwise, you're just as distracted because you must instruct your assistant.

- Your design choices are severely limited. Because most overhead transparencies are printed on inkjet or black-and-white laser printers, you can't incorporate a great deal of color, fancy gradients from one color to another, or full-color photographs.

  You can improve your design choices by printing the transparencies on a thermal-wax or dye-sublimation printer, which increases quality. Another option is using high-resolution viewgraphs, which require special equipment similar to slide recorders. If you don't have one of these devices, you must take your presentation to a service bureau, which increases the cost of your transparencies dramatically. Thermal-wax transparencies cost about as much as 35mm slides (between $5 and $10). Dye-sublimation transparencies can cost as much as $25 to $40 each. Viewgraphs typically run between $10 and $20 each.

- Your audience size is limited. No matter what kind of printer you use for your transparencies, you can magnify them only so much without serious degradation of quality.

  How much you can magnify a transparency depends largely on what the slide contains and the resolution of the printing device. But if your audience is larger than, say, 500 people, you should consider another medium. Even if the image doesn't degrade, you cannot get a big enough image for people to see from the back of a large room.

- Except in small, intimate settings, transparencies are an unimpressive, almost goofy format, especially when you have so many other options.

- Transparencies are not as durable and as long-lasting as slides and electronic presentations; they can be scratched easily, and their colors fade quickly. An exception is viewgraphs printed at a service bureau, which don't fade too badly but are easily scratched and bent.

Color or Black-and-White Transparencies

Color is, of course, more dynamic and impressive than black and white. We suggest that you use it whenever you can. If you don't have a color printer, though, the only way to get color is to send your presentation out to a service bureau, which can be expensive. Most service bureaus don't output transparencies on inexpensive inkjet printers; instead, they use thermal-wax, dye-sublimation, and viewgraph transparency recorders.

The first two devices usually are 300-dpi printers that are capable of producing fairly good color. The relatively low resolution of these devices makes them good for transparencies aimed at small audiences; these transparencies aren't magnified much if they're projected on a screen. Viewgraphs are printed on transparency machines that work similarly to slide recorders. These devices are capable of high resolution and high quality.

The question is not really whether to use color, but how to use it. If you are printing on a low-resolution device — an inkjet, thermal-wax, or dye-sublimation printer — you should use color wisely, which means that you should not use gradients and dark backgrounds. Your transparencies project better if you use solid colors and light (or even clear) backgrounds.

The problem with using gradients on low-resolution devices is that you get a phenomenon known as *banding*. Instead of the desired effect — one color slowly blending into another — you get stripes of the various shades between the two colors. The problem with dark backgrounds is that they tend to distort the light that comes through the transparency, sometimes giving you colors that are dramatically different from the ones you expected.

> **TIP** If you design your presentation around a fancy colored background, you can change the background easily by applying a new SmartMaster look to the presentation; simply choose Presentation ➪ Different SmartMaster Look. Alternatively, you can tell Freelance Graphics not to print the background (or to print gradients as solids) by choosing certain options in the Option dialog box, as shown in Figure 13-1. To open Options, choose Print ➪ Options.

High-resolution viewgraphs are a different story; you can get pretty fancy with your gradients and fills. Because of the limitations of overhead projectors, however, you still should shy away from dark backgrounds and from light text and graphics.

> **TIP** Although we're not really subscribers to Murphy's Law, we must point out that you never know when things may go wrong, especially if you're working with technology. You never know when you may show up at a presentation site and find that the slide projector doesn't work or that your notebook computer is incompatible with the site's electronic screen-show system. Be safe — always carry a set of black-and-white transparencies of your presentation. Most places have overhead projectors.

Figure 13-1:
Use these options to print your transparencies without backgrounds.

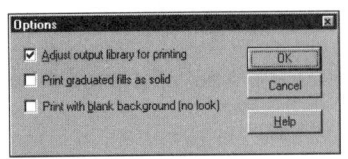

Another relatively good color solution is to use one of the high-end inkjet printers from Hewlett-Packard, Cannon, and a few other companies. These printers are capable of producing good color and high-quality, low-resolution output, especially if you use transparency film that is designed specifically for inkjet printers. Also, make sure that you use the transparency setting in the printer's Properties dialog box, as shown in Figure 13-2. To open Properties, choose Print⇨Properties.

Figure 13-2:
To get great results on transparencies with an inkjet printer, use film designed for inkjet printers and select Transparency as the paper type in the printer's Properties dialog box.

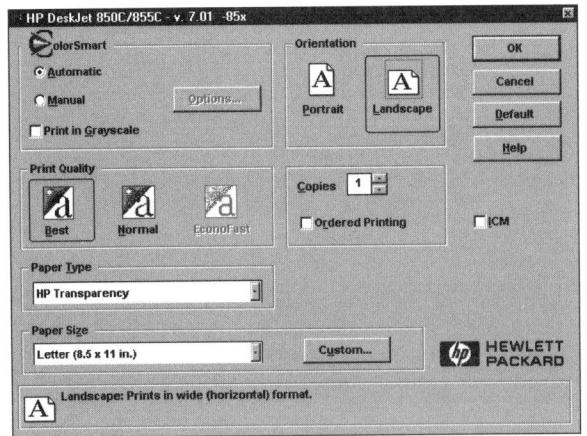

If you send your presentation to a service bureau for output, you should know several things about preparing and transporting or transmitting the file. The preceding chapter contains valuable information about working with service bureaus.

Chapter 13: Working with Overhead Transparencies **205**

How to Print Your Transparencies

Printing transparencies on a desktop laser or inkjet printer is not difficult; the process is pretty much like printing any other Windows document. The only real difference is that you should compensate for the printer's inherent limitations, which Freelance Graphics enables you to do during the printing process.

To print your transparencies, follow these steps:

1. **Choose File**⇨**Print.**

    The Print dialog box appears, as shown in Figure 13-3. This dialog box enables you to specify what to print, the range of pages to print, and so on.

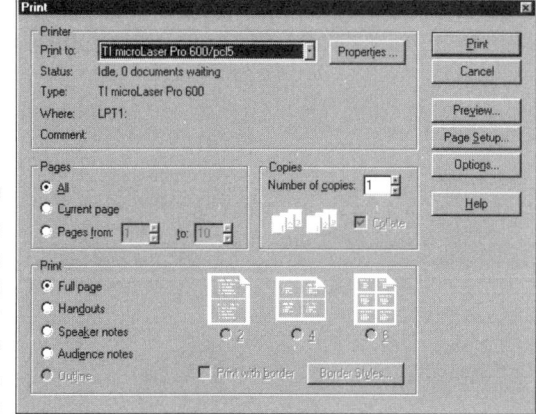

Figure 13-3:
Use this dialog box to print your transparencies.

2. Select the desired printer from the P<u>r</u>int to drop-down list.
3. In the Print section, make sure that Full page is selected.
4. Select the page range: <u>A</u>ll, C<u>u</u>rrent page, or Pages <u>f</u>rom.
5. If your printer supports multiple paper types — plain, premium inkjet, transparencies, and so on — click Propert<u>i</u>es; select the desired paper and other settings, such as print quality and resolution; and then click OK to return to the Print dialog box.
6. If you are printing to a black-and-white printer or if your pages contain dark or fancy backgrounds that don't print well on your transparencies, click the Optio<u>n</u>s button to display the Options dialog box and then choose either Print graduated fills as solid or Print with <u>b</u>lank background (no look) (see Figure 13-4).
7. Click <u>P</u>rint to print your transparencies.

Figure 13-4:
Use one of these options to control how your backgrounds print.

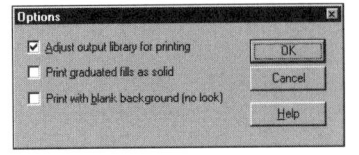

You can see a preview of the slide in your presentation before printing by clicking the Preview button in the Print dialog box. A screen like that shown in Figure 13-5 appears, enabling you to print the page, go to the next page, or return to the Print dialog box.

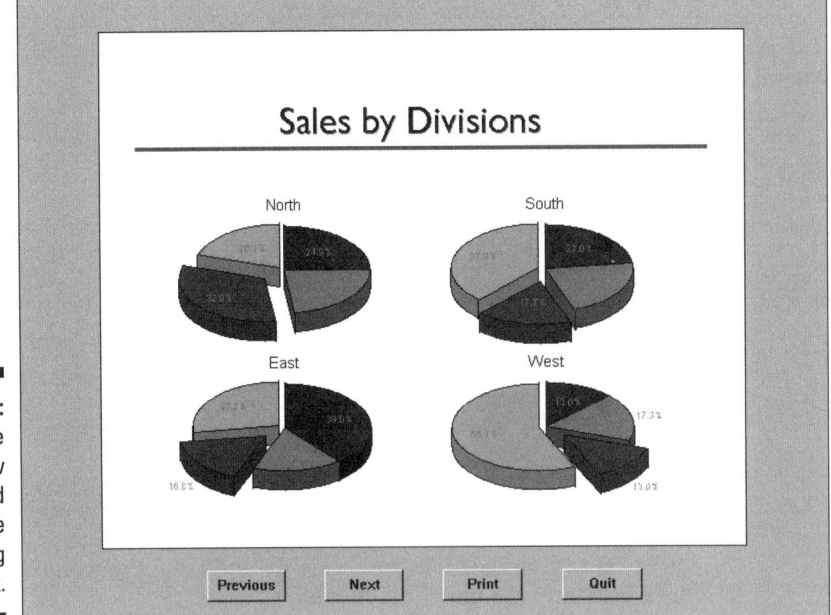

Figure 13-5:
An example of a preview displayed from the Print dialog box.

Chapter 14
Creating and Delivering Electronic Presentations

* *

In This Chapter
- Working with transition effects and builds
- Incorporating other applications and OLE2
- Incorporating sound, animation, and video
- Delivering your presentation

* *

*T*he change has been slow in coming, but many businesses are moving away from traditional hard-copy, slide-and-overhead presentations and toward more impressive (and sometimes more economical) electronic screen shows.

Imagine razzle-dazzling your audience with fancy fades, wipes, sounds, animated demonstrations, and video testimonials. All these features are elements at your disposal in Freelance Graphics. In this chapter, we show you how to assemble an electronic screen show — you discover how to incorporate builds and transitions, embed sound and motion, and deliver your presentation in-house and on the road.

Get ready. You're entering the exciting world of multimedia. After you get hooked, there's no return.

Using Builds and Transitions

One of the benefits of making presentations from a computer is that your slides are dynamic. You're not stuck with a passive image that hangs silently in front of your audience. Instead, your slides become active participants in your delivery and make your presentation more impressive, more interesting, and more memorable.

One important way to improve the content of your presentations is by using automatic builds and transitions. *Builds* add content to your slides by displaying one element at a time, helping you to build, one point at a time, the message conveyed on a slide. *Transitions* are different from builds in that, instead of having to add elements to a slide one at a time, you replace the entire slide with a new slide. In other words, you make a transition from one slide to another.

Freelance Graphics supports many kinds of builds and transitions, including the capability to build a slide by adding one element at a time. For example, you can have a page title slide in from the left and then have bullet points or graphics slide in, one at a time, from different directions. Or you can have them fade or wipe. The possibilities are nearly limitless.

Many people use transitions haphazardly. They clutter up their presentations with meaningless, distracting transitions rather than use meaningful content. When you incorporate builds and transitions, think about why you're using the transition.

When you're using builds, you can bring in elements in a manner that helps illuminate your points. On a two-chart slide, for example, display the first chart and talk about it and what it means. Then display the comparison chart — perhaps slide it in from the right or have it fade in beside the first chart.

One popular transition is to have new data fade in or wipe away old data. For example, you can display a chart that shows last year's sales numbers and then have this year's (much better) numbers wipe away the old (not-so-good) numbers.

The point is that you shouldn't use transitions just because they are there. Instead, use your imagination to incorporate them in a manner that enhances your message.

Using fancy transitions between slides

Freelance Graphics provides about 30 different transitions between slides — everything from wipes and fades to curtains that close on one slide and open on another. You control slide transitions by using Page Properties, which is an option on the Page menu. (Remember that the Page menu is available in Current Page view or Page Sorter view if no page elements are selected.)

You can also use the Set Up Screen Show command on the Presentation menu to assign the same effect to all slides and use the Screen Show Effects command on the Page menu to access the Screen Show Effects Properties dialog box.

After this Properties dialog box appears, follow these steps:

1. **Click the Screen Show Effects tab (the one with the movie projector, as shown in Figure 14-1).**

Figure 14-1: Click the little movie projector to assign transitions to pages.

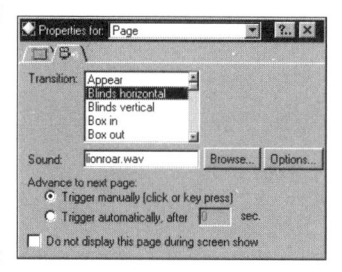

2. From the Transition list, choose the transition effect you want to use.

3. Use the Advance to next page option to determine whether the next slide appears after you click the mouse button or automatically after a specified number of seconds. You can also elect to exclude the slide from the screen show by checking the box labeled Do not display this page during screen show.

4. Use the Sound option to assign a sound to the transition.

    For a description of sound options, see the sidebar "Assigning sounds to transitions," in this chapter.

If you want to assign a transition to more than one slide or to several different slides at a time, switch to Page Sorter view, as shown in Figure 14-2. Every time you choose a new slide, the Properties dialog box changes to work with that slide. You can also choose multiple slides and assign transitions to all of them at the same time.

Creating bullet builds

A useful build effect is to have your bullets appear on a slide one at a time. From the Properties dialog box (display it either by choosing Bullet Build from the Page menu or by selecting the bullet block you want to assign a build to), choose the Page Properties dialog box.

This action opens the Screen Show Effects dialog box, as shown in Figure 14-3. The following list explains the sections in the Screen Show Effects dialog box:

- **Timing:** Defines the way bullets behave on a slide. You can choose whether the block of bullets appears with the slide or after the slide appears. If you choose the second option, you can also define whether the text appears after a mouse click or after a designated number of seconds. When you choose the Display page first, then display text option, the next section of the dialog box (Effect when text block is added) becomes available.

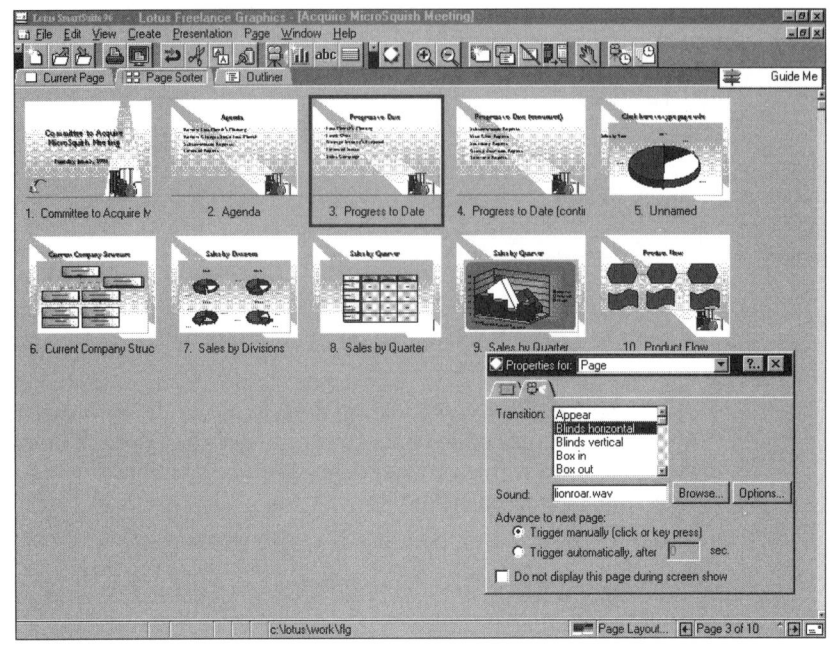

Figure 14-2: Switch to Page Sorter view to assign transitions to several slides.

Figure 14-3: Use the Properties dialog box to set up bullet builds.

- **Effect when text block is added:** Defines the way bullets appear on a slide: all at once or one at a time. If you choose one at a time, the Dim previous bullets option becomes available. If this option is active, as shown in Figure 14-4, previous points are dimmed after a new bullet appears. In this section, you can also assign a transition effect and a sound to the bullets.
- **Action when text block is clicked:** Determines what Freelance Graphics does when the presenter or viewer clicks the bullet block:

Chapter 14: Creating and Delivering Electronic Presentations *211*

> No action
>
> Jump (jumps to another slide in the current presentation)
>
> Run application (opens another Windows application)
>
> Play sound
>
> Play movie
>
> Run show (runs another Freelance Graphics presentation as a screen show)

Figure 14-4: A set of bullet builds. When a new point appears, the others are dimmed.

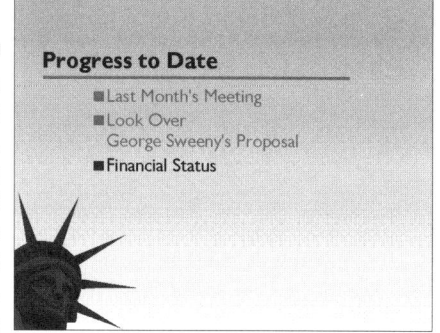

> ### Assigning sounds to transitions
>
> In addition to using fancy visual transitions, you can tell Freelance Graphics to play sounds when your new slides, bullet points, or other elements appear in a presentation. You can have the sound play repeatedly while the slide is displayed, or you can set several other options.
>
> You assign sounds to transitions from the Screen Show Effect tab of the Properties dialog box. You assign the sound by either typing the name of the file in the Sound field or clicking the Browse button to find the sound.
>
> Click the Options button to set the sound options. From the dialog box that appears, you can determine how the sound is played.
>
> - Start playing: Plays the sound as the transition occurs (During transition) or after the transition finishes (After transition). The second option makes the Play sound section of the dialog box available.
>
> - Play sound: Enables you to set the sound to play once or to play repeatedly until a new slide is displayed.
>
> - Sequencing: Enables you to tell Freelance Graphics to finish playing the sound before another automatic event occurs, such as displaying another slide or bullet point.

Building slide elements

In addition to building bullet slides, you can also build individual slide elements, such as titles, charts, and clip art. Freelance Graphics treats individual elements as transitional objects.

To set up builds for objects, follow these steps:

1. **Choose (Text, Chart, and so on)⇨Properties to open the Properties dialog box.**
2. **Click the Screen Show Effects tab (the movie projector).**
3. **Click the option labeled Display page first, then display object, and then define how the objects appear — by mouse click or after a designated time.**
4. **Use the rest of the Screen Show Effects tab to define how the object appears, such as with transitions and sound.**
5. **Click the object you want to appear next, and follow steps 1 through 4 to define how it appears.**
6. **Click Sequence.**

    When you see the Screen Show Sequence Overview dialog box, as shown in Figure 14-5, you can get an overview of how each object appears, including the transition, sound, and action. Use this dialog box to change the order in which objects appear by dragging the object names in the

Sequence list to their new positions. (If you don't change the sequence, Freelance Graphics displays them in the order in which they were created. Titles and "Click here" placeholders appear first.)

TIP: On slides that contain several objects, remembering what they are by their default names may be difficult. (Object 1 and Object 2 aren't meaningful names.) Use the Object name field to rename the objects with more meaningful names, such as Title and Chart.

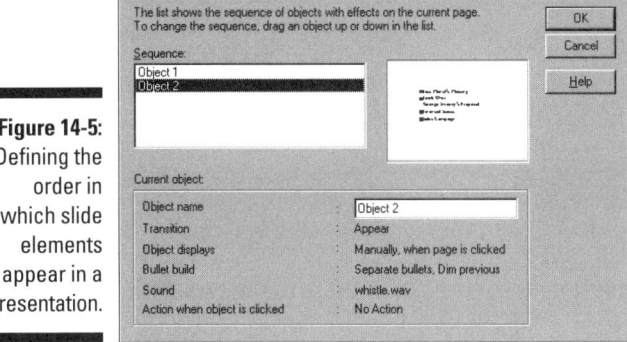

Figure 14-5: Defining the order in which slide elements appear in a presentation.

Assigning transitions to charts, tables, and diagrams

You can also assign transitions to your graphic elements, such as charts and diagrams. You can have a chart wipe or fade onto a slide, for example. If you read the first part of this chapter, you probably can figure out how to apply transition effects to these elements; but just in case, here's a description of the procedure:

1. **In Current Page view, choose the element you want to set up a transition for.**
2. **Choose (Chart, Table, and so on)➪Properties from the menu bar.**
3. **Click the Screen Show Effects (movie projector) tab.**
4. **Choose the transition options you want, as described in the preceding sections of this chapter.**

Launching Other Applications and Using OLE2

Freelance Graphics enables you to integrate your presentations with other Windows applications in two ways: Launch the application by clicking a hot object or use OLE2. The first method enables you to go to the other application and display an object in its native environment. The second method enables you to edit the element in place, in the Freelance Graphics presentation.

Launching another application from an electronic screen show

You make objects (text, charts, diagrams, drawings, clip art, and so on) *hot* (create links) in Freelance Graphics screen shows by using the Screen Show Effects tab in the Properties dialog box. To do so, follow these steps:

1. **Choose the element on the slide you want to make hot.**
2. **Choose (Chart, Text, and so on)➪Properties from the menu bar.**
3. **Click the Screen Show Effects tab.**
4. **In the section Action when object is clicked, choose Run application.**

    This step opens the Launch Application dialog box, as shown in Figure 14-6. Use this dialog box to find the application you want to run.

5. **Use the Browse button to find the application you want to run, or type the path and filename in the text box.**
6. **Click OK.**

While you run the screen show, you can click the object during the show to open the application. Then find the file you want to open and go to work. After you finish, you can close the application or leave it open.

Figure 14-6: Finding the application you want to run during the screen show.

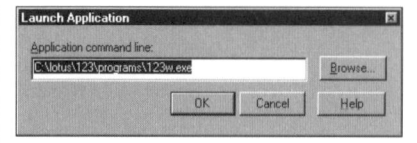

Chapter 14: Creating and Delivering Electronic Presentations *215*

TIP

Another way to launch an application from a Freelance Graphics presentation is by using the Paste Special command (as described in the section "Creating a hot link with Paste Special," later in this chapter). You can also use this method to launch other Freelance Graphics screen shows or to jump to various slides in the current presentation. Simply choose the appropriate option from the Action when object is clicked section.

Using OLE2 during screen shows

In some presentation environments, you may need to edit data that's linked to embedded charts and diagrams that originate in other applications. Suppose that, during a presentation, an audience member asks you how the numbers on a graph would appear if you change an assumption, such as fewer or greater sales within a given period. If the chart were created somewhere else — in Excel, for example — you would need to use Excel to change the chart.

In these cases, you can display a modified chart by using OLE2 to edit the data the chart is linked to in your spreadsheet. First you need to examine how to embed an OLE object, and then you need look at how to use OLE2 to edit the object.

TECHNICAL STUFF

Windows has always enabled users to use the Cut and Paste commands with the Clipboard to move graphics from one Windows application to another. OLE and OLE2 take this concept several steps farther, however. You not only can copy and paste graphics, text, and other objects between applications, but you also can create hot links between the originating application, or OLE *server,* and the receiving application, or OLE *client.*

The advantage of *object linking* is that you automatically update presentations, no matter how many applications or documents they're linked to. If you link an Excel chart to a Freelance Graphics presentation, the linked chart in the Freelance Graphics presentation is automatically updated every time you change the chart in Excel — without your having to import the object again.

Object embedding enables you to temporarily launch a second application from within a Windows program and use it to create a new object. You typically do this by using the client application's Object command. (In Freelance Graphics, Object is on the Create menu.) When you finish creating the object, the second application, the server, pastes it into the original, or client, application — in this case, Freelance Graphics. You can then edit the object at any time by simply double-clicking it in Freelance Graphics. The server application (in this case, a spreadsheet) then opens to enable you to edit the embedded object. (You embed the object either as a document or as an icon that opens the server application.)

After you close the server application, the object is updated. For linking and embedding to work, both applications must be OLE-aware. Nowadays most Windows applications support OLE2. Freelance Graphics does, as do Lotus 1-2-3 and Excel.

Creating a hot link with Paste Special

To create a link to a spreadsheet chart, you use the Paste Special command rather than Paste, 1-2-3 Named Chart, or Object. (You can create links to a wide range of objects, including text, drawings, charts, and multimedia applications.) The originating (client) application must support OLE2. Also, the file containing the chart must have been saved — it cannot be an "untitled" file. The source, or server, application must be kept open as you follow these steps.

Due to the tight integration between 1-2-3 and Freelance Graphics, when you paste a chart from 1-2-3 into Freelance Graphics, the chart becomes a Freelance Graphics chart. You don't have to use 1-2-3 to edit the data. Instead, you edit data in the Freelance Graphics Edit Data module the same way you edit any other Freelance Graphics chart. To create a link by using Paste Special, follow these steps:

1. **Start the spreadsheet application and open the file that contains the chart you want.**
2. **Copy the chart to which you want to link by choosing Edit➪Copy from the menu bar.**
3. **Open the Freelance Graphics presentation in Current Page view on the page where you want to paste the chart.**
4. **Choose Edit➪Copy➪Paste Special.**

    After the Paste Special dialog box appears, as shown in Figure 14-7, you determine how the object is to be pasted into your presentation.

Figure 14-7: Use Paste Special to import a chart or another type of document into a presentation with a link that updates the object every time it changes in the source application.

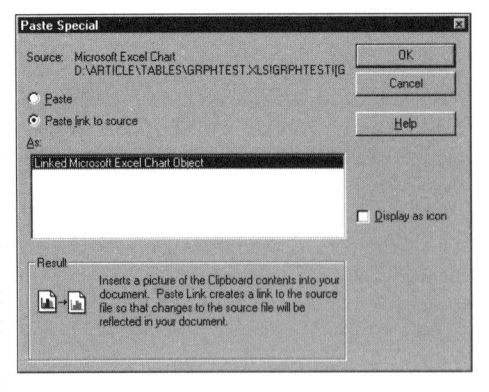

5. Choose Paste **l**ink to source.

6. Choose, in the **A**s box, how you want to import the data (as an object, an icon, and so on).

7. Click OK.

If you choose Display as icon in the Paste Special dialog box, Freelance Graphics displays an icon rather than the object on the page, as shown in Figure 14-8. You can then use the icon as a link to the client application only if necessary. In other words, if no one from your audience asks a question that requires you to open the other application, you can save delivery time by skipping that portion of your presentation.

When should you use links?

A *link* is a conduit through which data stored in a server file is displayed in a client file. When you update linked data in a client file, the latest data from the server file is displayed.

You should use links in these situations:

- When you want to share data between Windows applications
- When you expect the chart data to change
- When you need to update the chart when the original data changes

Suppose that you use a chart from a 1-2-3 file in a Freelance Graphics presentation, and the chart changes weekly. You can create OLE links in the Freelance Graphics presentation to the chart in the 1-2-3 file. Then, whenever you open the Freelance Graphics presentation, it automatically displays the latest 1-2-3 chart.

You should *not* use links in these situations:

- When you use the chart only in Freelance Graphics
- When you do not expect the chart to change
- When you do not need (or want) to update the chart when the original changes

When should you use embedded charts?

You can create an embedded chart by using a spreadsheet application, for example, stored in a file that's created by using Freelance Graphics (sometimes called the *container* file). The embedded object can be either a document or an icon that opens the server application.

You should embed objects in these situations:

- When you use a chart in only one application
- When you expect to edit or update the data

If you make a Freelance Graphics presentation that contains a chart from an Excel document, for example, you can embed the Excel chart into the presentation. When you distribute it for review online, if your reviewers want information from the Excel document, they can simply double-click the Excel icon to open Excel and the file.

Figure 14-8: In this example, the presenter created an Excel chart that depicts the same data as in the table. If necessary, the presenter can click the icon in the upper-right corner to open Excel and the spreadsheet that contains the chart and data.

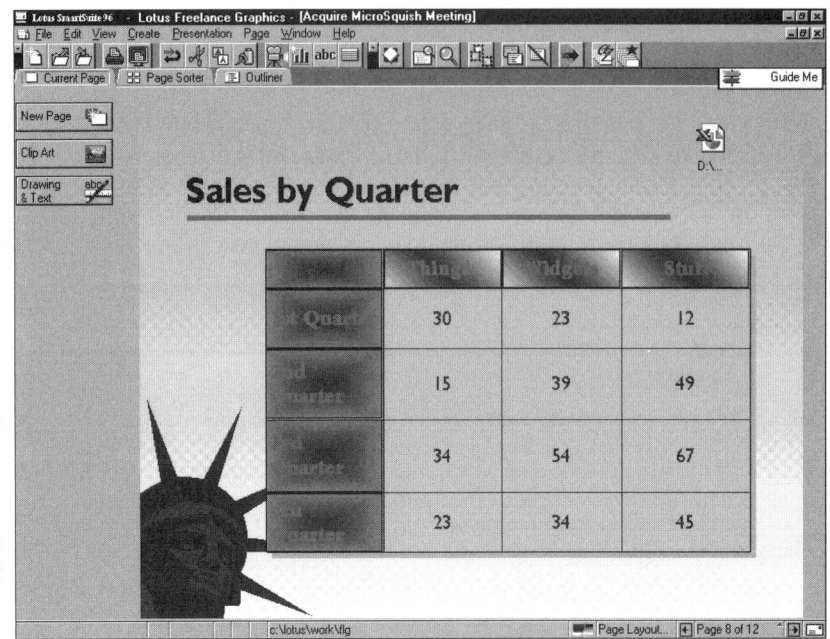

Editing an OLE2 object in Freelance Graphics

If you're using a Paste Special link, simply double-click the object (or icon, if you used the Display as icon option). This technique launches the client application and enables you to edit the object. Simple enough.

WARNING!

If you perform all this OLE magic, be mindful of your system resources. On any computer (even on a Pentium), opening several applications at a time can slow down the system — sometimes gruelingly so. Be sure to do a test run on the computer on which you intend to make your presentation. After you're finished with a supporting application, close it to free up memory.

TIP

A variation of this procedure is another OLE2 feature that enables you to edit the object directly in your Freelance Graphics presentation, as shown in Figure 14-9. To do so, choose Paste rather than Paste Special to bring the object to the page. Then, when you want to edit the object, double-click it. This step changes the Freelance Graphics menus and icons to those of the client application. To return to Freelance Graphics menus, deselect the object.

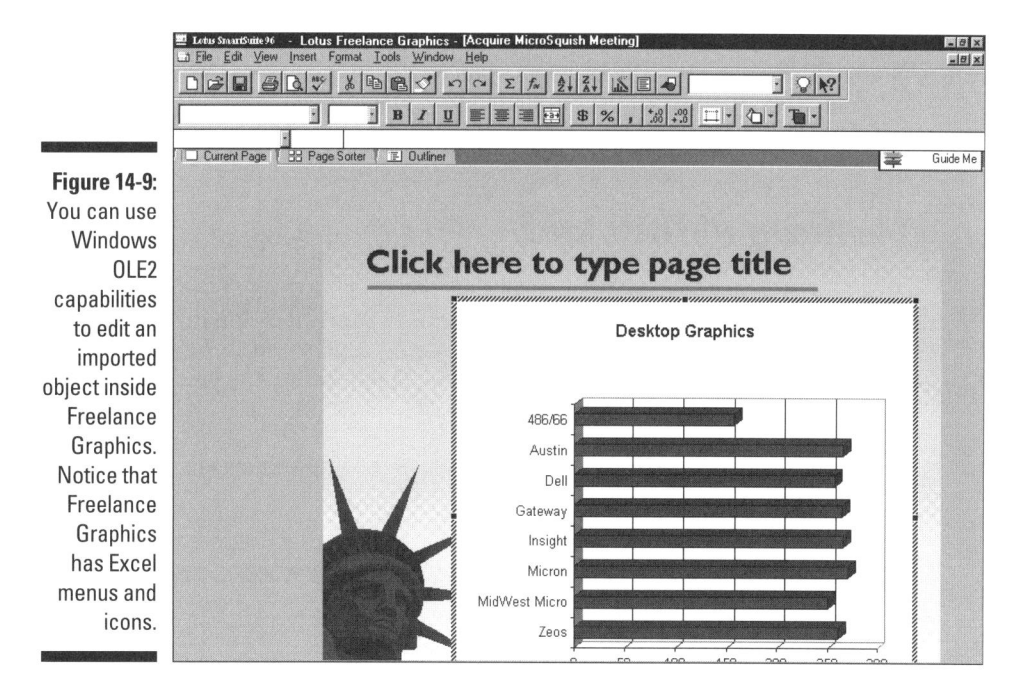

Figure 14-9:
You can use Windows OLE2 capabilities to edit an imported object inside Freelance Graphics. Notice that Freelance Graphics has Excel menus and icons.

Adding Sound and Movies

By adding movies and sound effects to a screen show, you turn it into a multimedia presentation. You can tell Freelance Graphics to play sounds or movies when a new slide appears, or you can assign them to objects on the page and run the sound when you click the object. You can also sequence sounds and movies so that they play one after the other.

> **NOTE:** Technically, there's a difference between video and animation. Video typically comes from analog sources, such as TVs, VCRs, laser discs, and camcorders; animation consists of computer graphics that move. Freelance Graphics calls them all movies. For the sake of this discussion, we don't argue.

Knowing which types of sounds and movies Freelance Graphics supports

Freelance Graphics comes with several wave (.WAV) sound files. You can also use your own wave files or MIDI clips (.MID). The program comes with a bunch of Gold Disk Add Impact Movies (.AIM), and you can play Gold Disk Add Impact or Animation Works (.AWM) movies of your own. The program supports all movie types that are supported by the Windows Media Control Interface (MCI), which includes the Windows AVI format.

Part IV: Printing and Rehearsing Your Presentation

> **NOTE:** In addition to the sound and movie formats supported directly by Freelance Graphics, you can also use the Object command on the Create menu to embed other formats, such as AutoDesk Animator (.FLI and .FLC) and other files. In these cases, the graphics run in a separate window.

Working with sound

To add sound to a presentation, you attach a sound file to an object on a page, as discussed in the sidebar "Assigning sounds to transitions," in this chapter. After you do so, you can control when the sound begins to play, how many times to play it, and whether it should finish playing before the presentation moves on to the next event.

Sounds are attached to objects by using the Screen Show Effects tab of the Properties dialog box, as shown in Figure 14-10.

Figure 14-10: From this dialog box, you assign sounds to objects on the current page.

Working with movies

You have a number of choices for how to make a movie begin playing. One way is to have the movie appear as an icon that you click during a screen show. Another is to have the movie begin playing after the slide appears. In the latter case, you can choose to have the movie play after you click the mouse or after a specified number of seconds.

Should I *embed* or *refer* to sound and movie files?

When you add a sound or a movie to a page, you have the choice of embedding the sound or movie or referring to the sound or movie. You define whether to embed or refer to a file from the Adding Sound to section or the Create Movie dialog boxes section, in the Store in presentation sections.

When you *embed* a movie, it becomes part of the presentation and increases the size of the presentation. You should embed movies and sound files if you want to create a presentation that's easily portable. For example, if you embed movies in your presentation and then send it to someone via the Mobile Screen Show Player (discussed in the next chapter) or TeamReview (discussed in Chapter 20), you can send the presentation complete with its movies. Unless you're on a network or have access to some sort of high-volume removable media (such as Syquest or Bernoulli), however, you can't embed many sound and movie files — they're very large.

If you want to keep the size of your presentation small, rather than embed sounds and movies, you can *refer* to movies and sound files, which essentially creates a link from the presentation to the movie or sound file. Then, rather than store a movie or sound file with the presentation, Freelance Graphics stores only the path and filename of the movie or sound file.

If you choose to link your files, deselect the Prepare for Mobile Screen Show Player option when you save your file the first time — or else Freelance Graphics converts the linked files to embedded files.

To change the look of the standard movie icon, you can attach a movie to an object or text the same way you attach a sound file or some other element. During a screen show, click the text or object and have the movie play. The Freelance Graphics Clip Art library has a selection of buttons, in fact, designed just for this purpose. Chapter 9 explains how to add clip art to pages.

Adding movies to slides

In addition to the capability to embed movies with OLE2, Freelance Graphics provides two ways to add movies to slides: by using the Add Movie command on the Create menu or by using the Screen Show Effects tab in the Properties dialog box.

To add a movie by using the Add Movie command, follow these steps:

1. **Choose Create⇨Add Movie from the menu bar.**

    This step opens the Add a Movie dialog box, as shown in Figure 14-11. Choose your movie and then determine whether to embed or create a link to the movie file. If you don't know which to choose, see the sidebar "Should I *embed* or *refer* to sound and movie files?" You can also see a preview of the movie by choosing the filename and clicking the Preview button.

Figure 14-11: Rocky Mountain high! Use the Add a Movie dialog box to find and open a movie file.

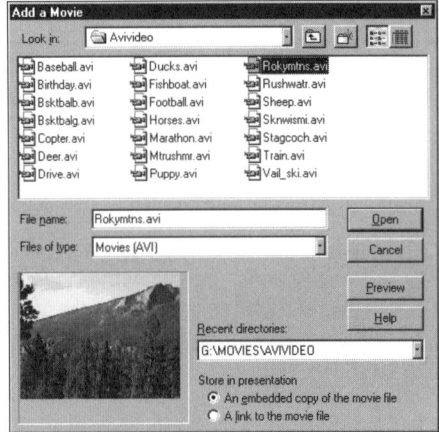

  2. **Find and choose the movie file.**
  3. **In the Store in presentation section, choose whether to embed or link the file.**
  4. **Click Open.**

     The movie is imported as an icon, as shown in Figure 14-12, and you can move it around or resize it. You can also control how and when the movie plays by choosing Movie⇨Movie Properties from the menu bar. From the Properties dialog box, as shown in Figure 14-13, you choose whether to play the movie by clicking an icon during the screen show or to play the movie after the slide appears. You can also click the Sequence button to determine when the movie plays in relation to other movies on the page or to sound files. This technique works only if you have more than one sound or movie on the page, of course. Movies initially are played in the order in which you add them to a page, but you can easily resequence them.

You assign movies to slide elements from the Screen Show Effects tab of the Properties dialog box, a process that's similar to launching an application or running another screen show. To assign a movie to a slide element so that it's played when you click the element, follow these steps:

  1. **Choose the object you want to assign the movie to.**
  2. **Choose (Text, Drawing, Chart, and so on)⇨Properties from the menu bar.**
  3. **Click the Screen Show Effects tab (the movie projector).**
  4. **Choose the option Display page first, then display object.**
  5. **In the box labeled Action when object is clicked, select Play movie.**

That's it. When you click the object during a screen show, the movie runs.

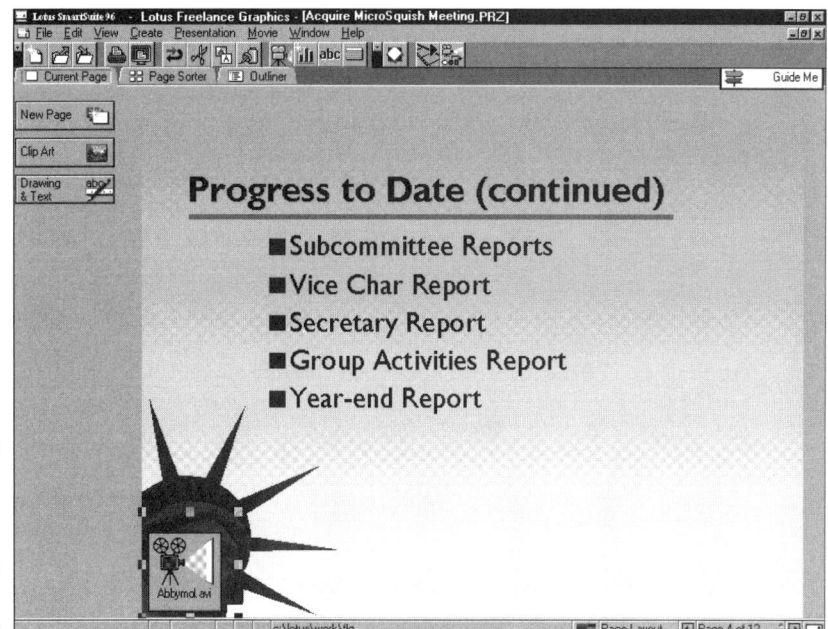

Chapter 14: Creating and Delivering Electronic Presentations

Figure 14-12: Movies are loaded on a page as icons.

Movie screen resolution and resizing

Not everyone uses the same monitor resolution. Fortunately, Freelance Graphics compensates by resizing movies according to the screen resolution on which a screen show is playing. In Gold Disk movies, for example, the bitmaps from which the movies are created are scaled, depending on the screen resolution at which you play them. Movies appear at the same size, relative to other objects on the page, when you play them in a screen resolution that differs from the one in which the presentation was created.

If you create a screen show with your monitor set to VGA (600 × 480) and show the screen show on a monitor set to 1024 × 786, movies (like other objects on the page) are enlarged to fit the higher resolution. The same is true for AVI movies: If you change screen resolutions and your presentation has AVI movies, the AVI movies are scaled along with everything else on the page.

When you add a movie to a page, the projector icon is displayed within a rectangle. The rectangle is the stage on which a movie plays. If a movie consists of an actor and a path — for example, a balloon (the actor) rises from bottom to top up the screen (the actor's path) — you can resize the rectangle to change the path.

Resizing the rectangle does not change the size of the actor. Instead, it alters the area in which the actor moves. AVI movies, on the other hand, scale the entire movie when you enlarge them. Some other MCI movie types, such as Apple QuickTime, do not scale at all. If you resize the rectangle, the movie continues to play in its original size.

Figure 14-13: You're in control: Choose when a movie plays.

> With the emergence of the Internet and cross-platform applications, many movie and animation file formats are available. You can either use some type of converter to turn the movie into an AVI format or, if you have the player applet for the movie format (QuickTime or MPEG, for example), you can embed the file as an object. After the object is embedded, you can assign transition effects (such as defining when to start the movie) the same way that you would with any other movie file supported by Freelance Graphics. The difference in this approach is that the movie is played in a separate window.

Delivering Your Presentation

Now that you have set up your screen show effects and added sounds and movies, it's time to put the finishing touches on your screen show and deliver it. Freelance Graphics provides a few tools (such as a control panel and the ability to draw on slides as you deliver your presentation) to make delivering the screen show easier. This section shows you how to set up your show and then deliver it.

Setting up your screen show

To add a control panel and drawing tool to your screen show, follow these steps:

1. **Choose Presentation⇨Set Up Screen Show.**

   This step opens the Set Up Screen Show dialog box. You can create a control panel and define a drawing tool for use during your presentation. You can also set a global screen show effect for the entire presentation. If you've gone to the trouble to set up transitions for specific slides, however, changes you make in this dialog box override these transitions.

2. **Click the Tools tab in the Set Up Screen Show dialog box.**
3. **In the Control panel box, check Display control panel.**
4. **In the Position drop-down box, choose where on-screen you want the control panel displayed.**
5. **Click OK to return to Current Page view.**

Chapter 14: Creating and Delivering Electronic Presentations 225

The control panel, shown in the upper-right corner of Figure 14-14, works like this:

- Click either the right or left arrow to advance forward or go backward one slide.
- Click the button with several pages on it (between the arrows) to open the Screen Show Pages dialog box. Then you can advance to any slide in the presentation or quit the screen show.
- Click the button with the black square on it to quit the screen show and return to the Freelance Graphics screen.

NOTE: The control panel buttons override any transition or automatic settings you've set up in the presentation.

To add a drawing tool to your delivery arsenal, follow these steps:

1. **Choose Presentation➪Set Up Screen Show.**
2. **In the Set Up Screen Show dialog box, click the Tools tab.**
3. **In the On-screen drawing area, select the Allow drawing on pages check box.**
4. **For Line color, choose the color you want for the lines.**
5. **For Line width, choose a line width.**
6. **Click OK to return to Current Page view.**

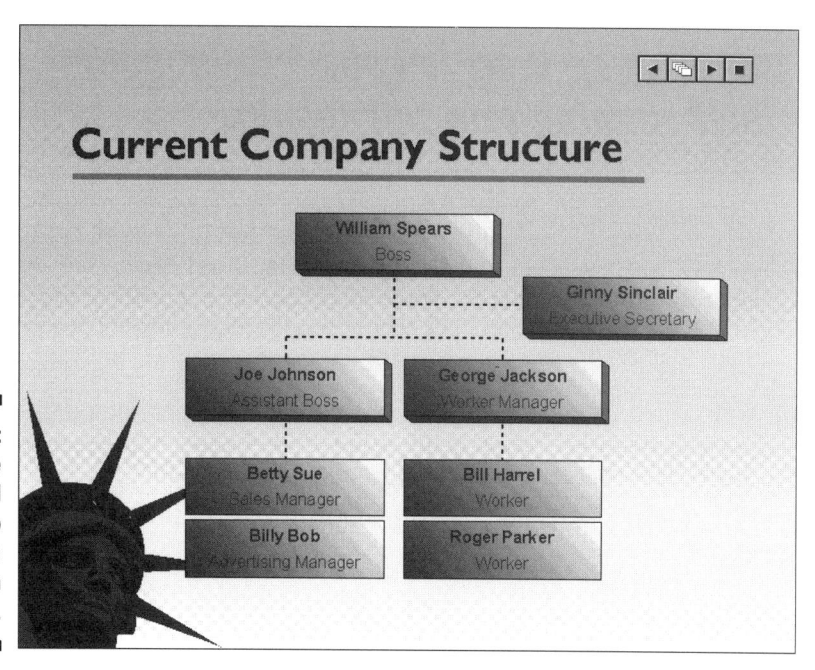

Figure 14-14: Use the control panel to navigate a screen show.

After you complete these steps, you can draw on your slides with your mouse during a screen show, as shown in Figure 14-15. Simply press and drag where you want to draw. To remove the lines, press the Alt key (all by itself).

Figure 14-15: Draw whatever you want on a slide during a screen show. (Pretend that you're John Madden during a football game!)

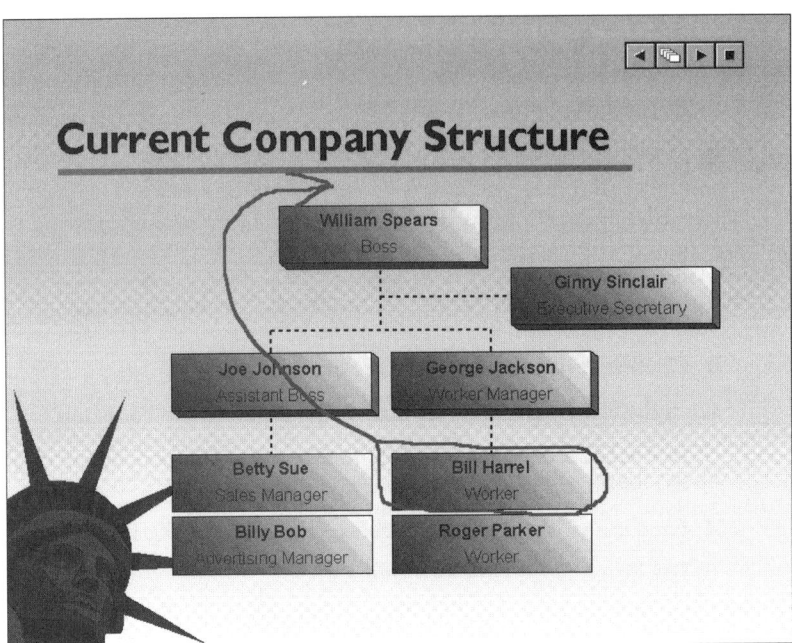

Setting up a screen show to be both self-running and self-looping

You use the Set Up Screen Show command on the Presentation menu to create a self-running screen show. *Self-running* means, of course, unattended. One slide appears and plays its multimedia events, and then the next slide appears, and so on. If you have a large number of fancy transitions, builds, movies, and sounds in your presentation, you've probably already defined the transitions from slide to slide. If you haven't, however, you can follow the next series of steps to make the show self-running.

When you use this method, you override any transitions you set up by using methods discussed earlier in this chapter. Sounds and movies are played, however, as long as you didn't assign them to objects that require clicking to execute the file.

1. **Begin with your presentation open; from Current Page view, choose Presentation⇨Set Up Screen Show from the menu bar.**

   This step displays the Set Up Screen Show dialog box, in which you can set the options for a self-running screen show and set up a screen show for an entire presentation or for all new slides. To make the screen show self-running, you want to set up the entire presentation. You can also set up a transition effect and a control panel to help navigate the show, as you see in a moment.

2. **On the Page Effects tab of the Set Up Screen Show dialog box, make sure that Apply to all existing pages is selected.**

   Any transition you set here affects all slides. Your builds and multimedia events still work, however, as long as you set the time between slides long enough to accommodate them.

3. **In the Transition list, choose Appear.**

4. **In the Display Next Page section, choose After _ Seconds.**

   This step tells Freelance Graphics to change from slide to slide automatically. The number you type in the field determines how many seconds elapse between each slide. Use a number that's large enough to enable audience members to see each slide but not so long that your screen show gets boring.

   You probably need about 30 seconds for each text slide and, depending on your graphics, longer for each chart and graph. If your charts and graphs take more than a minute of study to decipher, however, you should consider revising them. In the context of your presentation, when you're speaking to an audience and the audience is trying to read slides and listen to you at the same time, even a minute can be too long.

5. **Enter the number of seconds for each slide to be displayed.**

6. **To set up the *looping*, or repeating, action (to run the presentation repeatedly until you stop it), click the Options tab.**

7. **In the Run Options section, choose Run screen show in continuous loop.**

   That's it. If you set up a loop in the last two steps, you can press Shift+Esc to stop the presentation.

Delivering an electronic screen show

Here's the moment of truth — you're ready to begin your screen show. If you made it self-running and looping, all you do is sit back and watch the action. If you're delivering your presentation in front of an audience, however, you should read this section. It tells you how to navigate your presentation by using your mouse and keyboard.

Beginning a screen show

This part is easy. Click the Run Screen Show from Beginning (movie projector) SmartIcon or choose Presentation⇨Run Screen Show from the menu bar and then choose From Beginning from the submenu.

Navigating your screen show

If you have not set up automatic transitions between slides (and you have not included a control panel, as discussed earlier in this chapter), use these methods to navigate your screen show:

- **Advance one slide:** Press the left mouse button or PgDn on the keyboard.
- **Move back one slide:** Press the right mouse button or PgUp on the keyboard.
- **Jump to a slide out of sequence:** Press Shift+Esc and then, in the Screen Show Pages dialog box, double-click the slide you want in the list.
- **End a screen show:** Press Shift+Esc and then choose Quit Screen Show from the Screen Show Pages dialog box.

You can also run applications, launch movies, and perform other tasks, of course, depending on how you defined them when you set up your screen show.

Taking Your Presentation on the Road

Now you're ready to venture out into the world and deliver your presentation. The ideal situation is to deliver it from the machine on which you created it. Chances are that you've already tried everything more than once, all your movies and sounds work, and your slides look good.

Seldom do you carry your computer to a presentation site, however (unless you're using a notebook computer in front of a small audience). Instead, you may end up using the equipment provided on-site or connecting your notebook to an LCD panel or Barco large-screen system.

Whichever medium you plan to use, unless you're using your own equipment to deliver a presentation, the following chapter contains valuable information about how to prepare presentations on equipment other than what you create them on.

Chapter 15
Preparing Files for Remote Viewing

In This Chapter

▶ Creating presentations for distribution
▶ Distributing run-time versions of your presentations
▶ Delivering presentations remotely with TeamShow
▶ Creating self-running presentations for kiosks and trade shows

*Y*ou can deliver a presentation remotely, as either a self-running show or a user-interactive show or over a network, by using the Freelance Graphics TeamShow feature. Whichever method you choose, Freelance Graphics provides the tools you need.

That's the focus of this chapter — creating presentations you can distribute to others for viewing or reviewing. In this chapter, you discover how to use Freelance Graphics to become, in effect, a multimedia author.

Creating Presentations for Remote Viewing: An Overview

Before getting into the specifics of preparing files for remote viewing, we need to cover some technical ground. When you prepare a presentation for viewing on someone else's computer, you must keep some things in mind. What those things are depends on whose computer the presentation is played on. If you're distributing presentations to several people and perhaps you don't know how their computers are configured, you have additional considerations.

Confused yet? After you read this section, you'll be better equipped to distribute presentations for remote viewing.

Distributing a presentation to a few people you know

The ideal situation for distributing a presentation is that you know the people who will see the presentation and you know how their computers are configured. In this type of situation, you just tailor your presentation to their computers. When possible, find out about the configuration of the computers to which you are distributing your presentation. You need to be able to answer the questions in the following sections.

Which fonts are they using?

If you design a presentation with fonts that aren't installed on the computers on which the distributed presentation is to be viewed, the text doesn't appear correctly. In many cases, because fonts can be extremely different in shape and size, lines may break incorrectly and words can get cut off.

One way to eliminate this problem is by including with the presentation the fonts you use, in addition to instructions for installing them. Be careful, however: Some fonts are copyrighted, which means that you cannot legally copy and distribute them.

Another way to be reasonably sure that the fonts you use are on a remote computer is to use only the Arial and Times New Roman typefaces. Because these fonts are shipped with Windows, everyone who has Windows has them. If anyone who may see your presentation has uninstalled one or both fonts, all they need to do is install them again from their Windows installation disks.

What size is their display system?

Although Freelance Graphics has the capability to resize presentations to fit the screen on virtually any system, you don't always get the same results when you move among various resolutions. For example, if you design your presentation on a 17-inch monitor with a 1024×768 resolution (where elements are small), by the time your presentation gets to a 14-inch display at 640×400, elements may appear out of proportion. This situation is especially true when you go the other way and move to a larger resolution. Small text that's easily read on a 640×480 monitor cannot be read as easily on a 1024×768 monitor.

Another consideration is color depth. If you include a large number of 24-bit images in your presentation and users at the remote site can view only 8-bit images, the images don't look good. Figure 15-1 shows an image displayed in 24-bit color and the same image in 8-bit color.

If you plan to distribute your presentation to an audience that has inferior display systems, you should design it for the machines of your intended audience, not for your beautiful 24-bit powerhouse.

Figure 15-1: An example of the same image displayed in both 24-bit and 8-bit color.

How fast are their computers?

So now you have this magnificent Pentium that screams; it breezes through your presentations with ease. Don't be fooled, though: 386 and slower 486 machines don't handle your material well. The slower the system, the longer that slides take to display, especially if your presentation contains many bitmap images and sound and video effects.

Because the files with images and sounds are large and can take a long time to load, every time a slide with this type of file on it is displayed during a presentation, the tempo of your show can significantly slow down on slow computers. Nothing is more frustrating for a user than waiting while a computer's hard disk and display system churn.

By the same token, computers with a low complement of RAM can also slow down a presentation. A rule of thumb is that computers running Windows 95 should have about 16MB of RAM to run Freelance Graphics presentations that contain a great deal of graphics, multimedia files, builds, and transitions.

What kind of multimedia equipment and drivers do their systems have?

Most computers nowadays have sound cards and speakers. If any of the remote sites on your list don't have these items, however, they can't hear the sounds in your presentation. Keep this possibility in mind when you design a presentation for remote viewing. Don't bog down a presentation with bulky sound files if remote users can't hear them.

By the same token, if you embed multimedia files (such as QuickTime movies, AutoDesk .FLI and .FLC files, and sound files not supported directly by Freelance Graphics), you also must provide the drivers and viewers when you distribute the presentation file. The good news is that because the viewers for most multimedia files are not copyright-protected, you can distribute them freely. Also, most of them come compressed in self-extracting installation files. Users need only to double-click the icon, and the viewer installs itself. To be safe and avoid hassles, though, stick to the file types that Freelance Graphics supports directly: .AVI, .AIM, .WAV, and .MID.

Distributing presentations when you don't know where they'll be shown

A common marketing practice is to create self-running presentations that potential customers or clients can order and view on their computers. Unfortunately, your multimedia extravaganzas don't run optimally on every computer. Also, you want to confine your presentation to one disk (definitely no more than two!). For this reason, you can't include many multimedia files and large images.

When you design a presentation to be distributed on demand, assume that the computers it is viewed on are old, slow clunkers. Make transitions simple. Tailor colors to 256-color capabilities. (Most Freelance Graphics SmartMasters fit this bill. If you're unsure, however, turn down the color depth to 256 colors to see how the presentation looks at that level. You control color depth by using the Display option on the Windows 95 control panel.)

> **NOTE:** Many people create presentations to be viewed from CD-ROM discs. If you're one of these digital gurus, much of what you read in this section may not pertain to you. It's safe to assume that computers with CD-ROM drives also have sound cards and speakers. Also, most computers equipped in this way are usually fast enough to run anything you throw at them.

Creating a Run-Time Version of Your Presentation

You can distribute your presentations to two basic types of users: those who have Freelance Graphics on their computers and those who do not. (A third type is people who use Publish to Internet from the File menu, which is discussed in Chapter 20. This option creates large graphics files, however, which download slowly over phone lines. It works well only if users have fast connections, such as ISDN or a network.)

To give your presentation to people who have a copy of Freelance Graphics, simply copy the file to a floppy or post it on their network. (You can also use removable media, such as Syquest, Bernoulli, or backup tape, as long as both parties can read it — in the other words, as long as they have the appropriate hardware.) To provide presentations to users who don't have Freelance Graphics, use the Freelance Mobile Screen Show Player.

Chapter 15: Preparing Files for Remote Viewing   233

Using the Freelance Mobile Screen Show Player is a two-part process. You must copy the presentation file by using Prepare for Mobile Screen Show Player in the Save As dialog box to embed all linked files and then copy the viewer and the presentation to a disk (or disks).

The first step is easy. Make sure that the presentation you want to distribute remotely is open, and then choose File➪Save As from the menu bar. Make sure that Prepare for Mobile Screen Show Player is checked, and then save the file. If the presentation isn't too large (more than 1.4MB), you can copy it directly to a floppy disk. (You can use Windows Explorer to copy files.)

If the file doesn't fit on a floppy disk, you have two options: Compress the file or break it into pieces from Freelance Graphics. Figure 15-2 shows a file compressed by 77 percent.

Figure 15-2: Use WinZIP 95 to compress files that are too large to transmit in a reasonable amount of time or that can't fit on a floppy disk.

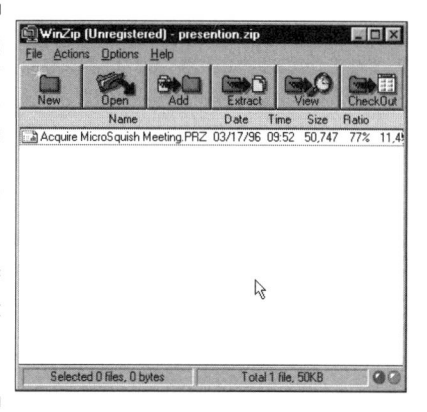

When you compress a file with PKZIP, the person to whom you distribute the file must have PKUNZIP (it's part of the PKZIP package) to decompress the file. You can ensure that the user at the other end can decompress the file if you use ZIP2EXE (also included in the PKZIP package) to turn the zipped file into an executable .EXE file. That way, all the user must do is double-click the file icon to decompress it.

To break your presentation into small chunks of slides, use the Cut or Clear command on the Edit menu to delete slides from the file and then save the file with a new name. Then save or copy the smaller files to floppy disks. The Mobile Screen Show Player enables users to chain together several presentations in one viewing session. If you find this necessary, you should give the files names that designate their order: Sales Proposal 1, Sales Proposal 2, and so on.

Distributing the Mobile Screen Show Player

Lotus has changed the procedure that Freelance Graphics uses to create run-time versions of presentations. In earlier versions of Freelance Graphics, you created a self-contained file that held both the presentation and the viewer. All users needed to do was double-click an icon to start a screen show.

In Freelance Graphics 96, you must copy the presentation and the Mobile Screen Show Player to disks separately. It's less convenient for users, but doing so enables you to distribute longer presentations because of the player's capability to play more than one presentation at a time.

Finding the Mobile Screen Show Player

After you have your presentation copied to floppy disks or another type of removable media, you should copy the viewer. Because the viewer takes a little more than 1MB of disk space, you can't get much of your presentation on the same disk with it. You probably should count on distributing the presentation and the viewer on separate disks.

When you installed Freelance Graphics, the Mobile Screen Show Player was installed in the Freelance Graphics directory. If you accepted the defaults during installation, the directory is C:\LOTUS\FLG. The Mobile Screen Show Player is a compressed file called MOBILESS.EXE, as shown in Figure 15-3. Simply select it and copy it to a floppy disk.

Figure 15-3: The Freelance Graphics remote player.

TIP

If you are posting the viewer and a presentation or two on a network or the Internet, use PKZIP to compress them into one file. This step saves your users from having to download and manage several files.

Using the Mobile Screen Show Player

After you distributed the presentation and the viewer, you must give recipients instructions for how to use it. This section describes how to install the viewer on a remote computer. We suggest that you create a README text file. (Because you're working with Windows 95, you can give the file a descriptive name, such as How to Install This Presentation.txt.)

Chapter 15: Preparing Files for Remote Viewing   235

Follow these steps:

1. **Place in the floppy disk drive the disk that contains MOBILESS.EXE.**
2. **In Windows, choose Start⇨Run.**
3. **In the Run dialog box, type** a:mobiless.
4. **Accept the default location for the files, or change the location, and then click OK.**

   This step installs the Mobile Screen Show Player and the TeamShow files in the designated directory and creates a Lotus Smart Suite menu entry on the Windows 95 Programs submenu. It also opens the Mobile Screen Show Player, as shown in Figure 15-4.

   You can make things easier for your remote users by creating a presentation list that tells them which presentations to run and in which order to run them. Use a text editor or word-processing application to create a presentation list file. The file must be an ASCII text file that has one filename per line, and it should be saved with a .PLZ extension. You can specify full pathnames for each file, but you'll have better luck if you save all presentation files in the same directory and then simply list the filenames in the text file. Just save the list in the same directories as the presentations. The benefit of this method is that remote viewers don't need to choose all the presentation names in the correct order — you do it for them.

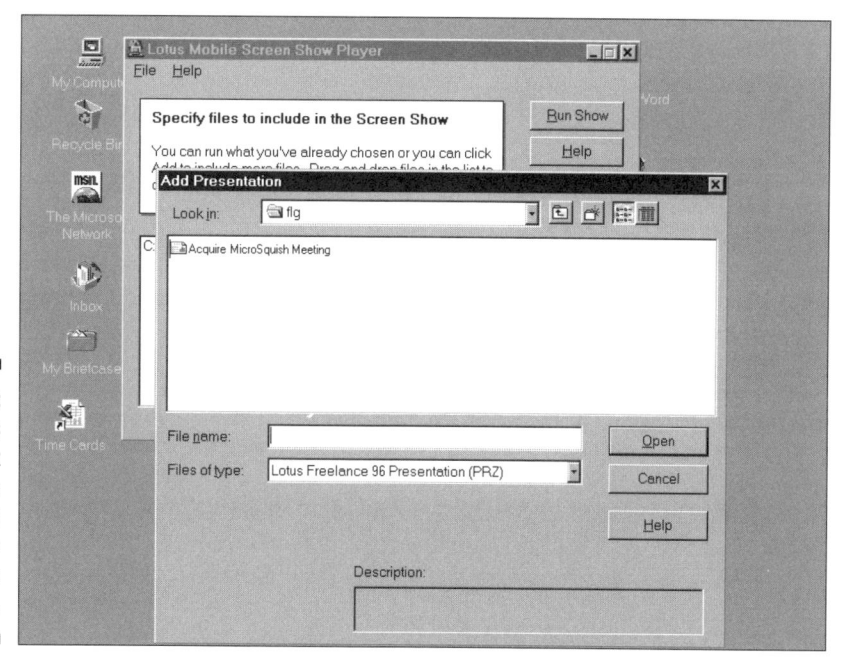

Figure 15-4: Use this dialog box to choose the presentation you want to show.

NOTE: In addition to installing the viewer, users should also copy the presentations from the disks (or network) to their hard disk. Instruct them to copy all the presentations to the same directory.

5. **Choose the presentation (or presentations) you want to show, or select a presentation list.**

   To add multiple presentations, choose one and then click Open. Click Add to return to the Add Presentations dialog box, choose another presentation, click Open, and so on. After you have your presentations listed in the Lotus Mobile Screen Show Player, you can click the Remove button to remove them from the list, and you can drag and drop the presentations in the list to rearrange them.

6. **Arrange the presentations the way you want.**

7. **Click Run Show.**

From now on, the presentation runs exactly as you set it up in Freelance Graphics. If you made it self-running and looping, that's what it does. If it's interactive, users have the options of advancing the show and initiating events.

TIP: If you're distributing a presentation to remote users who have no experience with electronic presentations, you can help them out by placing on the first screen some instructions for using the presentation.

After you install the viewer on a system, you can use it to show any Freelance Graphics 96 presentation. Simply choose Freelance Mobile Screen Show Player from the Lotus Smart Suite submenu on the Windows Start⇨Programs menu.

Delivering Presentations Remotely with TeamShow

You or a remote site can deliver a presentation over your company's network, between two computers connected by a serial or parallel cable or between two computers connected by a modem with the TeamShow feature. This option is easy to use. When you install MOBILESS.EXE, a copy of TeamShow is also installed. TeamShow works from a context-sensitive wizard. Simply invoke a TeamShow session, which opens the TeamShow dialog box, and then follow the steps shown on-screen. Between the prompts and the context-sensitive Help, this feature is a snap to use — if the computers are connected and talking to each other *before* you start up TeamShow.

Are you a sender or a receiver?

If you present a screen show to someone else, you are the TeamShow *sender*. Use the Send a Screen Show to a Remote Viewer option of the TeamShow dialog box to designate yourself the sender. Speaker notes, if you created them, are displayed only on your computer. As the sender, you control the flow of the presentation on both computers. If you view a screen show presented by someone else, you are the TeamShow *receiver*.

Connecting and sending a file

As the TeamShow sender, you choose the presentation file and control the flow of the show. As the sender, you have the following two options:

- If you start TeamShow from within Freelance Graphics (choose File⇨TeamShow), the open presentation file is the only file you can share with a receiver.

- If you start up Mobile TeamShow (which was installed on the Lotus Smart Suite menu when you installed MOBILESS.EXE), you must find the presentation file and identify it, as shown in Figure 15-5.

Regardless of how you start TeamShow, you must identify the computer that is to receive the presentation. You also must agree with the receiver about how to connect the two computers. If you're not close enough to talk to the receiver directly, you should call the person on the phone to coordinate connecting the computers.

File, file, who's got the file?

You can use TeamShow to show a presentation in three ways:

- Share a copy of the presentation file from a server.
- Send a copy of the file to the receiver.
- Tell TeamShow that both users already have copies of the presentation.

Armed with this information, you're ready to use TeamShow to show your presentation remotely.

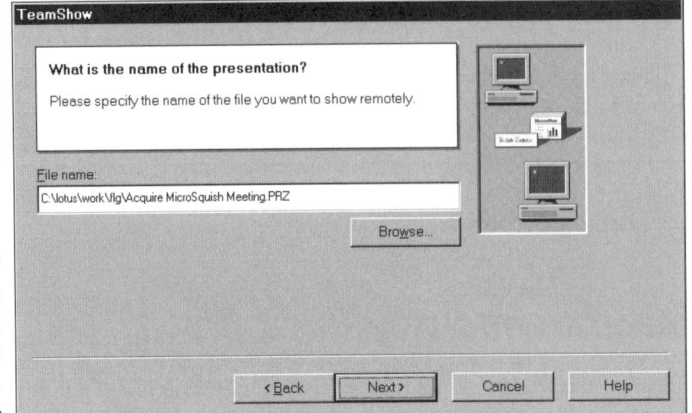

Figure 15-5: Choosing a presentation file.

Creating Self-running Presentations for Kiosks and Trade Shows

Self-running kiosks are, of course, presentations with no interaction from users. They just sit there and run and (you hope!) attract attention and an audience. If you've ever been to the computer section of a department store, you've seen self-running demonstrations on the computers. Each machine has its own presentation that churns away, vying for attention.

You can use the Freelance Graphics Mobile Screen Show Player or Freelance Graphics itself to run these shows. We show you, in Chapter 14, how to create automatic transitions between slides and make a presentation run in a continuous loop, so we don't cover that ground here.

The difference between a self-running presentation (one you run on a computer you most likely carry to the site and set up) and one you distribute on floppy disks or by modem is that, with the former, you probably don't need to worry about space and file size constraints — within reason.

Chapter 16
Preparing and Printing Speaker's Notes

In This Chapter
- Understanding why speaker's notes are important
- Creating and formatting speaker's notes
- Knowing what to include in your speaker's notes
- Printing speaker's notes

Few things are more distracting to an audience than a presenter repeatedly turning around to refer to slides. When a presenter looks away to refer to slides while speaking, the audience may have difficulty hearing what's being said. Worse yet, the presenter appears unprepared.

Whether you are making a presentation on slides or overheads or during a screen show, you should create and use *speaker's notes,* which are the focus of this chapter. No one should go on stage without a script, so consider speaker's notes your script.

Understanding Why Speaker's Notes Are Important

You may as well ask, "Why is preparation important?" The answer — as stated throughout this book — is that better-prepared presenters are better presenters. Poise and confidence should be the look you're after. Having a script in front of you to refer to helps instill you with poise and confidence.

Many presenters make the mistake of relying too heavily on their notes. Speaker's notes are *not* a substitute for rehearsing — period. Use all the tools in your arsenal to ensure that your presentations are successful. Speaker's notes are only one of many tools. They're part of the overall picture.

Part IV: Printing and Rehearsing Your Presentation

You probably wouldn't think of giving a speech without notes. Well, what's a presentation? It's a speech with props — slides, overheads, and other elements. The props help convey your message. Speaker's notes help you stay on track and cue you to what's coming next. When you're interrupted by questions or other distractions, you can use them to get back on course.

You can also use speaker's notes to help you rehearse and hone your delivery. We can't think of a single reason not to use speaker's notes.

Creating and Formatting Speaker's Notes

Freelance Graphics enables you to create speaker's notes for every slide in your presentation. You can format the text (typeface, type size, attributes, and bullets, for example) of each note. Remember, though, that your purpose is to make the notes easier for *you* to read, not to make them attractive. You're the audience. Design them so that they make sense to you.

To create speaker's notes, follow these steps:

1. **Begin on the first slide in the presentation for which you want to create a speaker's note.**

2. **Choose Create⇨Speaker Note from the menu bar or click the Speaker Note SmartIcon (the one that looks like a 3 × 5 note card).**

    This step opens the Speaker Note dialog box, in which you can create a speaker's note for the current slide, format text, create bullets and numbered lists, and so on (see Figure 16-1). Freelance Graphics provides a great deal of flexibility for formatting speaker's notes.

Figure 16-1: The Speaker Note dialog box.

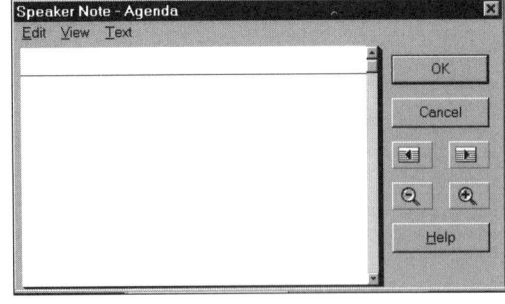

3. **Type the speaker's note or copy and paste text from some other source, such as a word processor, a slide, or the Freelance Graphics Outliner.**

4. **Format the text the way you want.**

Chapter 16: Preparing and Printing Speaker's Notes

The following list describes the menus and options in the Speaker Note dialog box:

- **Edit menu:** Contains the standard Copy, Cut, Paste, and Clear commands for working with the Windows Clipboard.

- **View menu:** Enables you to control the zoom level on the speaker's note page. As with presentation pages, you can choose to see less or more of the page according to how much you zoom in or out on it, respectively. The Next and Previous commands enable you to move forward and backward in the presentation.

- **Text menu:** Enables you to format your speaker's note text, including text properties, numbers, and bullets. (By default, the speaker's notes text is printed in small type. You probably want to enlarge it a little.)

- **Previous and Next buttons:** On the right side of the dialog box, underneath the Cancel button; these buttons move both the speaker's note and the presentation backward or forward one slide.

- **Zoom Out and Zoom In (magnifying glass) buttons:** Enable you to zoom in and out on the speaker's note page.

Most of the commands on the Text menu open the Text Properties for Speaker Note dialog box, as shown in Figure 16-2. You can change typefaces, attributes, size, and so on. You can also add a bullet to the current paragraph or to all selected paragraphs. Clicking the Bullet drop-down list displays a palette of bullets similar to the one in the Bullets portion of the Properties dialog box for formatting slides. To number lists, choose either the *1* or the Roman numeral *I* from the bullet palette, depending on which numbering style you want.

Figure 16-2: Use the Text Properties for Speaker Note dialog box to format speaker's note text.

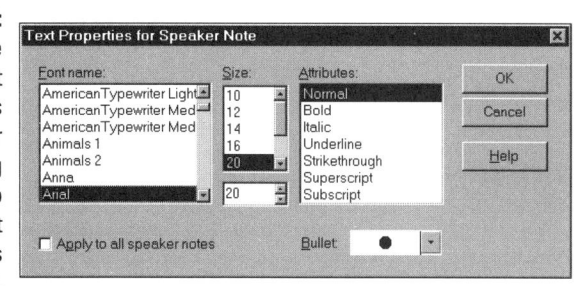

You can also use the Reset to Defaults command on the Text menu to remove all formatting. Choose the Apply Style to All Speaker Notes command to use the same formatting for all the speaker's notes you create for the current presentation. In addition, because the standard Windows formatting shortcut keys (such as Ctrl+B for bold) also work in this dialog box, you can easily format, cut, copy, and paste text.

> **TIP:** In Current Page view, you can tell whether a slide already has a speaker's note attached by looking at the speaker's note SmartIcon. If no speaker's note for the current slide exists, the icon displays a blank 3 × 5 card; when you move the mouse cursor over the icon, the Bubble Help message appears. If a speaker's note has already been created for the current slide, the icon displays a 3 × 5 card with the letters *ABC* on it. When you move the mouse cursor over this icon, the Bubble Help message reads `Edit speaker note`.

Knowing What to Include in Your Speaker's Notes

We say in a number of places in this book that your speaker's notes, not your slides, are the places for ancillary data (the things you want to talk about but don't necessarily want your audience to see).

Having said that, we should point out that speaker's notes that contain too much detail are difficult to read and follow. Although you can include additional data on speaker's notes, you should not write out exactly what you want to say. You may find yourself reading to the audience instead of *speaking* to them. That's a no-no — a *big* no-no. It's boring, and it shows that you're unprepared.

You can choose from many approaches for creating speaker's notes, but this section describes the one that works best for us.

Using an outline format

If you use a line-by-line outline format rather than full paragraphs, your speaker's notes are easier to read. We like to use key words and phrases rather than entire sentences. Check out the two examples in Figure 16-3. Notice in the first example how much easier you can find information and stay on track.

> **TIP:** When you get ready to print speaker's notes, print two sets so that you can mark one up as you rehearse and use the other to deliver your presentation. Use the marked-up set to review and refresh your memory before you begin your delivery.

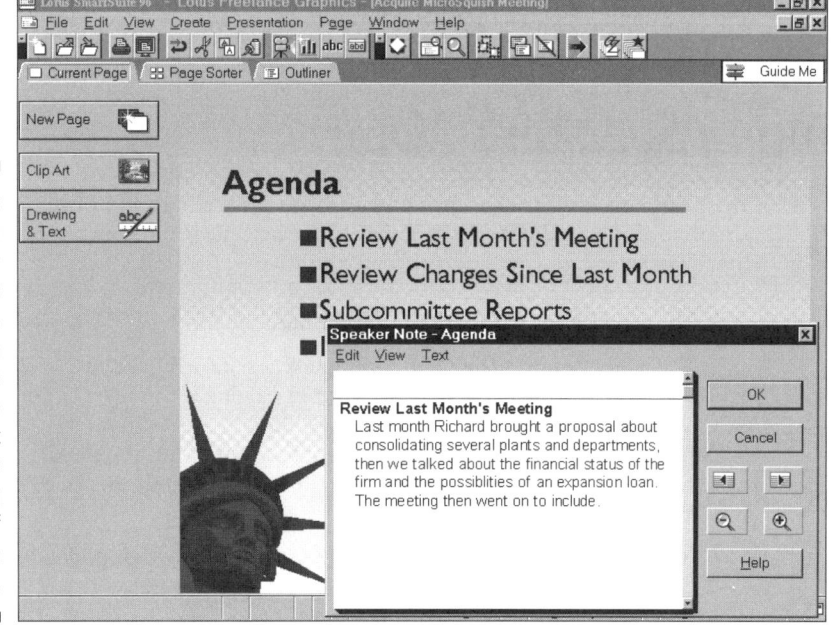

Chapter 16: Preparing and Printing Speaker's Notes *243*

Figure 16-3: When you create speaker's notes, format them in a simple outline format that makes maintaining a flow of information easy.

Including information that doesn't fit on a slide

The speaker's note is where you put subpoints and other information that doesn't fit on a slide — the things you need to talk about to support, enhance, or clear up points you make. You can also include reminders about which parts of charts and graphs you want to call attention to.

Suppose that the point of presenting a bar chart is to show how well a certain product is doing compared to others. You also want to point out, however, the growth of a second, not-so-glamorous product. Rather than clutter up the slide with a callout, include a note to yourself on the speaker's note to point out the second product.

Also include notes to yourself about things you want to talk about if time permits. Ideally, your slide should be tailored to the shortest delivery time, and your speaker's notes should contain extra stuff.

Your speaker's notes should remind you of how you defined the hot spots (*links*) on your slides and what they do. For example, if you have a hot spot that jumps to a slide or displays a slide not in the normal information flow, your speaker's note can remind you that you have the slide and how to get to it (which object to click). This capability is especially handy if you use normal slide elements, such as titles or charts, as hot spots.

Printing Speaker's Notes

You print speaker's notes the same way you print slides and other Freelance Graphics documents: from the Print dialog box. To print speaker's notes, follow these steps:

1. **Choose File⇨Print from the menu bar.**

   This step displays the Print dialog box, as shown in Figure 16-4. In this dialog box, you set up the way your speaker's notes are printed. You can set a page range and determine how many notes (slides) to put on a page (one, two, or three). Freelance Graphics prints thumbnails of the slides and prints the notes either beside the slides or underneath them, depending on the option you choose.

2. **In the Pages section of the dialog box, choose which pages to print: All, Current page, or Pages from (choose a page range).**

3. **In the Print section, choose Speaker notes.**

Chapter 16: Preparing and Printing Speaker's Notes ***245***

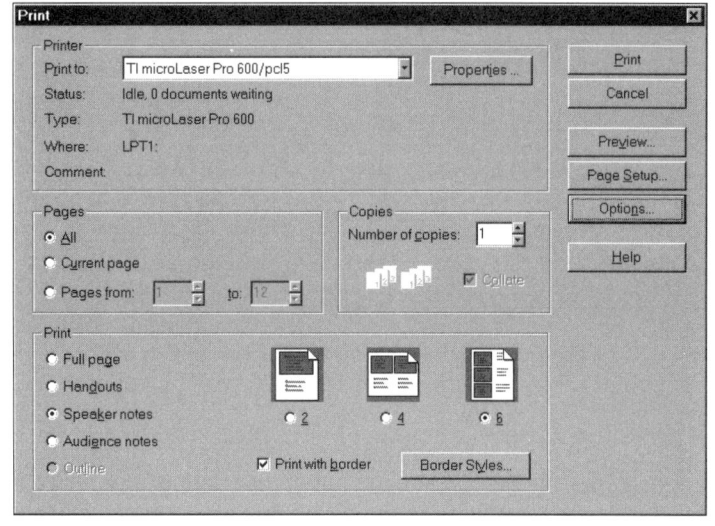

Figure 16-4:
Use the expansive Print dialog box to print your speaker's notes.

The dialog box changes to enable you to set your speaker's notes options. You can choose one of the three options shown in Figure 16-5.

Figure 16-5:
Choose one of these three options for formatting your speaker's notes.

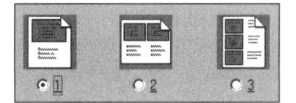

4. **Choose a formatting option.**

    You can also choose whether to print a border around your speaker's notes by selecting the Print with border check box and then clicking the Border Styles button, which opens the Select Print Border Style dialog box, as shown in Figure 16-6. However, we can't understand how placing a border around speaker's notes serves a purpose. The slide thumbnails are printed with borders. This option puts a border around the entire page.

5. **Click Print.**

Figure 16-6:
Use the cryptic names in this dialog box to place a border around your speaker's notes.

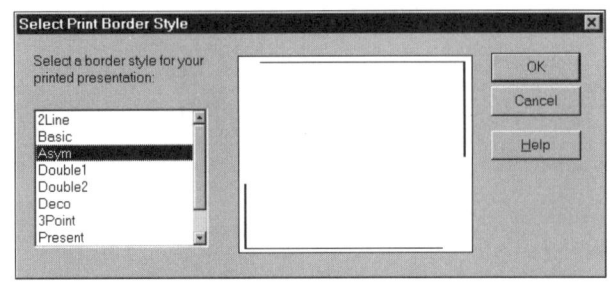

Got nothing to do on your way to the presentation site — on the plane or while sitting at the airport? Whip out those speaker's notes, and go over your presentation. We know that this may be the hundredth time you've heard this, but the better you know your presentation, the better your delivery will be (and the better your life will be).

Chapter 17
Preparing and Printing Audience Handouts

In This Chapter
▶ Why you should use audience handouts
▶ Formatting and printing audience handouts

*I*n addition to printing speaker's notes and outlines, with Freelance Graphics you can print audience handouts — thumbnails of your slides that audience members can use to follow along and then take home. That's the subject of this chapter — understanding the benefits of using audience handouts and how to format and print them.

Understanding Why You Should Use Audience Handouts

Think of audience handouts as a program guide — a list of program highlights and the cast of characters. Handouts not only make your presentation easier for audience members to follow along with (especially if they're sitting in the back of the room or behind someone with big hair) but also provide them with something tangible to take home with them.

You have two compelling reasons — audience convenience and tangibility — to print and distribute handouts. The first reason speaks for itself: The easier you make your presentation for the audience to see and follow, the more they relax and listen to (and understand) your message.

The second reason is not so apparent. Picture this: You just gave a whopping performance, and someone in your audience is thrilled and can't wait to get back to her company to sell your ideas to *her* boss. Because she scribbled notes while listening to you, she missed some of your more important points. Now she must go back to her office and prepare a presentation for her coworkers.

How can audience handouts help you? Here are some ways in which the members of your audience can come to your rescue:

- They don't need to be as diligent in their note-taking, which enables them to concentrate on your message.
- They can take your presentation back to their offices and use it in preparing their own presentations.
- They can show *your* presentation to their co-workers, directly from the handouts you provide. What better way to convey *your* version of your message?
- They can review the presentation at their leisure to refresh their memory, answer questions that come up, and become more familiar with the message in the material.

What other reasons can you think of?

Formatting and Printing Audience Handouts

Unfortunately, Freelance Graphics doesn't provide extensive formatting controls over audience handouts. Basically, you can determine how many slides should appear on each page. You have a choice of two, four, or six slides per page. You can also place headers and footers that contain virtually any information you choose, such as page number, date, and presentation name. You can put borders on the page, and you can choose whether to print the handouts in black-and-white or in color. (Freelance Graphics automatically prints color handouts on color printers and black-and-white handouts on black-and-white printers. But you can change the settings by using the Print⇨Properties command.)

Figure 17-1 shows an audience handout page with headers and footers.

You control all your handout formatting from the Print dialog box. Follow these steps to format and print audience handouts:

1. **With the presentation you want to print open and active, choose File⇨Print from the menu bar.**

    This step displays the Print dialog box, as shown in Figure 17-2. You can format your audience handouts and determine how many copies to print.

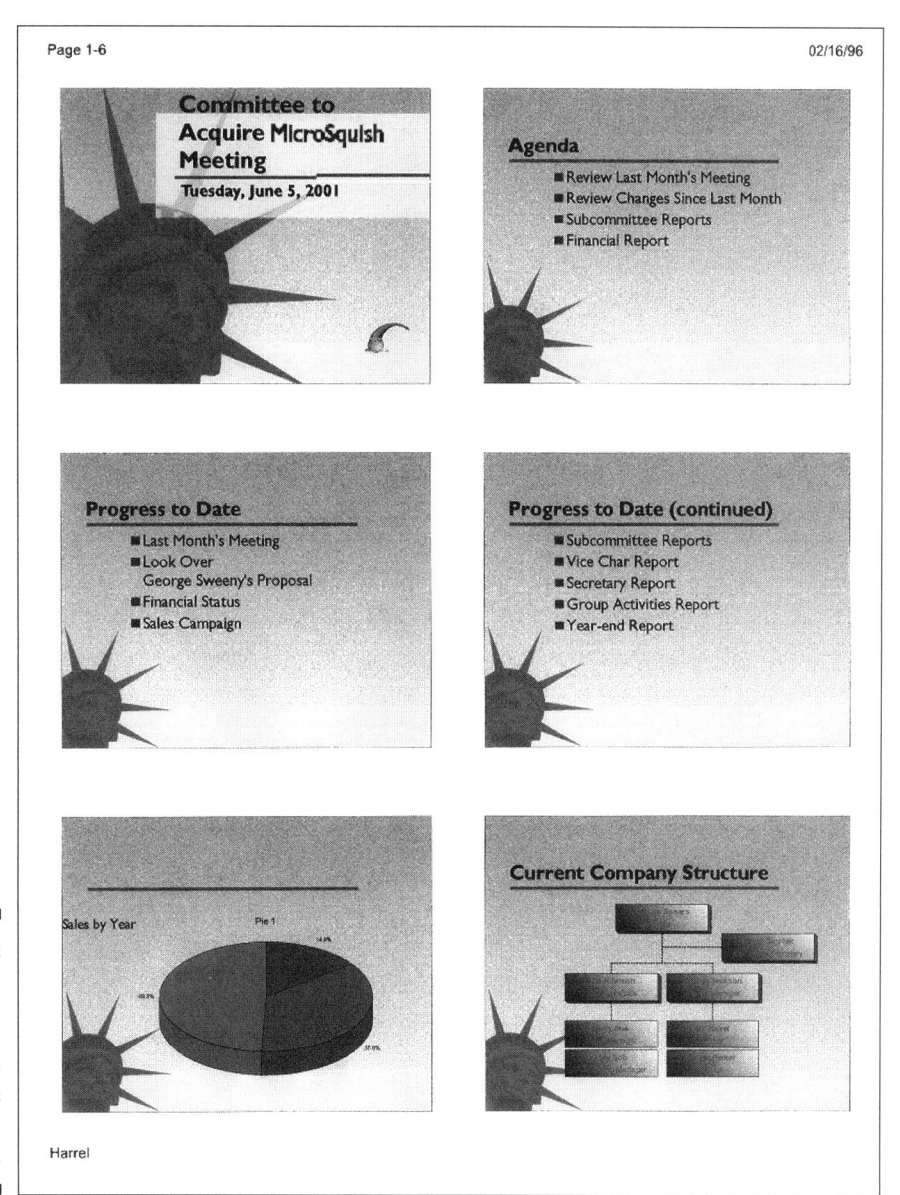

Figure 17-1: This six-slide-per-page audience handout has headers and footers.

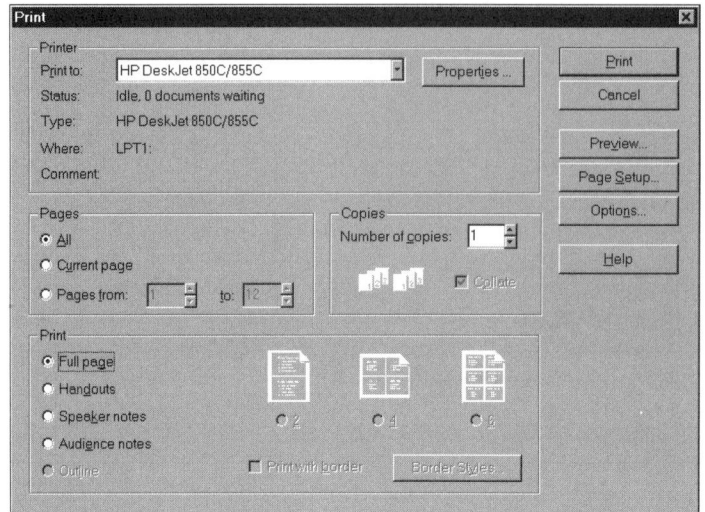

Figure 17-2: Use this dialog box to format and print audience handouts.

2. **In the Print section of the dialog box, choose Handouts.**

   The dialog box changes to work with audience handouts. You have three choices of how many slides to include on each page: two, four, or six slides per page, as shown in Figure 17-3.

Figure 17-3: Choose one of these three options for formatting your audience handouts.

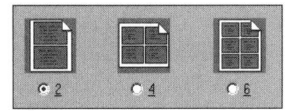

3. **Choose which slides-per-page option you want.**
4. **In the Copies section, choose the Number of copies you want to print.**

   If you're printing all copies on a desktop printer, use the copies option. If your audience is larger than about 50 people, you may want to take your printout to a copy shop — it may be cheaper than using up your desktop printer's consumables.

Chapter 17: Preparing and Printing Audience Handouts

TIP

If you have your choice of using a desktop laser or color ink-jet printer, we suggest that you choose to print your audience handouts in color. They're much more attractive and memorable. Unfortunately, because Freelance Graphics doesn't support color separations, you can't get your color handouts printed on an offset press in full color (not without having separations created at a print shop or service, which can be expensive). Another option is color photocopying, which is also relatively costly.

You can also set up headers and footers on your audience handout pages.

5. **Click Print.**

   The handouts are printed.

Adding page numbers, dates, and other information to handout pages

Print sequential page numbers, a presentation name, and the current date on your pages to personalize your audience handouts. Use the Freelance Graphics Page Setup feature in the Print dialog box.

WARNING!

If you use the following option to set up the headers and footers on your audience handouts, Freelance Graphics saves the setup with your presentation. When you print your slides or transparencies, they also contain the headers and footers. If you don't want this information on your slides, print them before you print handouts or go back and delete the Page Setup entries.

Follow these steps to place headers and footers on your handouts:

1. **In the Print dialog box, click the Page Setup button.**

   This step displays the Page Setup dialog box. Create a header or footer that contains a page number, filename, date and time, and any additional text you want to include, such as the word *Page* preceding the page number or the title of your presentation.

2. **Place the text cursor in the Header & footers field (Left, Center, or Right) where you want the page number printed.**

3. **Type any additional text you want to include.**

   When you include text, make sure to type any spaces or dashes necessary to keep the page number separated from the optional text.

4. **Click the Page, File name, Date, or Time icon to include the appropriate code, as shown in Figure 17-4.**

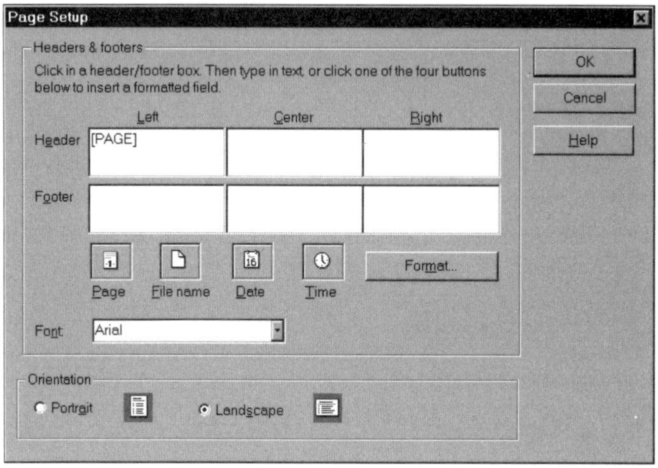

Figure 17-4: When you click an icon, Freelance Graphics inserts a code in the box containing the text cursor.

5. From the Font drop-down list, choose the font you want to use. (The font change doesn't show in this dialog box.)
6. Click OK.

    Note: The header or footer doesn't appear on the presentation on-screen. Freelance Graphics prints the header or footer on the slide or page when you print the presentation. You can change the header or footer font but not the type size. The header or footer is printed in 10-point type.

7. Click Print.

Adding a border to handouts

Freelance Graphics enables you to decorate your handout pages with one of several page borders, which can make your handouts look more polished. To print a border around each page, follow these steps:

1. In the Print dialog box, choose Print with border.
2. Click the Border Styles button.

    This step opens the Select Print Border Style dialog box. Choose a style from the list on the left. The preview window shows what the border looks like. After you find the one you want, you can click OK to choose it.

3. Choose from the list the border style you want.
4. Click OK to return to the Print dialog box.

    When you print the handouts, they contain borders.

Part V
The Part of Tens

In this part...

This Part of Tens is a collection of ten or so morsels of interesting information you can use to enhance your work in Freelance Graphics — or improve your presentation skills. The part has questions to help you plan your presentation, tips for polishing that presentation, and things you need to know to use TeamReview (Freelance Graphics' feature for working as teams). Finally, we threw in our suggestions for making the number one fear of American society, getting up in front of others, a little less intimidating.

Chapter 18

Ten Questions to Help You Define Your Presentation Goals and Strategies

....

In This Chapter
▶ Who is your audience?
▶ How much does your audience know about the topic of your presentation?
▶ What action do you want your audience to take?
▶ What is your audience's position on this subject?
▶ What top three points do you want your audience to remember?
▶ What questions and objections are your audience members likely to have?
▶ What control do you have over the presentation environment?

....

*F*rom the title of this chapter, you may think that we're advocating talking to yourself. Well, that's right. Before you can plan, create, and deliver an effective presentation, you first must ask yourself some probing questions. Essentially, making a presentation is selling yourself and your message — marketing. Like all good marketing people, you need to define your audience and find a way to convince them that they need what you're selling. That's what this chapter is about — the preliminary stages of the presentation process, defining the market, and creating an effective strategy to sell your message. Oh, and we have only seven questions, not ten. That's why this section is titled "The Part of Tens."

Who Is Your Audience?

Seldom do you begin creating a presentation in Freelance Graphics without first having an idea as to whom you intend to deliver the presentation. Most presentations are designed to get a certain group of people to do something specific, such as buy a product, approve a proposal, or simply see things your way.

Getting your audience to see things your way is much easier if you know as much as you can about the audience's members. Knowing who they are, what they think and feel about specific subjects, about their lifestyles, and so on enables you to tailor your message toward *that* group of people. This knowledge also enables you to use examples and analogies pertinent to *their* experiences. Knowing what the audience is likely to find distasteful, too, can help you avoid saying something offensive. Ouch!

Granted, sometimes presentations are created for generic audiences, such as, say, a sales seminar you're taking around the country. But even then, you need a general idea of who is likely to comprise your audience. First, you know that if people show up, they're interested in your topic. So, hey, get out there and find out what kind of people care about the topic you're presenting!

Oh, yeah. One more thing. All the other questions in this chapter relate to this one. You can't answer the rest of them if you can't nail this one down. Period.

How Much Does Your Audience Know about the Topic of Your Presentation?

Do yourself a huge favor: Know your audience's level of expertise *before* creating your presentation. Why? Because if you rehash information they already know, you waste time and bore them. And if your presentation is over the audience's head, you're sure to lose them because they're going to be frustrated and resentful. Either way, you can expect to have a great deal of trouble just getting the presentation across. In fact, even hearing yourself talk over the sounds of fidgeting and snoring may prove difficult.

On a higher plane, if you understand your audience's level of familiarity with the topic, you can deliver a presentation that respects their knowledge and doesn't insult their intelligence. And you can use examples they can relate to, establishing rapport. You can spend your valuable time (and theirs) conveying meaningful information instead of lulling them with an all-to-familiar re-education. You're more effective, and your audience is impressed with how well-prepared you are — everybody likes people who seem to have their acts together.

You are happy. They are happy. Life is good. All is well with the universe.

What Action Do You Want Your Audience to Take?

What's the purpose of your presentation? What do you want the members of your audience to do? Buy stock in your company? Finance a project? Become more informed? Elect you as president? Whatever the goal, you must know exactly what that goal is before you can tailor a presentation to obtain it.

After you determine the goal, you can create a presentation designed to pull it off. Looking good and knowledgeable is secondary and, besides, happens automatically if you deliver a clear, concise message targeted with precision at your audience.

You probably learned somewhere in your illustrious education that jokes and anecdotes are important aids to presenting information because they help keep the audience engaged. True. But *only* if you stay on target. Telling shaggy-dog stories that have no relevance to the proposal you're making serves only to detract from your message.

What Is Your Audience's Position on This Subject?

Most presenters are lucky enough to deliver their messages to audiences that are — if not receptive — at least open-minded to the information. But not always. Sometimes the purpose of your presentation is to persuade a skeptical audience. (If you're lucky, you may never experience the torment of giving a presentation to an audience hostile to your message — unless, of course, you're into that kind of stress.) Knowing where your audience stands on the subject of your presentation enables you to tailor your message more precisely. You don't waste your time trying to sell people who are already sold. If your audience needs persuading, you can tailor your argument toward the merits of your proposal.

Beware of trying to convince people who are dead-set against your message. You are unlikely, for example, to be well-received when delivering a presentation on the merits of legalizing heroin to an audience of police officers. You'd need to be a strong presenter, indeed, to convince an audience comprised of National Rifle Association members to give up their weapons. Why set yourself up to fail? *Not* good for the ol' self-esteem.

What Top Three Points Do You Want Your Audience to Remember?

Most presentations convey a lot of information. The *successful* presentation, however, typically focuses on just a few major points, using minor points to support the major ones. Along the same lines as the earlier question regarding what action you want your audience to take, ask yourself what is the most important information that you want your audience to remember. Then tailor your information accordingly, stressing the major points repeatedly, even from different angles whenever you can.

Often, however, what you want your audience to do is not the only important point you must make. From the standpoint of your message, *why* you want them to take a specific action or feel a certain way also is a major point. Sometimes you want your audience to choose between several courses of action or options. In this situation, your important, memorable points may be the options themselves, with minor points being the pros and cons of the options.

If only life were more simple!

What Questions and Objections Are Your Audience Members Likely to Have?

Okay, so you know to whom you're making your presentation as well as their stance on your topic. You have your three important topics to emphasize. Armed with this information, now look at the *components* of your message. Which points are not clear or can be interpreted in more than one way? Which options could have undesirable consequences and why? What arguments against your proposal have surfaced in the past, and are they likely to come up again? Do you know members of the audience and think that they may question you about certain assumptions and points your presentation makes?

Get the picture? Be prepared to circle the wagons to protect yourself and your message from attack. If you don't know the answer to a question or have a reasonable rebuttal to an objection, doubt creeps into your audience members' minds. Unanswered concerns can kill the effectiveness of your message. If, for example, you anticipate that somebody may question how you came up with a certain set of figures, prepare a chart and link it to the slide containing the questionable data. You may not need it, but isn't it comforting to know that you have the backup information you need — just in case?

Chapter 18: Ten Questions to Help You Define Your Presentation Goals . . .

TIP

Okay. I can hear you thinking. *Anticipating every question that may come up is impossible.* Right, sometimes you can't. But you'd be surprised how many questions you *can* predict if you just step back and look at your information from your audience's perspective. (You already know who they are and have gathered as much information about them as you can, right?) If you deliver the same presentation more than once and you're asked a certain question at one presentation, you can assume that the same question is likely to come up again at other presentations. Prepare to answer that question or address that concern the next time.

What Control Do You Have over the Presentation Environment?

This question pertains more to *where* you make your presentation rather than to whom. We can't emphasize this point enough. Whenever possible, go to the presentation site *before* you start creating the presentation itself. Check out factors such as lighting, stage and screen size, the availability of equipment, and so on. Keep these things in mind while planning and creating your presentation and work accordingly.

You and your audience both are sure to be happier if the show goes on without a hitch.

Chapter 19
Ten Tips for Polishing Presentation Content

In This Chapter
- Avoiding awkward formatting
- Getting the words right

We maintain throughout this book that the presenter's credibility is a key factor in how well a presentation is received. One way you can enhance credibility is to weed out unsightly formatting and pretentious wordiness.

This chapter focuses on finding errors and content problems and then using Freelance Graphics' editing tools to fix them. Use the ten (well, really more than ten) tips in this chapter, and your presentations are sure to sparkle.

Avoid Awkward Formatting

Computers make people more creative and enable them to do things that they normally couldn't. But computers do not automatically imbue people with knowledge and experience as designers and typesetters, which is why guys like us get to hack out a living writing these how-to books. And we wouldn't be doing our jobs if we didn't warn you about the most common design-and-typesetting pitfalls.

The following tips show you how to fine-tune your presentation by looking for little flaws, such as overly long lines of text, improper line breaks, and improper use of typesetting characters (or the lack thereof). The first part of this section covers some common-sense topics that you may have figured out on your own (or you may not have). The next part describes some tricks of the typesetting trade that can help you make your presentations appear more polished and professional.

Avoid Incorrect and Awkward Line Breaks

A *line break* is the end of a line of text, where text wraps to the next line. The three most common pitfalls in breaking lines of text are the following:

- Lines that stick out too far in relation to the other lines
- Lines that are broken between proper names and company names
- Hyphenated lines

Correct Lines That Stick out Too Far

You may find that one of the lines on a slide is much too long, making the entire slide unattractive. You can handle this situation in two ways: Edit the line so that it has fewer words or put part of the bullet point on the next line.

Assuming that the bullet point says exactly what it's supposed to, the first option isn't really an option. So how do you move half that line to the next line without inserting another bullet point? The process is easier than you may think. Simply place the cursor behind the word where you want the line to break and then press Ctrl+Enter. This action invokes Freelance Graphics' line-break feature, overriding the levels and bulleted formatting.

Avoid Breaking Lines between Proper Names and Company Names

Now that you know how to break lines, you need to make sure that you don't break them in all the wrong places. A presentation page contains so little text that you really should avoid breaking lines between people's proper names and company names. (We know, of course, that some company names are too long for you to avoid breaking them sometimes.)

Avoid Hyphenation

Although hyphenated words have their place in text-heavy documents, such as books and reports, they really have no place on a presentation slide. Hyphenation looks terrible on a slide and does nothing to enhance the readability of the text. If you must choose between using hyphens and breaking a line, choose the latter option every time.

Look Professional by Using Special Characters

Your presentations demonstrate more polish if you use the typesetting conventions described in this section.

Many software publishers call uncommon characters *special characters*. Nothing is *really* special about these characters; they just aren't on the keyboard (a fact that does give them a certain distinction). If you're not familiar with how to access these characters, the process may seem like magic.

You can access special characters in several ways, but the easiest method is to use the Windows Character Map to look up font addresses. To find a character's address, select a font in the Font list and then select the desired character. If that character can be accessed from the keyboard, the keystroke combination is displayed in the bottom-right corner of the Character Map window. If a decimal address is required, the address is displayed.

Most Windows applications enable you to enter special characters from the numeric keypad on the keyboard. Hold down the Alt key and then type the character's ANSI (decimal) address.

You can use the Character Map (usually located in the Accessories program group in the Windows Program Manager) to insert a character into a presentation. Select the character and click the Copy button to copy it to the Clipboard. Then return to Freelance Graphics, select the name of the font that you selected in the Character Map, and choose Edit⇨Paste from the menu bar.

Use Em Dashes

You should use an em dash character (—) instead of the double-hyphen dash (--) that you probably use on a typewriter or in your word processing program. The Character Map contains an em dash among its characters.

Use Typesetter Fractions

Most people make fractions by separating two regular numbers with a slash character, as follows: 3/4. This format not only can be confusing, but also doesn't look right (compare 22 3/4 with $22^3/_4$). Your character set probably has fraction characters for all quarter-inch and eighth-inch increments; you can make others by using your software's superscript and subscript features (for example, $^{16}/_{32}$).

Use Legal Characters

The trademark (™) and registered mark (®) symbols should be set in superscript next to the product or company name — for example, MicroSquish® Wonders™. The copyright symbol (©) usually appears after the word *copyright*, as in Copyright © IDG Books 1996.

Get Rid of Excess Modifiers

In a presentation, brevity is bliss. The more precise and to the point your words are, the more effect your message has.

Excess words, especially adverbs and adjectives, add little to your message except flab. Beef up your message by using strong nouns and verbs that don't require modifiers. Instead of *trotting quickly,* the boy *ran. Very big* seldom is bigger than *big.* And sometimes a thing is only *smaller,* not *very much smaller.* Know what we mean?

Get Rid of Idle, Nonworking Words

During revision, always question whether you really need *basically, ultimately, inevitably, essentially,* and other words in this vein. These words say little and add too much fat to your message, so whack them out.

Whenever you can, do away with articles and prepositions: *the, there, of, to,* and so on. These words don't do much except take up space. Use tight, short phrases rather than complete sentences.

Get Rid of Flabby, Long Words

Perhaps the worst offense is using a pretentious long word where a nice, short, to-the-point word does the trick. The purpose of your presentation is not to make you seem erudite (smart), but to convey a message. Use language that everybody readily understands.

Check out the following list of offenders (and the simpler words you should replace them with):

- *abatement* (for *decrease*)
- *abbreviate* (for *shorten*)
- *abdicate* (for *give up*)
- *ventilate* (for *air*)
- *venturous* (for *bold*)

This list could go on and on. Surely you get the idea: Don't be boorish.

Chapter 20
Ten Things You Need to Know to Use TeamReview Effectively

In This Chapter

▶ Sharing presentation drafts with other people to solicit input
▶ Viewing presentations that other people have marked up
▶ Sending presentations via e-mail

As we noted elsewhere in this book, everybody needs an editor. And that's the subject of this chapter: soliciting and incorporating second opinions.

Freelance Graphics provides a powerful review tool called *TeamReview,* which enables you to distribute drafts to reviewers. The review drafts contain a set of tools for marking up the presentation. When the reviewers return their comments to you, you can review the comments and make changes in the presentation.

How You Can Begin a Review Session

After you finish the draft of your presentation, you can begin a review session by following these steps:

1. **Choose File⇨TeamReview⇨Distribute for Review.**

   The Distribute for TeamReview dialog box appears.

   Because not all Freelance Graphics users are on networks or use e-mail, the remainder of this procedure uses floppy disks as the distribution method.

2. **If Save to a Floppy Disk(s) is not already selected in Distribute presentation by drop-down list box, open the list, select it, and click OK.**

   The Distribute Presentation on Floppy Disk dialog box appears.

3. **If you want, change the name of the file in the File Name text box and click OK.**

    You return to the Distribute for TeamReview dialog box.

 4. **Insert a formatted floppy disk into the designated drive and click OK.**

    After it finishes saving the file, Freelance Graphics displays another dialog box in which you can elect to make another copy or go on to the next step.

 5. **Click Yes to make another copy (make as many copies as you need), or click No to go to the next step.**

    Freelance Graphics displays the Distribution Complete dialog box. At this point, you can save and close the presentation or save and continue editing the presentation. The ideal scenario is to wait for your reviews to come back before you do any more editing. If you continue editing the presentation, it may get out of sync with the review drafts, and the reviewers' comments may not be relevant.

 6. **Click OK and distribute your disks to the reviewers.**

> Reviewers must have Freelance Graphics on their computers before they can view and make comments on the review copies. If your reviewers are not familiar with the Reviewer's Desktop and how to use it, refer them to the TeamReview section of Freelance Graphics Help. To get to that section, you choose Help➪Help Topics and then type **TeamReview** in the Type the Words You Want to Find text box.

How You Can Distribute Review Drafts to Coworkers Electronically

If you're using Freelance Graphics on a network, you can distribute review drafts to coworkers electronically. You have two options: post the drafts to a Lotus Notes database, or post them to a public directory on the network. Your network and/or Lotus Notes must be installed and operating correctly for either of these procedures to work.

How You Can Post a Presentation Draft to a Notes Database

To post a presentation draft to a Notes database, follow these steps:

Chapter 20: Ten Things You Need to Know to Use TeamReview Effectively

1. **Choose Edit⇨TeamReview⇨Distribute for Review.**

    The Distribute for TeamReview dialog box appears.

2. **Select Posting in a Notes Database from the Distribute Presentation By drop-down list.**

3. **If you want, select the Notify Reviewers by E-Mail check box; under Notes Database, type the name of the Notes database where you want to post the presentation draft (or use Browse to find the database) and click OK.**

4. **If you chose the e-mail option, fill out and route the e-mail notification in the TeamMail dialog box that appears.**

How You Can Post a Presentation Draft to a Public Network Directory

To post a presentation draft to a public network directory, follow these steps:

1. **Choose Edit⇨TeamReview⇨Distribute for Review.**

    The Distribute for TeamReview dialog box appears.

2. **Select Posting in a Public Directory from the Distribute Presentation By drop-down list and, if you want, select the Notify Reviewers by E-Mail check box.**

3. **Under Notes Database, type the name of the Notes database where you want to post the presentation draft (or use Browse to find the database) and click OK.**

4. **If you chose the e-mail option, fill out and route the e-mail notification in the TeamMail dialog box that appears.**

How You Can Preview Reviewers' Comments

After your reviewers return the floppy disks that contain the marked-up presentation drafts, consolidate those drafts with the main (or *parent*) presentation to review the comments. To consolidate reviewers' comments into the parent presentation, follow these steps:

1. **Open the parent presentation from which you made the drafts.**

    Freelance Graphics displays a warning dialog box, informing you that you have opened a presentation that is under review.

2. **Click Open.**

   The presentation opens. Notice the new option buttons on the left side of the screen. This area is known as the *Author's Desktop*.

3. **Choose File➪TeamReview➪Consolidate Comments.**

   The Consolidate Comments dialog box appears. In this dialog box, you choose the reviewer's draft file that you want to consolidate into the parent presentation.

4. **Type the path and filename of the review draft in the text box or use the Browse button to find the file.**

5. **Repeat steps 3 and 4 for each reviewer's draft that you want to consolidate; then save the parent presentation file.**

After you consolidate all the reviewers' drafts, you're ready to preview the comments and make changes in your presentation based on those comments. The tools that you use to review the comments are on the Author's Desktop.

How You Can Complete the Review Process

To complete the review process, follow these steps:

1. **Review the comments, using the buttons on the Author's Desktop.**

2. **Make changes to the presentation the way that you normally edit a Freelance Graphics presentation, incorporating comments that you like and ignoring comments that you don't want to use.**

3. **After you finish the review, choose File➪TeamReview➪End Review.**

   The End Review dialog box appears.

4. **Click OK.**

The last step returns the presentation to its original state, deleting all comments and ending the review process. You can repeat this process as often as necessary.

How You Can Publish Your Presentation on the Internet

Everybody is excited about the opportunities to publish on the Internet's *World Wide Web* (henceforth abbreviated as *WWW*). Freelance Graphics provides a utility for turning your presentations into WWW documents that you can upload to your Internet server. To do so, follow these steps:

1. **Choose File⇨Publish to Internet.**

   The Publish to Internet dialog box appears. This dialog box enables you to choose a directory in which to save your WWW pages and to name the file.

2. **Choose a directory, name the file, and click OK.**

   Freelance Graphics creates an HTML document and converts the slide images to GIF format (a graphics format that is used on the Web).

Keep the following factors in mind as you publish presentations in HTML format:

- Use your display system's lowest resolution (640 by 480).
- Use your display system's 256-color (8-bit) color setting.
- Don't use fancy backgrounds and gradients (the fewer colors you use, the better).
- Use smaller-than-normal page sizes. The smaller the image, the better.

How You Can Send a Presentation via E-Mail

Nowadays, almost everybody uses electronic mail. Freelance Graphics enables you to send your presentations via e-mail in two ways: TeamMail and TeamReview.

TeamMail enables you to send a message and selected pages of a presentation or a message and all of a presentation, but the presentation is not a review draft. TeamReview enables you to send review drafts. Except for that distinction, the method of sending presentations via e-mail is mostly the same for both options.

> **NOTE:** For either TeamMail or TeamReview e-mail to work, you must have an e-mail system (such as Lotus cc:Mail, Microsoft Mail, or Microsoft Network) installed and working correctly. Depending on your e-mail setup, you may not be able to send e-mail directly from Freelance Graphics.

How You Can Start TeamMail or TeamReview to Send a Presentation

To e-mail a presentation to one or more people with TeamMail, you can begin by choosing File⇨TeamMail or by clicking the small e-mail icon in the bottom-right corner of the Freelance Graphics screen. Either action opens the TeamMail for Lotus Freelance dialog box. The TeamMail dialog box appears.

To send a presentation over an e-mail system by using TeamReview, choose File⇨TeamReview⇨Distribute for Review to open the Distribute for TeamReview dialog box, select the Routing via E-Mail check box, and click OK. The TeamMail dialog box appears.

Some of the functions of TeamMail are dependent on Lotus Notes and are beyond the scope of this book.

How You Can Route a TeamMail Presentation

To route your presentation, follow these steps:

1. **Type the names of the recipients under the Recipient column head, pressing Enter after each name.**

   Use your e-mail system's required format for the recipient names. For Lotus Notes, for example, type the first name first; for cc:Mail, type the last name first.

2. **Select a Send Mode from the drop-down list: either select Route from one address to the next or select Send to all addresses at once.**

   If you're using Lotus Notes, all reviewers can annotate the same file, thereby making your job easier.

3. **Type a Subject and a General Message in the appropriate text boxes and select a message priority from the Delivery Priority drop-down list.**

   Depending on your e-mail system, the message is treated differently according to the priority that you set.

4. **Set your Tracking and Options preferences and click Send.**

The message is sent. Now just kick back and wait for your reviewers' comments.

You also can deliver (show) a presentation over your company's network by using the TeamShow feature. To deliver a presentation over the network, choose File⇨TeamShow⇨Send; then follow the steps in the ensuing dialog boxes.

Chapter 21
Ten Ways to Look and Feel More Confident

In This Chapter
- Rehearsing your presentation and fine-tuning your timing
- Using Freelance Graphics' Screen Show feature to review your presentation from the audience's point of view
- Anticipating objections and preparing optional slides
- Preparing notes and handouts
- Getting a good night's sleep
- Introducing yourself to audience members ahead of time
- Focusing your eyes on potential supporters
- Learning to ignore people who leave or look bored
- Answering questions correctly
- Learning when to bluff (never)

By now, you are likely to have created at least one presentation with Freelance Graphics 96. Time now to go out into the world and deliver your presentation to an audience. If you're like most people, you probably feel a little anxious and may be experiencing a little stage fright. Or maybe you're just plain petrified.

Relax. (Easy for us to say.) Presenting your material is not that hard. People with much less intelligence and ability than you have do it all the time. What separates you from them is *confidence* — they *know* that they know their material and how to deliver it.

Confidence is not, however, a quality most people are born with, especially in getting up in front of an audience and giving a presentation. This kind of confidence comes primarily from being prepared, from knowing your material, and from practicing your delivery. Armed with this kind of preparation, you look and feel more confident. And looking and feeling confident is half the battle.

This chapter lists and describes several things you can do before and during your presentation to look and feel more confident. If you seem confident, your audience is much more receptive to your message.

Practice Makes Perfect

If you've read others chapters of this book, you've probably heard our spiel on rehearsing. We can't emphasize this point enough. You should be familiar with your material and how it is to unfold during the presentation. Although you created the presentation yourself, before going into battle, you should switch hats, from designer to presenter. The more you know the material, the better.

Freelance Graphics provides a Rehearse feature that enables you to go through the presentation, slide by slide. As you practice, a counter times how long you spend on each slide and also times the entire length of the presentation. You can pause the slide show if you need to (say, if the phone rings). And you can display your speaker notes for each slide as you practice. After you leave Rehearse mode, the program gives you a report depicting the time you spent on each slide and the overall presentation time. Virtually everything you need to practice effectively is supplied in this mode.

You can also use the Rehearse mode on your laptop on a plane or in your hotel room.

Use the Rehearse mode not only to fine-tune your timing, but also to familiarize yourself with the presentation material. Each time you go through the presentation, you are better equipped to deliver it. Here are some important points about using the Rehearse feature:

- To enter Rehearse mode, choose Presentation⇔Rehearse/Start from the menu bar.
- On entering Rehearse mode, the two counters — Page Time and Total Time — automatically begin timing your delivery.
- You can advance through the presentation by clicking the left mouse button or by clicking the arrow to the right of the Pause button.
- You can restart your rehearsal at any point by clicking the Restart button.
- The Pause button, of course, stops the counters.
- Continue resumes the counters.
- The Speaker Note button displays speaker notes you create for the current slide. (Speaker notes are covered in Chapter 16.)
- The Done button stops the rehearsal.

After you finish rehearsing, you can use the report Freelance Graphics displays to adjust your timing. Figure out which points you're overemphasizing and which are not getting enough attention. If your delivery is too long, figure out where you can trim some fat. If the presentation is too short, decide where you can add material.

You can also use Rehearse mode to check the continuity of the information flow — do you have enough material? Too little? Is everything in the right order? Where can you add a new slide to make a point clearer? Where can you delete a slide to save some time? As you go through this rehearsal process, ask yourself these questions. You get more and more familiar with your material as you rehearse it.

In working with the Rehearse feature, try to resist staring at the screen. In fact, if you can, you should rehearse standing up, looking at the screen only when changing from one slide to another or to glance at a speaker note. During your presentation you want to be looking at your audience, not at the presentation screen. Don't use the presentation itself as a crutch for remembering your material during rehearsal, and you're less likely to do so during delivery. The best presenters don't look at the presentation screen at all. They know what's there from practice and their notes.

Another effective way to practice is with printouts of your speaker notes, as discussed in Chapter 16.

Watch Your Presentation from the Audience's Perspective

What if you could just kick back and passively watch your presentation from an audience's perspective, without worrying about when to advance a slide or other administrative distractions. Well, you can — by using Freelance Graphics' Screen Show option. All you need to do is make the show self-running. Then you can sit there and watch the show pass by on your computer screen, observing the effectiveness of the presentation instead of worrying about when to display the next slide. Chapter 14 explains more about using the Screen Show option.

To use this feature, follow these steps:

1. **With the presentation open in the Current Page view, choose Presentation⇨Set Up Screen Show from the menu bar.**

    This menu command opens the Set Up Screen Show dialog box. This dialog box enables you to make global screen show settings (for all slides) for your presentation. This dialog box contains several options, as discussed in Chapter 14. To set up a self-running screen show, however, these steps are all you need to know.

2. **In the Page Effects section of the dialog box, under Apply, make sure that the All Existing Pages option is selected.**
3. **For the Display Next Page option, select After _ seconds.**

   The text field enables you to select the length of time you want each slide to displayed. If your slides are complex, allow 10 or 15 seconds to look at them. If the pages in your presentation are short and sweet, set the display to less time.

4. **Set the number of seconds you want your slides to display by typing the number of seconds.**
5. **If you want, select a transition effect from the Transition list.**

   You can elect to use one of this dialog box's transition effect options to set up various transition effects between slides. (As explained in Chapter 14, a *transition* is a fancy way to display new slides, by using such effects as wipes, checkerboards, and so on.) From this dialog box, however, the changes you make apply to the entire presentation (or to all new slides, if you select that option). To set effects separately for each slide, you must use the Page⇨Screen Show Effects command on the menu bar.

6. **After you finish in this dialog box, click OK.**
7. **To run the screen show, click the Run Screen Show From Beginning SmartIcon.**

> **NOTE:** If you include *builds* (build bullet points as discussed in Chapter 18) in your presentations, the procedure described in these steps does not cause each new point to appear. Your automatic screen show pauses at the title of the build slide You must then use the mouse or keyboard (the Page Down key) to advance from slide to slide. The automatic screen show resumes after you click through the bullet points on the build slide. You can, however, tell Freelance Graphics to display all the bullet points at once by selecting the Run Entire Screen Show Automatically check box in the Options section of the Set Up Screen Show dialog box.

Anticipating Objections and Preparing Optional Slides

You can save yourself a mountain of frustration if you try to anticipate beforehand what objections are likely to arise during your presentation. Look at the components of your message. Which points are not clear or can be interpreted in more than one way? Which options could have undesirable consequences and why? What arguments against your proposal have surfaced in the past, and are they likely to come up again? Do you know members of the audience and think that they may question you about certain assumptions and points your presentation makes?

Chapter 21: Ten Ways to Look and Feel More Confident

Be prepared to protect yourself and your message from attack. If you don't know the answer to a question or have a reasonable rebuttal to an objection, doubt creeps into your audience's minds. Unanswered concerns can kill the effectiveness of your message. If, for example, you anticipate that somebody may question how you arrived at a certain set of figures, prepare a chart and link that chart to the slide containing the potentially questionable data. You may not need this extra information, but knowing that you have it as a backup — just in case — can be a real comfort in such situations.

Okay. I can hear you thinking. *Anticipating every question that may come up is impossible.* Right. Sometimes you can't. But you'd be surprised how many questions you *can* predict if you just step back and look at your information from your audience's perspective. (You already know who they are and have gathered as much information about them as you can, right?) If you deliver the same presentation more than once and you're asked a certain question at one presentation, you can assume that the same question is likely to come up again at other presentations. Prepare to answer that question or address that concern the next time.

Looking Good by Preparing Notes and Handouts

All presenters use notes. Notes are like a script. They keep you and your message focused. Notes help keep you on track. They help you avoid going off on irrelevant tangents about the cost of tea in China when what you should be talking about is the cost-effectiveness of using CD-ROM discs for backing up your company's data.

Your speaker's notes, rather than your slides, is where you include all the topics you want to discuss. Audience handouts are printouts — either black and white or inkjet color — of the slides in the presentation. Speaker notes are discussed in Chapter 16. Audience handouts are covered in Chapter 17.

Looking Good by Getting a Good Night's Sleep

Okay, so you're giving a presentation at a convention of your peers. The night before your part of the show, everybody stays out late whooping it up. Where are you? If you're no dummy, you're in your hotel room sleeping, getting well-rested and clear-headed for the next day. You and your audience will be glad that you did.

Looking Good by Introducing Yourself to Audience Members Ahead of Time

If you get a chance, circulate among the audience *before* the presentation. Introduce yourself. Shake hands. Make small talk. That way, at least, you're not delivering your presentation to total strangers. You're more confident, and the people who meet you are a little more receptive to your message. They already know that you're a nice guy.

Looking Good by Focusing Your Eyes on Potential Supporters

Your audience contains three types of listeners: *supporters, objectors,* and *neutrals.* If you did your homework, you already know why your supporters support your message. Tailor your message to reinforce your supporters' point of view. If you know in advance who your supporters are, talk directly to them, making eye-contact, engaging them. This practice makes you more confident and animated. You seem more sure of yourself to the rest of the audience.

This practice also works if you're trying to persuade the neutral and objecting members of your audience. Project your arguments to the potential supporters. If your argument is strong, the dissenters follow suit.

Looking Good by Ignoring People Who Leave or Look Bored

Surely you heard the anecdote about imagining your audience in their underwear? This idea is somehow supposed to neutralize the presenter's fear. Well, we don't know if that works. We've never tried it. New presenters, however, often fall into the trap of paying too much attention to people who walk out during the presentation. Another distraction is concentrating on audience members who seem bored.

Keep in mind that people leave presentations for many reasons. Sometimes, they just need to go to the restroom. Other times, they simply have somewhere else they need to be. Seldom do people leave a presentation simply because they disagree with what's being said, especially in business presentations.

Keep in mind also that, just because certain people *look* bored or distracted, those people aren't necessarily bored or distracted in reality. They could be thinking intently about what you're saying. Even if they are thinking about something else, their state of mind is no reflection on your presentation. Maybe they just have something serious going on in their lives right now.

In any case, this tip relates to the previous one. If you concentrate on your supporters, you don't have time to be distracted by walkouts and sleepers.

Looking Good by Answering Questions Properly

Have you ever been in a presentation where an audience member asks a question and, in response, the presenter answers simply "Yes" or "No"? Or worse, the presenter just nods. You may have no idea what the question was (and perhaps couldn't even hear it), so the entire exchange means nothing to you. To make matters worse, you then raise your hand and proceed to ask the same question.

Sounds annoying, doesn't it? What's more, you appear not to have been paying attention. To avoid such embarrassing moments, presenters need to accommodate their audiences however they can. One way to do so is to *answer questions properly*. Answering a question properly means that, before answering, you thank the questioner and then repeat the question so that the rest of the audience can hear it.

Next, you answer the question clearly and precisely. Seldom does a simple *No* suffice as an answer. By itself, such an answer sounds sultry and curt. Whenever you answer a question negatively, elaborate. State clearly why the answer is *No*. Do not, however, drag your answers out with irrelevant material, and don't rehash information, except where necessary to provide the appropriate answer.

Looking Good by Never Bluffing

Bluffing is, of course, a form of lying. Saying that you intend to do something that you have no intention of doing (or providing a false answer to appear more knowledgeable than you really are) almost always catches up with you, degrading your credibility. Nothing can undermine your delivery more severely than a lack of integrity.

Here's a list of integrity-degrading pitfalls you need to avoid:

- Never promise to do something on which you can't deliver.
- Never purposely provide false information.
- Never deliver idle threats.
- Never exaggerate benefits to persuade.
- Never falsely accuse or debase a competitor.
- Never be afraid to admit that you don't know an answer, rather than make one up.

Chapter 22
Ten Things You'll Like about Freelance Graphics 96

In This Chapter
- Attractive, all-purpose SmartMasters
- Content SmartMasters
- Easy-to-use, "Click here" slide creation
- Three easy-to-navigate views
- Presentation previews in either color or black and white
- Rehearse mode
- AutoBuilds and flying bullets
- Fancy electronic transitions
- Work group collaboration
- SmartSuite integration

*H*ere's a bunch of reasons (ten, in fact) why Freelance Graphics 96 makes creating presentations a breeze.

Attractive, All-Purpose SmartMasters

Face it — most people who step up to the Freelance Graphics presentation plate haven't the foggiest about art and design. Here's where Freelance Graphics' professionally designed *SmartMasters* come into play. You can choose from among more than 120 prefabricated templates varying in themes from Australia to medicine to construction.

Choosing a SmartMaster look is easy. You can choose a SmartMaster to begin your presentation right from the Welcome to Lotus Freelance Graphics dialog box that appears as soon as you open the program. Or you can change a SmartMaster look at any time by choosing Presentation➪Choose a New SmartMaster Look from the menu bar. You can even edit a SmartMaster to fine-tune it to your specific needs.

Content SmartMasters

People, especially businesspeople, have been making presentations for a long time — so long, in fact, that basic formats are established as accepted and reliable for conveying such specific types of information as business plans, corporate strategies, brainstorming, and other topics. Freelance Graphics comes with more than 30 *content SmartMasters* that guide you through the process of creating presentations that contain specific types of information.

You choose a content SmartMaster after you begin a new presentation, either on opening Freelance Graphics or after choosing File⇨New from the menu bar. You select your content SmartMasters from the Welcome to Lotus Freelance Graphics dialog box. (*Note:* This dialog box doubles as the New Presentation dialog box after you choose File⇨New from the menu bar.)

You can create your own content SmartMaster templates by choosing SmartMaster Content on saving the presentation file.

Easy-to-Use "Click Here" Slide Creation

Freelance Graphics invented the "click here" approach to creating presentations. All you do is click the Page Layout button at the bottom of the screen, choose the slide layout you want, and then click the placeholders to enter text, clip art, tables, or charts. The program then switches to the appropriate mode to help you perform the task at hand.

Three Easy-to-Navigate Views

Depending on what you're doing in Freelance Graphics, the program provides three easy-to-use views: *Current Page, Slide Sorter,* and *Outliner*. You can easily switch between each view by clicking the tabs below the SmartIcons button bar. Each view makes designing your presentations easier. The following list provides an overview of each view:

- **Current Page view:** In Current Page, you design your slides by adding titles, clip art, graphs, tables, and so on. Think of this view as your layout table.
- **Slide Sorter view:** This view displays your presentation in thumbnails. Depending on the resolution of your monitor, you can see as many as ten or so slides on-screen at once. This view is used primarily to rearrange the slides in your presentation. Think of this view as a light box for arranging the information flow.

✔ **Outliner view:** The Outliner enables you to control the flow of text information from slide to slide. Use it as you would the outliner in your favorite word processor. The Outliner contains six outline levels: the title level and five topic levels. You could actually type your entire presentation from Outliner.

View Presentations in Color or Black and White

If you print to a black-and-white laser or inkjet for proofing or transparencies, seeing your slides in black and white on-screen before you print can often be helpful. You can switch between black-and-white and color views by clicking the toggle button at the bottom of the screen. You can also choose the View➪Display in Color command from the menu bar.

Rehearsing Made Easy by Rehearse Mode

How well-rehearsed you, the presenter, are is vitally important to the success of any presentation. Freelance Graphics helps you rehearse your presentation with its *Rehearse mode.* Just choose Presentation➪Rehearse/Start from the menu bar. The Rehearse screen times your delivery for each slide and for the entire presentation. You can also review your speaker notes while rehearsing, and Freelance Graphics provides a summary, or overview, at the end of the rehearsal.

Bullet Magic with AutoBuilds and Flying Bullets

Freelance Graphics enables you to do creative things with bullet points. *AutoBuilds* are a series of electronic slides in which a new bullet point is automatically displayed after you finish one bullet point, and any preceding points are dimmed. This option adds a level of sophistication to your presentations, making you look good, and helps your audience stay focused on the topic at hand. To use AutoBuilds, choose Page➪Build Bullets from the menu bar.

Flying bullets enable you to define dynamic bullet transitions during an electronic screen show. Bullets can "fly" onto the screen from any direction you choose or use dramatic transition effects, such as fades or blinds effects. Flying bullets also are defined from the Build Bullets command.

Looking Good with Fancy Electronic Transitions

If you plan to do electronic screen shows with Freelance Graphics, you need to know about the program's *transition effects*. A transition effect is the manner in which one slide replaces another. You can, for example, have the new slide fade in behind the existing slide or have it wipe away the existing slide from the right or left. Freelance Graphics supports glitter effects and blinds — just a whole bunch of neat, magiclike transitions. Why, you can even apply sounds to transitions — you know, such as a fanfare as your boss' picture appears on-screen. You apply transitions by choosing the Page⇨Screen Show Effects command from the menu bar, which opens a Page Properties dialog box.

Working with Team Members

If you are a member of a work group, you can appreciate Freelance Graphics' team presentation features. By using these features, you can perform the following functions:

- Mail a presentation to team members for review, comments, and revisions.
- Distribute a presentation on a network, the Internet, or on floppy disk for review, comments, and revisions. (Freelance Graphics enables you to compile the revisions and adapt or reject them without a lot of extra work.)
- Show a presentation over the network to other computer users.
- Publish to the Internet as a World Wide Web page.

These and other team collaboration tasks are available on the File menu.

Lotus SmartSuite Integration

Nothing is handier than having your word processor, presentation program, and spreadsheet work hand-in-hand. As part of the Lotus SmartSuite, Freelance Graphics is well-integrated with Lotus Word Pro and 1-2-3. Wherever possible, these programs work alike, right down to using the same handy SmartIcons.

You can also easily swap data between Freelance Graphics and the other two programs. Charting data from a 1-2-3 spreadsheet in the Freelance Graphics' charting module, for example, is quite easy. Or you can just use your 1-2-3 charts in your Freelance Graphics presentations. You can also copy and paste Word Pro outlines into the Freelance Graphics Outliner to create instant presentations.

Chapter 23
The Ten Most Important SmartIcons

In This Chapter
- The New SmartIcon
- The Open SmartIcon
- The Save SmartIcon
- The Print SmartIcon
- The Create a Chart SmartIcon
- The Check Spelling SmartIcon
- The Create a Text Block SmartIcon
- The Run Screen Show SmartIcon
- The Place Logo on Every Page SmartIcon

*T*he purpose for all those SmartIcons at the top of the Freelance Graphics screen is to put often-used commands at your disposal. They also save you from having to wade knee-deep into the menu and dialog box structure. This chapter lists and describes several SmartIcons that are crucial to survival in Freelance Graphics.

The New SmartIcon

Use the New SmartIcon to start a new presentation. It's that simple. No matter what you're doing anywhere in the program, the New SmartIcon opens the New Presentation dialog box. From here, you can choose a content SmartMaster, select a look SmartMaster, and then get on with your new presentation.

> Remember that Freelance Graphics enables you to work with several presentations at once. This capability is great for copying data between presentations, but you need to keep in mind that the more (and the bigger) the files that you have open, the more memory Windows 95 requires. If you have several presentations open and your computer is running too slowly, close some of them. This tip also works if you have too many programs open. Close some of the programs to perk up your computer.

The Open SmartIcon

Use the Open SmartIcon to open existing presentations. You can also use this SmartIcon to open presentations created in earlier versions of Freelance Graphics, open SmartMaster content and look templates, and open several different types of graphics files.

Clicking this SmartIcon accesses the Open dialog box, which is similar to most Windows 95 Open dialog boxes. Use this dialog box to navigate to wherever you store presentations on your hard disk, and then double-click the presentation's filename. To open a file type other than one for Freelance Graphics 96, use the Files of Type drop-down list to select a supported file type.

The Save SmartIcon

Use the Save dialog box to save the current presentation. Clicking this icon before the current file is titled (or if the file was not previously saved) opens the Save As dialog box, which enables you to name and save the file. Clicking this SmartIcon after a file is named and saved simply saves the presentation to the current filename, overwriting the previous version. Using this icon (or pressing Ctrl+S) is a good way to ensure against a loss of work from mishaps.

> So hey, with all these great SmartIcons, what if you wanted to display more icons than can fit on that little bar across the top of the screen? No problem. Freelance Graphics enables you to tear away (ouch!), or *float,* SmartIcon palettes anywhere in the Freelance Graphics window. To float an icon bar, simply drag from the small title bar below the drop-down menu for the specific SmartIcon bar.

The Print SmartIcon

Use the Print SmartIcon to print the current presentation. You can also use it to print individual slides, speaker notes, audience handouts, an outline — whatever. Clicking this button opens the Print dialog box, which provides a plethora of print options — more than you can shake a stick at.

The Create a Chart SmartIcon

Clicking this SmartIcon enables you to place a chart on the current slide. After you click the Create a Chart SmartIcon, the Freelance Graphics charting module opens. From here, you can create a new chart from scratch, use one of the programs charting templates, or use data from your 1-2-3 or Microsoft Excel spreadsheets.

After you finish working in the charting module, Freelance Graphics returns you to the Current Page view so that you can place and resize the chart on the slide as desired.

The Check Spelling SmartIcon

Few things, if any, are more embarrassing than standing before a hundred or so people with a word misspelled on one of your slides. Freelance Graphics' spell checker can help you avoid this trauma. Clicking this SmartIcon opens the Spell Check dialog box. From here, you can run a spell-check session on the currently selected block of text, the current slide, or the entire presentation.

Be aware that, by default, the Check Spelling icon does not reside on any of the Freelance Graphics SmartIcon bars. You must go into SmartIcon Setup, as described in Chapter 1, to place this icon on the icon bars where you want it to appear. We suggest that you place it on the Outliner SmartIcon bar and on the Universal SmartIcon bar.

The Create a Text Block SmartIcon

Clicking the Create a Text Block SmartIcon enables you to insert text anywhere on the current slide. All you do is click the icon and then click the spot on the slide where you want the text block to appear. Then just start typing. You can use the Level and size controls to resize the text and the Selection (arrow) tool to resize the box containing the text.

The Run Screen Show SmartIcon

Use the Run Screen Show icon to display your presentation in full-screen mode. You can then advance from slide to slide by using the left mouse button. To go back a slide, you press the right mouse button. If you set up electronic screen show transitions (by choosing Page⇨Screen Show Effects from the menu bar), Freelance Graphics runs the entire show, complete with effects, just as you designed it.

You can create a screen show that advances with mouse clicks or one that moves from slide to slide automatically after a specified period.

The Place Logo on Every Page SmartIcon

If you ever had to go through a document placing the same graphic page after page, you are sure to appreciate what a time-saver the Place Logo on Every Page SmartIcon can be. Clicking this icon displays a screen for drawing (by using Freelance Graphics' drawing tools) or importing an icon onto a SmartMaster page. After you finish and return to your presentation, the logo you import or create appears on every page of your presentation.

Chapter 24
Ten Keys to Good-Looking, Easy-to-Read Overheads

In This Chapter
- Why you should use the right transparency film
- Why you should use light backgrounds
- Why you should use dark text
- Why you should use sans-serif type
- Why you should use simple (or no) borders and clip art
- Why you should avoid using portrait page orientation

Despite all the high-tech slide and multimedia screen show hype, sometimes you still need a quick and dirty low-tech overhead transparency presentation. Because of the special nature of the overhead transparency medium — typically transparency film printed on an inkjet printer — getting good results isn't always easy. So this chapter provides a list of things you can do to make creating overheads more successful.

Why You Should Use the Right Transparency Film

Not all transparency film is created equal. And some is more equal than others. When looking for transparency film, match the film to the output device. Some film is designed specifically for laser printers and some is designed specifically for inkjets.

This distinction is important. The composition of the plastic is slightly different for each medium. Laser printers heat up the transparency film much more than do inkjets. One device uses toner, similar to that of a copy machine, and the other uses ink. Toner is powder, and ink is liquid — a significant difference.

Get the picture? The two different kinds of film hold the image and absorb differently. So make sure that you read the box before waltzing off to the cash register. Okay?

> If you use a Hewlett-Packard DeskJet series printer, you can't go wrong by using the transparencies and paper designed specifically for these printers. These materials may cost a little more than others, but the print quality that results is excellent.

Why You Should Use Light Backgrounds

Unlike slides, transparencies are printed at relatively low resolutions — about 300 dpi for color and between 300 and 700 dpi for black and white. If you shine a projector light through them and then magnify the image onto a screen, you are, in effect, dramatically increasing the size without increasing the resolution. This situation can greatly degrade the quality of the image, distorting the relationship between the elements — text and graphics — on your transparencies.

For this reason, you should always use light backgrounds or no backgrounds at all. Although your deep blues, purples, and gradients may look beautiful rolling out of the printer, you could be in for a sloppy-looking mess when you project the transparency onto a wall.

Why You Should Use Dark Text

If you skipped over the explanation in the preceding section about light backgrounds, go back and read it before reading this section.

Back now?

Good. You already have a darn good reason to use black or dark-colored text. Here's another reason: The lighter the text, the more translucent is the ink. If you get into light-colored yellows and pinks, the ink can become almost clear, making your text very difficult indeed to read when projected onto a screen, especially for large audiences.

You need to make the text as comfortable to read as possible for your audience. You want them listening to you, not straining to see what's on the presentation screen.

Why You Should Use Sans-Serif Type

Sans-serif typestyles are the ones without the tiny feet on the ends of the letters. (Chapter 11 goes into detail about serif and sans-serif type; if you aren't sure of the differences between these typestyles, take a look at that chapter.) Even at large point sizes, serifs tend to be quite thin, as do the points on the characters that join with the serifs. (Check out the *w*'s, and *y*'s in this book, for example.) If you're working with low-resolution transparencies (especially from earlier model printers with not-so-hot print quality), these thin spots on the text can become broken up, making your text (at best) look jagged, something like the appearance of broken teeth. If blown up too much, serif type can even become unreadable. Bummer!

Why You Should Use Simple (or No) Borders and Clip Art

If you read this chapter from the beginning, you can probably answer this question without our help. Sure, the fancy border or clip art may look great on-screen — even on the transparency itself. But after you project the stuff up on the screen, it appears jagged and messy-looking.

So use simple borders, without a lot of colors and twists and turns. The best borders for transparencies consist of straight, thin lines of about 4 to 10 points thickness. Anything smaller may break up during projection, and anything larger is just too wide a border.

The same is true for clip art. Use it sparingly, and when you do use it, be highly selective. Use solid line art without light colors and a lot of thin lines or curves. You (and your audience) will be glad that you did.

Why You Should Avoid Using Portrait Page Orientation

Here's an easy one. If you've ever seen an overhead projector, you know that, on most of them, the glass where you lay your transparency is designed for wide, 11-x-$8^1/_2$-inch orientation, rather than the other way around. Although you *can* lay the sheet the other way, if you put any information at the extreme top or bottom of the page, that information doesn't get displayed.

Another reason to keep your overheads in portrait orientation is that you can get more data onto the sheet and you don't need to squeeze elements onto the page, which makes the pages in your presentation easier to read and more attractive.

An attractive presentation is a happy presentation.

Index

• A •

Add a Movie dialog box, 221–222
Add Clip Art or Diagram to the Page
 dialog box, 40, 144–145
Add Presentations dialog box, 236
Adobe Illustrator, 122, 148
Adobe Photoshop, 122, 181
Advance One Slide (PgDn) key, 228
AIM (Add Impact) movies, 219, 231
Align dialog box, 136–137
aligning Text Shapes, 136–137
alternate color libraries, 46–47
animation files, 18, 219
applications launching from electronic
 screen shows, 214–215
Arc tool, 141
arcs, 141
area charts, 65
Arrow tool, 141
arrows, 141
artwork, 26–27
attention-grabbing text effects
 wrapping text around shapes, 142–143
 wrapping text around user-created
  shapes, 143–144
audience
 action they should take, 257
 answering questions properly, 279
 anticipating objections, 276–277
 different sized and output media, 9–10
 focusing eyes on supporters, 278
 how much they know about topic, 256
 ignoring those who are leave or are
  bored, 278–279
 impressing, 8
 introducing yourself before
  presentation, 278
 never bluffing, 280
 position on topic, 257
 questions and objections, 258–259
 watching presentation from their
  perspective, 275–276
 what three points do they remember, 258
 who they are, 255–256
audience handouts, 277
 border, 252
 convenience, 247–248
 enhancing, 251–252
 formatting, 248–250
 headers and footers, 251
 printing, 248–251
 tangibility, 247–248
Author's Desktop, 270
AutoBuilds, 283
automatically saving files, 33, 45
AVI file format, 219, 231
AWM (Animation Works) movies, 219
axes
 making information easier to read, 95–98
 modification, 88–92
 modifying labels, 90–91
 showing/hiding, 90

• B •

Back One Slide (PgUp) key, 228
backdrop
  adding bitmapped graphics to, 181–182
  changing colors and patterns, 183
backgrounds
  cells, 111
  changing, 203
  charts, 81–84
  fills, 83
  gradients, 83
  modifying SmartMasters, 174–175
  not printing, 203
  organizational charts, 118–119
  patterns, 83
  tints, 83
  turning off, 47
backup files, 32
banding, 203
bar charts, 65
Bernoulli drives, 194
Bitmap Properties dialog box, 149–150
Bitmap⇨Bitmap Properties command, 149
Bitmap⇨Crop Bitmap command, 150
bitmapped graphics, 148–150, 153
  adding to SmartMasters backdrop, 181–182
  contrast, sharpness, and brightness, 149
  cropping, 150
  device dependent, 148
  importing, 182–183
  inverting colors, 150
  linking, 182
  modifying, 149–150
  resizing, 182
  tiled, 182
  transparent, 150
black-and-white presentations, 283
black-and-white transparencies, 203–204

BLANK.MAS SmartMaster Look file, 180–181
blocks, 184–186
BMP file format, 147, 149, 181
borders
  audience handouts, 252
  chart series, 86–87
  charts, 81–84
  organizational charts, 118
  speakers notes, 245
  tables, 110–111
brightness, 149
Browse dialog box, 182
Bubble Help feature, 21
build bullet, 64
builds, 207–208, 276
  bullets, 209–211
  elements, 212–213
bullet charts, 64, 79
bullet slides, 79
Bulleted List SmartMaster, 80
bulleted lists, 80–81
bullets, 283
  builds, 209–211
  modifying SmartMaster, 177

• C •

cell backgrounds, 111
Change Named Style dialog box, 176–177
Character Maps, 263
Chart menu, 29
Chart Properties dialog box options, 82–83, 85–87
Chart⇨Axes and Grids command, 97
Chart⇨Chart Properties command, 82
Chart⇨Legend Properties command, 84
Chart⇨Series command, 86

Chart⇨X-Axis properties command, 84–85
charts, 16, 42, 63–77
　area, 65
　axes, 95–98
　axes and gridlines modification, 88–92
　backgrounds, 81–84
　bar, 65
　borders, 81–84
　build bullet, 64
　bullet, 64, 79
　combining types, 100–101
　converting color of imported, 71
　creation, 65–68
　data from other programs, 68–77
　defining imported data, 70
　defining on current chart settings, 102
　defining X- and Y-axis labels, 70
　Excel linked, 73–74
　embedded, 77
　gridlines, 94–95
　importing data, 68–76
　importing from spreadsheet, 70–74
　line graph, 65
　linking, 69, 73–76
　Lotus 1-2-3 data, 71–72
　mixing series on, 101
　multiple on slide, 101
　organizational, 64
　pie, 65
　placing on slide, 287
　previewing, 65
　rounding border corners, 83
　saving settings as style, 101–102
　scale, 90, 93
　selecting type, 66
　series borders and colors, 86–87
　tables, 64
　text enhancement, 84–85
　tick marks, 88–92
　titles and legends, 66–67
　transitions, 213
　X-axis, 90
　Y-axis, 90, 99
Charts⇨Axes and Grids command, 90
Charts⇨Series Labels command, 99
Check Spelling SmartIcon, 287
Choose Multiple Content Pages option button, 42
circles, 140
Click Here menu, 176
Click here placeholders, 20, 282
　adding, 185
　automatic placement, 187
　changing typeface, 176
　ID numbers, 187
　modifying properties, 185–186
　styles, 186
Click Here⇨Click Here Properties command, 177, 185
Click Here⇨Font & Color command, 176
ClickArt, 122
client, 69
clip art
　adding, 40–41
　adding to library, 145
　bitmapped graphics, 148–150
　bringing into document, 144–145
　catalog symbols and diagrams, 40
　enlarging, 41
　groups, 145–146
　importing, 121–122, 147–150
　included with Freelance Graphics, 121
　modifying, 145–147
　placing, 41
　recoloring images, 147
　selecting, 145
　speeding up search for, 145
　storing, 32
　ungrouping, 145–147
　vector graphics, 148

Freelance Graphics 96 For Windows 95 For Dummies

Clip Art button, 144
closed path, 141
closing presentations, 49
collapsed view, 57
Collection menu, 29, 146
Collection⇨Group command, 145
Collection⇨Space command, 136
Collection⇨Text Properties command, 144
color
  alternate color library, 46
  chart series, 86–87
  converting to black-and-white format, 47
  monitors, 152–153
  organizational chart text, 118
  presentations, 283
  SmartMaster backgrounds, 174–175
  solid rather than changing, 46
  text in tables, 110
  transparencies, 203–204
Color button, 127
color depth, 17, 230
color palettes, 183–184
color/monochrome button, 22
columns
  adding, 105
  cutting and pasting, 107
  defining, 104
  moving, 107
  removing, 105
  resizing, 108
combining chart types, 100–101
commands
  Bitmap⇨Bitmap Properties, 149
  Bitmap⇨Crop Bitmap, 150
  Chart⇨Axes and Grids, 90, 97
  Chart⇨Chart Properties, 82
  Chart⇨Legend Properties, 84
  Chart⇨Series, 86
  Chart⇨Series Labels, 99
  Chart⇨X-Axis Properties, 84–85

Click Here⇨Click Here Properties, 177, 185
Click Here⇨Font & Color, 176
Collection⇨Group, 145
Collection⇨Space, 136
Collection⇨Text Properties, 144
Create⇨1-2-3 Named Chart, 71
Create⇨Add Bitmap, 149
Create⇨Add Clip Art, 121, 144
Create⇨Add Movie, 221
Create⇨Add to Library⇨Clipart Library, 145
Create⇨Chart, 101
Create⇨Click here Block, 185
Create⇨Fonts & Colors, 125
Create⇨Object, 75, 220
Create⇨Organization Chart, 112
Create⇨Page, 56, 163
Create⇨Speaker Note, 240
Create⇨Table, 104
Create⇨Text Shape Properties, 125
Drawing⇨Group, 145
Drawing⇨Line/Curve Properties, 141
Edit⇨Check Spelling, 167, 169
Edit⇨Clear, 163, 196, 233
Edit⇨Copy, 72, 75, 216
Edit⇨Cut, 107, 196, 233
Edit⇨GoTo, 35
Edit⇨Paste, 72, 107, 263
Edit⇨Paste Special, 75, 217
Edit⇨Staff, 115
Edit⇨TeamReview⇨Distribute for Review, 269
File⇨Close, 173
File⇨New, 282
File⇨Open, 172, 180
File⇨Print, 45, 48, 59, 197–198, 205, 244, 248
File⇨Publish to Internet, 271
File⇨Save, 43

Index 297

File⇨Save As, 173, 233
File⇨TeamMail, 271
File⇨TeamReview⇨Consolidate Comments, 270
File⇨TeamReview⇨Distribute for Review, 267, 272
File⇨TeamReview⇨End Review, 270
File⇨TeamShow, 237
File⇨TeamShow⇨Send, 272
File⇨User Setup⇨Freelance Preferences, 145
Freelance Preferences, 31
Group⇨Ungroup, 145
Help⇨Help Topics, 268
Movie⇨Movie Properties, 222
Org Chart⇨Connecting Lines, 119
Org Chart⇨Edit Data, 116
Page⇨Build Bullets, 209, 283
Page⇨Go To Page, 35
Page⇨Next Page, 35
Page⇨Page Properties, 174, 181, 208
Page⇨Previous Page, 35
Page⇨Screen Show Effects, 208, 284, 288
Page⇨Switch Page Layout, 101
Presentation⇨Change Typefaces Globally, 176
Presentation⇨Choose a New SmartMaster Look, 281
Presentation⇨Different SmartMaster Look, 203
Presentation⇨Edit Backdrop, 178, 180, 183, 185
Presentation⇨Edit Page Layouts, 174, 176–180
Presentation⇨Edit Palette, 183
Presentation⇨Rehearse/Start, 274
Presentation⇨Run Screen Show, 159, 228
Presentation⇨Set Up Screen Show, 157–158, 208, 224–225, 227, 275
Presentation⇨Switch Palette, 183
Presentation⇨Units & Grids, 185
Print⇨Options, 46, 203
Print⇨Properties, 204, 248
Table⇨Cell Properties, 108
Table⇨Move Column/Row, 107
Table⇨Size Column/Row, 108
Table⇨Table Properties, 108
Text Shape⇨Align, 136
Text Shape⇨Fast Format, 132
Text Shape⇨Fast Format/Apply Attributes, 132
Text Shape⇨Fast Format/Pickup Attributes, 132
Text Shape⇨Font & Colors, 125, 127
Text Shape⇨Group, 137
Text Shape⇨Named Styles, 128
Text Shape⇨Priority, 135
Text Shape⇨Rotate, 134
Text Shape⇨Switch Text Shape Type, 125
Text Shape⇨Text Shape Properties, 125, 127, 130
Text Shape⇨Ungroup, 137
Text⇨Apply Style to All Speaker Notes, 242
Text⇨Reset to Defaults, 242
Text⇨Text Properties, 80, 108, 143
Text⇨Text Properties by Level, 80
User Setup, 21
View⇨Last Zoom, 35
View⇨Show Rulers, 185
View⇨Zoom Out, 35
View⇨Zoom to Actual Size, 35
company names, 262
compressing files, 195
computer screens, 8
connecting lines in organizational charts, 119
Connector menu, 29

Freelance Graphics 96 For Windows 95 For Dummies

connectors, 27
Consolidate Comments dialog box, 270
container file, 77
context sensitive, 21
contrast, 149
Control menu icon, 49
Copy (Ctrl+C) key combination, 54
Copy SmartIcon, 54
copyright symbol, 264
CorelDRAW, 122, 148
CorelPhoto-Paint, 148, 181
Create a 1-2-3 Named Chart dialog box, 71
Create a Chart SmartIcon, 101, 287
Create a Chart SmartMaster, 65
Create a Text Block SmartIcon, 288
Create Chart dialog box, 65–66
Create Chart Style dialog box, 102
Create New Page Layout dialog box, 180, 185
Create Page (F7) function key, 56
Create Text Style dialog box, 128
Create⇨1-2-3 Named Chart command, 71
Create⇨Add Bitmap command, 149
Create⇨Add Clip Art command, 121, 144
Create⇨Add Movie command, 221
Create⇨Add to Library⇨Clipart Library command, 145
Create⇨Chart command, 101
Create⇨Click here Block command, 185
Create⇨Fonts & Colors command, 125
Create⇨Object command, 75, 220
Create⇨Organization Chart command, 112
Create⇨Page command, 56, 163
Create⇨Speaker Note command, 240
Create⇨Table command, 104
Create⇨Text Shape Properties command, 125
Crop Bitmap dialog box, 150
cropping, 150
Current Page view, 34, 213, 227, 282
  navigating, 34–35

Curve tool, 141
Curved Text dialog box, 143–144
curves, 141–143
CUSTOM.SYM file, 145
customized SmartMasters
  adding bitmapped graphics to backdrop, 181–182
  Click here placeholders, 184–186
  new color palettes, 183–184
  SmartMaster Look file, 180
  standard presentation, 180
  starting from scratch, 180–181
customizing
  active set of SmartIcons, 30–31
  preferences, 31–33
  SmartIcons bar, 29–31
  work environment, 29–33

• D •

data
  importing, 68–77
  linking, 69
  organized in groups, 103–112
date, 21
decorative typefaces, 175
defaults. *See* preferences
Delete Column/Row dialog box, 105
Delete Columns SmartIcon, 105
Delete key, 163
Delete Rows SmartIcon, 105
desktop publishing service bureaus. *See* service bureaus
device dependent, 148
device independent, 148
diagrams, 42, 213
dictionaries, 169–170
directory/time-date/cursor position button, 21

Index

display adapters, 151
display system size, 230
display typefaces, 175
Distribute for TeamReview dialog box, 267–269, 272
Distribute Presentation on Floppy Disk dialog box, 267
Distribution Complete dialog box, 268
Down One Level (Tab) key, 56
dragging, 24
Drawing & Text button, 27, 121–122, 140
Drawing menu, 26, 29, 133, 146
drawing tools, 26–27, 139–144
Drawing⇨Convert submenu, 143
Drawing⇨Group command, 145
Drawing⇨Line/Curve Properties command, 141
drawings, 140–141
  attention-grabbing text effects, 142–144
  linking to spreadsheet, 74–76
drop shadows and tables, 111
dye-sublimation transparencies, 202

• E •

e-mail and sending presentations, 271
e-mail icon, 271
Edit Backdrop mode, 176, 178–179, 185
Edit Backdrop screen, 181
Edit Data dialog box, 66–68
Edit Links dialog box, 68–70
Edit Page Layouts dialog box, 180
Edit Palette dialog box, 183–184
Edit Titles dialog box, 67
Edit⇨Check Spelling command, 167, 169
Edit⇨Clear command, 163, 196, 233
Edit⇨Copy command, 72, 75, 216
Edit⇨Cut command, 107, 196, 233
Edit⇨GoTo command, 35
Edit⇨Paste command, 72, 107, 263
Edit⇨Paste Special command, 75, 217
Edit⇨Staff command, 115
Edit⇨TeamReview⇨Distribute for Review command, 269
electronic screen shows
  adding sound, 219–220
  advancing one slide, 228
  animation and video files, 18
  back one slide, 228
  beginning, 228
  builds, 207–211
  color depth, 17
  control panel, 224–226
  delivering, 224–228
  drawing tool, 224–226
  ending, 228
  equipment necessary, 9
  floppy disks, 18
  hot links, 216–217
  jumping to slide, 228
  launching other applications, 214–215
  LCD panel, 14
  monitor resolution, 18
  movies, 219–224
  navigating, 228
  negative aspects, 17
  OLE2 (Object Linking and Embedding), 215–216
  Page Sorter navigation, 15
  photographs, 17
  positive aspects, 13–14
  running, 288
  self-looping, 226–227
  self-running, 226–227
  setting up, 224–226
  taking on the road, 228
  transitions, 207–209
  when to use, 13–16
elements
  adding to SmartMasters, 178–179
  transitions, 213

Freelance Graphics 96 For Windows 95 For Dummies

ellipses, 140
Ellipses tool, 140
em dashes, 263
embedded charts, 77
embedding
  deciding when to use, 77
  when to use, 217
End Review dialog box, 270
Enlarge SmartIcon, 24, 133
environment and presentations, 259
EPS (Encapsulated PostScript) file format, 147–148
Equal SmartIcon, 24, 133
equipment, 8–10
Excel, 73–74
excess modifiers, 264

• F •

File Locations dialog box, 32
File menu, 21, 30–31
File⇨Close command, 173
File⇨New command, 282
File⇨Open command, 172, 180
File⇨Print command, 45, 48, 59, 197–198, 205, 244, 248
File⇨Properties⇨Details Windows command, 197
File⇨Publish to Internet command, 271
File⇨Save As command, 173, 233
File⇨Save command, 43
File⇨TeamMail command, 271
File⇨TeamReview⇨Consolidate Comments command, 270
File⇨TeamReview⇨Distribute for Review command, 267, 272
File⇨TeamReview⇨End Review command, 270
File⇨TeamShow command, 237
File⇨TeamShow⇨Send command, 272
File⇨User Setup⇨Freelance Preferences command, 145
filenames, 33, 44
files
  automatically saving, 33
  compressing, 195
  printing to, 196–198
  saving, 43–45
  storing, 32–33
  transferring by modem, 195
  transporting large with removable media, 194
fill, 130–131
first presentation
  adding slides, 42
  adding text to page, 40
  charts and diagrams, 42
  clip art, 40–41
  closing, 49
  incremental saves, 45
  multiple page creation, 42
  naming, 43
  next page, 41
  notes about presentation, 43
  previewing pages, 49–50
  printing, 45–48
  reopening, 49
  saving, 43–44
  selecting first page, 39
FLC (AutoDesk Animator) format, 220
FLI (AutoDesk Animator) format, 220
floppy disks and electronic screen shows, 18
flowcharts
  showing relationships between objects, 27
  Text Shapes, 27, 122
flying bullets, 283
Font button, 125

Index

fonts, 17
  including with presentations, 230
  modifying SmartMaster, 175–176
  organizational charts, 118
  point size, 175
  remote viewing presentations, 230
  tables, 110
  Text Shapes, 125–127
formats, choosing appropriate, 7–16
formatting
  audience handouts, 248–250
  awkward, 261
  organizational chart text, 117–118
  speakers notes, 240–241
  tables, 108–110
fractions, 263
freehand drawing, 141
Freehand tool, 141
Freelance Graphics 96
  compatibility, 19
  customizing work environment, 29–33
  familiarizing yourself with, 19
  integration with Lotus 1-2-3, 216
  main screen, 19–22
  menus, 28–29
  navigation, 34–36
  saving in different version, 44
  starting, 38, 49, 54
  ten things you'll like, 281–284
  tools, 22–27
  view tabs, 21
Freelance Graphics Preferences dialog
    box, 31–33
Freelance Preferences command, 31

• G •

GIF file format, 181
Go To (Ctrl+G) key combination, 35
Go To Page dialog box, 35
Go To SmartIcon, 35
gradients, 83
graphics
  bad coloring, 153
  bitmapped, 148–150, 153
  monitors, 151–154
  pace and timing, 153
  preparing for presentations, 151–154
  preparing for slides, 154
  printing, 154
  vector, 148, 153
graphics cards, 152–153
graphs, 16, 63–77. *See also* charts
gridlines
  modification, 88–92, 94–95
  showing/hiding, 90
Group menu, 29, 146
Group⇨Ungroup command, 145
grouping
  clip art, 145
  Text Shapes, 137–138
groups, 145–146
GUI (graphical user interface), 19

• H •

handles, 23–24
handouts. *See* audience handouts
help, 33
Help⇨Help Topics command, 268
homonyms, 166
hot links, 75
  electronic screen shows, 216–217
hyphenation, 262

Freelance Graphics 96 For Windows 95 For Dummies

• I •

icons used in this book, 4
images, 121–137
Images with Impact, 122
importing
 bitmapped graphics, 182–183
 clip art, 121–122, 147–150
importing data
 charts, 68–70
 charts from spreadsheets, 70–74
impressing audience, 8
incremental backups, 33
information, organizing, 51–53
inkjet printers, 205
Insert a Row SmartIcon, 105
Insert a Table SmartIcon, 105
installing
 Mobile Screen Show Player, 235
 TeamShow files, 235

• J •

Jaz drives, 194
Jump to Slide (Shift+Esc) key combination, 228

• K •

key combinations
 Ctrl+C (Copy), 54
 Ctrl+Enter (Line Break), 113
 Ctrl+F2 (Spell Check), 167
 Ctrl+G (Go To), 35
 Ctrl+O (Open), 172
 Ctrl+S (Save), 43, 45
 Ctrl+V (Paste), 54
 Shift+Esc (Jump to Slide), 228
 Shift+Tab (Superiors), 113, 116
 Shift+Tab (Up One Level), 56

• L •

laser printers, 205
Launch Application dialog box, 214
layering multiple Text Shapes, 135–136
LCD panel, 14
leading, 80
legends, 66–67, 69
levels, 56, 80
Line Break (Ctrl+Enter) key
 combination, 113
line breaks, 262
line graph, 65
Line tool, 140
line weight, 130–131
lines, 130–131, 140
linking, 69, 73–76
 bitmapped graphics, 182
 client, 69
 deciding when to use, 76–77, 217
 OLE2 (Object Linking and Embedding), 71
 Paste Special command, 74–76
 server, 69
logos, 178, 288
long words, 264–265
Lotus 1-2-3
 importing charts from, 71
 integration with Freelance Graphics
  96, 216
 making Freelance Graphics chart out of
  data, 71–72
 pasting chart from, 72
Lotus SmartSuite integration, 284
LOTUS/SMASTER/FLG subdirectory, 172

• M •

main screen, 19–22
marquee selecting, 23, 162
MAS file extension, 172–173
MCI (Media Control Interface) movies, 219
menu bar, 21
menus, 28–29
messages, 22
metafiles, 76
Micrografx Designer, 148
MID (MIDI) sound files, 219, 231
Mobile Screen Show Player, 221, 232–235
Mobile TeamShow, 237
MOBILESS.EXE file, 234–236
modifying
  bitmapped graphics, 149–150
  Click here placeholders, 184–186
  clip art, 145–147
  SmartMasters, 172–179
monitors, 151–154
mouse, 56
  cursor position, 21–22
Move Column SmartIcon, 107
Move Column/Row dialog box, 107
Move Row SmartIcon, 107
Movie menu, 29
Movie⇨Movie Properties command, 222
movies, 219–224
moving objects, 23–24
multi-sided shapes, 141
multimedia drivers, 231
multimedia equipment, 231
multimedia viewers, 231
multiple
  objects, 23–24
  presentations, 286
  slides, 36, 209

multiple-segment arrows, 141
multiple-segment lines, 140–141
My Computer shortcuts, 50

• N •

Named Styles submenu, 129
naming presentations, 43
navigation, 34–36
networks and delivering presentations, 236–237, 272
New Page button, 42, 65
New Page dialog box, 41–42, 163
  2 Chart template, 101
  Choose Multiple Content Pages option button, 42
  Content Pages section, 65
  New Page button, 42
  Page Layouts section, 101
  selecting first page of presentation, 39
  Title option, 54
New Presentation dialog box, 38–39, 172–173, 181
New SmartIcon, 285
Next Cell (Tab) key, 108
nonworking words, 264
Notes database and posting presentation draft to, 268–269
numbering pages, 22
numbers translating into visuals, 63–77

• O •

object embedding, 75, 215, 217
object linking, 215, 217
  advantages, 75
Object Size submenu, 125, 133

objects
  aligning, 136–137
  assigning movies to, 222
  attaching movies, 221
  builds, 212–213
  dragging, 24
  editing OLE2 (Object Linking and
    Embedding), 218
  grouping, 137–138
  handles, 23–24
  layering multiple, 135–136
  moving, 23–24
  placing, 185
  resizing, 23–24, 133
  rotating, 134, 147
  selecting, 23
  showing relationships between, 27
OLE (Object Linking and Embedding), 75
OLE2 (Object Linking and Embedding),
    71, 75
  client, 75, 215
  editing objects, 218
  electronic screen shows, 215–216
  object embedding, 75, 215
  object linking, 75, 215
  server, 75, 215
Open (Ctrl+O) key combination, 172
Open dialog box, 68, 172, 286
Open SmartIcon, 286
opening
  presentations, 286
  SmartMaster Look files, 172
Options dialog box, 203, 205
Org Chart menu, 29, 117
Org Chart⇨Connecting Lines command,
    119
Org Chart⇨Edit Data command, 116
org charts. See organizational charts
Organization Chart Gallery dialog box,
    112–113
Organization Chart SmartMaster, 112
Organizational Chart Entry List dialog
    box, 113, 115–116
Organizational Chart Staff dialog box, 115
organizational charts, 64, 103
  adding staff member, 115
  backgrounds, 118–119
  borders, 118
  connecting lines, 119
  creation, 112–113
  enhancing, 116–119
  fonts, 118
  formatting text, 117–118
  labels for entries, 113
  previewing, 115
  styles, 120
  subordinates, 113–114
  superiors, 113–114
  typing entries, 113
  updating, 116
Outline view, 21, 51
  moving slides around, 164–165
Outliner, 283
  adding elements, 58
  adding slides, 56
  breaking slide into two slides, 164
  changing slide layouts, 56
  deciding to work in, 51–53
  expanding and collapsing outline, 57–58
  levels, 56
  moving text from WordPro into, 54
  new presentation, 54–56
  printing outline, 59
  promoting and demoting topics, 56
  rearranging slides, 57, 163–164
  speakers notes, 58
  text attributes, 58
  text down one level, 56
  text up one level, 56

Index

outlines
  expanding and collapsing, 57–58
  printing, 59
  Text Shapes, 130–131
overhead transparencies.
    See transparencies

• P •

Page # of # button, 35
page coordinates, 21, 22
Page menu, 28–29
page numbering buttons, 22
Page Properties dialog box, 284
Page Setup dialog box, 251
Page Sorter, 15, 21
  moving slides around, 162, 163
  navigation, 35–36
Page⇨Build Bullets command, 209, 283
Page⇨Go To Page command, 35
Page⇨Next Page command, 35
Page⇨Page Properties command, 174, 181, 208
Page⇨Previous Page command, 35
Page⇨Screen Show Effects command, 208, 284, 288
Page⇨Switch Page Layout command, 101
PageDown key, 35
pages, 20
  adding text, 40
  numbering, 22
  placing Text Shapes on, 123–124
  previewing, 48–50
  printing, 48
  sending to team, 22
  zooming in and out, 35
PageUp key, 35
Paste (Ctrl+V) key combination, 54
Paste SmartIcon, 54

Paste Special dialog box, 217
PCX file extension, 147, 149, 181
photographs, 17
pie charts, 65
PKUNZIP, 233
PKZIP, 195, 198, 233
Place Logo on Every Page SmartIcon, 288
PLZ extension, 235
point size, 175
Pointer tool, 23–24, 133, 162
points, 175
Polygon tool, 141
polygons, 141
Polyline tool, 140–141
PostScript slide recorders, 192
predefined styles, 129
preferences, 31–33
Presentation Backdrop layout, 174
presentation files, 32–33
presentation formats
  choosing appropriate, 7–16
  computer screens, 8
  electronic screen shows, 13–16
  planning ahead, 17
  presentation medium, 17
  razzle-dazzle effect, 8
  slides, 8–11
  transparencies, 8–13
Presentation⇨Change Typefaces Globally command, 176
Presentation⇨Choose a New SmartMaster Look command, 281
Presentation⇨Different SmartMaster Look command, 203
Presentation⇨Edit Backdrop command, 178, 183, 185
Presentation⇨Edit Page Layouts command, 174, 176–180
Presentation⇨Edit Palette command, 183
Presentation⇨Rehearse/Start command, 274

Presentation➪Run Screen Show command, 159, 228
Presentation➪Set Up Screen Show command, 157–158, 208, 224–225, 227, 275
Presentation➪Switch Palette command, 183
Presentation➪Units & Grids command, 185
presentations
  action audience should take, 257
  adding slides, 56
  answering questions properly, 279
  anticipating objections, 276–277
  audience handouts, 277
  audience position, 257
  avoiding awkward formatting, 261
  best chances of success, 8–9
  black-and-white, 283
  breaking into chunks of slides, 196, 233
  breaking proper names and company names, 262
  builds, 276
  closing, 49
  color, 283
  color to black-and-white format, 47
  compression, 195
  control over environment, 259
  delivering remotely, 236–237
  directory, 21
  em dashes, 263
  equipment, 8–10
  excess modifiers, 264
  filename, 21
  first, 37–50
  focusing eyes on supporters, 278
  good night's sleep before, 277
  how many slides you need, 161
  how much audience knows about topic, 256
  HTML format, 271
  hyphenation, 262
  ignoring people who leave or are bored, 278–279
  incremental backups, 33, 45
  introducing yourself to audience before, 278
  legal characters, 264
  line breaks, 262
  lines that stick out too far, 262
  long words, 264–265
  multiple, 286
  naming, 43
  never bluffing, 280
  new, 54–56
  nonworking words, 264
  notes about, 43
  numbering pages, 22
  on other computers, 17–18
  opening, 286
  optional slides, 276–277
  planning, 51–53
  planning formats ahead, 17–18
  polishing tips, 261–265
  practicing, 274–275
  preparing for service bureaus, 195–198
  preparing graphics for, 151–154
  printing, 45–48, 287
  printing in-house, 198–199
  printing to file, 196–198
  publishing on WWW (World Wide Web), 270–271
  questions and objections from audience, 258–259
  questions defining goals and strategies, 255–259
  remote viewing, 229–236
  reopening, 49
  review drafts, 267–268
  reviewing, 157–170
  revising, 162–165
  routing TeamMail, 272

Index 307

saving, 43–45, 286
sending through e-mail, 271
sending to team, 22
shortcuts, 50
speakers notes, 277
special characters, 263
starting, 285
typesetter fractions, 263
visuals, 63–77
watching from audience's perspective, 275–276
ways to be more confident, 273–280
what three points should audience remember, 258
where delivered, 8–9
who audience is, 255–256
previewing
  charts, 65
  color changes in color palettes, 184
  organizational charts, 115
  pages, 49–50
  printing selected pages, 48
  reviewer's presentation comments, 269–270
  slides, 199
  transparencies, 206
Print dialog box, 45, 59, 198–199, 205, 244, 248
  Copies section, 250
  Number of copies option, 46
  Page Setup button, 251
  Pages section, 46, 244
  Preview button, 206
  Preview option, 48
  Print section, 244, 250
  Print to drop-down list, 46
  Print with border option, 252
print file, 196–198
Print Preview dialog box, 48
Print SmartIcon, 287

Print to File dialog box, 197
Print⇔Options command, 46, 203
Print⇔Properties command, 204, 248
printer drivers, 197
printers, 46–47
printing
  Adjust output library for printing option, 46
  audience handouts, 248–251
  banding, 203
  graphics, 154
  matching displayed color, 46
  number of copies, 46
  number of pages, 46
  outline, 59
  presentations, 45–48, 287
  presentations at service bureaus, 195–198
  presentations in-house, 198–199
  previewing selected pages, 48
  Print graduated fills as solid option, 46
  Print with blank background option, 47
  slides in-house, 193–194
  speakers notes, 244–245
  to file, 196–198
  transparencies, 17, 203–206
  turning off backgrounds, 47
projector icon, 223
proper names, 262
Properties dialog box, 108–109, 116–117, 176–177, 181
  Basics section of Properties option, 185
  collapsing, 186
  Font & Color tab, 117
  Line & Fill Color tab, 86, 110–111, 118, 141, 174
  Pattern Color drop-down list, 174
  Pattern drop-down list, 174, 181
  playing movies, 222
  Properties for drop-down list, 110

Properties dialog box *(continued)*
  Screen Show Effects tab, 212–214, 220–222
  Style tab, 186
  transparency setting, 204
Properties for Bitmap dialog box, 149
Properties for Chart dialog box, 102
Properties for Connecting Lines dialog box, 119
Properties for Organizational Chart dialog box, 120
Properties for Selected Cells dialog box, 110
Properties for Series Label dialog box, 99
Properties for Text Shape dialog box, 125, 127, 129–132
Properties for X-Axis dialog box, 90–91, 93, 97
Properties for Y-Axis dialog box, 90–91, 93–95, 97–99
proportionally resizing objects, 24
proprietary-language slide recorders, 192
PRZ file extension, 43
public network directory, 269
Publish to Internet dialog box, 271

• *Q* •

QuickTime movies, 18

• *R* •

razzle-dazzle effect, 8
rearranging slides, 57
recoloring
  clip art, 147
  Text Shapes, 130–131
Rectangle tool, 140

rectangles, 140
Reduce SmartIcon, 24, 133
refresh rate, 153
register marks, 264
Rehearse mode, 274–275, 283
relationships between objects, 27
remote viewing presentations
  breaking into small chunks, 233
  color depth, 230
  computer speed, 231
  display system size, 230
  distributing, 230–232
  fonts, 230
  Mobile Screen Show Player, 234–235
  multimedia, 231
  multiple presentations, 236
  presentation list, 235–236
  README text file, 234
  run-time version, 232–233
  unknown computers, 232
removable media, 194
Remove Drawn Lines (Alt) key, 226
reopening presentations, 49
resizing
  objects, 23–24
  Text Shapes, 27, 122–123, 133
resolution, 151–152
  movies, 223
  slide recorders, 192
review drafts, 267–268
review session, 267–268
reviewing presentations
  logical data flow, 160–161
  revising presentation, 162–165
  self-running screen show, 157–160
  spelling errors, 165–170
  weak points in argument, 160–162
  wordy slides, 160
revising presentations, 162–165
rotating
  objects, 147
  Text Shapes, 134

Index

rows, 104–105, 107–108
rulers, 185
Run dialog box, 235
Run Screen Show From Beginning SmartIcon, 276
Run Screen Show SmartIcon, 50, 288
run-time presentation version, 232–233

• S •

sans-serif typefaces, 175, 291
Save (Ctrl+S) key combination, 43, 45
Save As dialog box, 43–44, 173
  naming styles, 102
  Prepare for Mobile Screen Show Player option, 233
Save dialog box, 286
Save SmartIcon, 286
saving
  color palettes, 184
  files, 33, 43–45
  presentations, 43–45, 286
  SmartMaster Look files, 173
scales, 90, 93
Screen Show, 275
Screen Show Effects dialog box, 209–211
Screen Show Effects Properties dialog box, 208–209
Show Page dialog box, 50
Screen Show Pages dialog box, 225, 228
Screen Show Sequence Overview dialog box, 212–213
screen shows. *See* electronic screen shows
screens, 8–9
Select Print Border Style dialog box, 245, 252
selecting objects, 23
Selection tool, 140

self-looping electronic screen show, 226–227
self-running electronic screen show, 157–160, 226–227
self-running kiosks, 238
self-running presentations, 17–18, 238
series, 86–87
  mixing on charts, 101
serif typefaces, 175
server, 69
service bureau slide output, 17–18
service bureaus, 193, 195–198
  transparencies, 202
Set Up Screen Show dialog box, 158, 224–225, 275
  Display Next Page option, 158, 227, 276
  Options tab, 159, 227
  Page Effects section, 158, 276
  Page Effects tab, 227
  Position drop-down box, 224
  Run Options section, 227
  Run Screen Show in Continuous Loop option, 159
  Tools tab, 159, 224–225
  Transition list, 158, 227, 276
sharpness, 149
shortcuts, 50
Slide Design view, 21
slide recorders, 191–192
Slide Sorter view, 282
slides, 8, 20, 191–194
  adding, 42, 163
  adding logos, 178
  adding movies, 221–222
  black and white, 22
  breaking into chunks, 164, 196
  bullet, 79
  bulleted lists, 80–81
  changing layouts, 56
  chart placeholder, 66
  Click here placeholders, 282

slides *(continued)*
  collapsed view, 57
  color, 22
  deleting, 163
  displaying one element at a time, 208–211
  dragging, 36
  drawings, 26–27
  element builds, 212–213
  element transitions, 213
  entering text, 25–26
  equipment necessary, 9
  expanding and collapsing outline, 57–58
  going to specific and returning to Current Page, 36
  how many you need, 161
  inserting text, 288
  levels, 56, 80
  lines that stick out too far, 262
  listing, 35
  logical data flow, 160–161
  moving around, 162–165
  moving between, 34–35
  moving objects, 23
  moving to another location, 36
  multiple charts, 101
  negative aspects, 11
  next, 35
  optional, 276–277
  organizing information, 52–53
  placing charts, 287
  positive aspects, 10–11
  preparing graphics for, 154
  previewing, 49–50, 199
  previous, 35
  printing in-house, 193–194, 198–199
  printing selected, 48
  rearranging, 57, 163–164
  resizing objects, 23
  selecting objects, 23
  service bureaus, 18, 193
  slide recorders, 191–192
  Speaker's Note SmartIcon, 242
  spelling errors, 165–170
  subtitles, 56
  text placeholder, 25
  thumbnails, 21, 35–36, 55
  time between, 158–159
  titles, 20, 55
  too much information on, 18
  transitioning between, 208–209
  weak points in argument, 160–162
  when to use, 10–11
  where they come from, 191–192
  wordy, 160
SmartCharts, 66
SmartIcons, 21
  active set customization, 30–31
  display resolution and, 30
  floating palette, 286
  most important, 285–288
  when context-sensitive sets are to appear, 31
SmartIcons bar, 29–31
SmartIcons Setup command, 30
SmartIcons Setup dialog box, 30–31
SmartMaster content templates, 37–44, 282
  charts and diagrams, 42
  information flows, 40
  modifying, 172
  saving files as, 44
  selecting template, 38
SmartMaster Look files
  modifying, 172–173
  opening, 172
  renaming edited, 173
  saving files as, 44
  saving, 173
SmartMasters, 171, 281
  adding to SmartMaster Look library, 181

Index 311

automatic Click here placeholder
  placement, 187
chart backgrounds, 82
customized, 179–187
default, 186–187
formatting charts, 71–72
logical data flow, 161
modifying, 172–179
storing, 32
Sound menu, 29
sounds
  assigning to transitions, 212
  electronic screen show, 219–220
  embedding or referring to files, 221
  formats supported, 219–220
Speaker Note dialog box, 240–241
Speaker Note SmartIcon, 240
Speaker's Note SmartIcon, 58, 242
speaker's notes, 58, 246, 277
  border, 245
  creation, 240
  formatting, 240–242
  hot spots, 244
  importance, 239–240
  information that doesn't fit on slide, 244
  outline format, 242–243
  printing, 244–245
  what to include in, 242–244
  zooming in or out, 241
special characters, 263
Spell Check (Ctrl+F2) key combination, 167
Spell Check dialog box, 167–169, 287
spell checker, 287
  dictionaries, 169–170
  removing formatting, 242
  spelling errors, 165–170
  starting session, 168–169
  views, 167
Spell Checker User's Dictionary dialog
  box, 169

spreadsheets
  importing charts from, 70–74
  linking to, 74–76
squares, 140
stacking order, 135–136
staff member, 115
Start menu, 49–50
Start⇨Run Windows command, 235
Start⇨Settings⇨Control Panels⇨Printer
  Windows command, 197
Start⇨Settings⇨Printer Windows
  command, 197
starting Freelance Graphics 96, 38
startup dialog boxes, 32
startup view, 32
styles, 176
  Click here placeholders, 186
  predefined, 129
  saving chart settings as, 101–102
  Text Shapes, 127–129
  typefaces, 175
subordinates, 113–114
Subordinates (Tab) key, 113, 116
subtitles, 56
Super VGA monitors, 151
superiors, 113–114
Superiors (Shift+Tab) key combination,
  113, 116
Switch Page Layout dialog box, 56
Switch Palette dialog box, 183
SyJet drives, 194
symbols, 121–137
Syquest drives, 194
Syquest EZ135 drives, 194

• T •

Table Gallery dialog box, 104–105
Table menu, 105, 108
Table Properties dialog box, 108
Table SmartMaster, 104
Table⇨Cell Properties command, 108
Table⇨Move Column/Row command, 107
Table⇨Size Column/Row command, 108
Table⇨Table Properties command, 108
tables, 64, 103–112
  adding columns and rows, 105
  adding text, 108
  borders, 110–111
  cell backgrounds, 111
  changing fonts, 110
  creation, 104–105
  cutting and pasting multiple rows or columns, 107
  defining rows and columns, 104
  drop shadow, 111
  formatting, 108–110
  manipulating columns and rows, 105–108
  moving columns and rows, 107
  removing columns and rows, 105
  resizing columns and rows, 108
  shadows for text, 110
  style, 104–105
  text attributes, 109–110
  text color, 110
  transitions, 213
tasks, 21
team members, 284
TeamMail, 271–272
TeamMail button, 22
TeamMail dialog box, 22, 269, 271–272
TeamReview, 221, 267–272
teams, 22
TeamShow, 235–237, 272
TeamShow dialog box, 236–237
templates. *See* SmartMaster content templates
  modifying, 172
  storing, 32
ten keys to great transparencies, 289–292
ten most important SmartIcons, 285–288
ten presentation polishing content tips, 261–265
ten questions defining presentation goals and strategies, 255–259
ten TeamReview effective uses, 267–270
ten things you'll like about Freelance Graphics 96, 281–284
ten ways to be more confident, 273–280
Test tool, 140
text
  adding to page, 40
  adding to tables, 108
  alignment, 25
  attention-grabbing effects, 142–144
  attributes, 58
  changing fonts, 110
  chart enhancement, 84–85
  color, 110, 118
  editing curved, 144
  entering, 25–26
  inserting, 288
  linking to spreadsheet, 74–76
  moving from WordPro into Freelance Graphics Outliner, 54
  object mode, 143
  organizational chart formatting, 117–118
  shadows, 110
  style, 25
  table attributes, 109–110
  Text Shapes, 123–129
  wrapping around shapes, 142–143
  wrapping around user-created shapes, 143–144

Index 313

text charts, 79–81
Text menu, 25, 28, 108, 241
Text mode bar, 125
text placeholder, 25
Text Properties dialog box, 80–81
Text Properties for Speaker Note dialog box, 241
Text Shape buttons, 27
Text Shape menu, 27, 29, 123–124, 133
Text Shape palette, 122
Text Shape⇨Align command, 136
Text Shape⇨Fast Format command, 132
Text Shape⇨Fast Format/Apply Attributes command, 132
Text Shape⇨Fast Format/Pickup Attributes command, 132
Text Shape⇨Font & Colors command, 125, 127
Text Shape⇨Group command, 137
Text Shape⇨Named Styles command, 128
Text Shape⇨Priority command, 135
Text Shape⇨Rotate command, 134
Text Shape⇨Switch Text Shape Type command, 125
Text Shape⇨Text Shape Properties command, 125, 127, 130
Text Shape⇨Ungroup command, 137
Text Shapes, 27
  aligning, 136–137
  applying attributes to other objects, 132
  automatically making fill color same as border, 132
  changing fonts, 125–126
  fill, 130–131
  flowcharts, 122
  font colors, 127
  grouping, 137–138
  layering multiple objects, 135–136
  line, 130–131
  line weight, 130–131
  manipulating, 133–137
  placing on page, 123–124
  previewing alignment, 137
  recoloring, 130–131
  resizing, 27, 122–123, 133
  resizing text, 125
  rotating, 134
  styles, 127–129
  text, 123–127
  Text mode, 124
Text tool, 25–26, 124, 127
Text⇨Apply Style to All Speaker Notes command, 242
Text⇨Reset to Defaults command, 242
Text⇨Text Properties by Level command, 80
Text⇨Text Properties command, 80, 108, 143
TGA file extension, 149, 181
thermal-wax transparencies, 202
35mm slides. *See* slides
thumbnails, 21, 35–36, 55, 57
tick marks, 88–92
TIF file extension, 147, 149, 181
time, 21
title slide, 20
titles, 55
  charts, 66–67
tool palette, 22
tools, 22–27
ToolTips, 105
top-down charts.
  See organizational charts
trademarks, 264
transitions, 207–209, 212–213, 284
transparencies, 8, 201–202
  as backup presentation, 203
  banding, 203–204

transparencies *(continued)*
  black-and-white, 203–204
  color, 203–204
  correct film, 289–290
  dark text, 290
  disadvantages, 202
  dye-sublimation, 202
  equipment necessary, 9
  high-end inkjet printers, 204
  high-resolution viewgraphs, 202
  keys to great, 289–292
  light backgrounds, 290
  negative aspects, 12–13
  portrait page orientation, 291–292
  positive aspects, 12
  previewing, 206
  printing, 17, 203–206
  reasons to use, 201–202
  sans-serif type, 291
  simple borders and clip art, 291
  thermal-wax, 202
  when to use, 11–13
typefaces, 175–176
typesetter fractions, 263

• U •

Ultra (Extended) VGA monitors, 151
ungrouping clip art, 145–147
Up One Level (Shift+Tab) key combination, 56
Use Bitmap for Page Background dialog box, 181–182
User Setup command, 21
User Setup submenu, 30–31

• V •

vector graphics, 148, 153
VGA monitors, 151
video, 219
video files, 18
view tabs, 21
View➪Last Zoom command, 35
View➪Show Rulers command, 185
View➪Zoom Out command, 35
View➪Zoom to Actual Size command, 35
viewgraphs, 202–203
views
  changing, 34
  Current Page, 282
  Outliner, 283
  Slide Sorter, 282
  spell checker, 167
  startup, 32

• W •

WAV (wave) sound files, 219, 231
Welcome to Lotus Freelance Graphics dialog box
  Create a New Presentation Using a SmartMaster tab, 38, 54
  opening presentations, 49
  Select a Content Topic list, 54
  Select a Look list, 54
  SmartMaster content, 282
Windows 95
  Add New Printer icon, 197
  Bubble Help feature, 21
  GUI (graphical user interface), 19
  installing printer drivers, 197
  moving graphics between applications, 215

Index

Windows commands
  File⇨Properties⇨Details, 197
  Start⇨Run, 235
  Start⇨Settings⇨Control Panels⇨Printer, 197
  Start⇨Settings⇨Printer, 197
Windows' Explorer shortcuts, 50
WinZIP, 195
WordPro moving text into Outliner, 54
wordy slides, 160
work environment, 29–33
wrapping text around shapes, 142–143
WWW (World Wide Web), 270–271
WYSIWYG (what-you-see-is-what-you-get), 151

• X •

X- and Y-coordinate, 21–22
X-axis, 21–22, 90, 97

• Y •

Y-axis, 21–22, 90, 97–99

• Z •

Zip drives, 194
ZIP2EXE, 233
Zoom In SmartIcon, 35
Zoom to Full Page SmartIcon, 35

Notes

Notes

Notes

Notes

DUMMIES PRESS™

The Fun & Easy Way™ to learn about computers and more!

10/31/95

Windows® 3.11 For Dummies,® 3rd Edition
by Andy Rathbone
ISBN: 1-56884-370-4
$16.95 USA/
$22.95 Canada

Mutual Funds For Dummies™
by Eric Tyson
ISBN: 1-56884-226-0
$16.99 USA/
$22.99 Canada

DOS For Dummies,® 2nd Edition
by Dan Gookin
ISBN: 1-878058-75-4
$16.95 USA/
$22.95 Canada

The Internet For Dummies,® 2nd Edition
by John Levine & Carol Baroudi
ISBN: 1-56884-222-8
$19.99 USA/
$26.99 Canada

Personal Finance For Dummies™
by Eric Tyson
ISBN: 1-56884-150-7
$16.95 USA/
$22.95 Canada

PCs For Dummies,® 3rd Edition
by Dan Gookin & Andy Rathbone
ISBN: 1-56884-904-5
$16.99 USA/
$22.99 Canada

Macs® For Dummies,® 3rd Edition
by David Pogue
ISBN: 1-56884-239-2
$19.99 USA/
$26.99 Canada

The SAT® I For Dummies™
by Suzee Vlk
ISBN: 1-56884-213-9
$14.99 USA/
$20.99 Canada

Here's a complete listing of IDG Books' ...For Dummies® titles

Title	Author	ISBN	Price
DATABASE			
Access 2 For Dummies®	by Scott Palmer	ISBN: 1-56884-090-X	$19.95 USA/$26.95 Canada
Access Programming For Dummies®	by Rob Krumm	ISBN: 1-56884-091-8	$19.95 USA/$26.95 Canada
Approach 3 For Windows® For Dummies®	by Doug Lowe	ISBN: 1-56884-233-3	$19.99 USA/$26.99 Canada
dBASE For DOS For Dummies®	by Scott Palmer & Michael Stabler	ISBN: 1-56884-188-4	$19.95 USA/$26.95 Canada
dBASE For Windows® For Dummies®	by Scott Palmer	ISBN: 1-56884-179-5	$19.95 USA/$26.95 Canada
dBASE 5 For Windows® Programming For Dummies®	by Ted Coombs & Jason Coombs	ISBN: 1-56884-215-5	$19.99 USA/$26.99 Canada
FoxPro 2.6 For Windows® For Dummies®	by John Kaufeld	ISBN: 1-56884-187-6	$19.95 USA/$26.95 Canada
Paradox 5 For Windows® For Dummies®	by John Kaufeld	ISBN: 1-56884-185-X	$19.95 USA/$26.95 Canada
DESKTOP PUBLISHING/ILLUSTRATION/GRAPHICS			
CorelDRAW! 5 For Dummies®	by Deke McClelland	ISBN: 1-56884-157-4	$19.95 USA/$26.95 Canada
CorelDRAW! For Dummies®	by Deke McClelland	ISBN: 1-56884-042-X	$19.95 USA/$26.95 Canada
Desktop Publishing & Design For Dummies®	by Roger C. Parker	ISBN: 1-56884-234-1	$19.99 USA/$26.99 Canada
Harvard Graphics 2 For Windows® For Dummies®	by Roger C. Parker	ISBN: 1-56884-092-6	$19.95 USA/$26.95 Canada
PageMaker 5 For Macs® For Dummies®	by Galen Gruman & Deke McClelland	ISBN: 1-56884-178-7	$19.95 USA/$26.95 Canada
PageMaker 5 For Windows® For Dummies®	by Deke McClelland & Galen Gruman	ISBN: 1-56884-160-4	$19.95 USA/$26.95 Canada
Photoshop 3 For Macs® For Dummies®	by Deke McClelland	ISBN: 1-56884-208-2	$19.99 USA/$26.99 Canada
QuarkXPress 3.3 For Dummies®	by Galen Gruman & Barbara Assadi	ISBN: 1-56884-217-1	$19.99 USA/$26.99 Canada
FINANCE/PERSONAL FINANCE/TEST TAKING REFERENCE			
Everyday Math For Dummies™	by Charles Seiter	ISBN: 1-56884-248-1	$14.99 USA/$22.99 Canada
Personal Finance For Dummies™ For Canadians	by Eric Tyson & Tony Martin	ISBN: 1-56884-378-X	$18.99 USA/$24.99 Canada
QuickBooks 3 For Dummies®	by Stephen L. Nelson	ISBN: 1-56884-227-9	$19.99 USA/$26.99 Canada
Quicken 8 For DOS For Dummies,® 2nd Edition	by Stephen L. Nelson	ISBN: 1-56884-210-4	$19.95 USA/$26.95 Canada
Quicken 5 For Macs® For Dummies®	by Stephen L. Nelson	ISBN: 1-56884-211-2	$19.95 USA/$26.95 Canada
Quicken 4 For Windows® For Dummies,® 2nd Edition	by Stephen L. Nelson	ISBN: 1-56884-209-0	$19.95 USA/$26.95 Canada
Taxes For Dummies,™ 1995 Edition	by Eric Tyson & David J. Silverman	ISBN: 1-56884-220-1	$14.99 USA/$20.99 Canada
The GMAT® For Dummies™	by Suzee Vlk, Series Editor	ISBN: 1-56884-376-3	$14.99 USA/$20.99 Canada
The GRE® For Dummies™	by Suzee Vlk, Series Editor	ISBN: 1-56884-375-5	$14.99 USA/$20.99 Canada
Time Management For Dummies™	by Jeffrey J. Mayer	ISBN: 1-56884-360-7	$16.99 USA/$22.99 Canada
TurboTax For Windows® For Dummies®	by Gail A. Helsel, CPA	ISBN: 1-56884-228-7	$19.99 USA/$26.99 Canada
GROUPWARE/INTEGRATED			
ClarisWorks For Macs® For Dummies®	by Frank Higgins	ISBN: 1-56884-363-1	$19.99 USA/$26.99 Canada
Lotus Notes For Dummies®	by Pat Freeland & Stephen Londergan	ISBN: 1-56884-212-0	$19.95 USA/$26.95 Canada
Microsoft® Office 4 For Windows® For Dummies®	by Roger C. Parker	ISBN: 1-56884-183-3	$19.95 USA/$26.95 Canada
Microsoft® Works 3 For Windows® For Dummies®	by David C. Kay	ISBN: 1-56884-214-7	$19.99 USA/$26.99 Canada
SmartSuite 3 For Dummies®	by Jan Weingarten & John Weingarten	ISBN: 1-56884-367-4	$19.99 USA/$26.99 Canada
INTERNET/COMMUNICATIONS/NETWORKING			
America Online® For Dummies,® 2nd Edition	by John Kaufeld	ISBN: 1-56884-933-8	$19.99 USA/$26.99 Canada
CompuServe For Dummies,® 2nd Edition	by Wallace Wang	ISBN: 1-56884-937-0	$19.99 USA/$26.99 Canada
Modems For Dummies,® 2nd Edition	by Tina Rathbone	ISBN: 1-56884-223-6	$19.99 USA/$26.99 Canada
MORE Internet For Dummies®	by John R. Levine & Margaret Levine Young	ISBN: 1-56884-164-7	$19.95 USA/$26.95 Canada
MORE Modems & On-line Services For Dummies®	by Tina Rathbone	ISBN: 1-56884-365-8	$19.99 USA/$26.99 Canada
Mosaic For Dummies,® Windows Edition	by David Angell & Brent Heslop	ISBN: 1-56884-242-2	$19.99 USA/$26.99 Canada
NetWare For Dummies,® 2nd Edition	by Ed Tittel, Deni Connor & Earl Follis	ISBN: 1-56884-369-0	$19.99 USA/$26.99 Canada
Networking For Dummies®	by Doug Lowe	ISBN: 1-56884-079-9	$19.95 USA/$26.95 Canada
PROCOMM PLUS 2 For Windows® For Dummies®	by Wallace Wang	ISBN: 1-56884-219-8	$19.99 USA/$26.99 Canada
TCP/IP For Dummies®	by Marshall Wilensky & Candace Leiden	ISBN: 1-56884-241-4	$19.99 USA/$26.99 Canada

Microsoft and Windows are registered trademarks of Microsoft Corporation. Mac is a registered trademark of Apple Computer. SAT is a registered trademark of the College Entrance Examination Board. GMAT is a registered trademark of the Graduate Management Admission Council. GRE is a registered trademark of the Educational Testing Service. America Online is a registered trademark of America Online, Inc. The "...For Dummies Book Series" logo, the IDG Books Worldwide logos, Dummies Press, and The Fun & Easy Way are trademarks, and ---- For Dummies and ... For Dummies are registered trademarks under exclusive license to IDG Books Worldwide, Inc., from International Data Group, Inc.

For scholastic requests & educational orders please call Educational Sales at 1. 800. 434. 2086

FOR MORE INFO OR TO ORDER, PLEASE CALL ▶ 800. 762. 2974

For volume discounts & special orders please call Tony Real, Special Sales, at 415. 655. 3048

DUMMIES PRESS™ — IDG BOOKS WORLDWIDE

The Internet For Macs® For Dummies,® 2nd Edition	by Charles Seiter	ISBN: 1-56884-371-2	$19.99 USA/$26.99 Canada
The Internet For Macs® For Dummies® Starter Kit	by Charles Seiter	ISBN: 1-56884-244-9	$29.99 USA/$39.99 Canada
The Internet For Macs® For Dummies® Starter Kit Bestseller Edition	by Charles Seiter	ISBN: 1-56884-245-7	$39.99 USA/$54.99 Canada
The Internet For Windows® For Dummies® Starter Kit	by John R. Levine & Margaret Levine Young	ISBN: 1-56884-237-6	$34.99 USA/$44.99 Canada
The Internet For Windows® For Dummies® Starter Kit, Bestseller Edition	by John R. Levine & Margaret Levine Young	ISBN: 1-56884-246-5	$39.99 USA/$54.99 Canada

MACINTOSH

Mac® Programming For Dummies®	by Dan Parks Sydow	ISBN: 1-56884-173-6	$19.95 USA/$26.95 Canada
Macintosh® System 7.5 For Dummies®	by Bob LeVitus	ISBN: 1-56884-197-3	$19.95 USA/$26.95 Canada
MORE Macs® For Dummies®	by David Pogue	ISBN: 1-56884-087-X	$19.95 USA/$26.95 Canada
PageMaker 5 For Macs® For Dummies®	by Galen Gruman & Deke McClelland	ISBN: 1-56884-178-7	$19.95 USA/$26.95 Canada
QuarkXPress 3.3 For Dummies®	by Galen Gruman & Barbara Assadi	ISBN: 1-56884-217-1	$19.99 USA/$26.99 Canada
Upgrading and Fixing Macs® For Dummies®	by Kearney Rietmann & Frank Higgins	ISBN: 1-56884-189-2	$19.95 USA/$26.95 Canada

MULTIMEDIA

Multimedia & CD-ROMs For Dummies,® 2nd Edition	by Andy Rathbone	ISBN: 1-56884-907-9	$19.99 USA/$26.99 Canada
Multimedia & CD-ROMs For Dummies,® Interactive Multimedia Value Pack, 2nd Edition	by Andy Rathbone	ISBN: 1-56884-909-5	$29.99 USA/$39.99 Canada

OPERATING SYSTEMS:

DOS

MORE DOS For Dummies®	by Dan Gookin	ISBN: 1-56884-046-2	$19.95 USA/$26.95 Canada
OS/2® Warp For Dummies,® 2nd Edition	by Andy Rathbone	ISBN: 1-56884-205-8	$19.99 USA/$26.99 Canada

UNIX

MORE UNIX® For Dummies®	by John R. Levine & Margaret Levine Young	ISBN: 1-56884-361-5	$19.99 USA/$26.99 Canada
UNIX® For Dummies®	by John R. Levine & Margaret Levine Young	ISBN: 1-878058-58-4	$19.95 USA/$26.95 Canada

WINDOWS

MORE Windows® For Dummies,® 2nd Edition	by Andy Rathbone	ISBN: 1-56884-048-9	$19.95 USA/$26.95 Canada
Windows® 95 For Dummies®	by Andy Rathbone	ISBN: 1-56884-240-6	$19.99 USA/$26.99 Canada

PCS/HARDWARE

Illustrated Computer Dictionary For Dummies,® 2nd Edition	by Dan Gookin & Wallace Wang	ISBN: 1-56884-218-X	$12.95 USA/$16.95 Canada
Upgrading and Fixing PCs For Dummies,® 2nd Edition	by Andy Rathbone	ISBN: 1-56884-903-6	$19.99 USA/$26.99 Canada

PRESENTATION/AUTOCAD

AutoCAD For Dummies®	by Bud Smith	ISBN: 1-56884-191-4	$19.95 USA/$26.95 Canada
PowerPoint 4 For Windows® For Dummies®	by Doug Lowe	ISBN: 1-56884-161-2	$16.99 USA/$22.99 Canada

PROGRAMMING

Borland C++ For Dummies®	by Michael Hyman	ISBN: 1-56884-162-0	$19.95 USA/$26.95 Canada
C For Dummies,® Volume 1	by Dan Gookin	ISBN: 1-878058-78-9	$19.95 USA/$26.95 Canada
C++ For Dummies®	by Stephen R. Davis	ISBN: 1-56884-163-9	$19.95 USA/$26.95 Canada
Delphi Programming For Dummies®	by Neil Rubenking	ISBN: 1-56884-200-7	$19.99 USA/$26.99 Canada
Mac® Programming For Dummies®	by Dan Parks Sydow	ISBN: 1-56884-173-6	$19.99 USA/$26.99 Canada
PowerBuilder 4 Programming For Dummies®	by Ted Coombs & Jason Coombs	ISBN: 1-56884-325-9	$19.99 USA/$26.99 Canada
QBasic Programming For Dummies®	by Douglas Hergert	ISBN: 1-56884-093-4	$19.95 USA/$26.95 Canada
Visual Basic 3 For Dummies®	by Wallace Wang	ISBN: 1-56884-076-4	$19.95 USA/$26.95 Canada
Visual Basic "X" For Dummies®	by Wallace Wang	ISBN: 1-56884-230-9	$19.99 USA/$26.99 Canada
Visual C++ 2 For Dummies®	by Michael Hyman & Bob Arnson	ISBN: 1-56884-328-3	$19.99 USA/$26.99 Canada
Windows® 95 Programming For Dummies®	by S. Randy Davis	ISBN: 1-56884-327-5	$19.99 USA/$26.99 Canada

SPREADSHEET

1-2-3 For Dummies®	by Greg Harvey	ISBN: 1-878058-60-6	$16.95 USA/$22.95 Canada
1-2-3 For Windows® 5 For Dummies,® 2nd Edition	by John Walkenbach	ISBN: 1-56884-216-3	$16.95 USA/$22.95 Canada
Excel 5 For Macs® For Dummies®	by Greg Harvey	ISBN: 1-56884-186-8	$19.95 USA/$26.95 Canada
Excel For Dummies,® 2nd Edition	by Greg Harvey	ISBN: 1-56884-050-0	$16.95 USA/$22.95 Canada
MORE 1-2-3 For DOS For Dummies®	by John Weingarten	ISBN: 1-56884-224-4	$19.99 USA/$26.99 Canada
MORE Excel 5 For Windows® For Dummies®	by Greg Harvey	ISBN: 1-56884-207-4	$19.95 USA/$26.95 Canada
Quattro Pro 6 For Windows® For Dummies®	by John Walkenbach	ISBN: 1-56884-174-4	$19.95 USA/$26.95 Canada
Quattro Pro For DOS For Dummies®	by John Walkenbach	ISBN: 1-56884-023-3	$16.95 USA/$22.95 Canada

UTILITIES

Norton Utilities 8 For Dummies®	by Beth Slick	ISBN: 1-56884-166-3	$19.99 USA/$26.95 Canada

VCRS/CAMCORDERS

VCRs & Camcorders For Dummies™	by Gordon McComb & Andy Rathbone	ISBN: 1-56884-229-5	$14.99 USA/$20.99 Canada

WORD PROCESSING

Ami Pro For Dummies®	by Jim Meade	ISBN: 1-56884-049-7	$19.99 USA/$26.95 Canada
MORE Word For Windows® 6 For Dummies®	by Doug Lowe	ISBN: 1-56884-165-5	$19.95 USA/$26.95 Canada
MORE WordPerfect® 6 For Windows® For Dummies®	by Margaret Levine Young & David C. Kay	ISBN: 1-56884-206-6	$19.95 USA/$26.95 Canada
MORE WordPerfect® 6 For DOS For Dummies®	by Wallace Wang, edited by Dan Gookin	ISBN: 1-56884-047-0	$19.95 USA/$26.95 Canada
Word 6 For Macs® For Dummies®	by Dan Gookin	ISBN: 1-56884-190-6	$19.95 USA/$26.95 Canada
Word For Windows® 6 For Dummies®	by Dan Gookin	ISBN: 1-56884-075-6	$16.95 USA/$22.95 Canada
Word For Windows® For Dummies®	by Dan Gookin & Ray Werner	ISBN: 1-878058-86-X	$16.95 USA/$22.95 Canada
WordPerfect® 6 For DOS For Dummies®	by Dan Gookin	ISBN: 1-878058-77-0	$16.95 USA/$22.95 Canada
WordPerfect® 6.1 For Windows® For Dummies,® 2nd Edition	by Margaret Levine Young & David Kay	ISBN: 1-56884-243-0	$16.95 USA/$22.95 Canada
WordPerfect® For Dummies®		ISBN: 1-878058-52-5	$16.95 USA/$22.95 Canada

Windows is a registered trademark of Microsoft Corporation. Mac is a registered trademark of Apple Computer. OS/2 is a registered trademark of IBM. UNIX is a registered trademark of AT&T. WordPerfect is a registered trademark of Novell. The "...For Dummies Book Series" logo, the IDG Books Worldwide logos, Dummies Press, and The Fun & Easy Way are trademarks, and ---- For Dummies and ... For Dummies are registered trademarks under exclusive license to IDG Books Worldwide, Inc., from International Data Group, Inc.

For scholastic requests & educational orders please call Educational Sales at 1. 800. 434. 2086

FOR MORE INFO OR TO ORDER, PLEASE CALL ▶ 800. 762. 2974

For volume discounts & special orders please call Tony Real, Special Sales, at 415. 655. 3048

DUMMIES PRESS™ QUICK REFERENCES

Fun, Fast, & Cheap!™

The Internet For Macs® For Dummies® Quick Reference
by Charles Seiter
ISBN:1-56884-967-2
$9.99 USA/$12.99 Canada

Windows® 95 For Dummies® Quick Reference
by Greg Harvey
ISBN: 1-56884-964-8
$9.99 USA/$12.99 Canada

Photoshop 3 For Macs® For Dummies® Quick Reference
by Deke McClelland
ISBN: 1-56884-968-0
$9.99 USA/$12.99 Canada

WordPerfect® For DOS For Dummies® Quick Reference
by Greg Harvey
ISBN: 1-56884-009-8
$8.95 USA/$12.95 Canada

Title	Author	ISBN	Price
DATABASE			
Access 2 For Dummies® Quick Reference	by Stuart J. Stuple	ISBN: 1-56884-167-1	$8.95 USA/$11.95 Canada
dBASE 5 For DOS For Dummies® Quick Reference	by Barrie Sosinsky	ISBN: 1-56884-954-0	$9.99 USA/$12.99 Canada
dBASE 5 For Windows® For Dummies® Quick Reference	by Stuart J. Stuple	ISBN: 1-56884-953-2	$9.99 USA/$12.99 Canada
Paradox 5 For Windows® For Dummies® Quick Reference	by Scott Palmer	ISBN: 1-56884-960-5	$9.99 USA/$12.99 Canada
DESKTOP PUBLISHING/ILLUSTRATION/GRAPHICS			
CorelDRAW! 5 For Dummies® Quick Reference	by Raymond E. Werner	ISBN: 1-56884-952-4	$9.99 USA/$12.99 Canada
Harvard Graphics For Windows® For Dummies® Quick Reference	by Raymond E. Werner	ISBN: 1-56884-962-1	$9.99 USA/$12.99 Canada
Photoshop 3 For Macs® For Dummies® Quick Reference	by Deke McClelland	ISBN: 1-56884-968-0	$9.99 USA/$12.99 Canada
FINANCE/PERSONAL FINANCE			
Quicken 4 For Windows® For Dummies® Quick Reference	by Stephen L. Nelson	ISBN: 1-56884-950-8	$9.95 USA/$12.95 Canada
GROUPWARE/INTEGRATED			
Microsoft® Office 4 For Windows® For Dummies® Quick Reference	by Doug Lowe	ISBN: 1-56884-958-3	$9.99 USA/$12.99 Canada
Microsoft® Works 3 For Windows® For Dummies® Quick Reference	by Michael Partington	ISBN: 1-56884-959-1	$9.99 USA/$12.99 Canada
INTERNET/COMMUNICATIONS/NETWORKING			
The Internet For Dummies® Quick Reference	by John R. Levine & Margaret Levine Young	ISBN: 1-56884-168-X	$8.95 USA/$11.95 Canada
MACINTOSH			
Macintosh® System 7.5 For Dummies® Quick Reference	by Stuart J. Stuple	ISBN: 1-56884-956-7	$9.99 USA/$12.99 Canada
OPERATING SYSTEMS:			
DOS			
DOS For Dummies® Quick Reference	by Greg Harvey	ISBN: 1-56884-007-1	$8.95 USA/$11.95 Canada
UNIX			
UNIX® For Dummies® Quick Reference	by John R. Levine & Margaret Levine Young	ISBN: 1-56884-094-2	$8.95 USA/$11.95 Canada
WINDOWS			
Windows® 3.1 For Dummies® Quick Reference, 2nd Edition	by Greg Harvey	ISBN: 1-56884-951-6	$8.95 USA/$11.95 Canada
PCs/HARDWARE			
Memory Management For Dummies® Quick Reference	by Doug Lowe	ISBN: 1-56884-362-3	$9.99 USA/$12.99 Canada
PRESENTATION/AUTOCAD			
AutoCAD For Dummies® Quick Reference	by Ellen Finkelstein	ISBN: 1-56884-198-1	$9.95 USA/$12.95 Canada
SPREADSHEET			
1-2-3 For Dummies® Quick Reference	by John Walkenbach	ISBN: 1-56884-027-6	$8.95 USA/$11.95 Canada
1-2-3 For Windows® 5 For Dummies® Quick Reference	by John Walkenbach	ISBN: 1-56884-957-5	$9.95 USA/$12.95 Canada
Excel For Windows® For Dummies® Quick Reference, 2nd Edition	by John Walkenbach	ISBN: 1-56884-096-9	$8.95 USA/$11.95 Canada
Quattro Pro 6 For Windows® For Dummies® Quick Reference	by Stuart J. Stuple	ISBN: 1-56884-172-8	$9.95 USA/$12.95 Canada
WORD PROCESSING			
Word For Windows® 6 For Dummies® Quick Reference	by George Lynch	ISBN: 1-56884-095-0	$8.95 USA/$11.95 Canada
Word For Windows® For Dummies® Quick Reference	by George Lynch	ISBN: 1-56884-029-2	$8.95 USA/$11.95 Canada
WordPerfect® 6.1 For Windows® For Dummies® Quick Reference, 2nd Edition	by Greg Harvey	ISBN: 1-56884-966-4	$9.99 USA/$12.99/Canada

Microsoft and Windows are registered trademarks of Microsoft Corporation. Mac and Macintosh are registered trademarks of Apple Computer. UNIX is a registered trademark of AT&T. WordPerfect is a registered trademark of Novell. The "...For Dummies Book Series" logo, the IDG Books Worldwide logos, Dummies Press, The Fun & Easy Way, and Fun, Fast, & Cheap! are trademarks, and ---- For Dummies and ... For Dummies are registered trademarks under exclusive license to IDG Books Worldwide, Inc., from International Data Group, Inc.

For scholastic requests & educational orders please call Educational Sales at 1. 800. 434. 2086

FOR MORE INFO OR TO ORDER, PLEASE CALL ▶ 800. 762. 2974

For volume discounts & special orders please call Tony Real, Special Sales, at 415. 655. 3048

PC PRESS

IDG BOOKS WORLDWIDE

3/26/96

Windows® 3.1 SECRETS™
by Brian Livingston
ISBN: 1-878058-43-6
$39.95 USA/$52.95 Canada
Includes software.

MORE Windows® 3.1 SECRETS™
by Brian Livingston
ISBN: 1-56884-019-5
$39.95 USA/$52.95 Canada
Includes software.

Windows® GIZMOS™
by Brian Livingston & Margie Livingston
ISBN: 1-878058-66-5
$39.95 USA/$52.95 Canada
Includes software.

Windows® 3.1 Connectivity SECRETS™
by Runnoe Connally, David Rorabaugh, & Sheldon Hall
ISBN: 1-56884-030-6
$49.95 USA/$64.95 Canada
Includes software.

Windows® 3.1 Configuration SECRETS™
by Valda Hilley & James Blakely
ISBN: 1-56884-026-8
$49.95 USA/$64.95 Canada
Includes software.

Internet SECRETS™
by John Levine & Carol Baroudi
ISBN: 1-56884-452-2
$39.99 USA/$54.99 Canada
Includes software.

Internet GIZMOS™ For Windows®
by Joel Diamond, Howard Sobel, & Valda Hilley
ISBN: 1-56884-451-4
$39.99 USA/$54.99 Canada
Includes software.

Network Security SECRETS™
by David Stang & Sylvia Moon
ISBN: 1-56884-021-7
Int'l. ISBN: 1-56884-151-5
$49.95 USA/$64.95 Canada
Includes software.

PC SECRETS™
by Caroline M. Halliday
ISBN: 1-878058-49-5
$39.95 USA/$52.95 Canada
Includes software.

WordPerfect® 6 SECRETS™
by Roger C. Parker & David A. Holzgang
ISBN: 1-56884-040-3
$39.95 USA/$52.95 Canada
Includes software.

DOS 6 SECRETS™
by Robert D. Ainsbury
ISBN: 1-878058-70-3
$39.95 USA/$52.95 Canada
Includes software.

Paradox 4 Power Programming SECRETS,™ 2nd Edition
by Gregory B. Salcedo & Martin W. Rudy
ISBN: 1-878058-54-1
$44.95 USA/$59.95 Canada
Includes software.

Paradox 5 For Windows® Power Programming SECRETS™
by Gregory B. Salcedo & Martin W. Rudy
ISBN: 1-56884-085-3
$44.95 USA/$59.95 Canada
Includes software.

Hard Disk SECRETS™
by John M. Goodman, Ph.D.
ISBN: 1-878058-64-9
$39.95 USA/$52.95 Canada
Includes software.

WordPerfect® 6 For Windows® Tips & Techniques Revealed
by David A. Holzgang & Roger C. Parker
ISBN: 1-56884-202-3
$39.95 USA/$52.95 Canada
Includes software.

Excel 5 For Windows® Power Programming Techniques
by John Walkenbach
ISBN: 1-56884-303-8
$39.95 USA/$52.95 Canada
Includes software.

...SECRETS®

INFO WORLD

Windows is a registered trademark of Microsoft Corporation. WordPerfect is a registered trademark of Novell. ----SECRETS, ----GIZMOS, and the IDG Books Worldwide logos are trademarks, and ...SECRETS is a registered trademark under exclusive license to IDG Books Worldwide, Inc., from International Data Group, Inc.

For scholastic requests & educational orders please call Educational Sales, at 1. 800. 434. 2086

FOR MORE INFO OR TO ORDER, PLEASE CALL ▶ 800. 762. 2974

For volume discounts & special orders please call Tony Real, Special Sales, at 415. 655. 3048

PC PRESS

IDG BOOKS WORLDWIDE

10/31/95

"A lot easier to use than the book Excel gives you!"

Lisa Schmeckpeper, New Berlin, WI, on PC World Excel 5 For Windows Handbook

Official Hayes Modem Communications Companion
by Caroline M. Halliday
ISBN: 1-56884-072-1
$29.95 USA/$39.95 Canada
Includes software.

1,001 Komputer Answers from Kim Komando
by Kim Komando
ISBN: 1-56884-460-3
$29.99 USA/$39.99 Canada
Includes software.

PC World DOS 6 Handbook, 2nd Edition
by John Socha, Clint Hicks, & Devra Hall
ISBN: 1-878058-79-7
$34.95 USA/$44.95 Canada
Includes software.

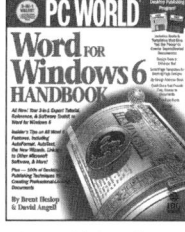

BESTSELLER!

PC World Word For Windows 6 Handbook
by Brent Heslop & David Angell
ISBN: 1-56884-054-3
$34.95 USA/$44.95 Canada
Includes software.

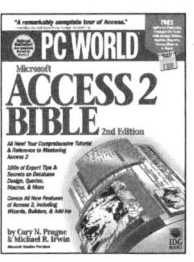

PC World Microsoft Access 2 Bible, 2nd Edition
by Cary N. Prague & Michael R. Irwin
ISBN: 1-56884-086-1
$39.95 USA/$52.95 Canada
Includes software.

BESTSELLER!

PC World Excel 5 For Windows Handbook, 2nd Edition
by John Walkenbach & Dave Maguiness
ISBN: 1-56884-056-X
$34.95 USA/$44.95 Canada
Includes software.

PC World WordPerfect 6 Handbook
by Greg Harvey
ISBN: 1-878058-80-0
$34.95 USA/$44.95 Canada
Includes software.

QuarkXPress For Windows Designer Handbook
by Barbara Assadi & Galen Gruman
ISBN: 1-878058-45-2
$29.95 USA/$39.95 Canada

Official XTree Companion, 3rd Edition
by Beth Slick
ISBN: 1-878058-57-6
$19.95 USA/$26.95 Canada

NATIONAL BESTSELLER!

PC World DOS 6 Command Reference and Problem Solver
by John Socha & Devra Hall
ISBN: 1-56884-055-1
$24.95 USA/$32.95 Canada

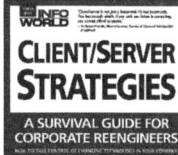

NATIONAL BESTSELLER!

Client/Server Strategies: A Survival Guide for Corporate Reengineers
by David Vaskevitch
ISBN: 1-56884-064-0
$29.95 USA/$39.95 Canada

SUPER STAR

"PC World Word For Windows 6 Handbook is very easy to follow with lots of 'hands on' examples. The 'Task at a Glance' is very helpful!"

Jacqueline Martens, Tacoma, WA

"Thanks for publishing this book! It's the best money I've spent this year!"

Robert D. Templeton, Ft. Worth, TX, on MORE Windows 3.1 SECRETS

Microsoft and Windows are registered trademarks of Microsoft Corporation. WordPerfect is a registered trademark of Novell. ----STRATEGIES and the IDG Books Worldwide logos are trademarks under exclusive license to IDG Books Worldwide, Inc., from International Data Group, Inc.

For scholastic requests & educational orders please call Educational Sales, at 1. 800. 434. 2086 | **FOR MORE INFO OR TO ORDER, PLEASE CALL ▶ 800. 762. 2974** | For volume discounts & special orders please call Tony Real, Special Sales, at 415. 655. 3048

MACWORLD® PRESS

10/31/95

Macworld® Mac & Power Mac SECRETS™, 2nd Edition
by David Pogue & Joseph Schorr

This is the definitive Mac reference for those who want to become power users! Includes three disks with 9MB of software!

ISBN: 1-56884-175-2
$39.95 USA/$54.95 Canada

Includes 3 disks chock full of software.

WINNERS 1994-95 TECHNICAL PUBLICATIONS AND ART COMPETITIONS OF THE SOCIETY FOR TECHNICAL COMMUNICATION

NEWBRIDGE BOOK CLUB SELECTION

HOT!

Macworld® Mac FAQs™
by David Pogue

Written by the hottest Macintosh author around, David Pogue, *Macworld Mac FAQs* gives users the ultimate Mac reference. Hundreds of Mac questions and answers side-by-side, right at your fingertips, and organized into six easy-to-reference sections with lots of sidebars and diagrams.

ISBN: 1-56884-480-8
$19.99 USA/$26.99 Canada

HOT!

Macworld® System 7.5 Bible, 3rd Edition
by Lon Poole

ISBN: 1-56884-098-5
$29.95 USA/$39.95 Canada

NATIONAL BESTSELLER!

Macworld® ClarisWorks 3.0 Companion, 3rd Edition
by Steven A. Schwartz

ISBN: 1-56884-481-6
$24.99 USA/$34.99 Canada

NATIONAL BESTSELLER!

Macworld® Complete Mac Handbook Plus Interactive CD, 3rd Edition
by Jim Heid

ISBN: 1-56884-192-2
$39.95 USA/$54.95 Canada

Includes an interactive CD-ROM.

BMUG SPRING 1995 CHOICE PRODUCT

NEWBRIDGE BOOK CLUB SELECTION

Macworld® Ultimate Mac® CD-ROM
by Jim Heid

ISBN: 1-56884-477-8
$19.99 USA/$26.99 Canada

CD-ROM includes version 2.0 of QuickTime, and over 65 MB of the best shareware, freeware, fonts, sounds, and more!

Macworld® Networking Bible, 2nd Edition
by Dave Kosiur & Joel M. Snyder

ISBN: 1-56884-194-9
$29.95 USA/$39.95 Canada

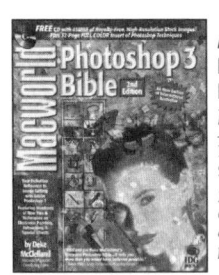

Macworld® Photoshop 3 Bible, 2nd Edition
by Deke McClelland

ISBN: 1-56884-158-2
$39.95 USA/$54.95 Canada

Includes stunning CD-ROM with add-ons, digitized photos and more.

WINNERS 1994-95 TECHNICAL PUBLICATIONS AND ART COMPETITIONS OF THE SOCIETY FOR TECHNICAL COMMUNICATION

NEW!

Macworld® Photoshop 2.5 Bible
by Deke McClelland

ISBN: 1-56884-022-5
$29.95 USA/$39.95 Canada

NATIONAL BESTSELLER!

Macworld® FreeHand 4 Bible
by Deke McClelland

ISBN: 1-56884-170-1
$29.95 USA/$39.95 Canada

Macworld® Illustrator 5.0/5.5 Bible
by Ted Alspach

ISBN: 1-56884-097-7
$39.95 USA/$54.95 Canada

Includes CD-ROM with QuickTime tutorials.

Mac is a registered trademark of Apple Computer. Macworld is a registered trademark of International Data Group, Inc. ----SECRETS, and ----FAQs are trademarks under exclusive license to IDG Books Worldwide, Inc., from International Data Group, Inc.

For scholastic requests & educational orders please call Educational Sales, at 1. 800. 434. 2086

FOR MORE INFO TO ORDER, PLEASE CALL ▶ 800. 762. 2974

For volume discounts & special orders please ca Tony Real, Special Sales, at 415. 655. 3048

MACWORLD® PRESS

"Macworld Complete Mac Handbook Plus CD covered everything I could think of and more!"

Peter Tsakiris, New York, NY

"Very useful for PageMaker beginners and veterans alike— contains a wealth of tips and tricks to make you a faster, more powerful PageMaker user."

Paul Brainerd, President and founder, Aldus Corporation

"Thanks for the best computer book I've ever read—Photoshop 2.5 Bible. Best $30 I ever spent. I love the detailed index....Yours blows them all out of the water. This is a great book. We must enlighten the masses!"

Kevin Lisankie, Chicago, Illinois

"Macworld Guide to ClarisWorks 2 is the easiest computer book to read that I have ever found!"

Steven Hanson, Lutz, FL

"...thanks to the Macworld Excel 5 Companion, 2nd Edition occupying a permanent position next to my computer, I'll be able to tap more of Excel's power."

Lauren Black, Lab Director, Macworld Magazine

Macworld® QuarkXPress 3.2/3.3 Bible
by Barbara Assadi & Galen Gruman
ISBN: 1-878058-85-1
$39.95 USA/$52.95 Canada
Includes disk with QuarkXPress XTensions and scripts.

Macworld® PageMaker 5 Bible
by Craig Danuloff
ISBN: 1-878058-84-3
$39.95 USA/$52.95 Canada
Includes 2 disks with PageMaker utilities, clip art, and more.

Macworld® FileMaker Pro 2.0/2.1 Bible
by Steven A. Schwartz
ISBN: 1-56884-201-5
$34.95 USA/$46.95 Canada
Includes disk with ready-to-run data bases.

Macworld® Word 6 Companion, 2nd Edition
by Jim Heid
ISBN: 1-56884-082-9
$24.95 USA/$34.95 Canada
NEWBRIDGE BOOK CLUB SELECTION

Macworld® Guide To Microsoft® Word 5/5.1
by Jim Heid
ISBN: 1-878058-39-8
$22.95 USA/$29.95 Canada

Macworld® ClarisWorks 2.0/2.1 Companion, 2nd Edition
by Steven A. Schwartz
ISBN: 1-56884-180-9
$24.95 USA/$34.95 Canada

Macworld® Guide To Microsoft® Works 3
by Barrie Sosinsky
ISBN: 1-878058-42-8
$22.95 USA/$29.95 Canada

Macworld® Excel 5 Companion, 2nd Edition
by Chris Van Buren & David Maguiness
ISBN: 1-56884-081-0
$24.95 USA/$34.95 Canada
NEWBRIDGE BOOK CLUB SELECTION

Macworld® Guide To Microsoft® Excel 4
by David Maguiness
ISBN: 1-878058-40-1
$22.95 USA/$29.95 Canada

Microsoft is a registered trademark of Microsoft Corporation. Macworld is a registered trademark of International Data Group, Inc.

For scholastic requests & educational orders please call Educational Sales, at 1. 800. 434. 2086

FOR MORE INFO OR TO ORDER, PLEASE CALL ▶ 800. 762. 2974

For volume discounts & special orders please call Tony Real, Special Sales, at 415. 655. 3048

ORDER FORM

IDG BOOKS WORLDWIDE

Order Center: **(800) 762-2974** (8 a.m.–6 p.m., EST, weekdays)

Quantity	ISBN	Title	Price	Total

Shipping & Handling Charges

	Description	First book	Each additional book	Total
Domestic	Normal	$4.50	$1.50	$
	Two Day Air	$8.50	$2.50	$
	Overnight	$18.00	$3.00	$
International	Surface	$8.00	$8.00	$
	Airmail	$16.00	$16.00	$
	DHL Air	$17.00	$17.00	$

*For large quantities call for shipping & handling charges.
**Prices are subject to change without notice.

Ship to:
Name _____
Company _____
Address _____
City/State/Zip _____
Daytime Phone _____

Payment: ☐ Check to IDG Books Worldwide (US Funds Only)
☐ VISA   ☐ MasterCard   ☐ American Express
Card # _____ Expires _____
Signature _____

Subtotal _____
CA residents add applicable sales tax _____
IN, MA, and MD residents add 5% sales tax _____
IL residents add 6.25% sales tax _____
RI residents add 7% sales tax _____
TX residents add 8.25% sales tax _____

Shipping _____

Total _____

Please send this order form to:
IDG Books Worldwide, Inc.
Attn: Order Entry Dept.
7260 Shadeland Station, Suite 100
Indianapolis, IN 46256

Allow up to 3 weeks for delivery.
Thank you!